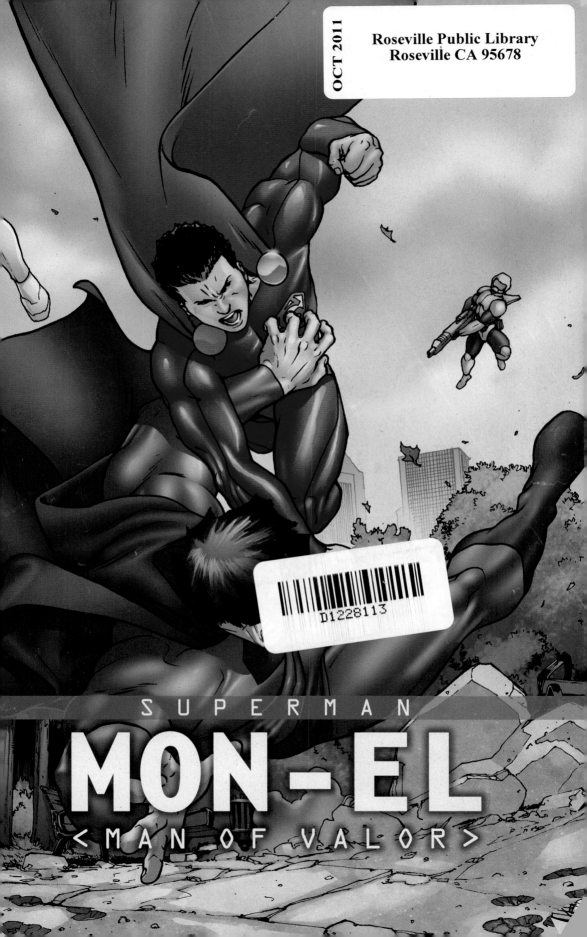

SUPERMAN
MON-EL
<MAN OF VALOR>

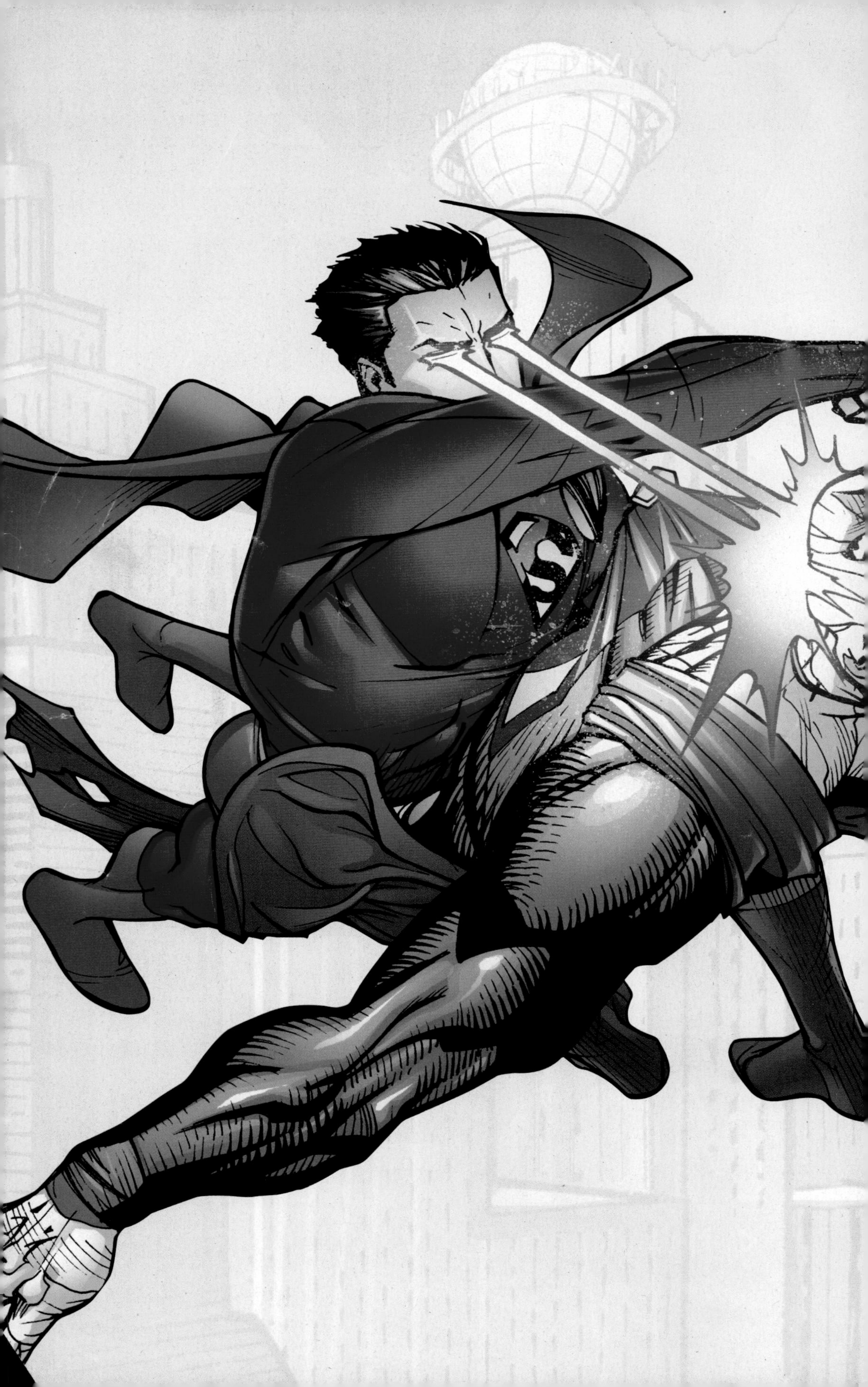

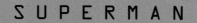

SUPERMAN

MON-EL

<MAN OF VALOR>

JAMES ROBINSON
<WRITER>

JAVIER PINA
FERNANDO DAGNINO & RAÚL FERNANDEZ
BERNARD CHANG
MATT CAMP
<ARTISTS>

BLOND
HI-FI
DAVID CURIEL
<COLORISTS>

JOHN J. HILL
TRAVIS LANHAM
SAL CIPRIANO
<LETTERERS>

RENATO GUEDES
<COLLECTION COVER ARTIST>

<SUPERMAN>
CREATED BY JERRY SIEGEL AND JOE SHUSTER

MATT IDELSON <EDITOR-ORIGINAL SERIES>
WIL MOSS <ASSISTANT EDITOR-ORIGINAL SERIES>
BOB HARRAS <GROUP EDITOR-COLLECTED EDITIONS>
SEAN MACKIEWICZ <EDITOR>
ROBBIN BROSTERMAN <DESIGN DIRECTOR-BOOKS>

DC COMICS
DIANE NELSON <PRESIDENT>
DAN DIDIO AND JIM LEE <CO-PUBLISHERS>
GEOFF JOHNS <CHIEF CREATIVE OFFICER>
PATRICK CALDON <EVP-FINANCE AND ADMINISTRATION>
JOHN ROOD <EVP-SALES, MARKETING AND BUSINESS DEVELOPMENT>
AMY GENKINS <SVP-BUSINESS AND LEGAL AFFAIRS>
STEVE ROTTERDAM <SVP-SALES AND MARKETING>
JOHN CUNNINGHAM <VP-MARKETING>
TERRI CUNNINGHAM <VP-MANAGING EDITOR>
ALISON GILL <VP-MANUFACTURING>
DAVID HYDE <VP-PUBLICITY>
SUE POHJA <VP-BOOK TRADE SALES>
ALYSSE SOLL <VP-ADVERTISING AND CUSTOM PUBLISHING>
BOB WAYNE <VP-SALES>
MARK CHIARELLO <ART DIRECTOR>

DC COMICS, 1700 BROADWAY, NEW YORK, NY 10019.
A WARNER BROS. ENTERTAINMENT COMPANY.
PRINTED BY RR DONNELLEY, SALEM, VA, USA.
9/15/11. FIRST PRINTING.
ISBN:978-1-4012-2938-2

SUSTAINABLE FORESTRY INITIATIVE
Certified Chain of Custody
Promoting Sustainable Forest Management
www.sfiprogram.org
Fiber used in this product line meets the sourcing requirements of the SFI program.
www.sfiprogram.org SGS-SFI/COC-US10/81072

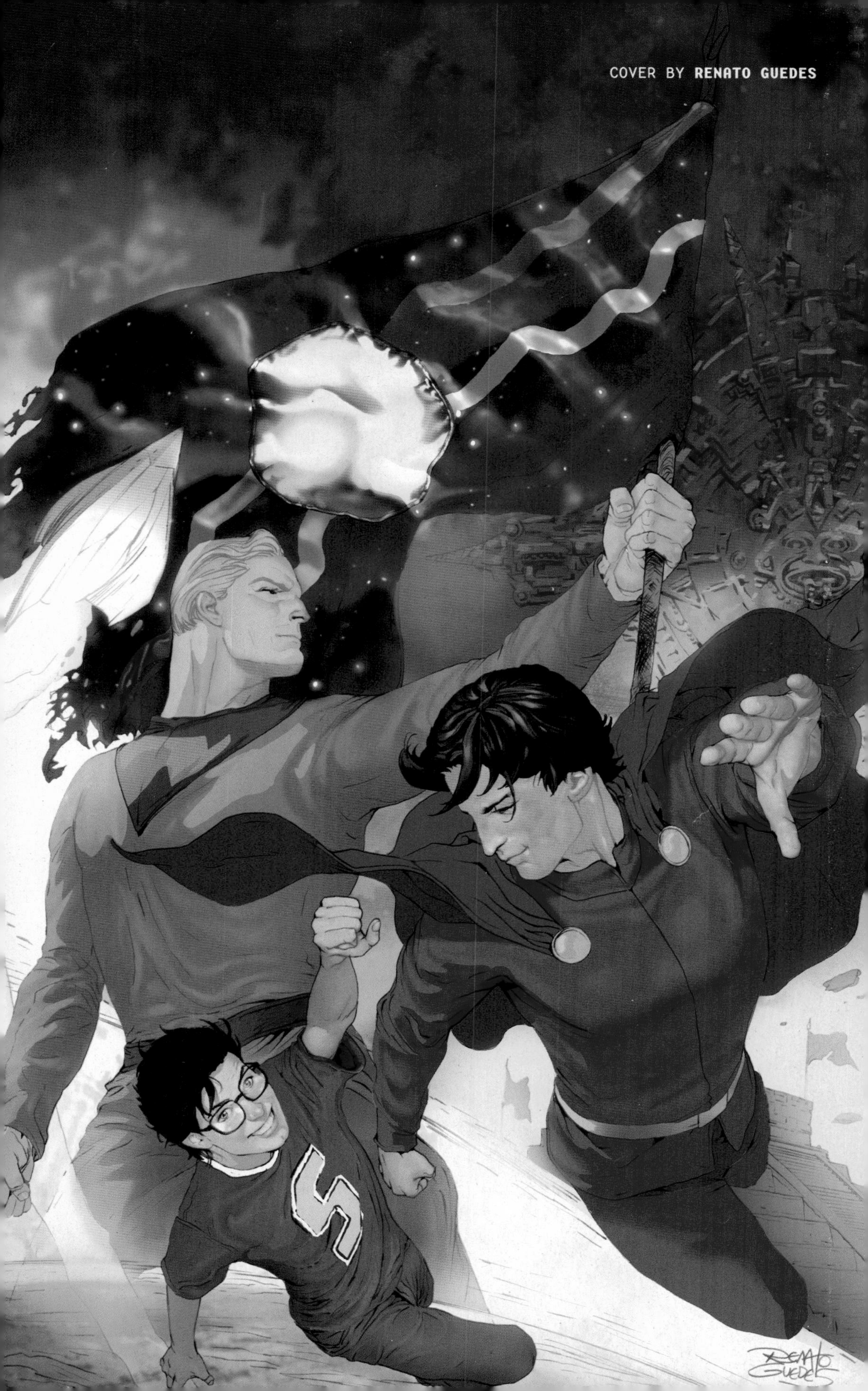

COVER BY **RENATO GUEDES**

THE HISTORY LESSON

JAVIER PINA <ARTIST>

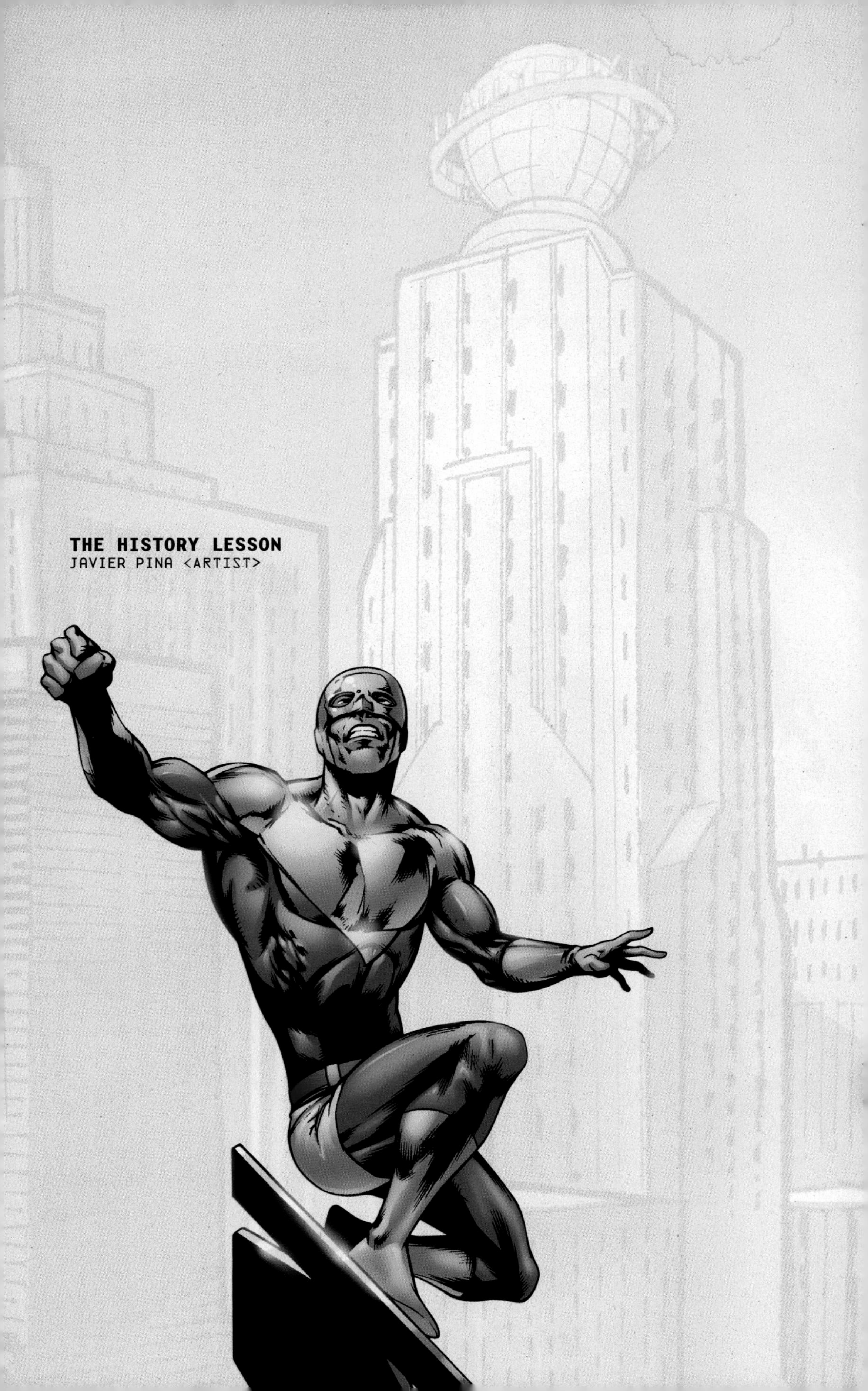

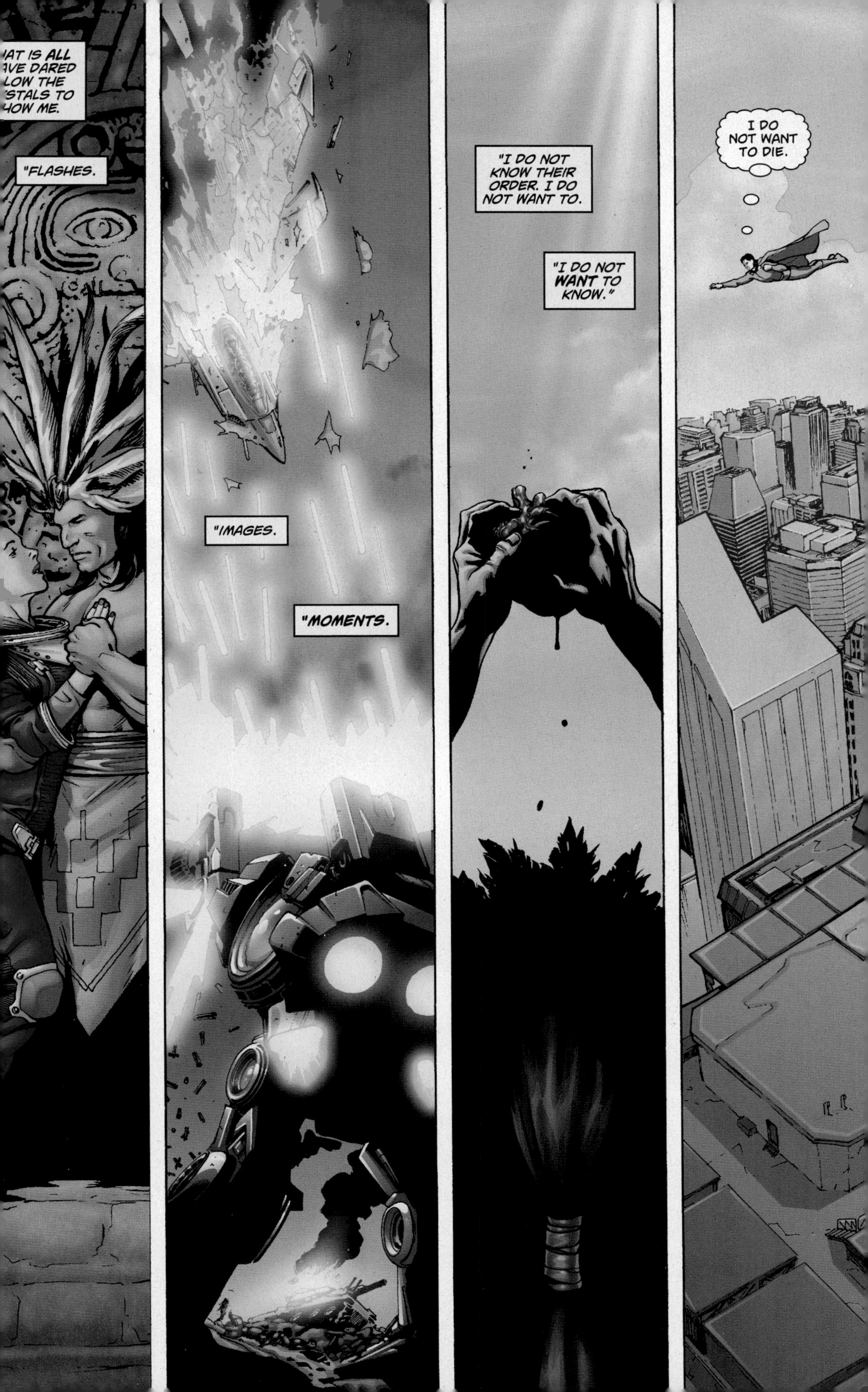

...HAT IS ALL ...AVE DARED ...LOW THE ...STALS TO ...HOW ME.
"FLASHES.
"IMAGES.
"MOMENTS.
"I DO NOT KNOW THEIR ORDER. I DO NOT WANT TO.
"I DO NOT WANT TO KNOW."
I DO NOT WANT TO DIE.

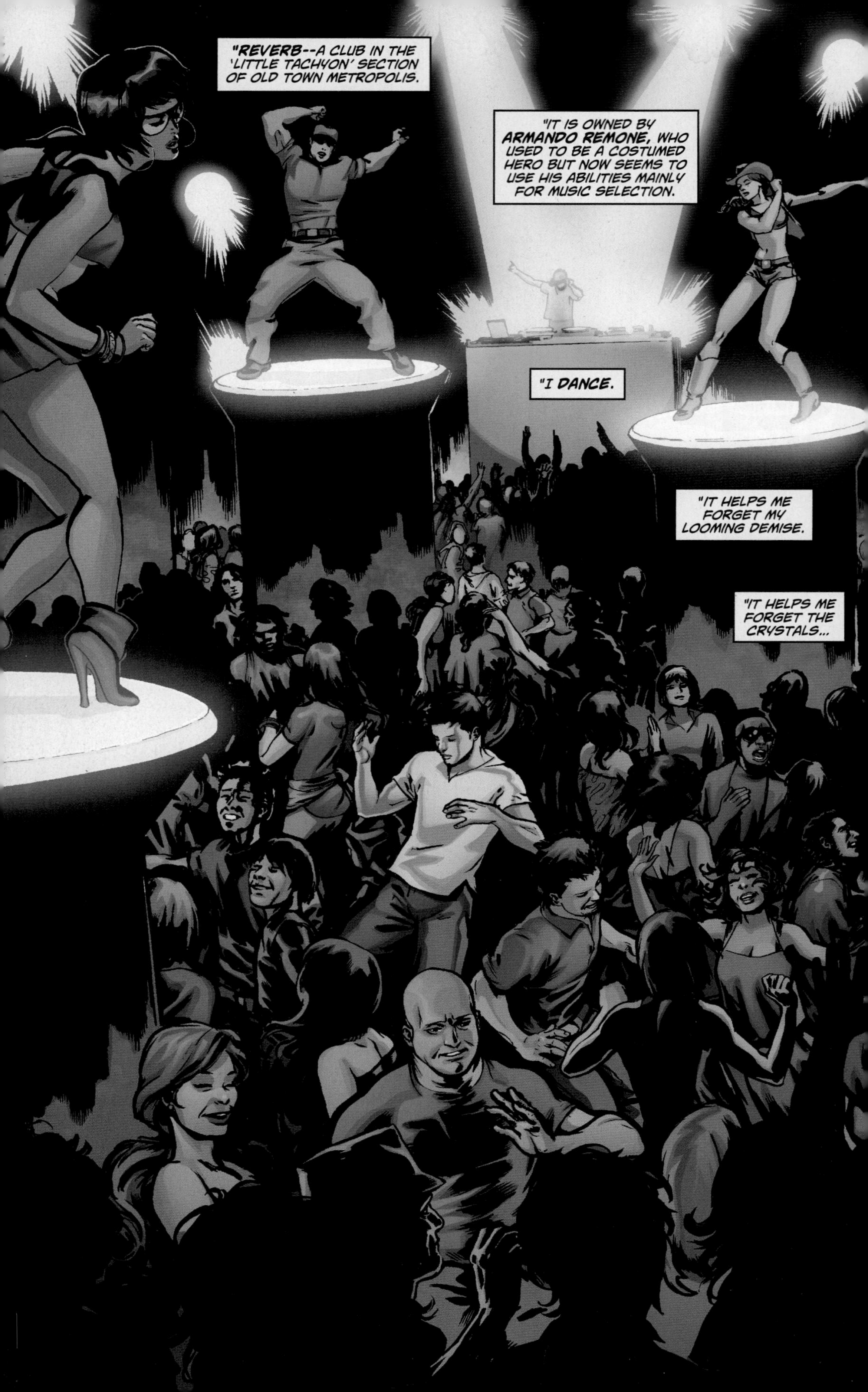
"REVERB--A CLUB IN THE 'LITTLE TACHYON' SECTION OF OLD TOWN METROPOLIS.
"IT IS OWNED BY ARMANDO REMONE, WHO USED TO BE A COSTUMED HERO BUT NOW SEEMS TO USE HIS ABILITIES MAINLY FOR MUSIC SELECTION.
"I DANCE.
"IT HELPS ME FORGET MY LOOMING DEMISE.
"IT HELPS ME FORGET THE CRYSTALS...

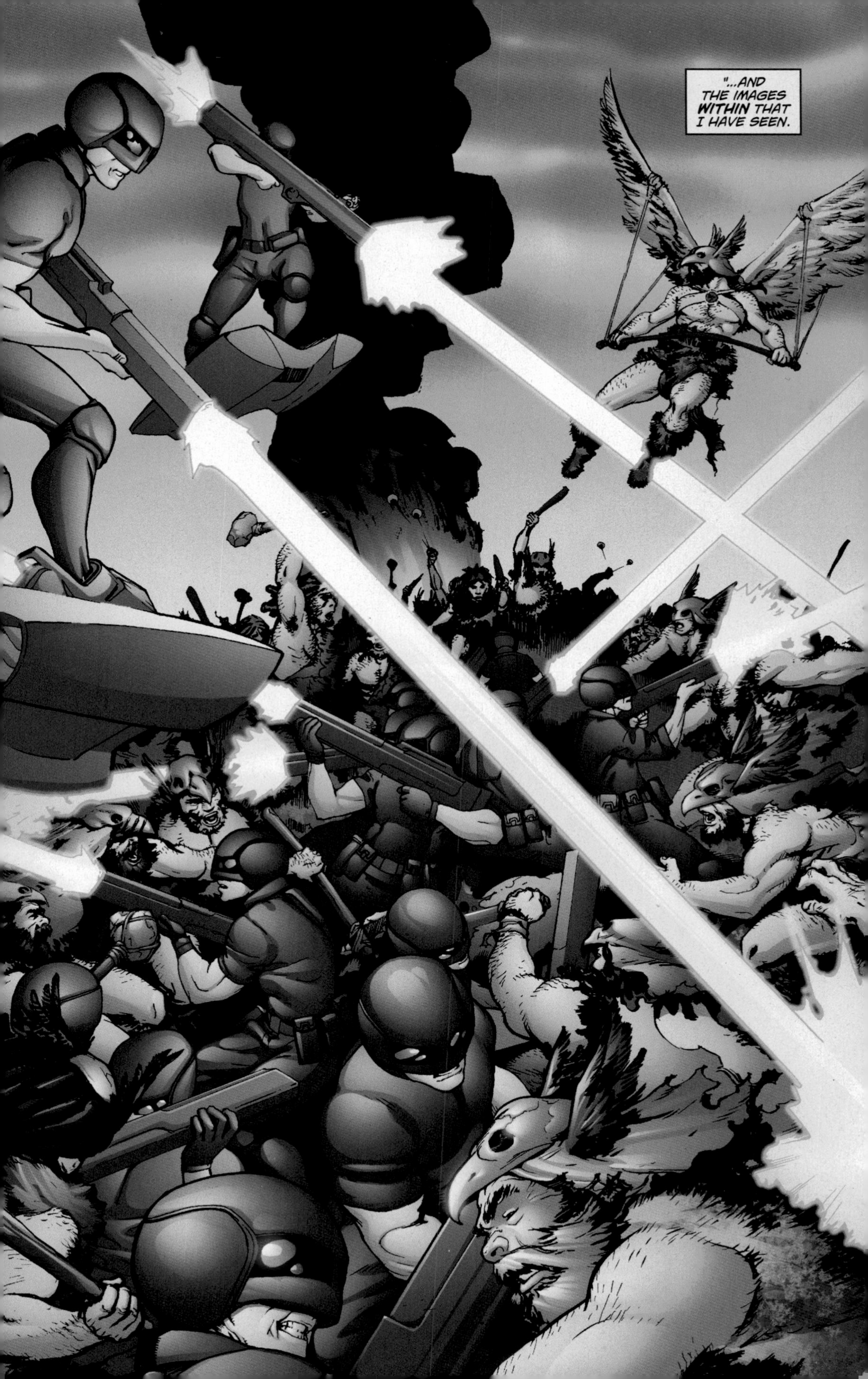
"...AND THE IMAGES WITHIN THAT I HAVE SEEN.

"ALL TOO EASILY THE MOMENTS THOSE CRYSTALS REVEAL REMIND ME OF MOMENTS IN MY OWN PAST.

"MY PAST."

WHAT IS THIS? SOMETHING *EXOTIC*?

MEATBALLS AND SPAGHETTI. EXOTIC, NOT AT ALL. COMFORT FOOD.

HERE, JON. EAT.

YOU LOOK LIKE YOU NEED COMFORTING.

YOU ARE WRONG, MITCH. AFTER THE LIFE I HAVE HAD, *ANYTHING* I EAT IS EXOTIC.

"MY LIFE."

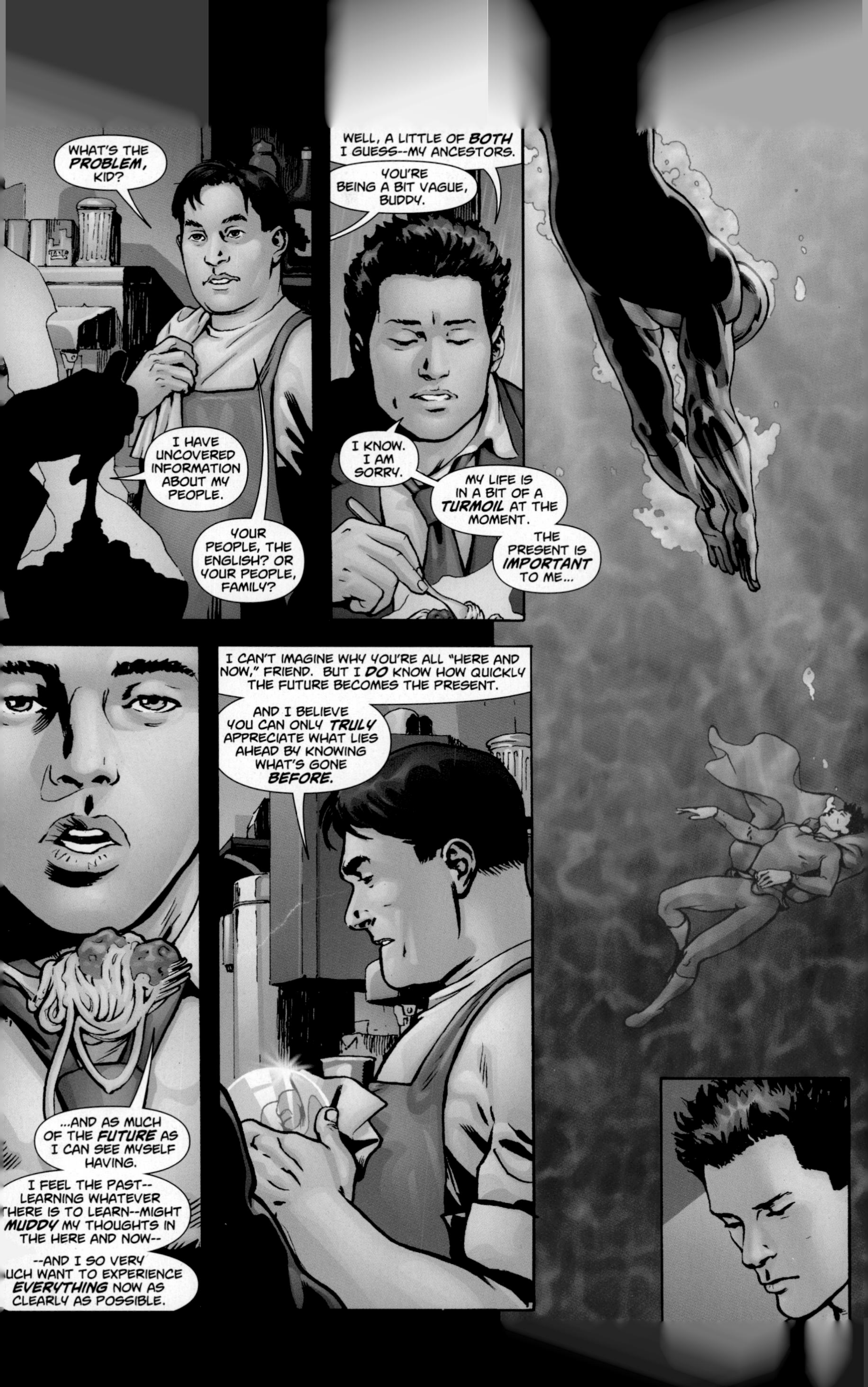
WHAT'S THE PROBLEM, KID?
I HAVE UNCOVERED INFORMATION ABOUT MY PEOPLE.
YOUR PEOPLE, THE ENGLISH? OR YOUR PEOPLE, FAMILY?
WELL, A LITTLE OF BOTH I GUESS--MY ANCESTORS.
YOU'RE BEING A BIT VAGUE, BUDDY.
I KNOW. I AM SORRY.
MY LIFE IS IN A BIT OF A TURMOIL AT THE MOMENT.
THE PRESENT IS IMPORTANT TO ME...
...AND AS MUCH OF THE FUTURE AS I CAN SEE MYSELF HAVING.
I FEEL THE PAST--LEARNING WHATEVER THERE IS TO LEARN--MIGHT MUDDY MY THOUGHTS IN THE HERE AND NOW--
--AND I SO VERY MUCH WANT TO EXPERIENCE EVERYTHING NOW AS CLEARLY AS POSSIBLE.
I CAN'T IMAGINE WHY YOU'RE ALL "HERE AND NOW," FRIEND. BUT I DO KNOW HOW QUICKLY THE FUTURE BECOMES THE PRESENT.
AND I BELIEVE YOU CAN ONLY TRULY APPRECIATE WHAT LIES AHEAD BY KNOWING WHAT'S GONE BEFORE.

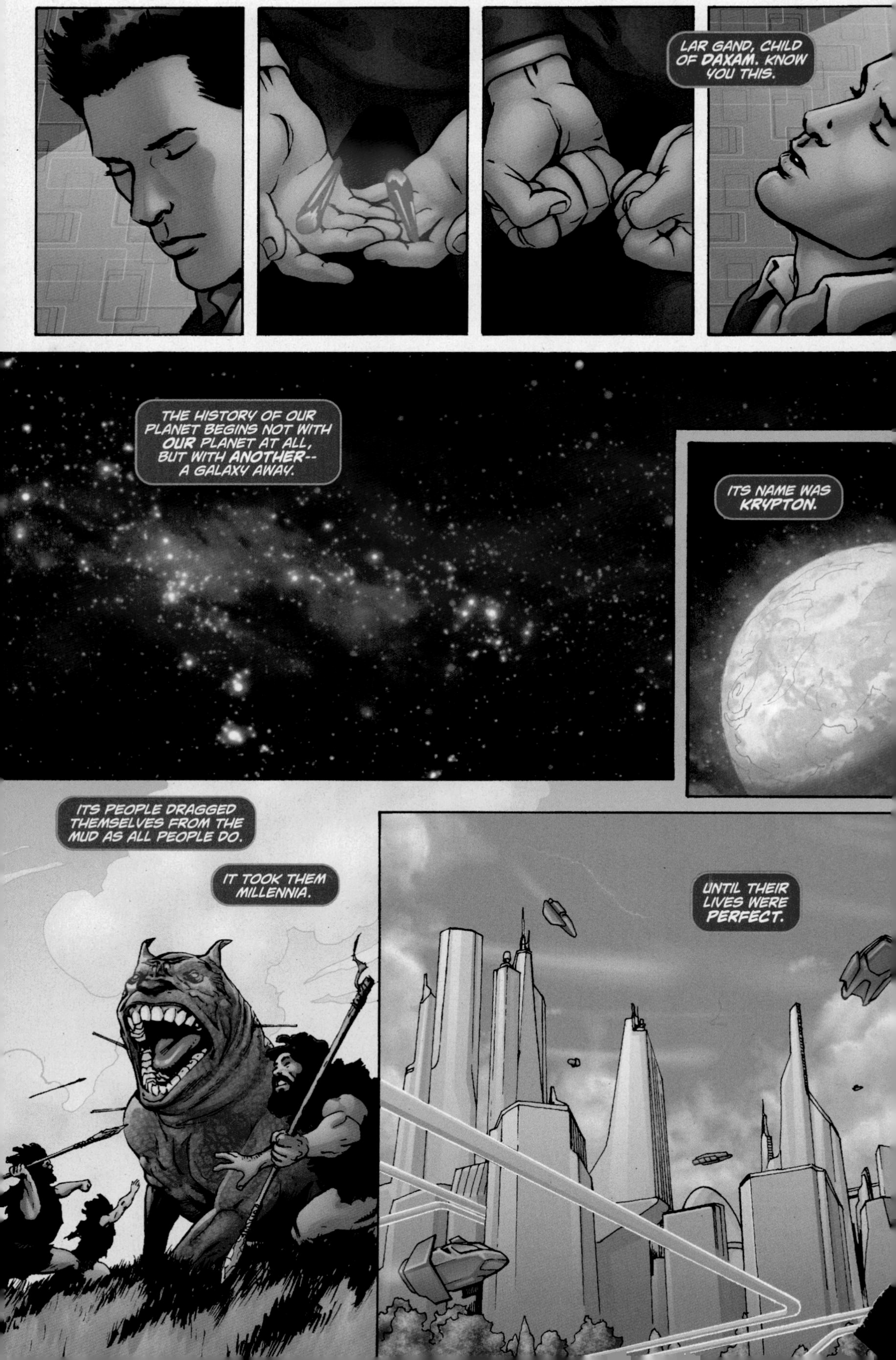
LAR GAND, CHILD OF DAXAM. KNOW YOU THIS.
THE HISTORY OF OUR PLANET BEGINS NOT WITH OUR PLANET AT ALL, BUT WITH ANOTHER-- A GALAXY AWAY.
ITS NAME WAS KRYPTON.
ITS PEOPLE DRAGGED THEMSELVES FROM THE MUD AS ALL PEOPLE DO.
IT TOOK THEM MILLENNIA.
UNTIL THEIR LIVES WERE PERFECT.

BORED WITH PERFECTION, THEY SOUGHT THE ENLIGHTENMENT OF OTHER WORLDS.

THOUGH THESE WERE NOT JOURNEYS OF EXPLORATION AND INQUIRY.

THIS WAS CONQUEST.

ALTHOUGH NOT ALL OF THE "GREAT INQUIRY" DREW THE BLOOD OF ABORIGINAL RACES.

A DISTANT SUN WAS DISCOVERED BY FAMED ASTRONOMER VAL-OR.

A YOUNG PILOT-CONSTABLE WAS SENT STAR-BOUND IN SEARCH OF ANY INHABITABLE WORLDS ORBITING IT.

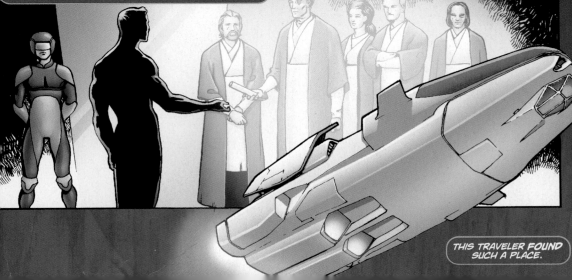

THIS TRAVELER FOUND SUCH A PLACE.

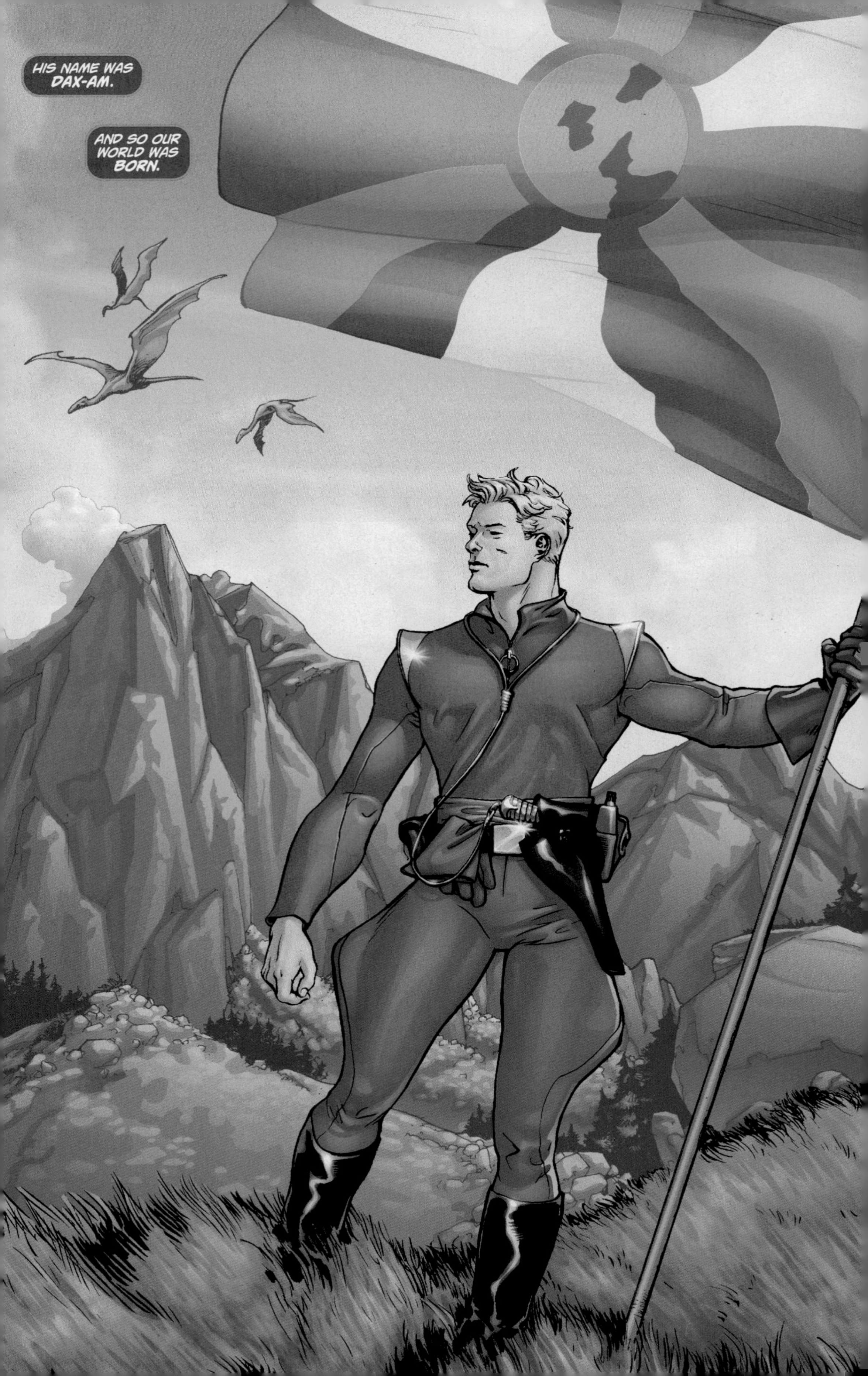
HIS NAME WAS DAX-AM.
AND SO OUR WORLD WAS BORN.

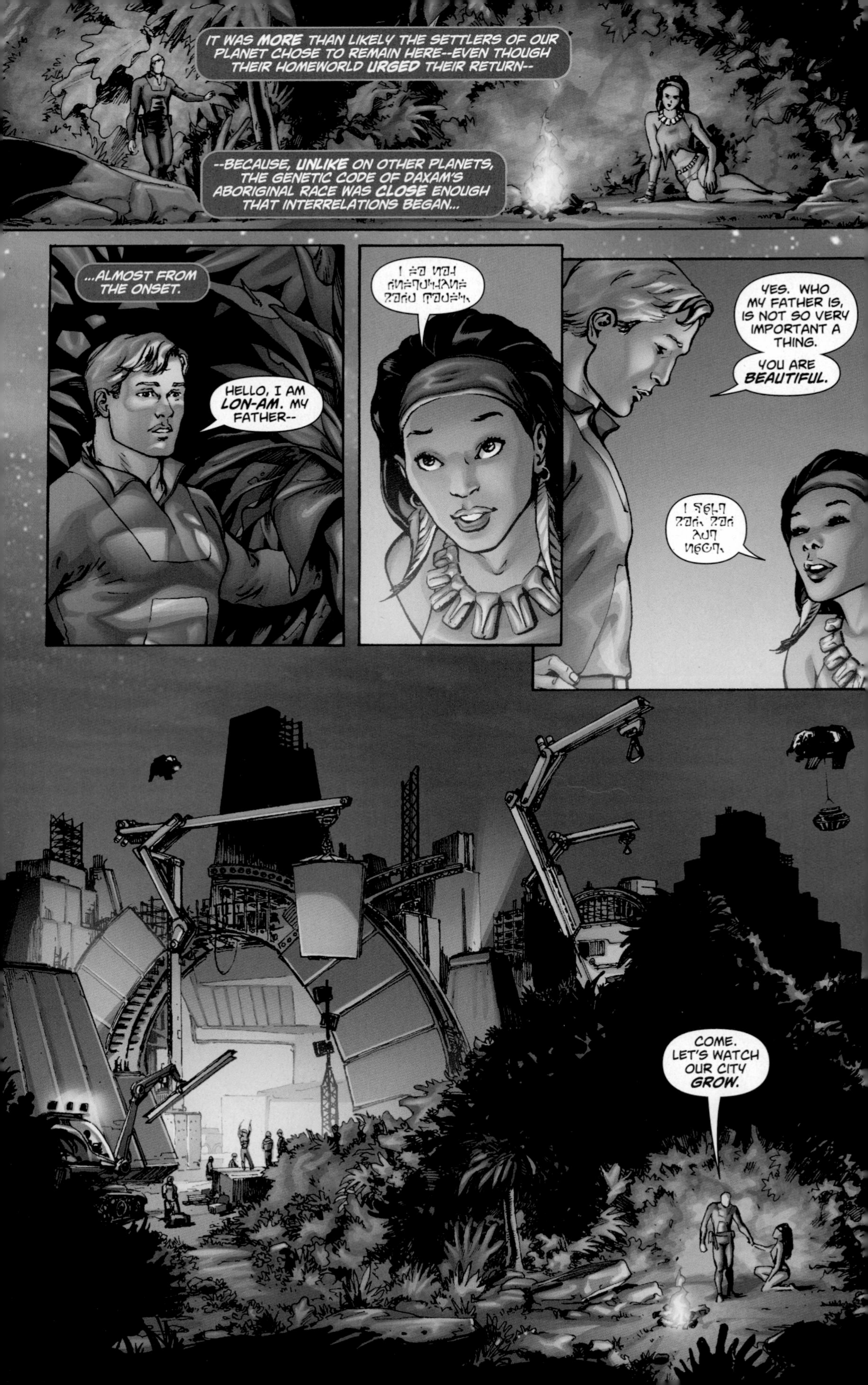
IT WAS MORE THAN LIKELY THE SETTLERS OF OUR PLANET CHOSE TO REMAIN HERE--EVEN THOUGH THEIR HOMEWORLD URGED THEIR RETURN--
--BECAUSE, UNLIKE ON OTHER PLANETS, THE GENETIC CODE OF DAXAM'S ABORIGINAL RACE WAS CLOSE ENOUGH THAT INTERRELATIONS BEGAN...
...ALMOST FROM THE ONSET.
HELLO, I AM LON-AM. MY FATHER--
YES. WHO MY FATHER IS, IS NOT SO VERY IMPORTANT A THING.
YOU ARE BEAUTIFUL.
COME. LET'S WATCH OUR CITY GROW.

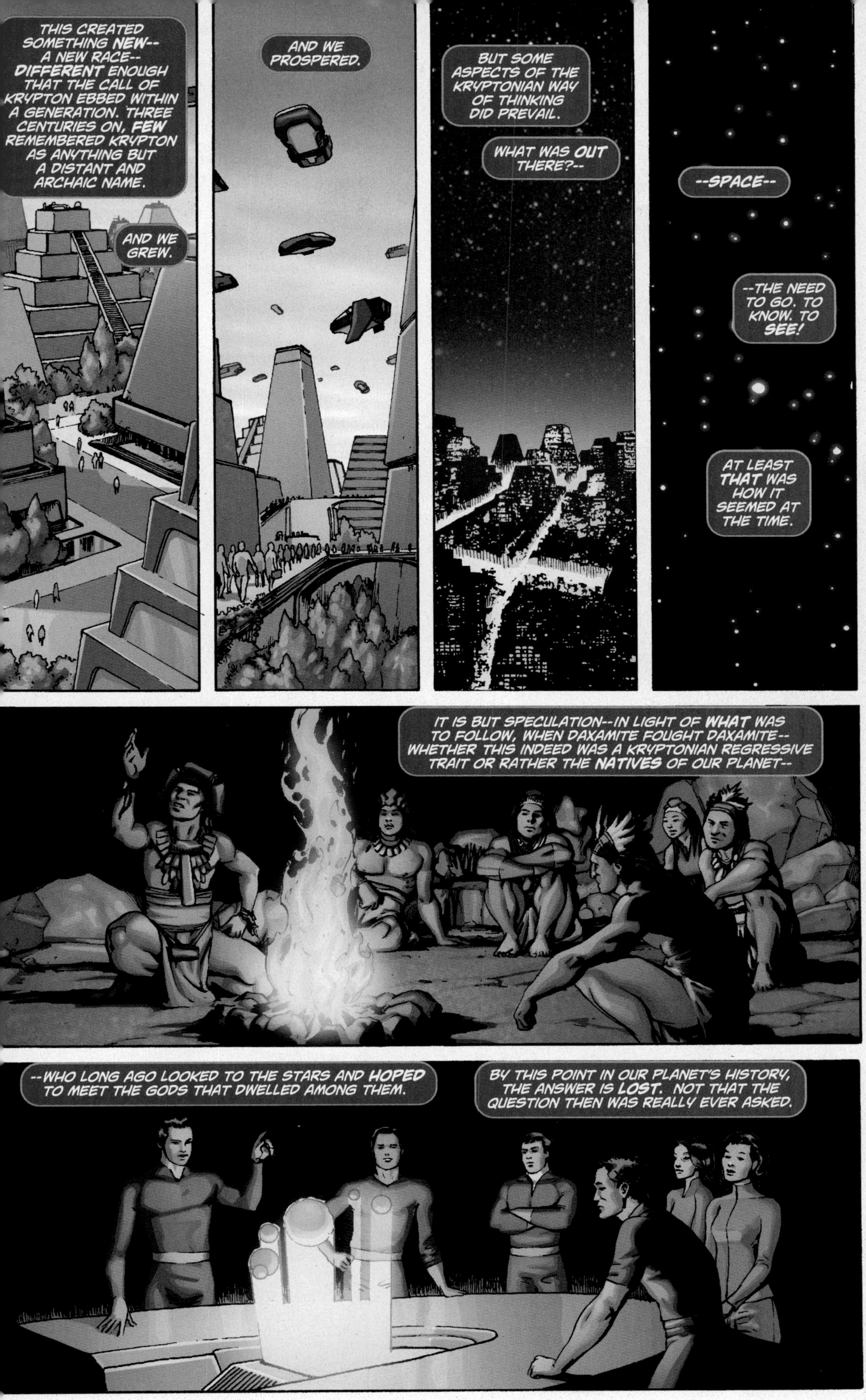
THIS CREATED SOMETHING NEW-- A NEW RACE-- DIFFERENT ENOUGH THAT THE CALL OF KRYPTON EBBED WITHIN A GENERATION. THREE CENTURIES ON, FEW REMEMBERED KRYPTON AS ANYTHING BUT A DISTANT AND ARCHAIC NAME.
AND WE GREW.
AND WE PROSPERED.
BUT SOME ASPECTS OF THE KRYPTONIAN WAY OF THINKING DID PREVAIL.
WHAT WAS OUT THERE?--
--SPACE--
--THE NEED TO GO. TO KNOW. TO SEE!
AT LEAST THAT WAS HOW IT SEEMED AT THE TIME.
IT IS BUT SPECULATION--IN LIGHT OF WHAT WAS TO FOLLOW, WHEN DAXAMITE FOUGHT DAXAMITE-- WHETHER THIS INDEED WAS A KRYPTONIAN REGRESSIVE TRAIT OR RATHER THE NATIVES OF OUR PLANET--
--WHO LONG AGO LOOKED TO THE STARS AND HOPED TO MEET THE GODS THAT DWELLED AMONG THEM.
BY THIS POINT IN OUR PLANET'S HISTORY, THE ANSWER IS LOST. NOT THAT THE QUESTION THEN WAS REALLY EVER ASKED.

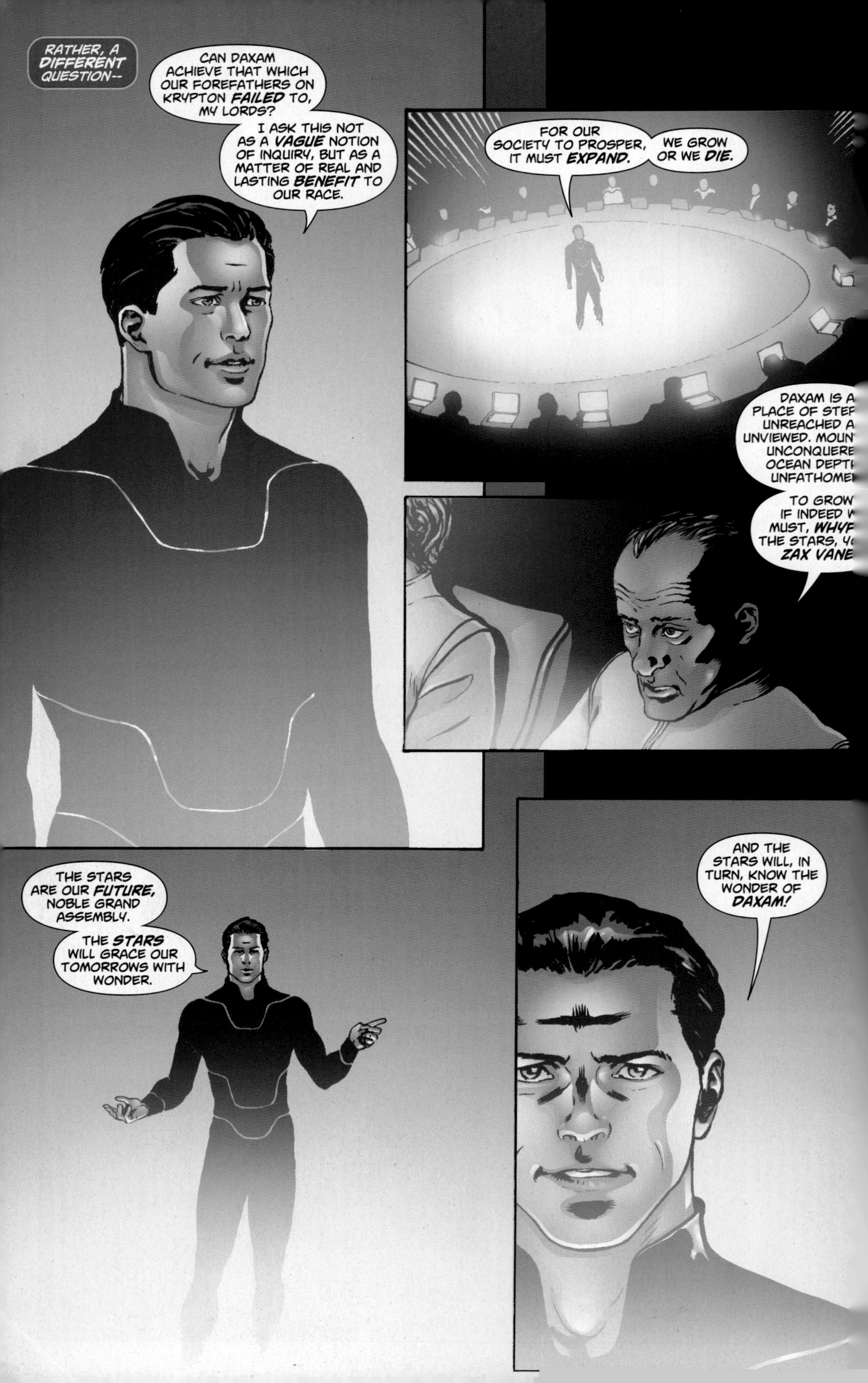
RATHER, A DIFFERENT QUESTION--
CAN DAXAM ACHIEVE THAT WHICH OUR FOREFATHERS ON KRYPTON FAILED TO, MY LORDS?
I ASK THIS NOT AS A VAGUE NOTION OF INQUIRY, BUT AS A MATTER OF REAL AND LASTING BENEFIT TO OUR RACE.
FOR OUR SOCIETY TO PROSPER, IT MUST EXPAND.
WE GROW OR WE DIE.
DAXAM IS A PLACE OF STEP UNREACHED A UNVIEWED. MOUNT UNCONQUERE OCEAN DEPTH UNFATHOME
TO GROW IF INDEED W MUST, WHY THE STARS, Y ZAX VANE
THE STARS ARE OUR FUTURE, NOBLE GRAND ASSEMBLY.
THE STARS WILL GRACE OUR TOMORROWS WITH WONDER.
AND THE STARS WILL, IN TURN, KNOW THE WONDER OF DAXAM!

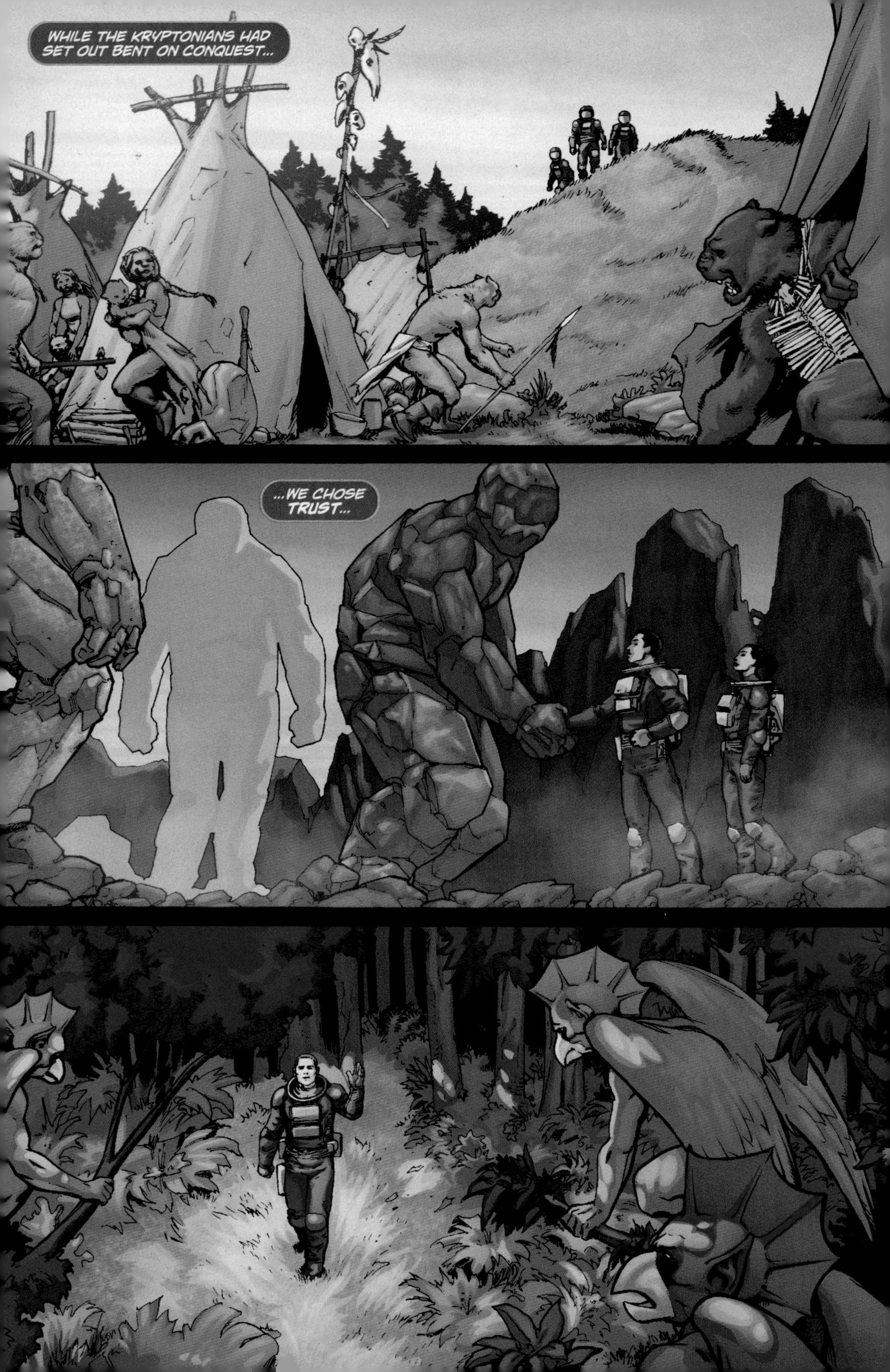
WHILE THE KRYPTONIANS HAD SET OUT BENT ON CONQUEST...
...WE CHOSE TRUST...

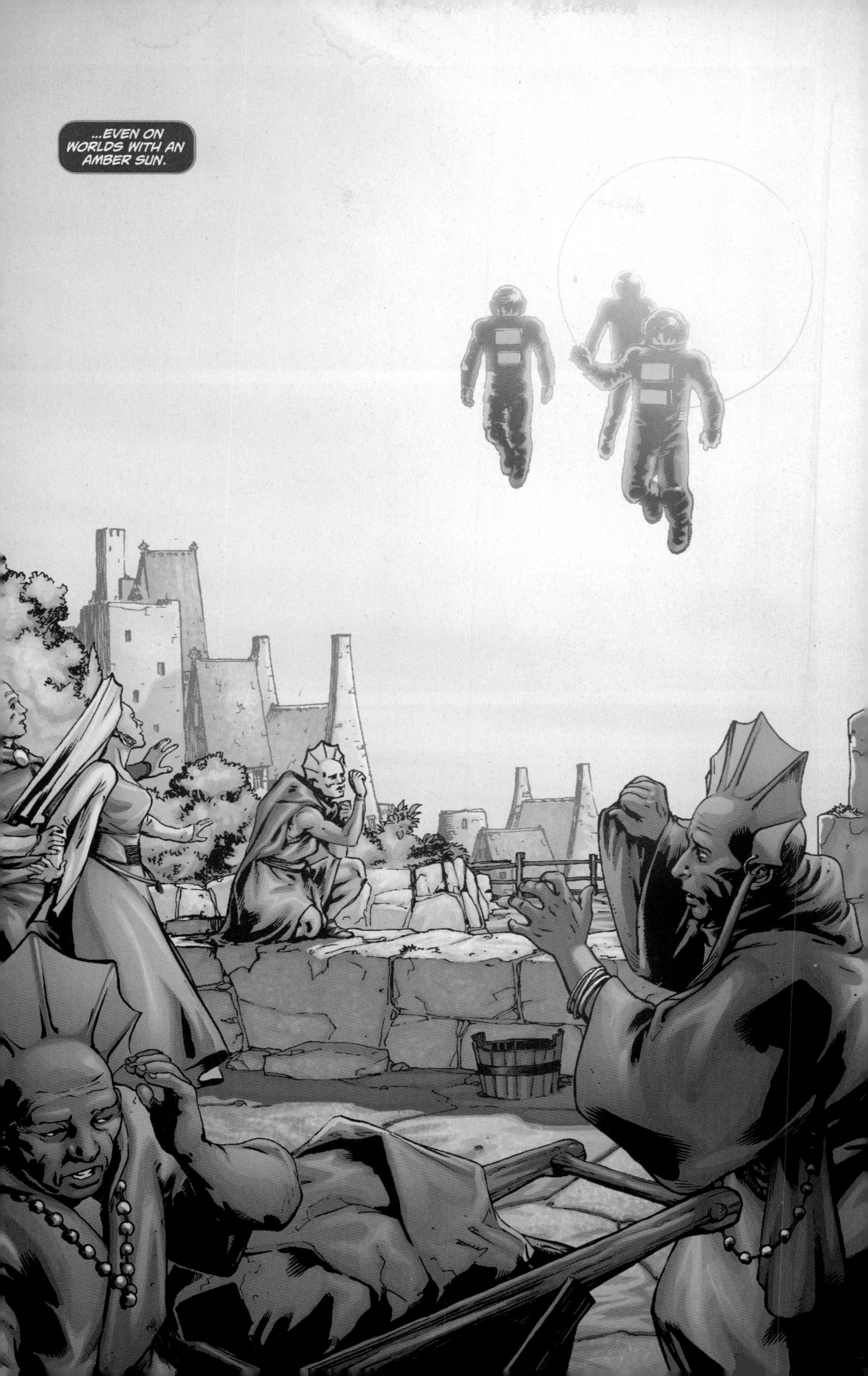
...EVEN ON WORLDS WITH AN AMBER SUN.

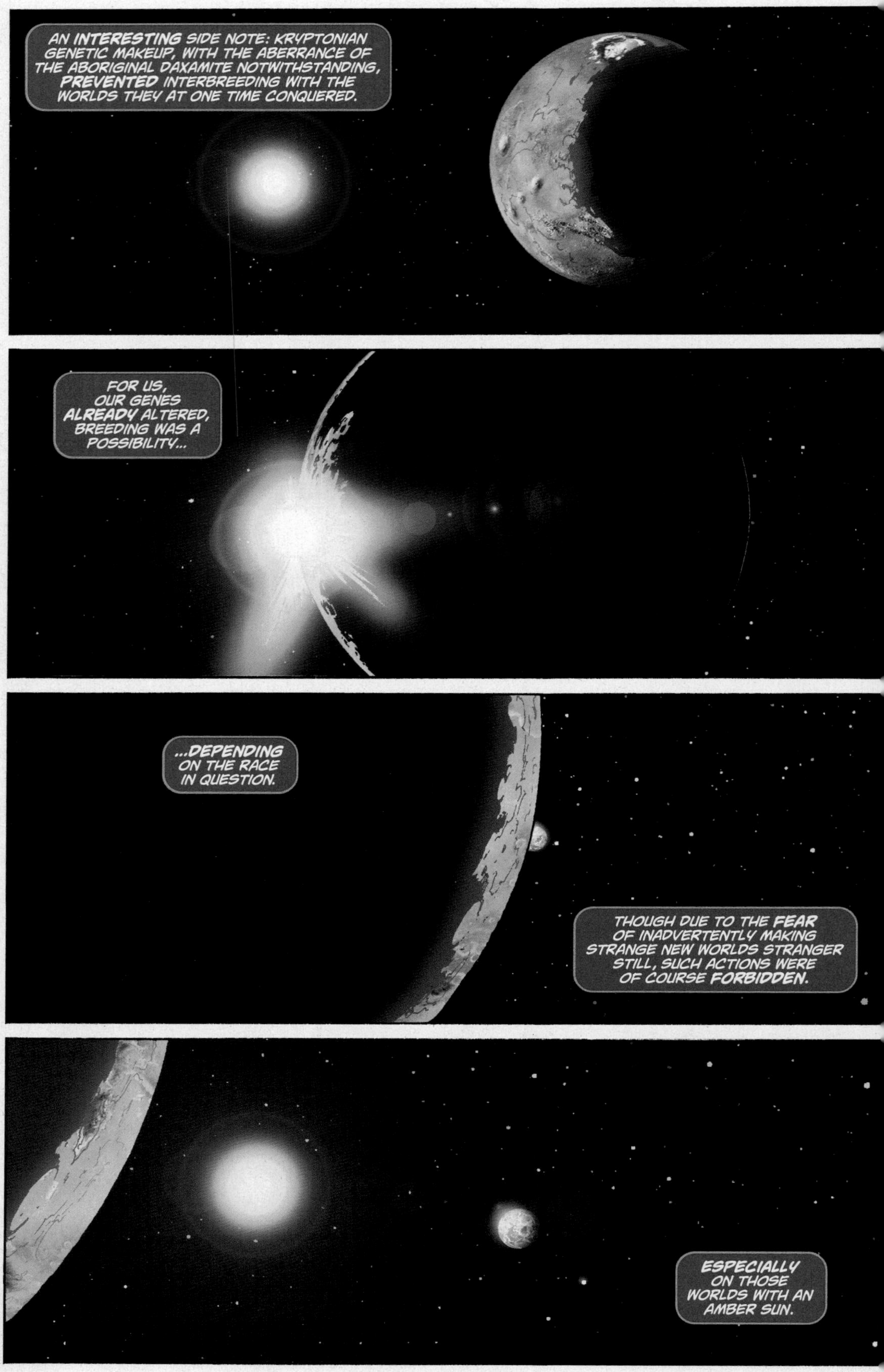
AN **INTERESTING** SIDE NOTE: KRYPTONIAN GENETIC MAKEUP, WITH THE ABERRANCE OF THE ABORIGINAL DAXAMITE NOTWITHSTANDING, **PREVENTED** INTERBREEDING WITH THE WORLDS THEY AT ONE TIME CONQUERED.
FOR US, OUR GENES **ALREADY** ALTERED, BREEDING WAS A POSSIBILITY...
...DEPENDING ON THE RACE IN QUESTION.
THOUGH DUE TO THE **FEAR** OF INADVERTENTLY MAKING STRANGE NEW WORLDS STRANGER STILL, SUCH ACTIONS WERE OF COURSE **FORBIDDEN**.
ESPECIALLY ON THOSE WORLDS WITH AN AMBER SUN.

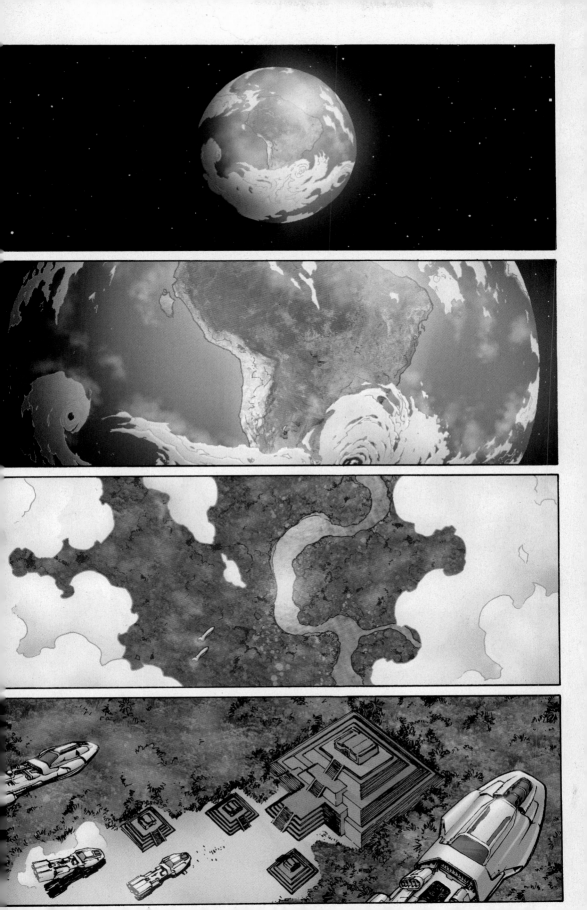

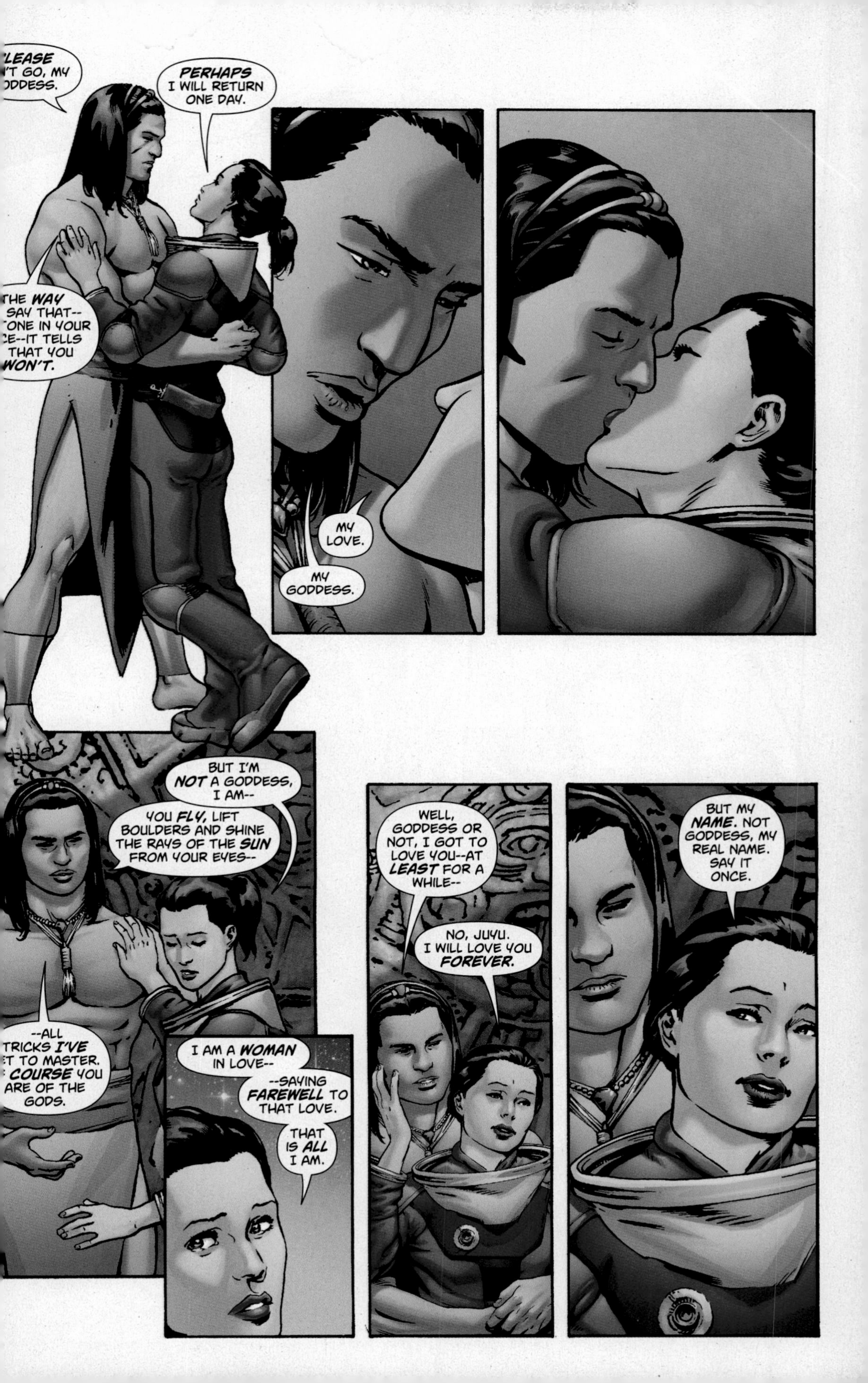

LEASE 'T GO, MY ODDESS.
PERHAPS I WILL RETURN ONE DAY.
THE WAY SAY THAT-- TONE IN YOUR CE--IT TELLS THAT YOU WON'T.
MY LOVE.
MY GODDESS.
BUT I'M NOT A GODDESS, I AM--
YOU FLY, LIFT BOULDERS AND SHINE THE RAYS OF THE SUN FROM YOUR EYES--
--ALL TRICKS I'VE ET TO MASTER. COURSE YOU ARE OF THE GODS.
I AM A WOMAN IN LOVE--
--SAYING FAREWELL TO THAT LOVE.
THAT IS ALL I AM.
WELL, GODDESS OR NOT, I GOT TO LOVE YOU--AT LEAST FOR A WHILE--
NO, JUYU. I WILL LOVE YOU FOREVER.
BUT MY NAME. NOT GODDESS, MY REAL NAME. SAY IT ONCE.

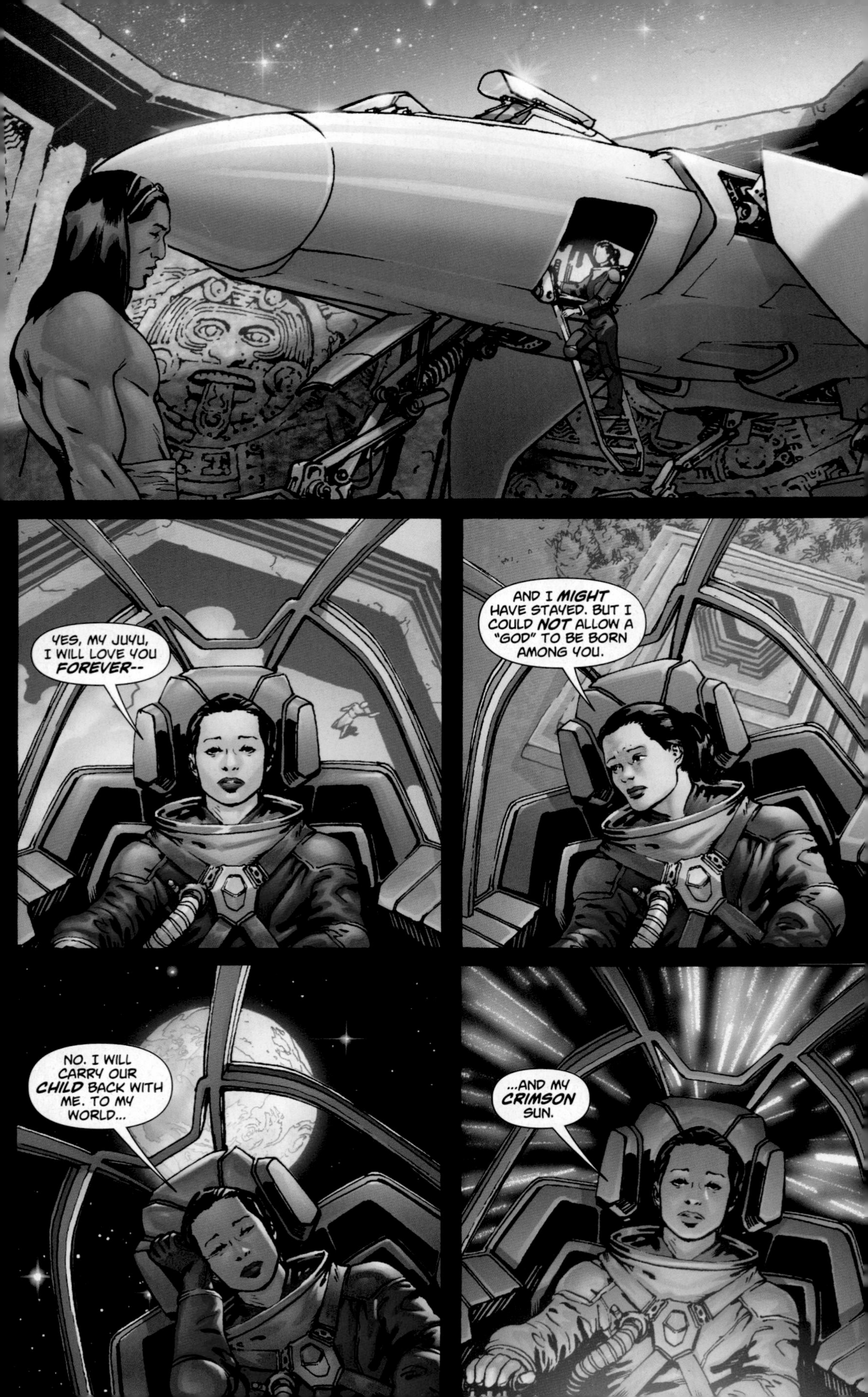
YES, MY JUYU, I WILL LOVE YOU FOREVER--
AND I MIGHT HAVE STAYED. BUT I COULD NOT ALLOW A "GOD" TO BE BORN AMONG YOU.
NO. I WILL CARRY OUR CHILD BACK WITH ME. TO MY WORLD...
...AND MY CRIMSON SUN.

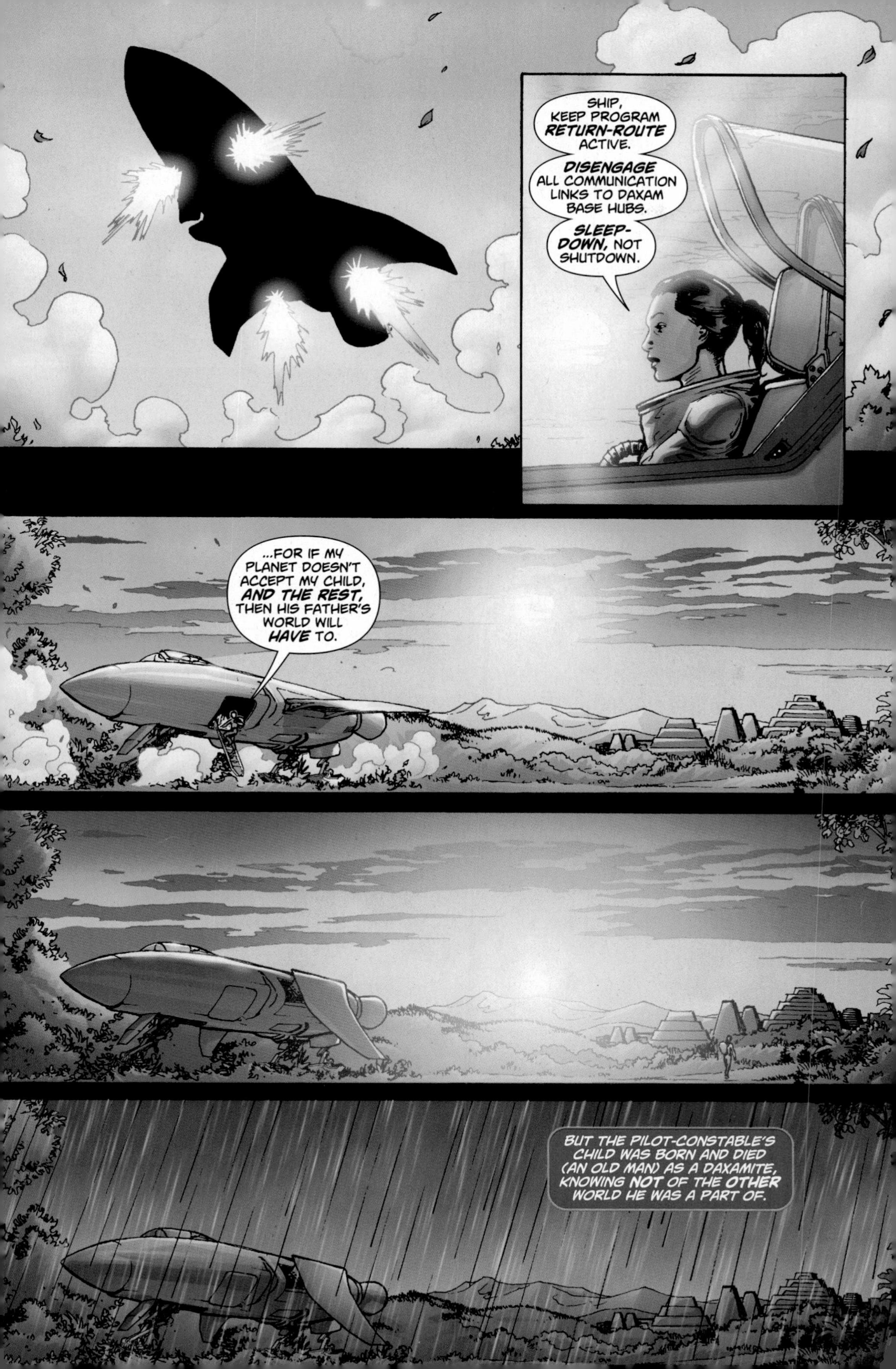
SHIP, KEEP PROGRAM RETURN-ROUTE ACTIVE.
DISENGAGE ALL COMMUNICATION LINKS TO DAXAM BASE HUBS.
SLEEP-DOWN, NOT SHUTDOWN.
...FOR IF MY PLANET DOESN'T ACCEPT MY CHILD, AND THE REST, THEN HIS FATHER'S WORLD WILL HAVE TO.
BUT THE PILOT-CONSTABLE'S CHILD WAS BORN AND DIED (AN OLD MAN) AS A DAXAMITE, KNOWING NOT OF THE OTHER WORLD HE WAS A PART OF.

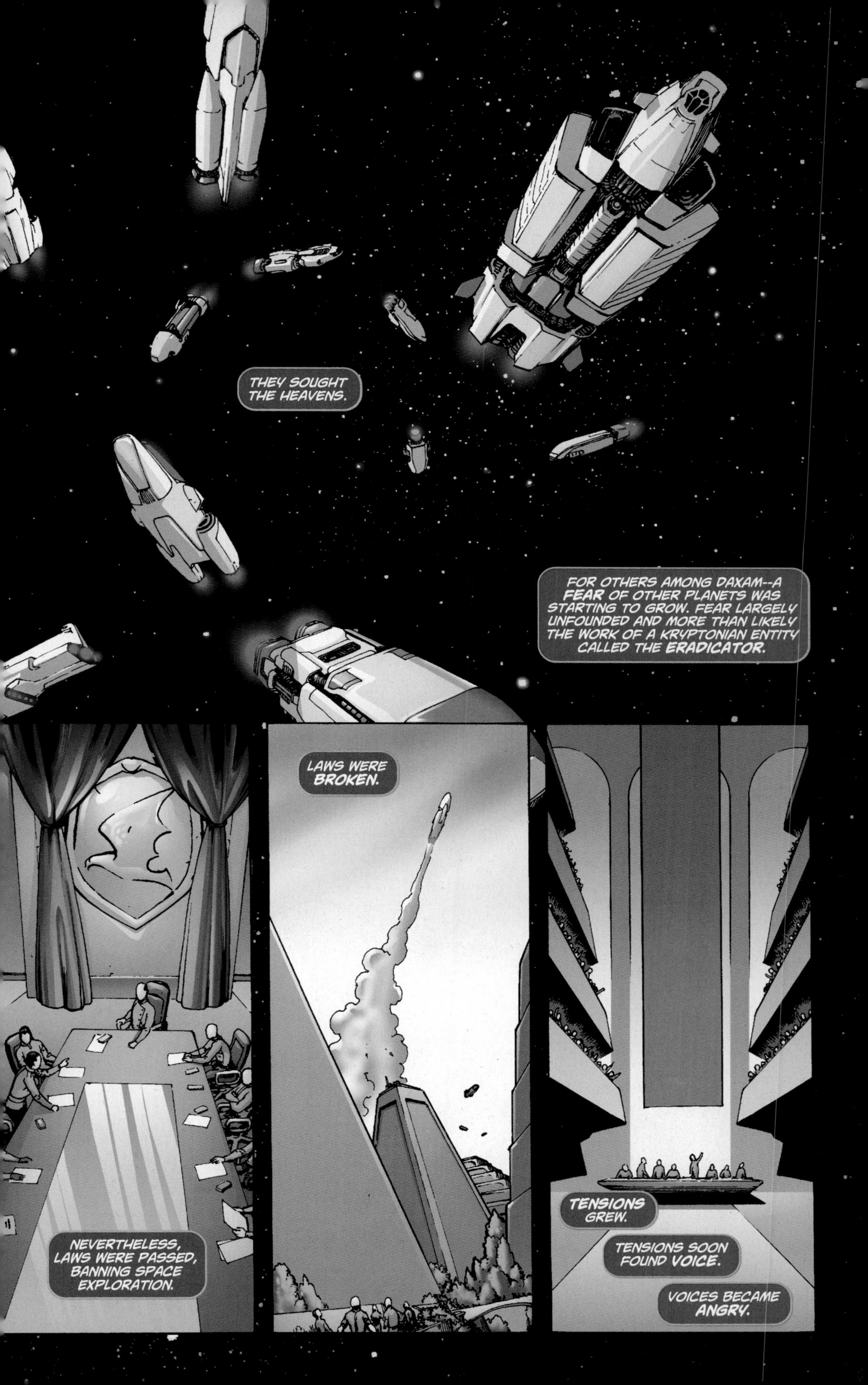
THEY SOUGHT THE HEAVENS.
FOR OTHERS AMONG DAXAM--A FEAR OF OTHER PLANETS WAS STARTING TO GROW. FEAR LARGELY UNFOUNDED AND MORE THAN LIKELY THE WORK OF A KRYPTONIAN ENTITY CALLED THE ERADICATOR.
NEVERTHELESS, LAWS WERE PASSED, BANNING SPACE EXPLORATION.
LAWS WERE BROKEN.
TENSIONS GREW.
TENSIONS SOON FOUND VOICE.
VOICES BECAME ANGRY.

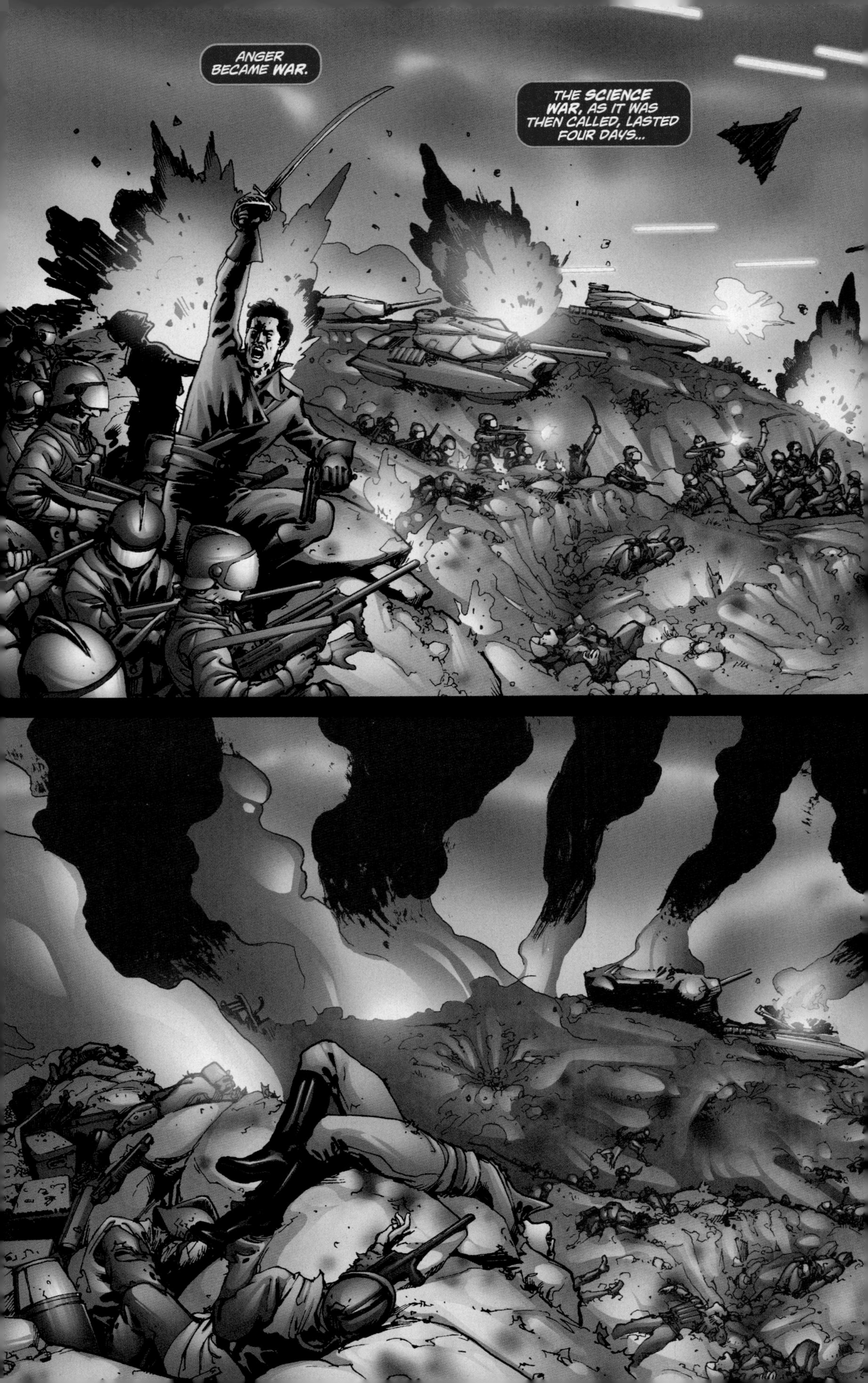
ANGER BECAME WAR.
THE SCIENCE WAR, AS IT WAS THEN CALLED, LASTED FOUR DAYS...

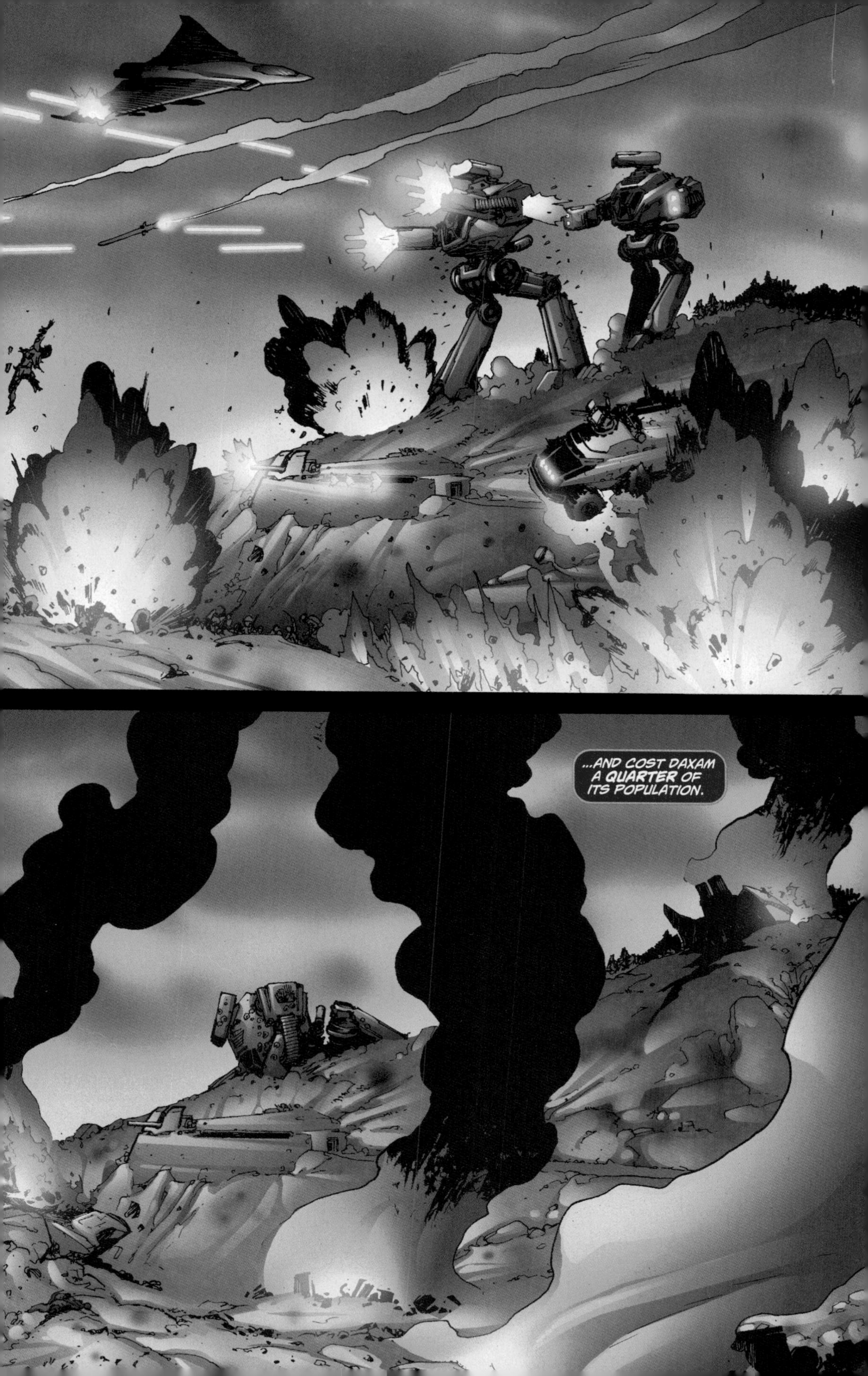
...AND COST DAXAM A QUARTER OF ITS POPULATION.

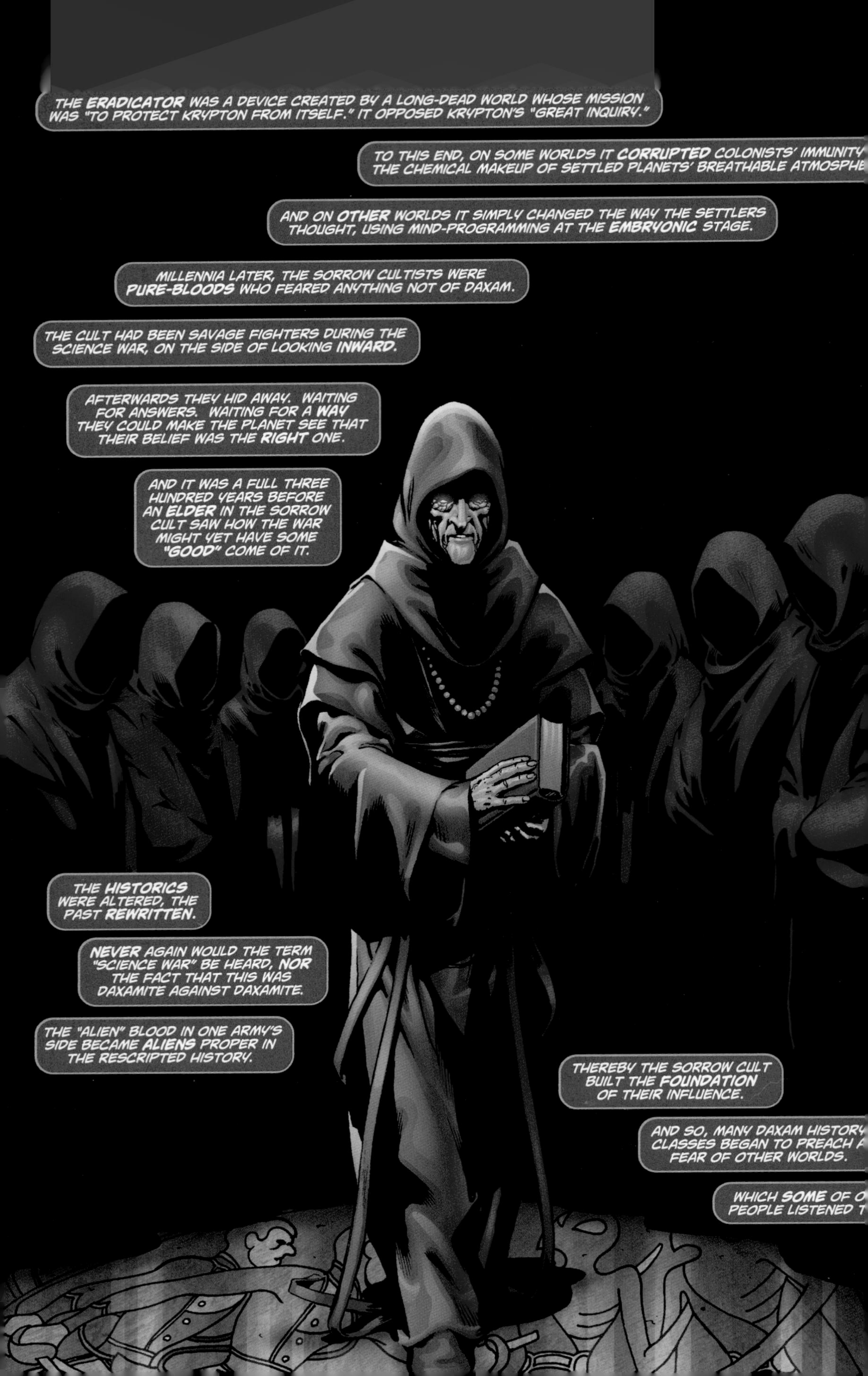

THE ERADICATOR WAS A DEVICE CREATED BY A LONG-DEAD WORLD WHOSE MISSION WAS "TO PROTECT KRYPTON FROM ITSELF." IT OPPOSED KRYPTON'S "GREAT INQUIRY."
TO THIS END, ON SOME WORLDS IT CORRUPTED COLONISTS' IMMUNITY THE CHEMICAL MAKEUP OF SETTLED PLANETS' BREATHABLE ATMOSPHE
AND ON OTHER WORLDS IT SIMPLY CHANGED THE WAY THE SETTLERS THOUGHT, USING MIND-PROGRAMMING AT THE EMBRYONIC STAGE.
MILLENNIA LATER, THE SORROW CULTISTS WERE PURE-BLOODS WHO FEARED ANYTHING NOT OF DAXAM.
THE CULT HAD BEEN SAVAGE FIGHTERS DURING THE SCIENCE WAR, ON THE SIDE OF LOOKING INWARD.
AFTERWARDS THEY HID AWAY. WAITING FOR ANSWERS. WAITING FOR A WAY THEY COULD MAKE THE PLANET SEE THAT THEIR BELIEF WAS THE RIGHT ONE.
AND IT WAS A FULL THREE HUNDRED YEARS BEFORE AN ELDER IN THE SORROW CULT SAW HOW THE WAR MIGHT YET HAVE SOME "GOOD" COME OF IT.
THE HISTORICS WERE ALTERED, THE PAST REWRITTEN.
NEVER AGAIN WOULD THE TERM "SCIENCE WAR" BE HEARD, NOR THE FACT THAT THIS WAS DAXAMITE AGAINST DAXAMITE.
THE "ALIEN" BLOOD IN ONE ARMY'S SIDE BECAME ALIENS PROPER IN THE RESCRIPTED HISTORY.
THEREBY THE SORROW CULT BUILT THE FOUNDATION OF THEIR INFLUENCE.
AND SO, MANY DAXAM HISTORY CLASSES BEGAN TO PREACH A FEAR OF OTHER WORLDS.
WHICH SOME OF O PEOPLE LISTENED T

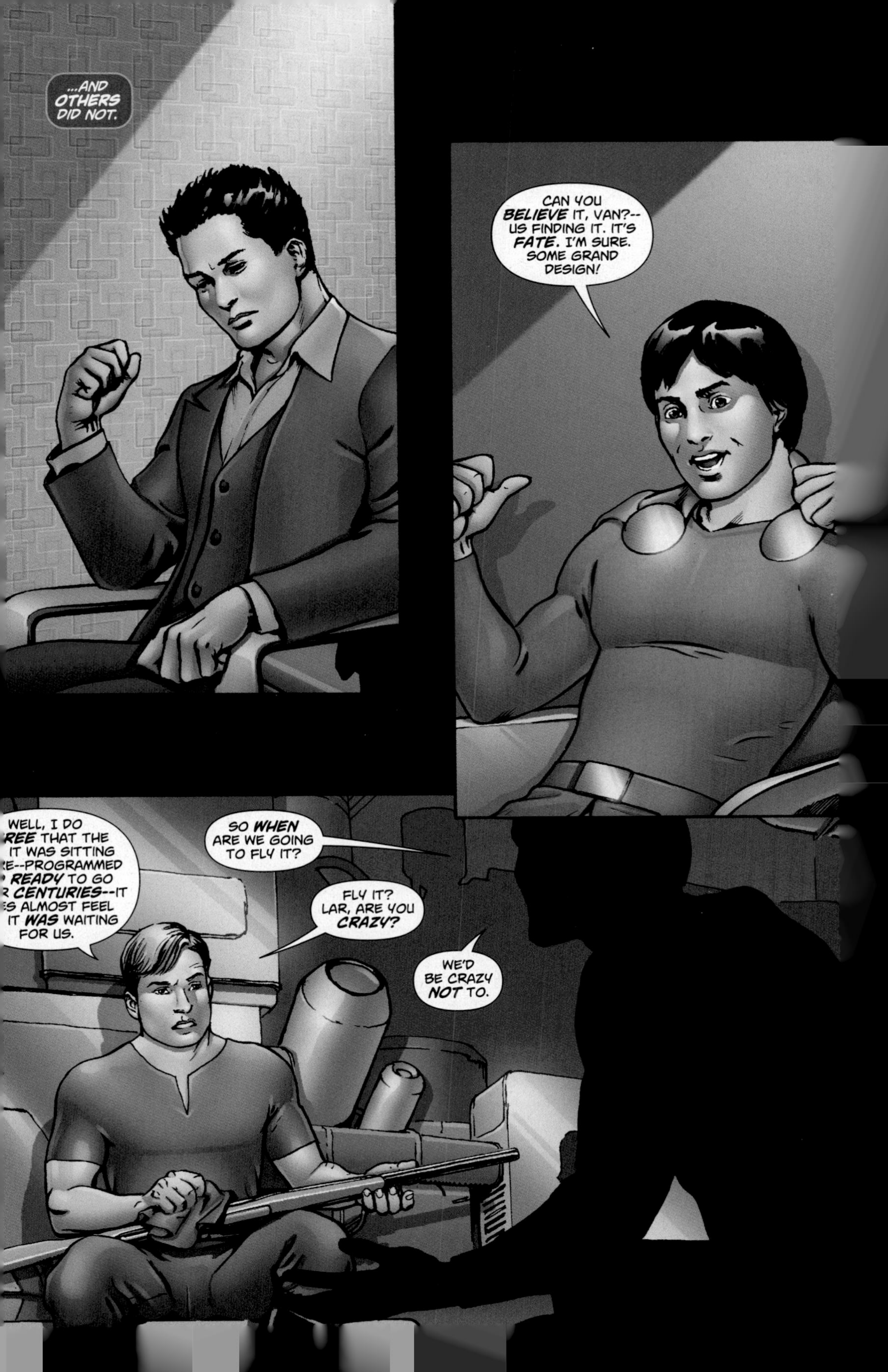
...AND OTHERS DID NOT.
CAN YOU BELIEVE IT, VAN?-- US FINDING IT. IT'S FATE. I'M SURE. SOME GRAND DESIGN!
WELL, I DO REE THAT THE IT WAS SITTING RE--PROGRAMMED READY TO GO R CENTURIES--IT ES ALMOST FEEL IT WAS WAITING FOR US.
SO WHEN ARE WE GOING TO FLY IT?
FLY IT? LAR, ARE YOU CRAZY?
WE'D BE CRAZY NOT TO.

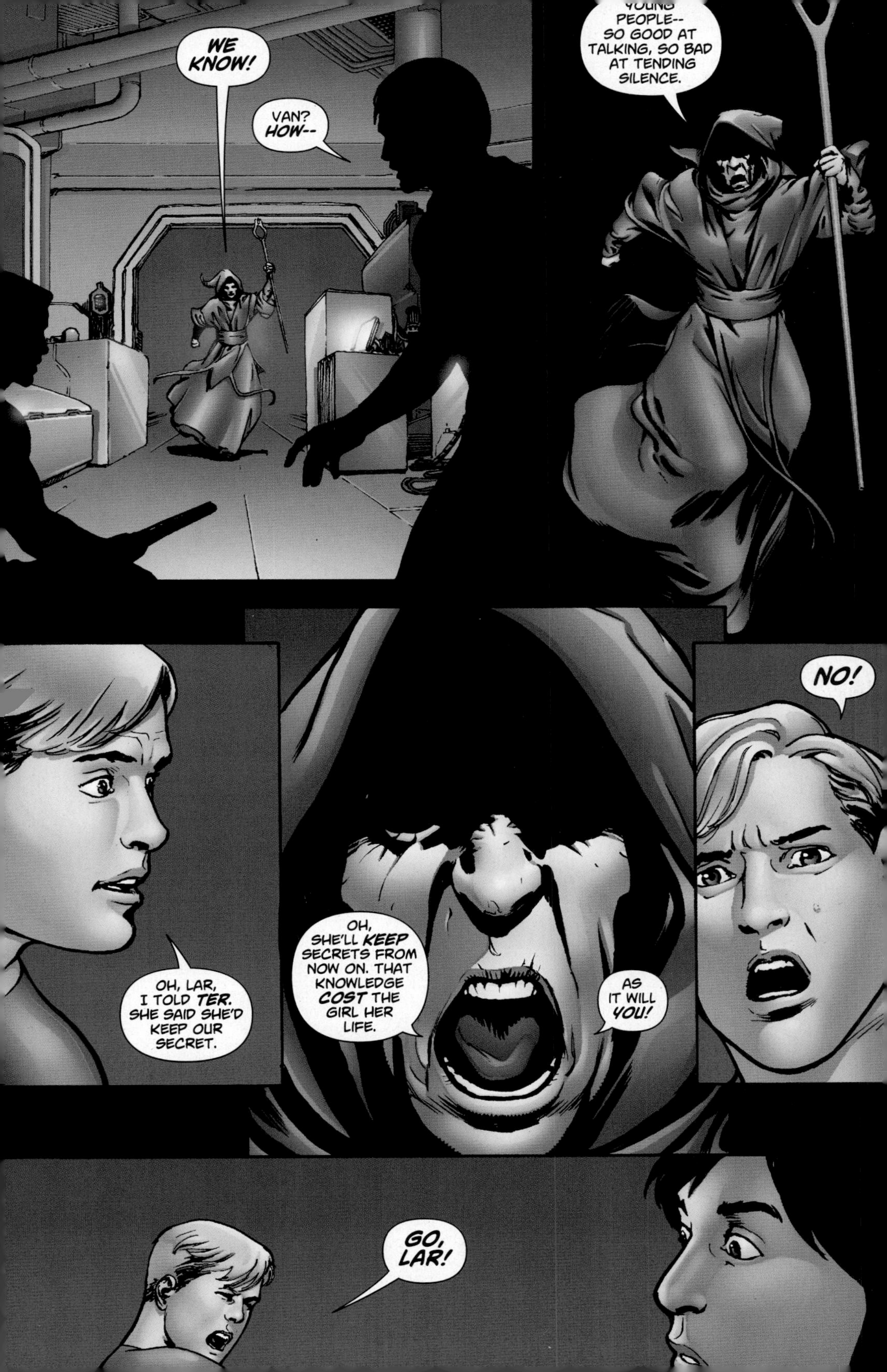
WE KNOW!
VAN? HOW--
YOUNG PEOPLE-- SO GOOD AT TALKING, SO BAD AT TENDING SILENCE.
OH, LAR, I TOLD TER. SHE SAID SHE'D KEEP OUR SECRET.
OH, SHE'LL KEEP SECRETS FROM NOW ON. THAT KNOWLEDGE COST THE GIRL HER LIFE.
AS IT WILL YOU!
NO!
GO, LAR!

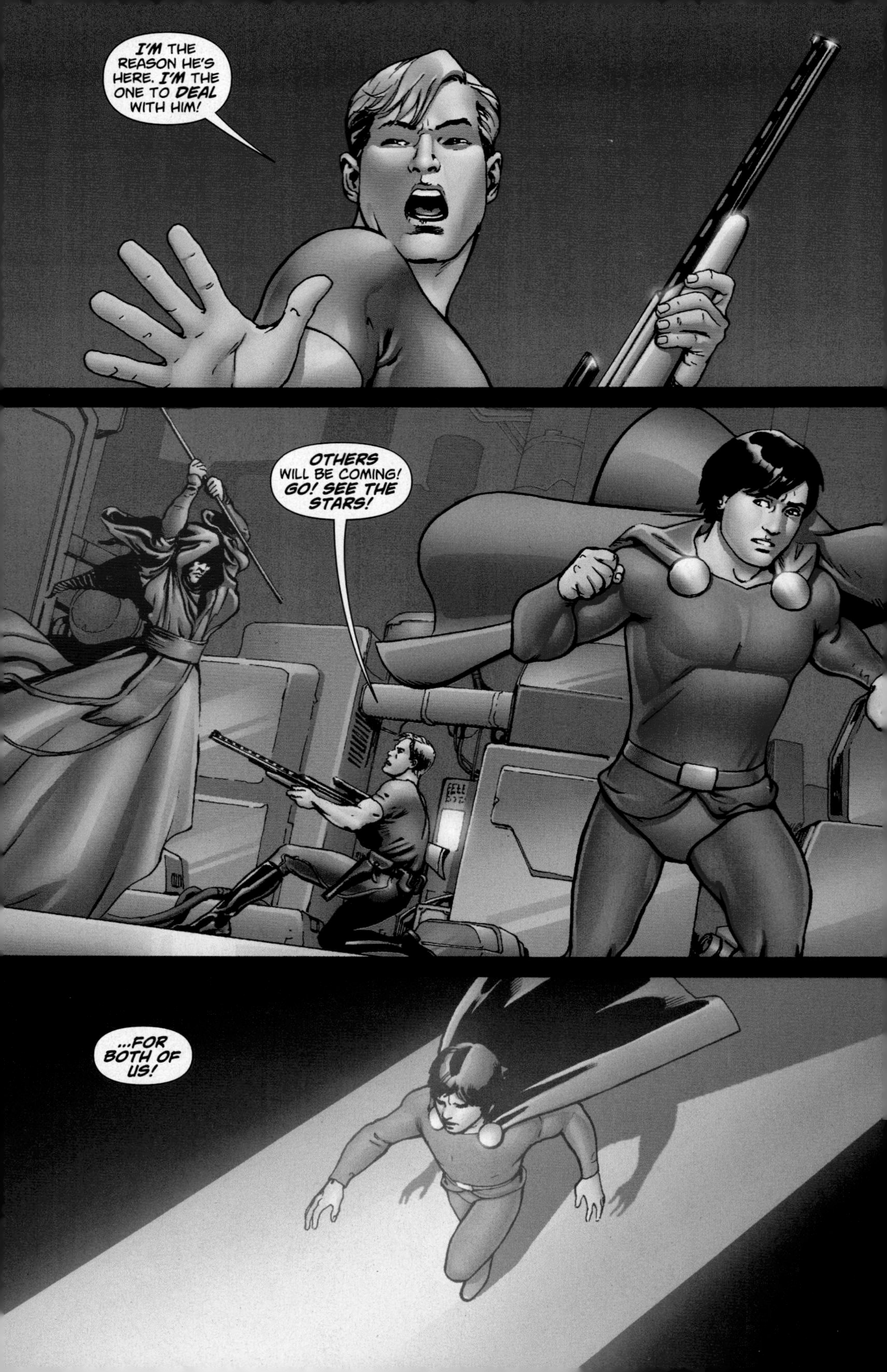
I'M THE REASON HE'S HERE. I'M THE ONE TO DEAL WITH HIM!
OTHERS WILL BE COMING! GO! SEE THE STARS!
...FOR BOTH OF US!

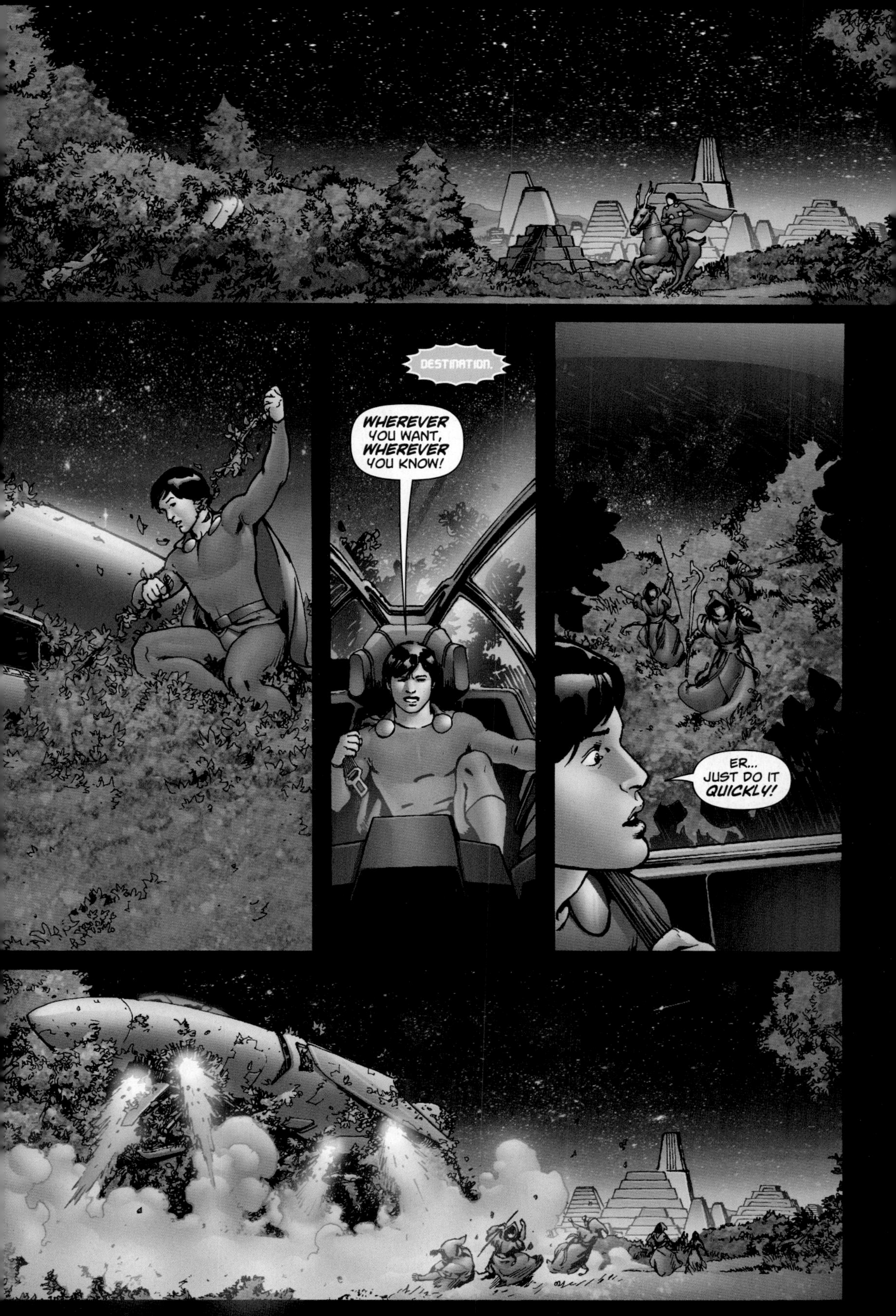
DESTINATION.
WHEREVER YOU WANT, WHEREVER YOU KNOW!
ER... JUST DO IT QUICKLY!

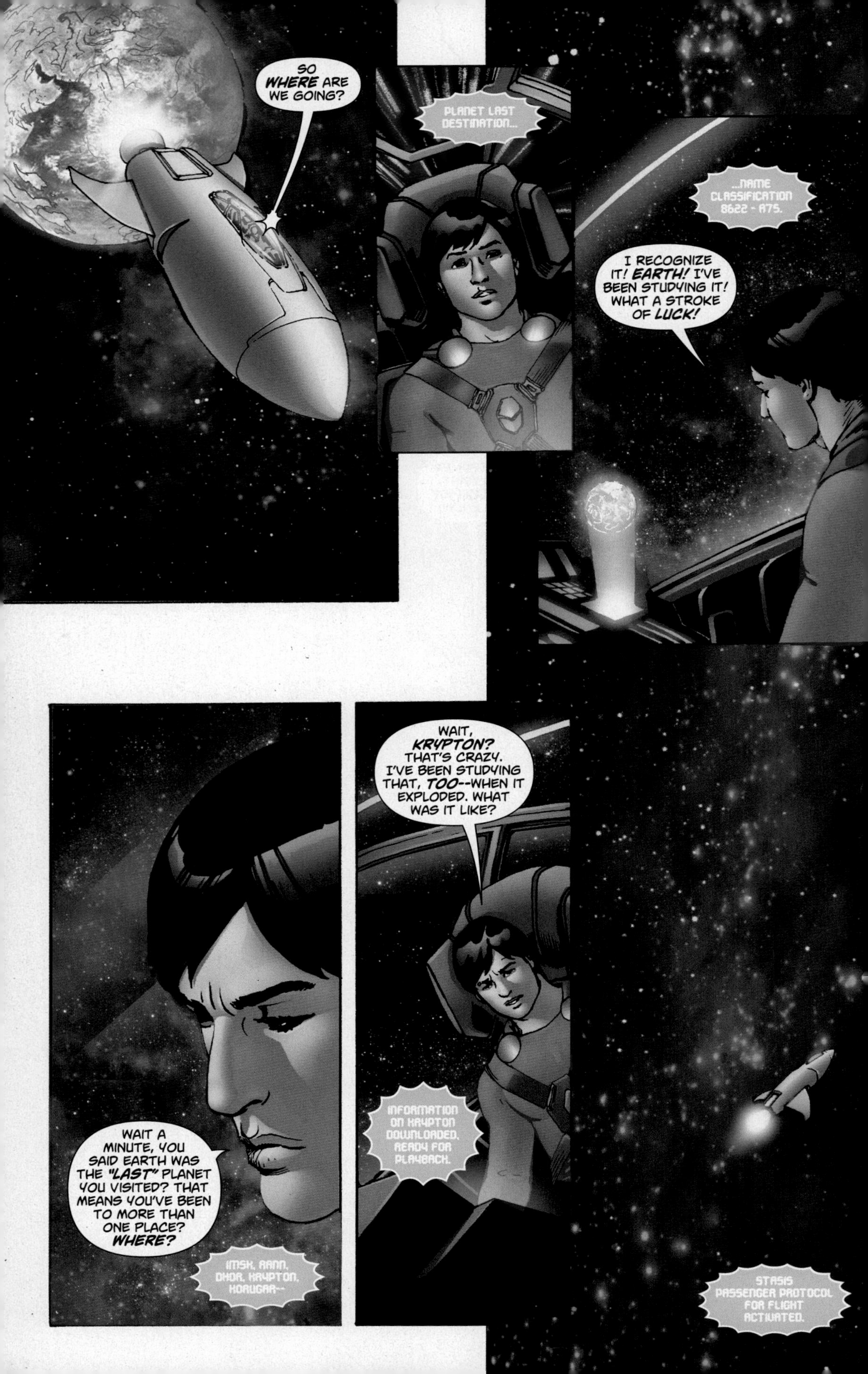
SO WHERE ARE WE GOING?
PLANET LAST DESTINATION...
...NAME CLASSIFICATION 8622 - A75.
I RECOGNIZE IT! EARTH! I'VE BEEN STUDYING IT! WHAT A STROKE OF LUCK!
WAIT A MINUTE, YOU SAID EARTH WAS THE "LAST" PLANET YOU VISITED? THAT MEANS YOU'VE BEEN TO MORE THAN ONE PLACE? WHERE?
IMSK, RANN, DHOR, KRYPTON, KORUGAR--
WAIT, KRYPTON? THAT'S CRAZY. I'VE BEEN STUDYING THAT, TOO--WHEN IT EXPLODED. WHAT WAS IT LIKE?
INFORMATION ON KRYPTON DOWNLOADED, READY FOR PLAYBACK.
STASIS PASSENGER PROTOCOL FOR FLIGHT ACTIVATED.

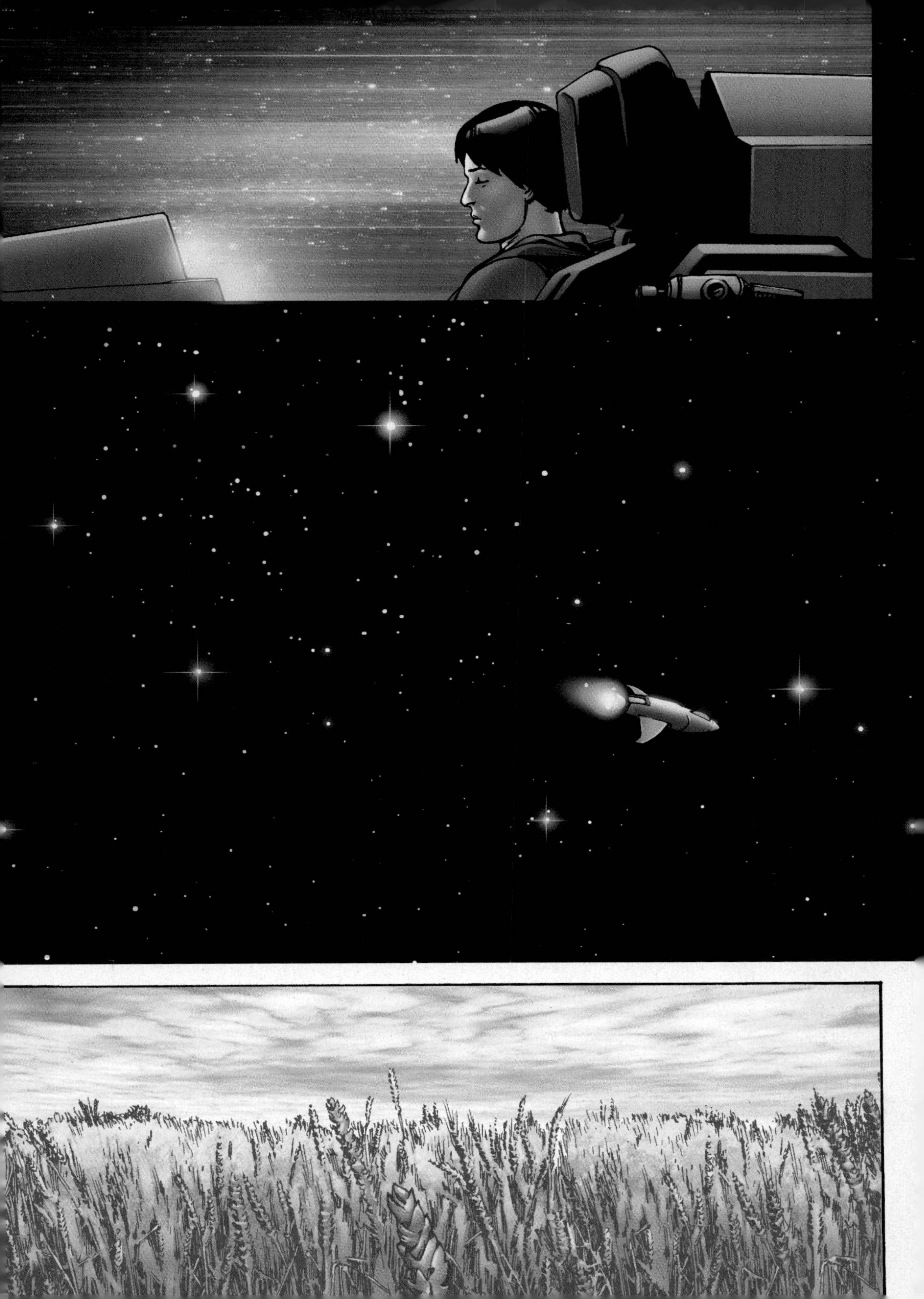

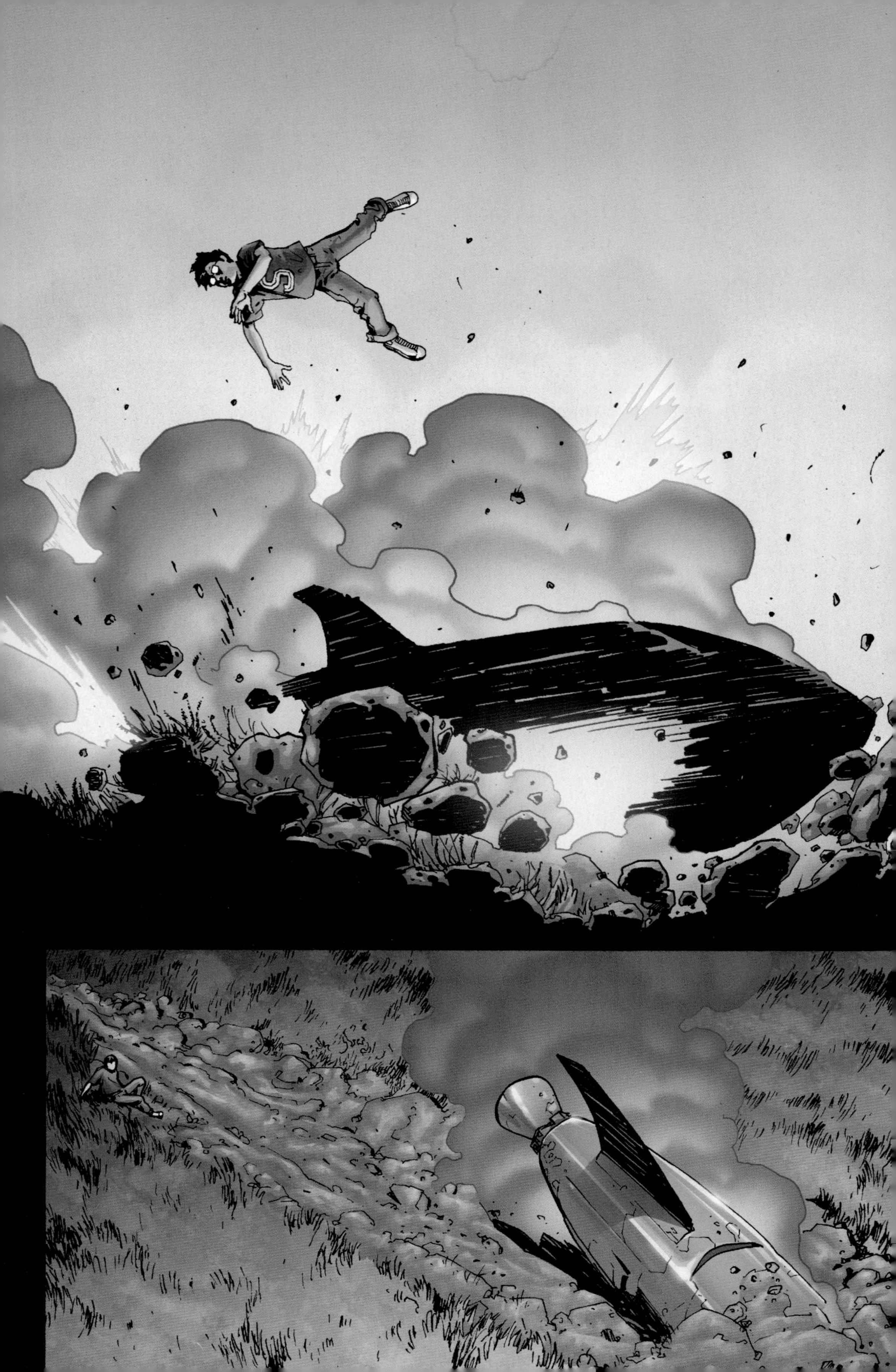

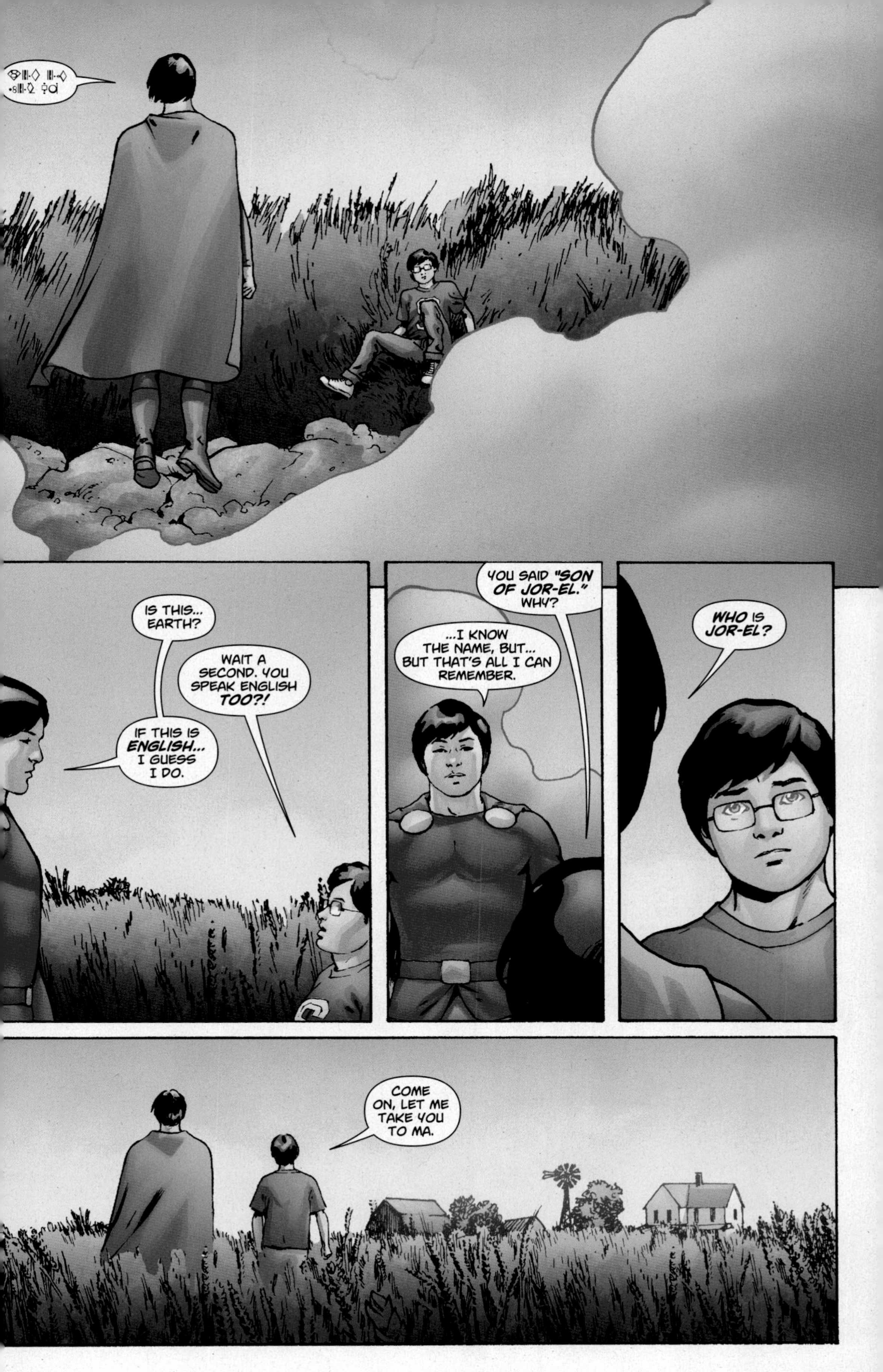
IS THIS... EARTH?
WAIT A SECOND. YOU SPEAK ENGLISH TOO?!
IF THIS IS ENGLISH... I GUESS I DO.
YOU SAID "SON OF JOR-EL." WHY?
...I KNOW THE NAME, BUT... BUT THAT'S ALL I CAN REMEMBER.
WHO IS JOR-EL?
COME ON, LET ME TAKE YOU TO MA.

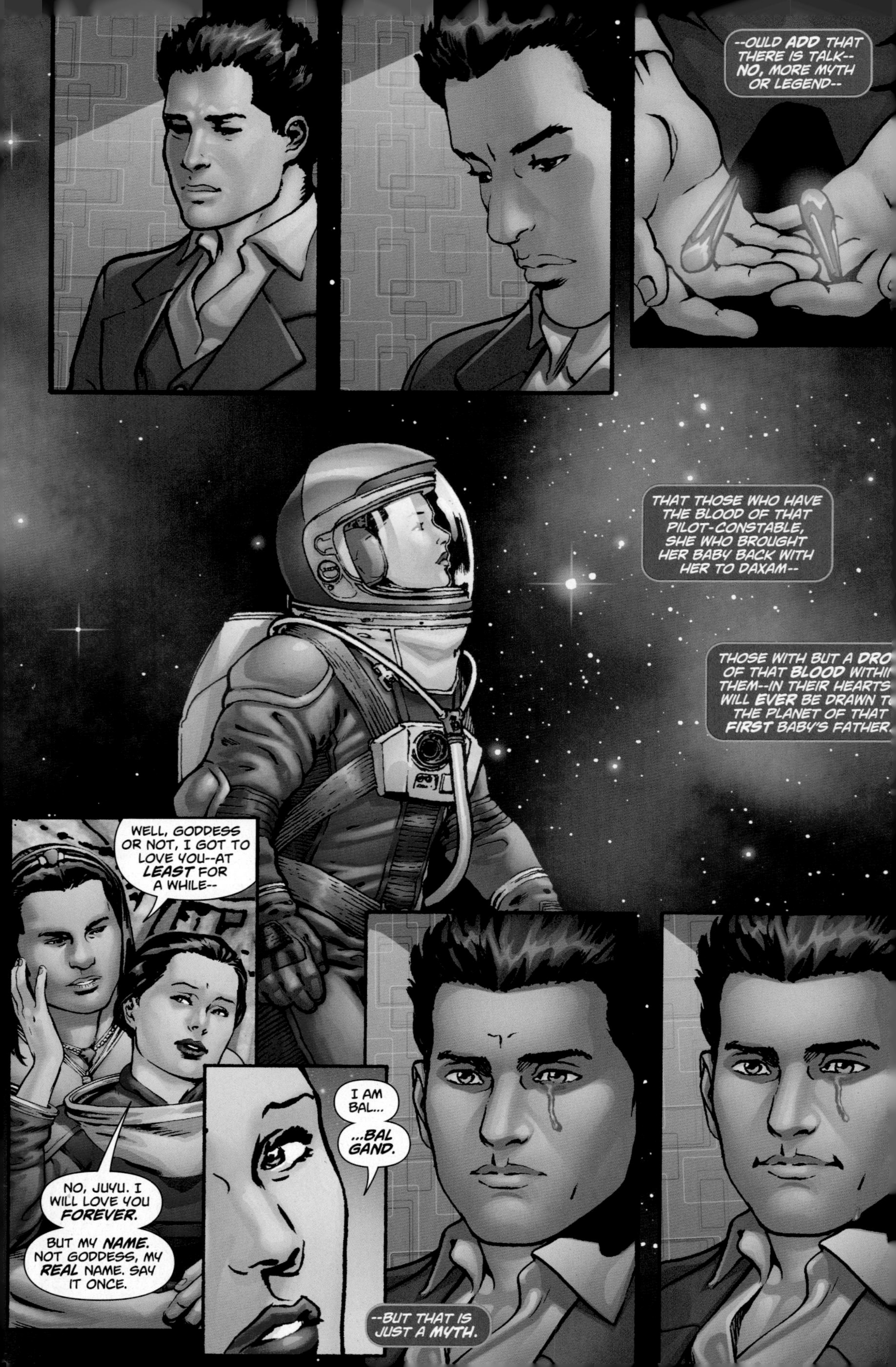
--OULD ADD THAT THERE IS TALK-- NO, MORE MYTH OR LEGEND--
THAT THOSE WHO HAVE THE BLOOD OF THAT PILOT-CONSTABLE, SHE WHO BROUGHT HER BABY BACK WITH HER TO DAXAM--
THOSE WITH BUT A DRO OF THAT BLOOD WITHI THEM--IN THEIR HEARTS WILL EVER BE DRAWN T THE PLANET OF THAT FIRST BABY'S FATHER.
WELL, GODDESS OR NOT, I GOT TO LOVE YOU--AT LEAST FOR A WHILE--
NO, JUYU. I WILL LOVE YOU FOREVER.
BUT MY NAME. NOT GODDESS, MY REAL NAME. SAY IT ONCE.
I AM BAL...
...BAL GAND.
--BUT THAT IS JUST A MYTH.

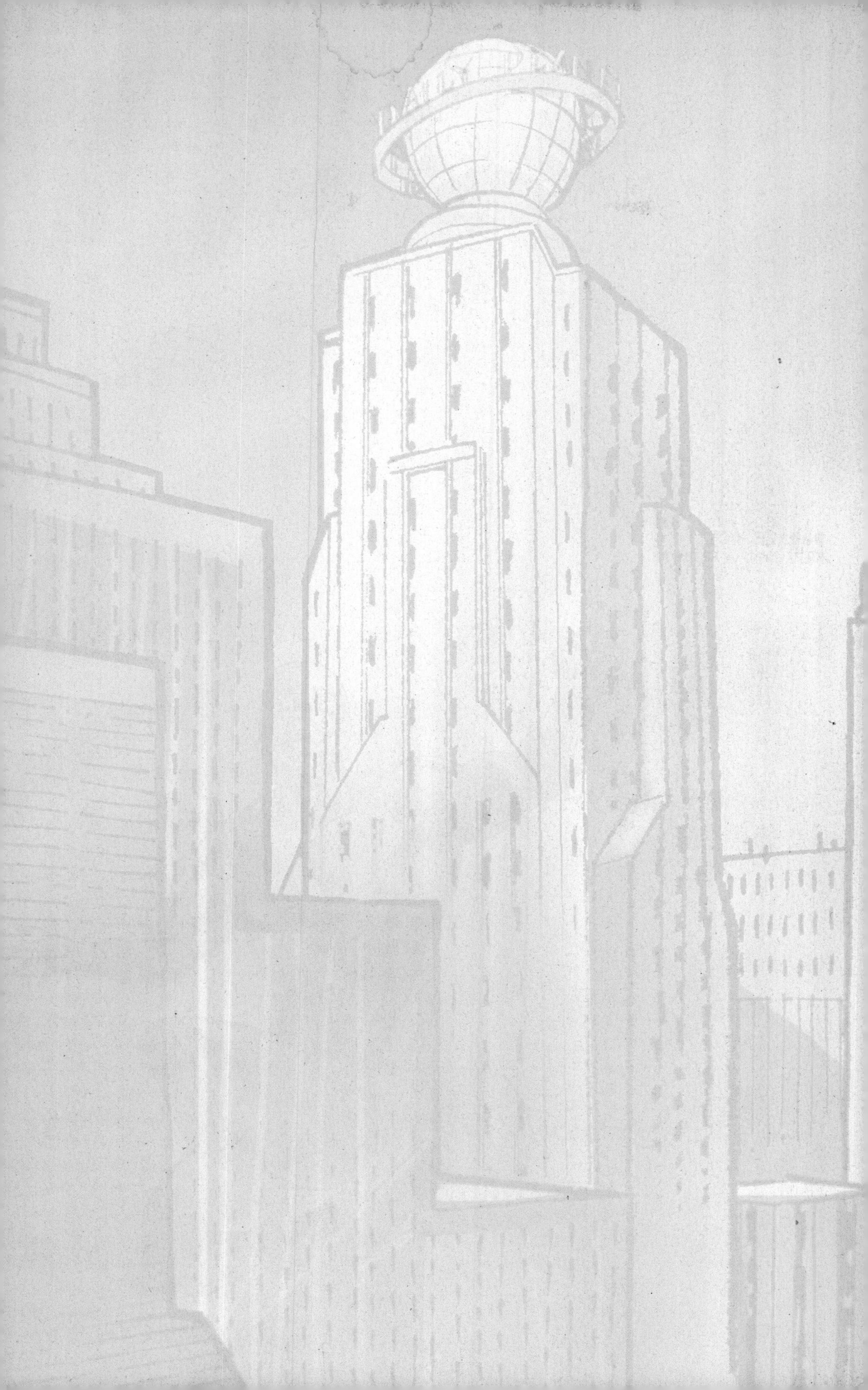

DOUBLE ACT
MATT CAMP <ARTIST>

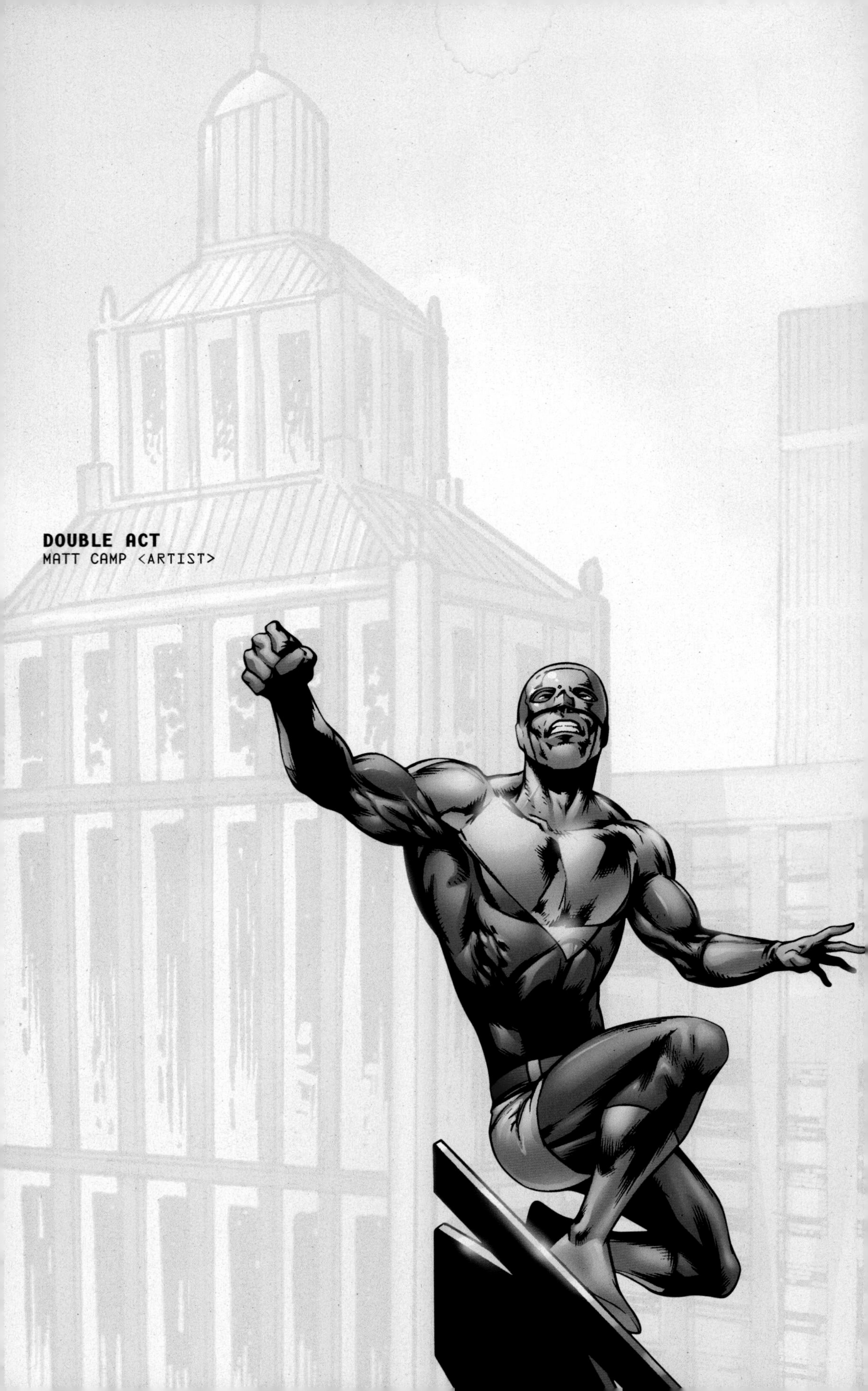

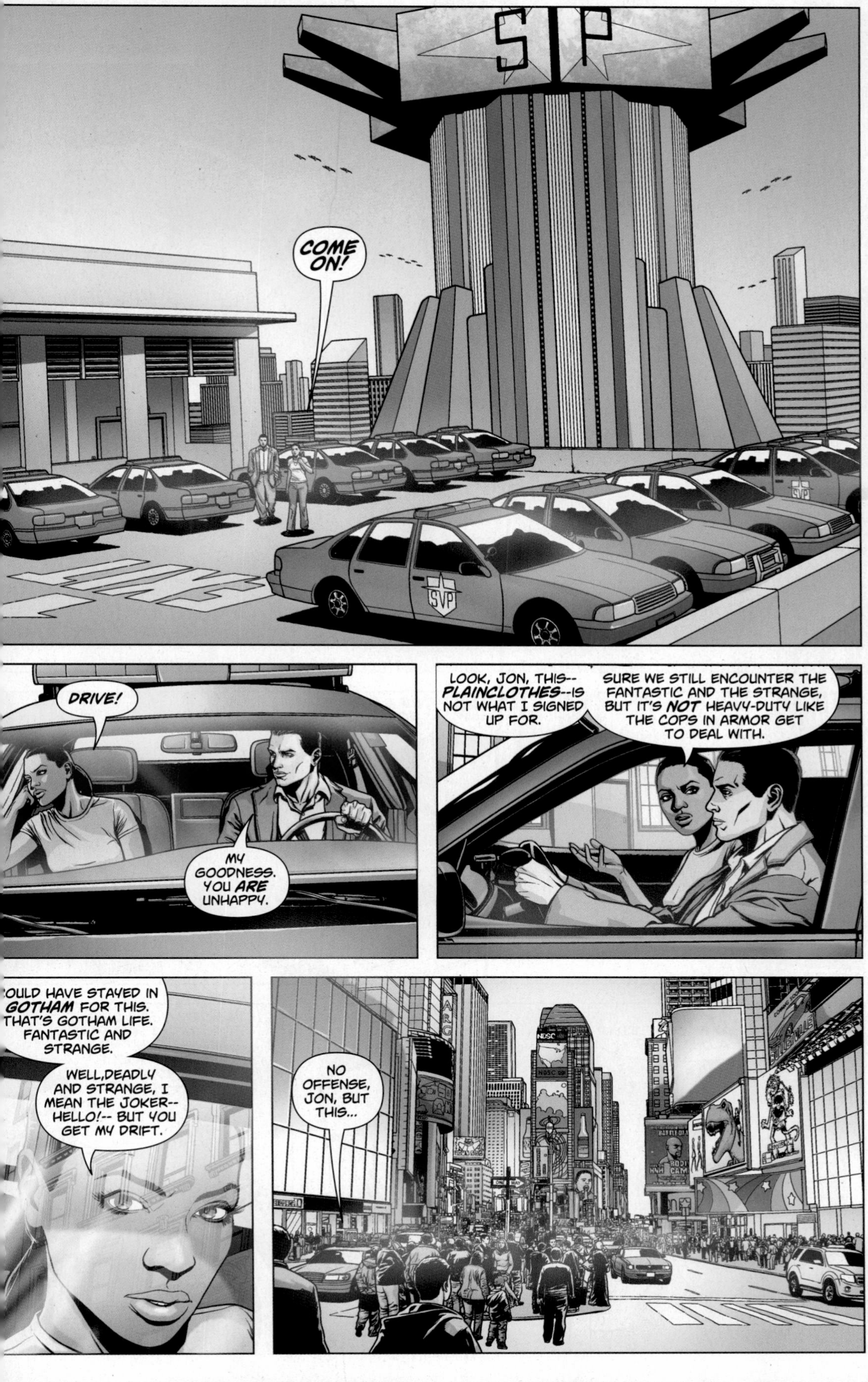
COME ON!
DRIVE!
MY GOODNESS. YOU ARE UNHAPPY.
LOOK, JON, THIS-- PLAINCLOTHES--IS NOT WHAT I SIGNED UP FOR.
SURE WE STILL ENCOUNTER THE FANTASTIC AND THE STRANGE, BUT IT'S NOT HEAVY-DUTY LIKE THE COPS IN ARMOR GET TO DEAL WITH.
COULD HAVE STAYED IN GOTHAM FOR THIS. THAT'S GOTHAM LIFE. FANTASTIC AND STRANGE.
WELL,DEADLY AND STRANGE, I MEAN THE JOKER-- HELLO!-- BUT YOU GET MY DRIFT.
NO OFFENSE, JON, BUT THIS...

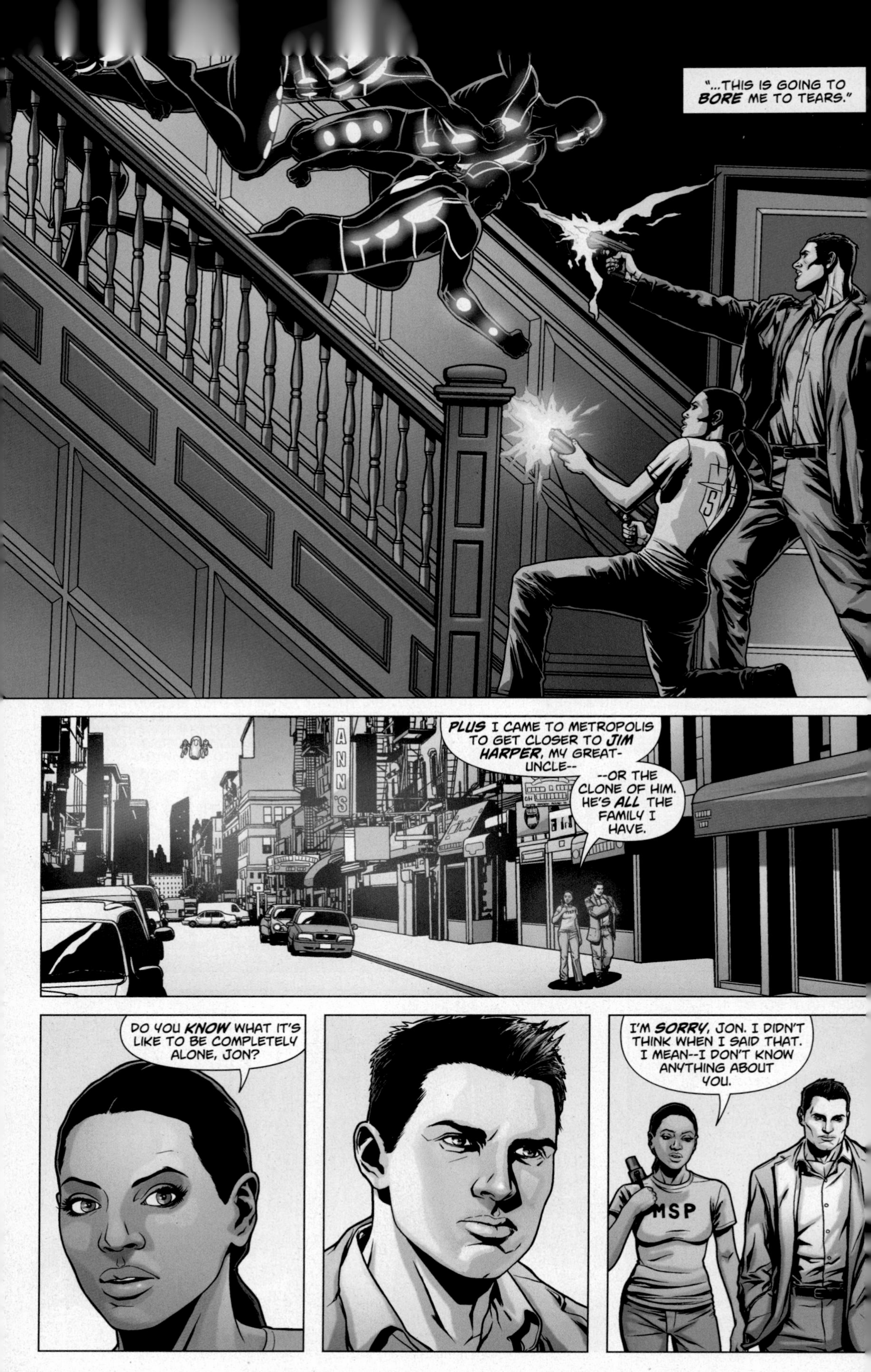
"...THIS IS GOING TO BORE ME TO TEARS."
PLUS I CAME TO METROPOLIS TO GET CLOSER TO JIM HARPER, MY GREAT-UNCLE--
--OR THE CLONE OF HIM. HE'S ALL THE FAMILY I HAVE.
DO YOU KNOW WHAT IT'S LIKE TO BE COMPLETELY ALONE, JON?
I'M SORRY, JON. I DIDN'T THINK WHEN I SAID THAT. I MEAN--I DON'T KNOW ANYTHING ABOUT YOU.
MSP

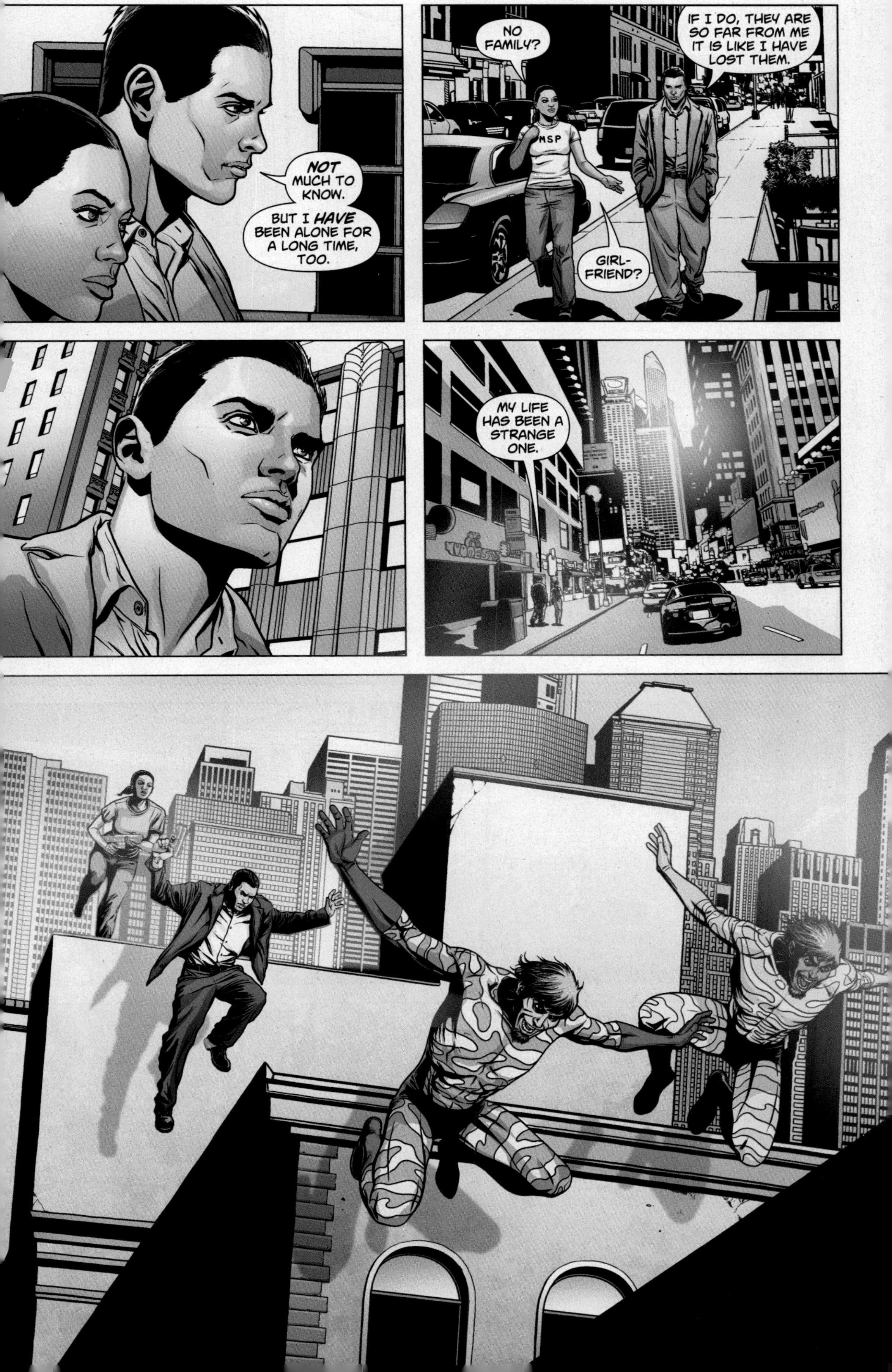
NOT MUCH TO KNOW.
BUT I HAVE BEEN ALONE FOR A LONG TIME, TOO.
NO FAMILY?
IF I DO, THEY ARE SO FAR FROM ME IT IS LIKE I HAVE LOST THEM.
MSP
GIRL-FRIEND?
MY LIFE HAS BEEN A STRANGE ONE.

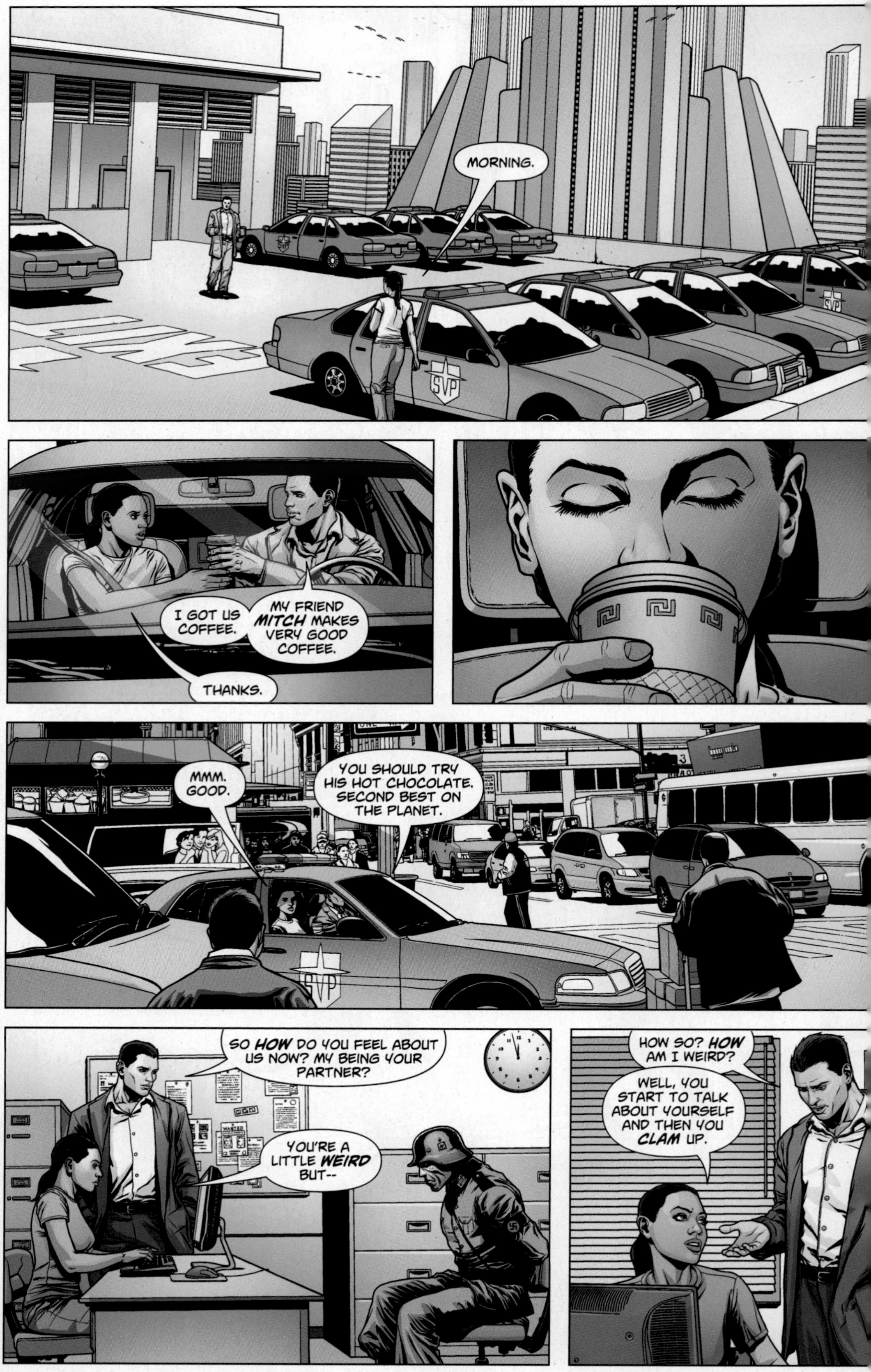
MORNING.
I GOT US COFFEE.
MY FRIEND MITCH MAKES VERY GOOD COFFEE.
THANKS.
MMM. GOOD.
YOU SHOULD TRY HIS HOT CHOCOLATE. SECOND BEST ON THE PLANET.
SO HOW DO YOU FEEL ABOUT US NOW? MY BEING YOUR PARTNER?
YOU'RE A LITTLE WEIRD BUT--
HOW SO? HOW AM I WEIRD?
WELL, YOU START TO TALK ABOUT YOURSELF AND THEN YOU CLAM UP.

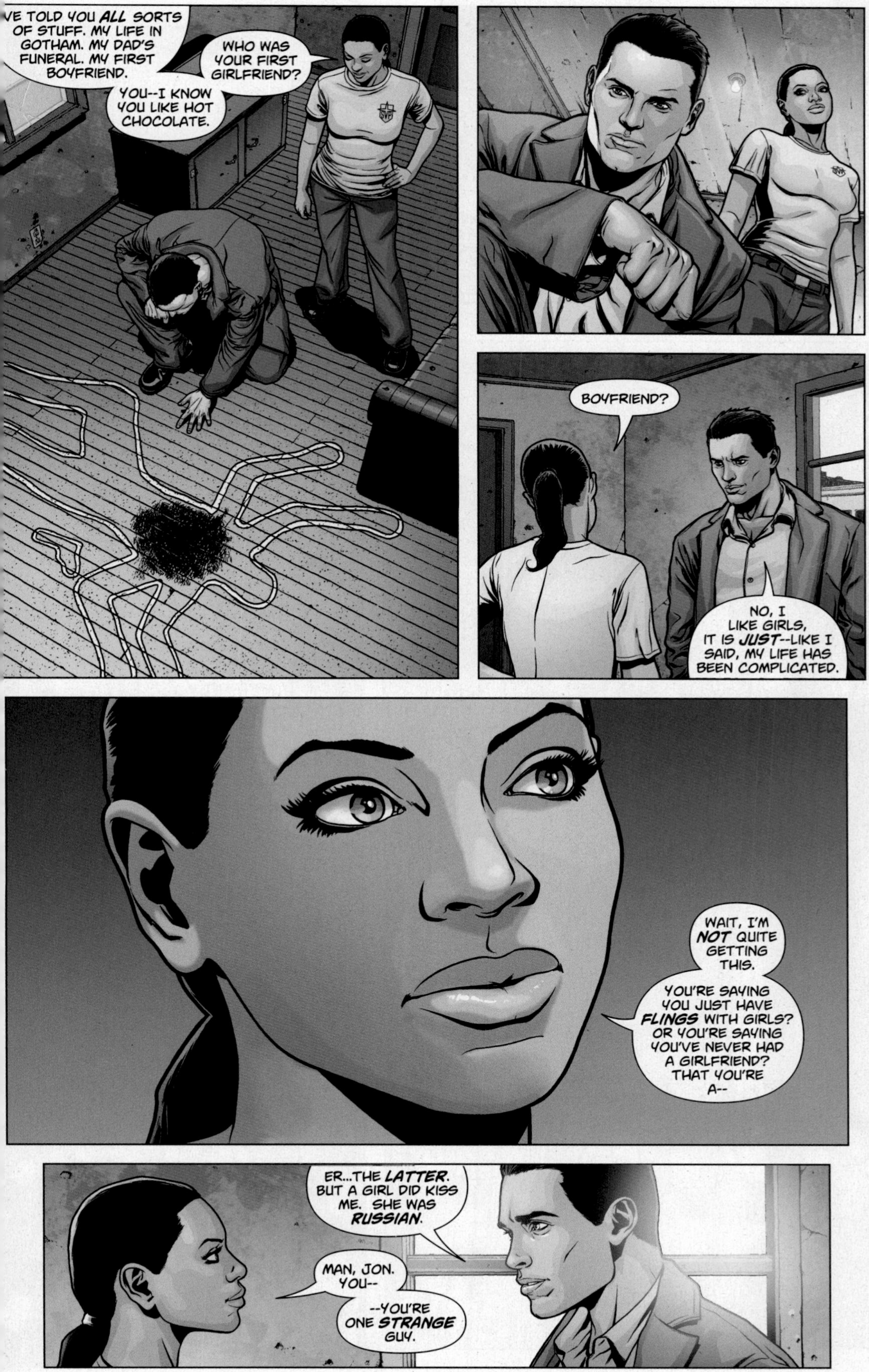

VE TOLD YOU ALL SORTS OF STUFF. MY LIFE IN GOTHAM. MY DAD'S FUNERAL. MY FIRST BOYFRIEND.
YOU--I KNOW YOU LIKE HOT CHOCOLATE.
WHO WAS YOUR FIRST GIRLFRIEND?
BOYFRIEND?
NO, I LIKE GIRLS, IT IS JUST--LIKE I SAID, MY LIFE HAS BEEN COMPLICATED.
WAIT, I'M NOT QUITE GETTING THIS.
YOU'RE SAYING YOU JUST HAVE FLINGS WITH GIRLS? OR YOU'RE SAYING YOU'VE NEVER HAD A GIRLFRIEND? THAT YOU'RE A--
ER...THE LATTER. BUT A GIRL DID KISS ME. SHE WAS RUSSIAN.
MAN, JON. YOU--
--YOU'RE ONE STRANGE GUY.

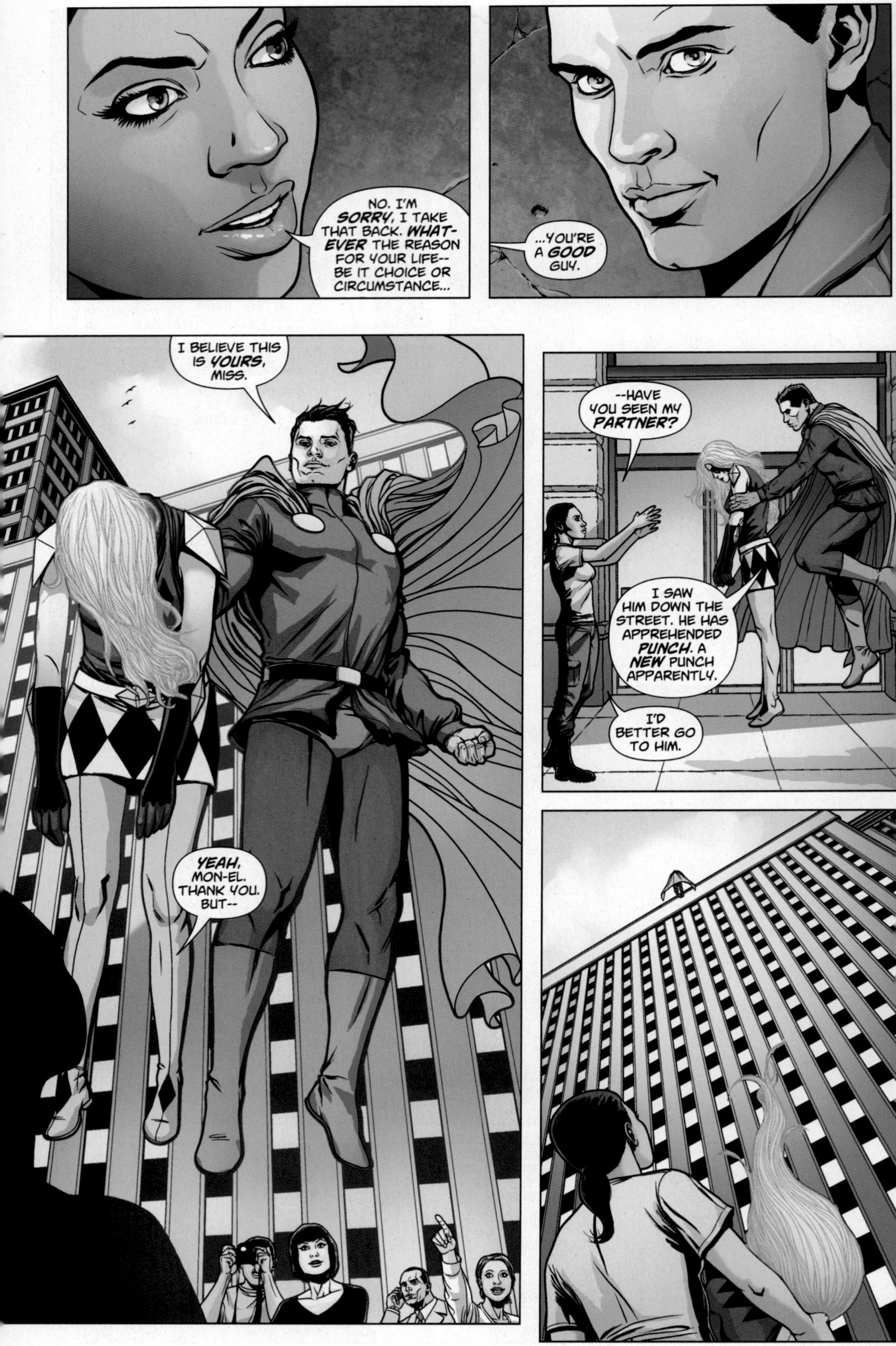
NO. I'M SORRY, I TAKE THAT BACK. WHATEVER THE REASON FOR YOUR LIFE-- BE IT CHOICE OR CIRCUMSTANCE...
...YOU'RE A GOOD GUY.
I BELIEVE THIS IS YOURS, MISS.
YEAH, MON-EL. THANK YOU. BUT--
--HAVE YOU SEEN MY PARTNER?
I SAW HIM DOWN THE STREET. HE HAS APPREHENDED PUNCH. A NEW PUNCH APPARENTLY.
I'D BETTER GO TO HIM.

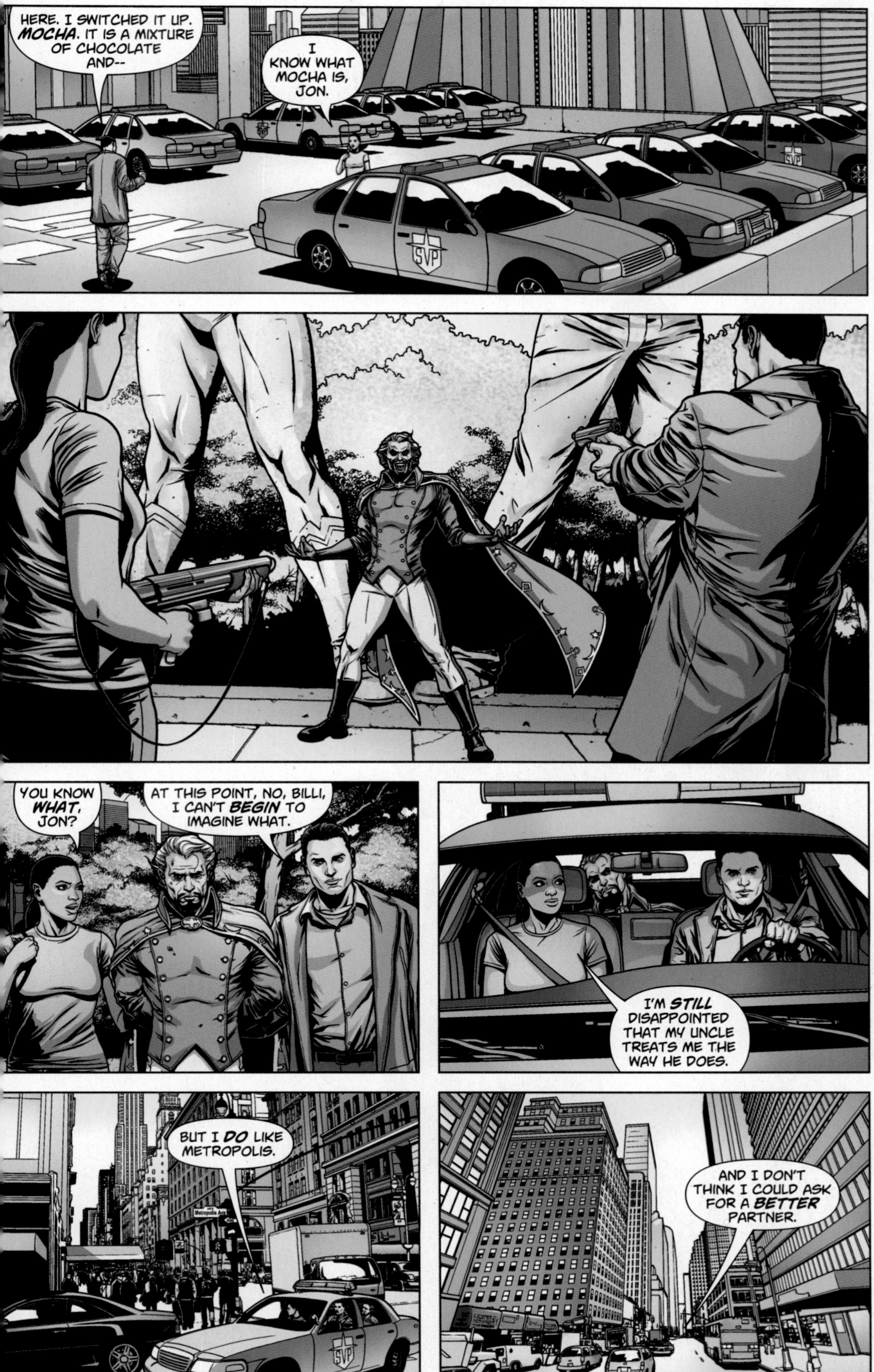

HERE. I SWITCHED IT UP. MOCHA. IT IS A MIXTURE OF CHOCOLATE AND--
I KNOW WHAT MOCHA IS, JON.
SVP
YOU KNOW WHAT, JON?
AT THIS POINT, NO, BILLI, I CAN'T BEGIN TO IMAGINE WHAT.
I'M STILL DISAPPOINTED THAT MY UNCLE TREATS ME THE WAY HE DOES.
BUT I DO LIKE METROPOLIS.
AND I DON'T THINK I COULD ASK FOR A BETTER PARTNER.

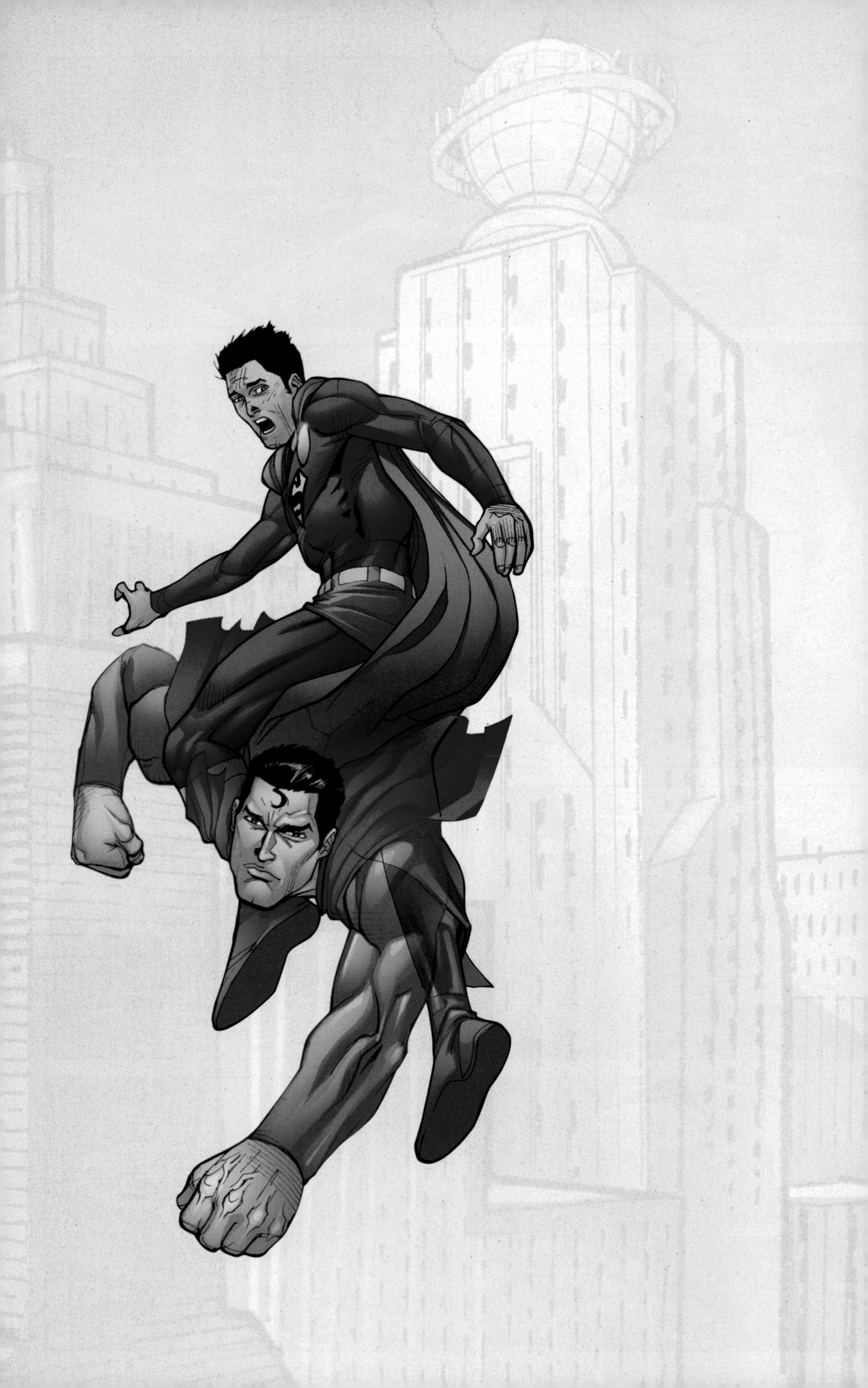

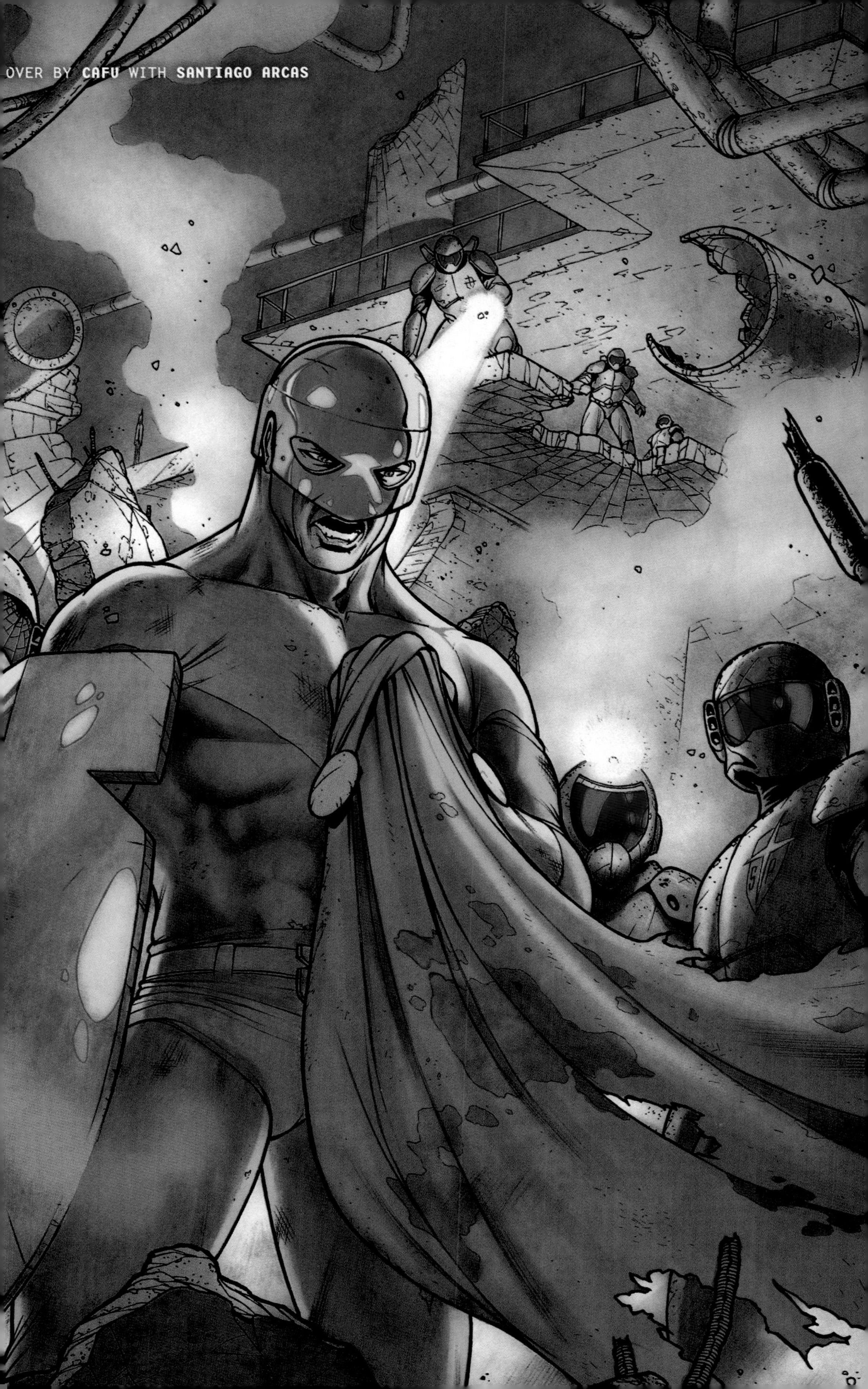

OVER BY **CAFU** WITH **SANTIAGO ARCAS**

‹PREVIOUSLY IN›
SUPERMAN:CODENAME: PATRIOT

In an effort to discredit Kryptonians in the eyes of the people of Earth, General Sam Lane, Lois Lane's father, staged a fight in the sewers of Metropolis so that it looked like the heroes Supergirl, Nightwing and Flamebird murdered Mon-El. In reality, Mon-El was fighting the villains Metallo, Reactron and Mirabai, who used her magic powers to make them appear to be the heroes. During the conflict, the trio detonated a bomb, destroying the sewers.

Meanwhile, General Lane stopped a rogue Kryptonian from killing the President of the United States in front of the world's media. What the public doesn't know is that Lane orchestrated the Kryptonian's attack. Now Lane is seen as the hero of Earth, and Kryptonians look like a bigger threat than ever.

As for Mon-El, his true fate remains a mystery…

DOWN TIME
FERNANDO DAGNINO ‹PENCILLER›
RAÚL FERNANDEZ ‹INKER›

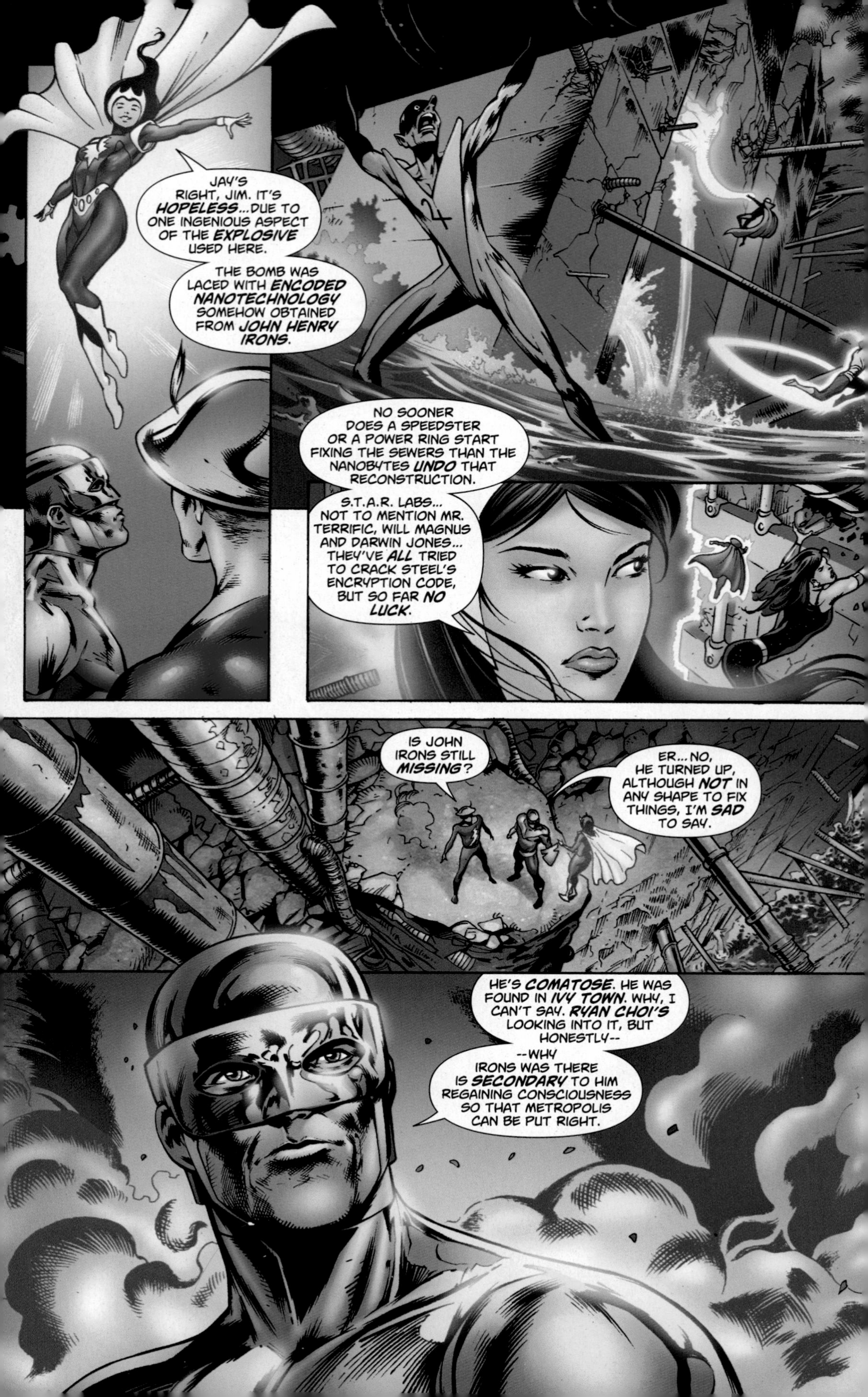

JAY'S RIGHT, JIM. IT'S HOPELESS...DUE TO ONE INGENIOUS ASPECT OF THE EXPLOSIVE USED HERE.
THE BOMB WAS LACED WITH ENCODED NANOTECHNOLOGY SOMEHOW OBTAINED FROM JOHN HENRY IRONS.
NO SOONER DOES A SPEEDSTER OR A POWER RING START FIXING THE SEWERS THAN THE NANOBYTES UNDO THAT RECONSTRUCTION.
S.T.A.R. LABS... NOT TO MENTION MR. TERRIFIC, WILL MAGNUS AND DARWIN JONES... THEY'VE ALL TRIED TO CRACK STEEL'S ENCRYPTION CODE, BUT SO FAR NO LUCK.
IS JOHN IRONS STILL MISSING?
ER...NO, HE TURNED UP, ALTHOUGH NOT IN ANY SHAPE TO FIX THINGS, I'M SAD TO SAY.
HE'S COMATOSE. HE WAS FOUND IN IVY TOWN. WHY, I CAN'T SAY. RYAN CHOI'S LOOKING INTO IT, BUT HONESTLY--
--WHY IRONS WAS THERE IS SECONDARY TO HIM REGAINING CONSCIOUSNESS SO THAT METROPOLIS CAN BE PUT RIGHT.

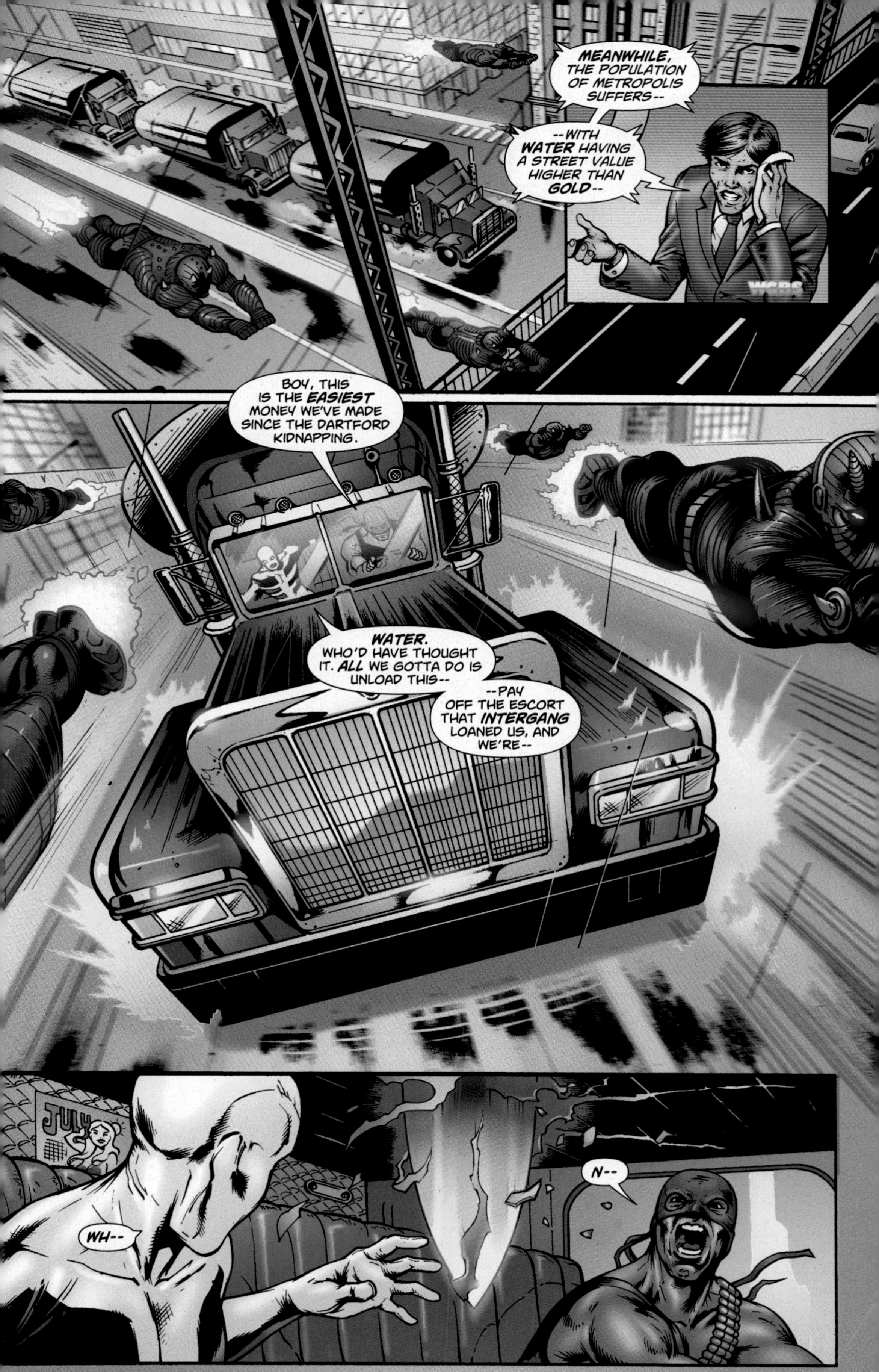
MEANWHILE, THE POPULATION OF METROPOLIS SUFFERS--
--WITH WATER HAVING A STREET VALUE HIGHER THAN GOLD--
WGBS
BOY, THIS IS THE EASIEST MONEY WE'VE MADE SINCE THE DARTFORD KIDNAPPING.
WATER. WHO'D HAVE THOUGHT IT. ALL WE GOTTA DO IS UNLOAD THIS--
--PAY OFF THE ESCORT THAT INTERGANG LOANED US, AND WE'RE--
JULY
WH--
N--

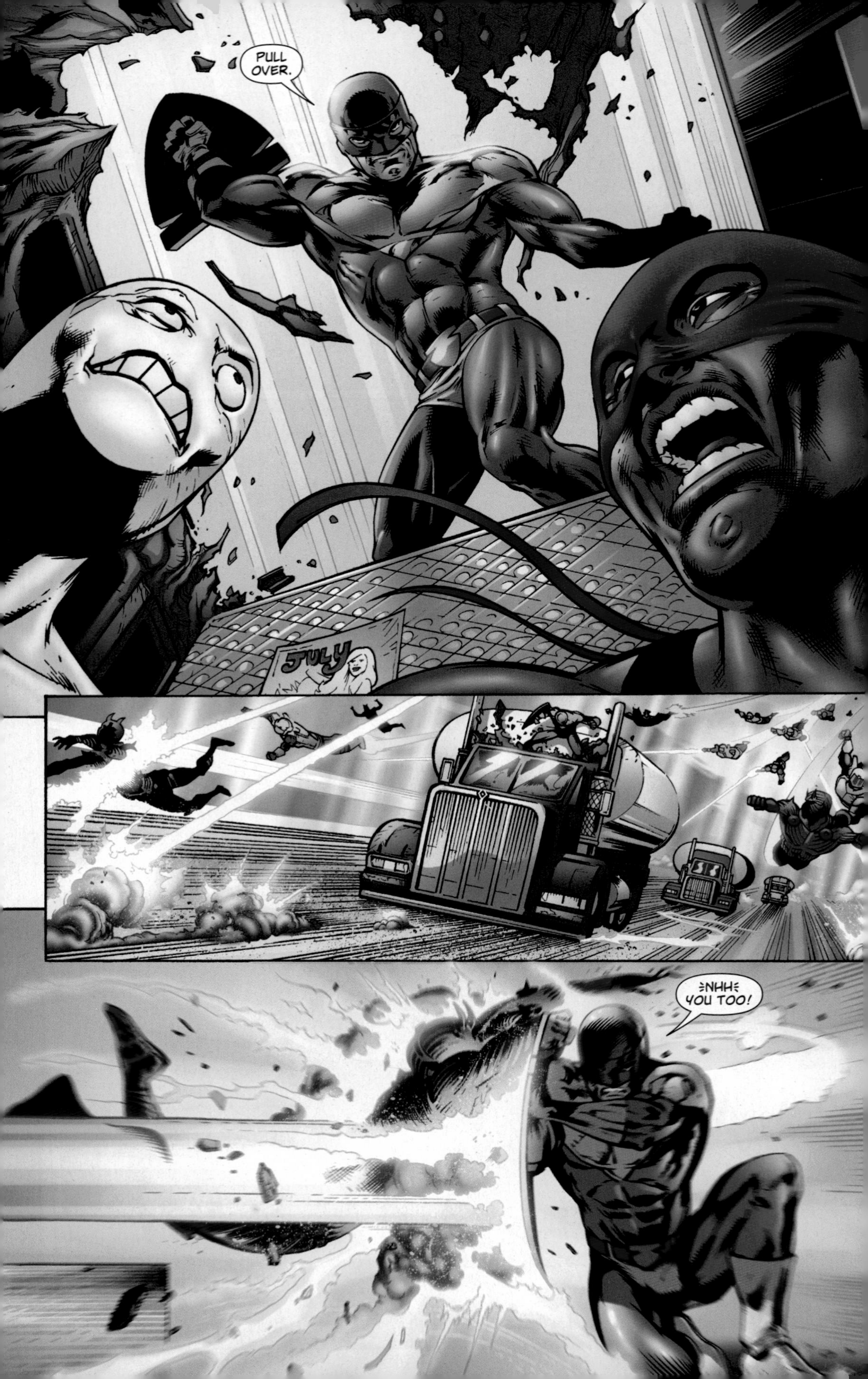
PULL OVER.
JULY
NHH YOU TOO!

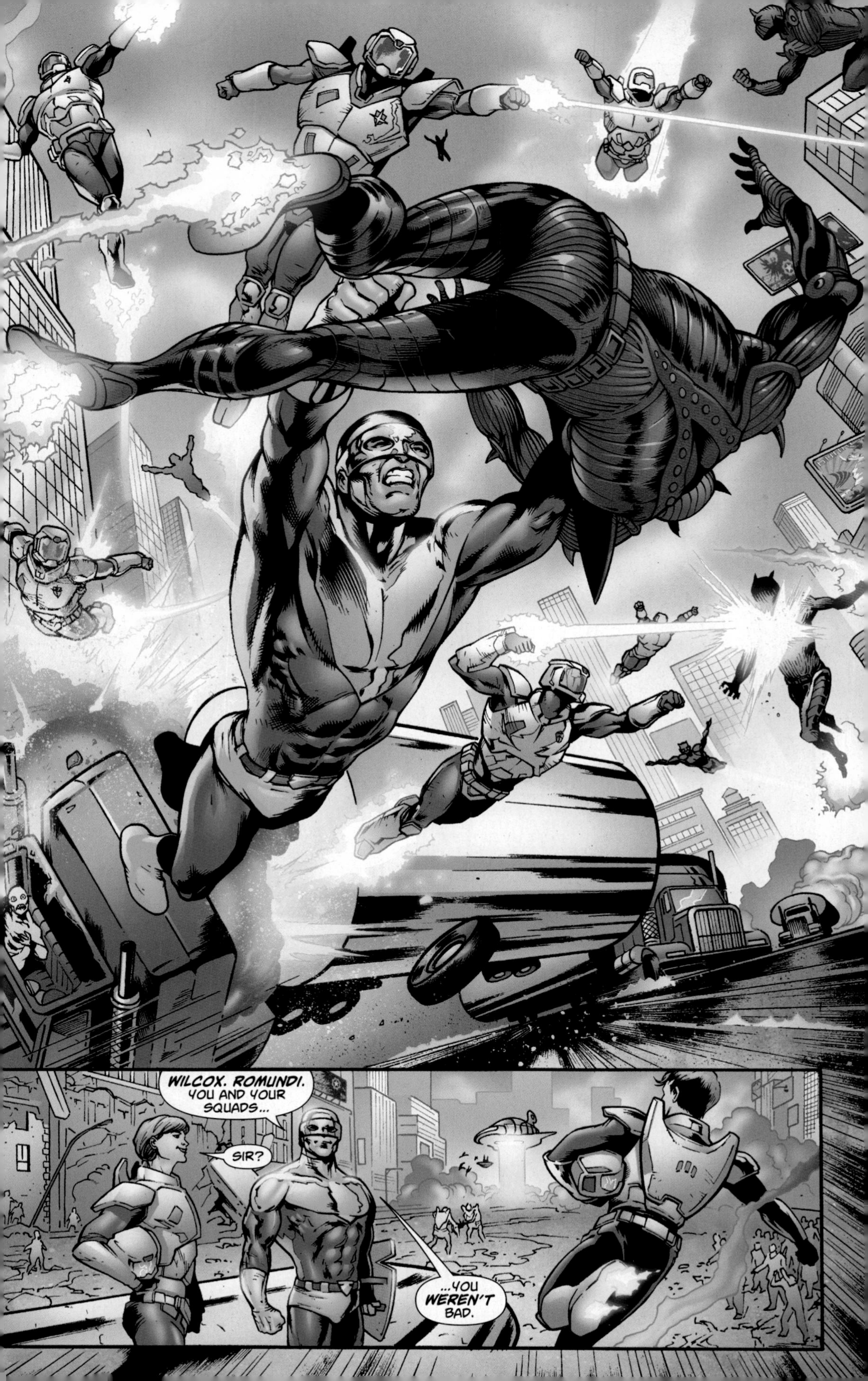
WILCOX. ROMUNDI. YOU AND YOUR SQUADS...
SIR?
...YOU WEREN'T BAD.

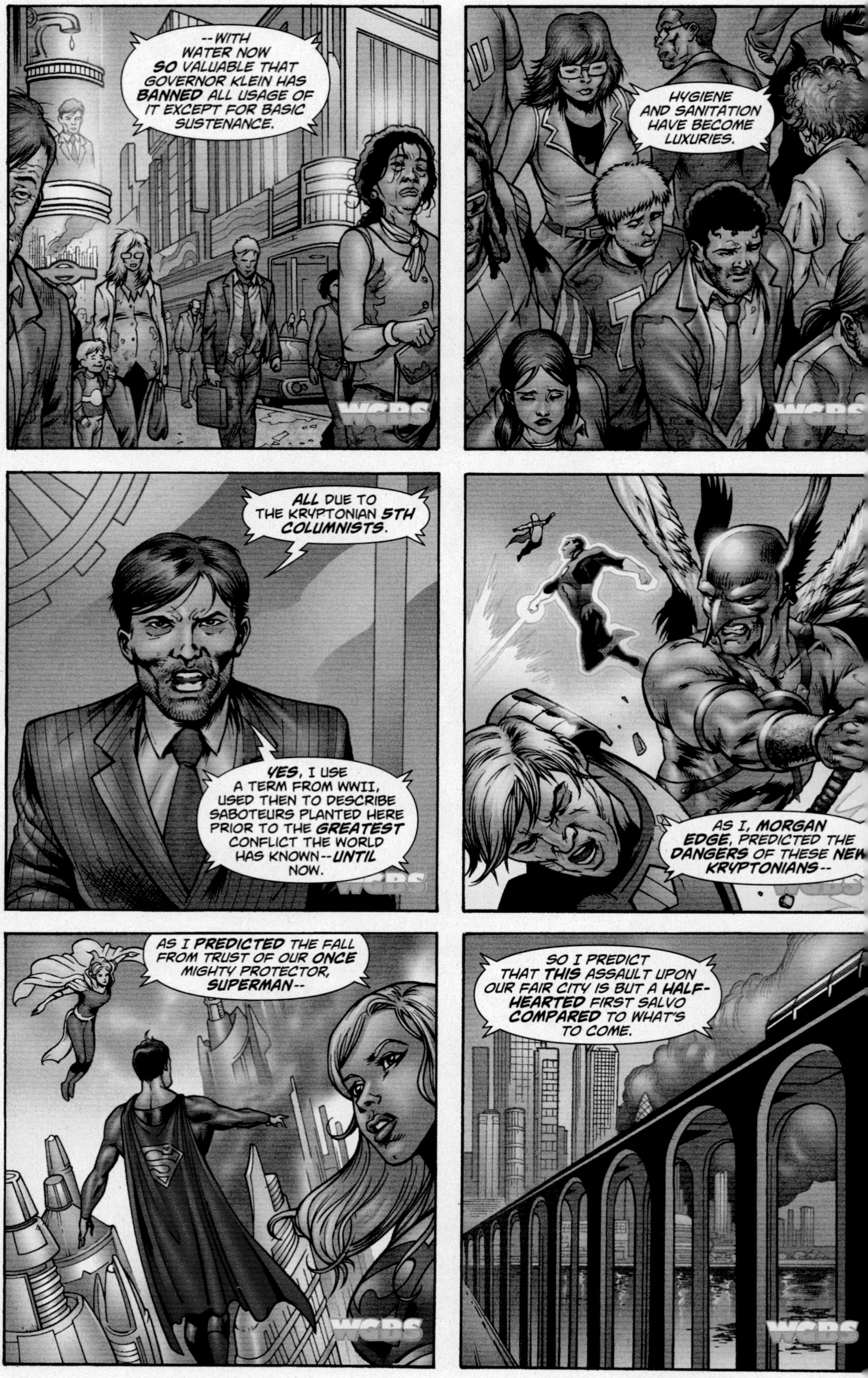
--WITH WATER NOW SO VALUABLE THAT GOVERNOR KLEIN HAS BANNED ALL USAGE OF IT EXCEPT FOR BASIC SUSTENANCE.
WGBS
HYGIENE AND SANITATION HAVE BECOME LUXURIES.
WGBS
ALL DUE TO THE KRYPTONIAN 5TH COLUMNISTS.
YES, I USE A TERM FROM WWII, USED THEN TO DESCRIBE SABOTEURS PLANTED HERE PRIOR TO THE GREATEST CONFLICT THE WORLD HAS KNOWN--UNTIL NOW.
WGBS
AS I, MORGAN EDGE, PREDICTED THE DANGERS OF THESE NEW KRYPTONIANS--
WGBS
AS I PREDICTED THE FALL FROM TRUST OF OUR ONCE MIGHTY PROTECTOR, SUPERMAN--
WGBS
SO I PREDICT THAT THIS ASSAULT UPON OUR FAIR CITY IS BUT A HALF-HEARTED FIRST SALVO COMPARED TO WHAT'S TO COME.
WGBS

THANK GOD! THANK GOD ALMIGHTY THAT THE ROAD TO SALVATION HAS BEEN PRESENTED TO US BY SOMEONE FROM OUR PLANET.

NOT AN ALIEN. NOT EVEN A META.

WCBS

GENERAL SAM LANE IS A HUMAN. AN AMERICAN. A HERO.

EMERGING FROM HIS SELF-IMPOSED EXILE, WHERE HE FORMULATED HIS "GOOD DEFENSE" AGAINST A THREAT FROM KRYPTON THAT HE FORESAW BEFORE ANY OF US.

IN LIGHT OF LANE'S INGENUITY IN FOILING THE ATTACK UPON PRESIDENT SUAREZ'S LIFE...

...BY EXECUTIVE ORDER, LANE HAS BEEN MADE THE FIVE STAR GENERAL OF THE HUMAN DEFENSE CORP.

THIS IS A BRANCH OF THE ARMED SERVICES THAT IS LITTLE KNOWN, BUT I FEAR WILL BE MORE READILY IN THE PUBLIC'S EYE WITH EACH COMING DAY!

DEFENSE

AD INFEROS ET RETRORSUM

WCBS

THEIR GOAL--AND LANE'S--TO DEFEND OUR WORLD FROM OTHERWORLDLY THREATS. SO BE IT SATAN OR SUPERMAN, GENERAL LANE WILL PROTECT US.

WCBS

THIS IS MORGAN EDGE SIGNING OFF BY SAYING GOD BLESS AMERICA AND GOD SAVE METROPOLIS.

WCBS

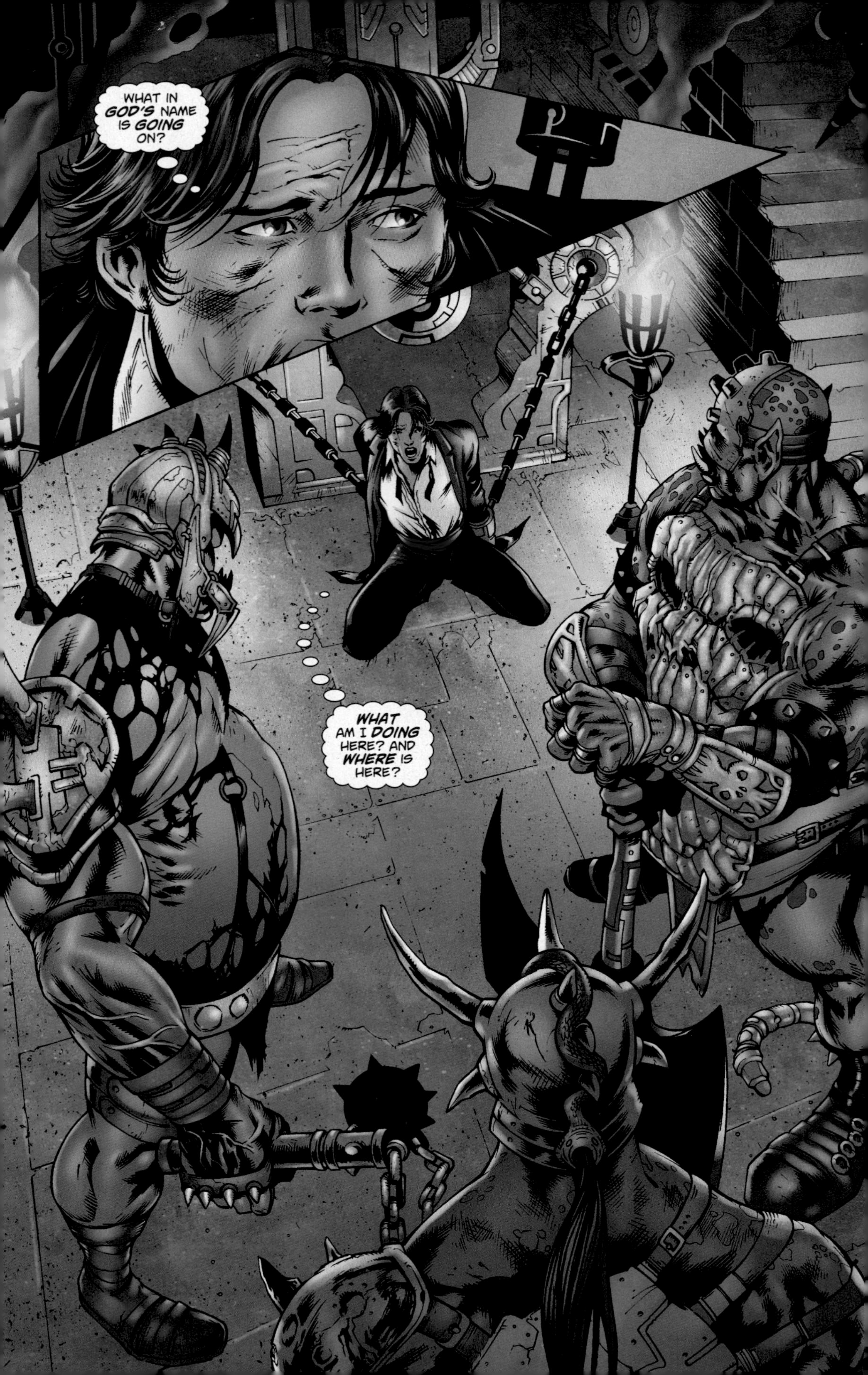
WHAT IN *GOD'S* NAME IS *GOING* ON?
WHAT AM I *DOING* HERE? AND *WHERE* IS HERE?

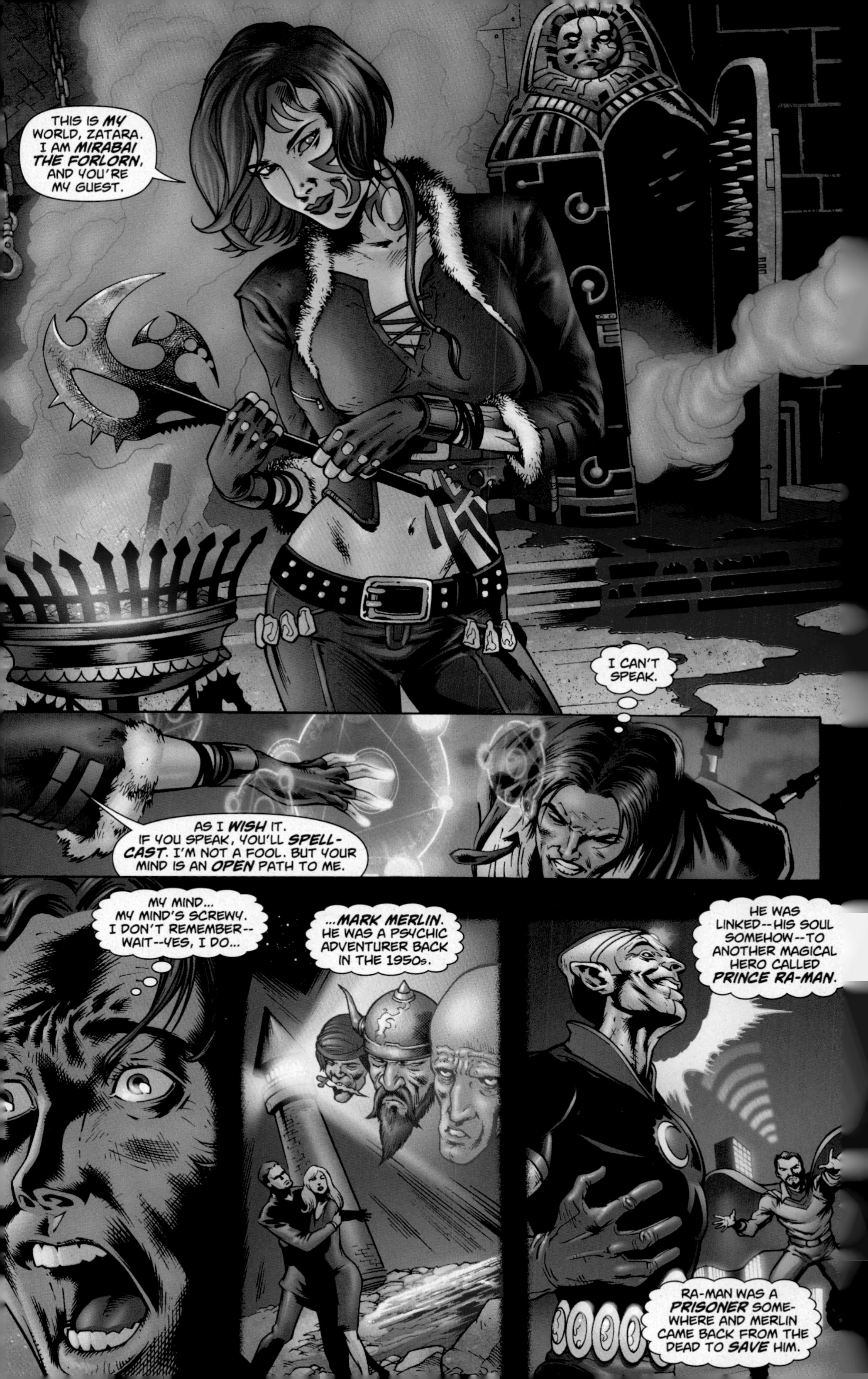
THIS IS MY WORLD, ZATARA. I AM MIRABAI THE FORLORN, AND YOU'RE MY GUEST.
I CAN'T SPEAK.
AS I WISH IT. IF YOU SPEAK, YOU'LL SPELL-CAST. I'M NOT A FOOL. BUT YOUR MIND IS AN OPEN PATH TO ME.
MY MIND... MY MIND'S SCREWY. I DON'T REMEMBER-- WAIT--YES, I DO...
...MARK MERLIN. HE WAS A PSYCHIC ADVENTURER BACK IN THE 1950s.
HE WAS LINKED--HIS SOUL SOMEHOW--TO ANOTHER MAGICAL HERO CALLED PRINCE RA-MAN.
RA-MAN WAS A PRISONER SOME-WHERE AND MERLIN CAME BACK FROM THE DEAD TO SAVE HIM.

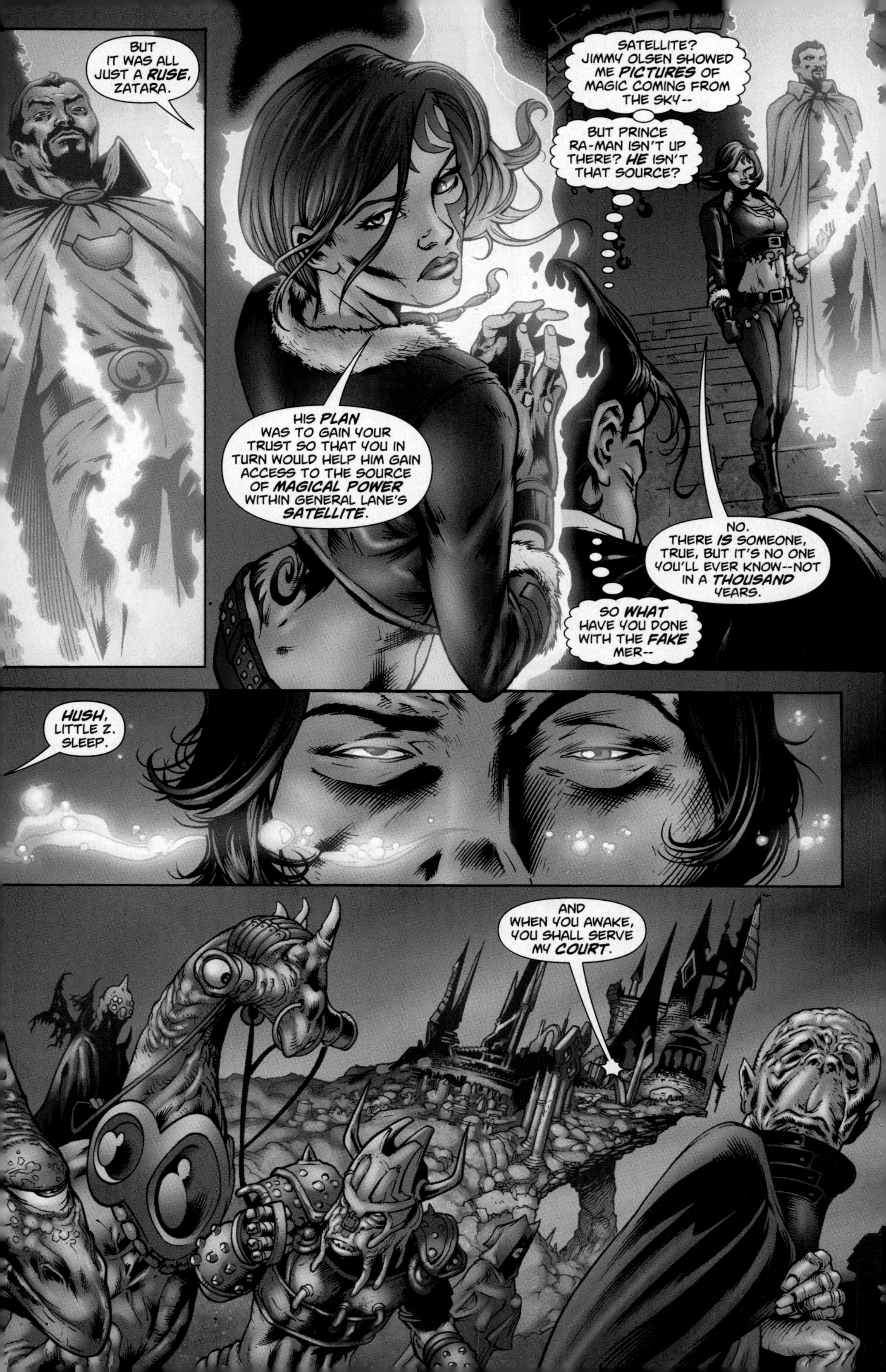
BUT IT WAS ALL JUST A *RUSE*, ZATARA.
SATELLITE? JIMMY OLSEN SHOWED ME *PICTURES* OF MAGIC COMING FROM THE SKY--
BUT PRINCE RA-MAN ISN'T UP THERE? *HE* ISN'T THAT SOURCE?
HIS *PLAN* WAS TO GAIN YOUR TRUST SO THAT YOU IN TURN WOULD HELP HIM GAIN ACCESS TO THE SOURCE OF *MAGICAL POWER* WITHIN GENERAL LANE'S *SATELLITE*.
NO. THERE *IS* SOMEONE, TRUE, BUT IT'S NO ONE YOU'LL EVER KNOW--NOT IN A *THOUSAND* YEARS.
SO *WHAT* HAVE YOU DONE WITH THE *FAKE* MER--
HUSH, LITTLE Z. SLEEP.
AND WHEN YOU AWAKE, YOU SHALL SERVE MY *COURT*.

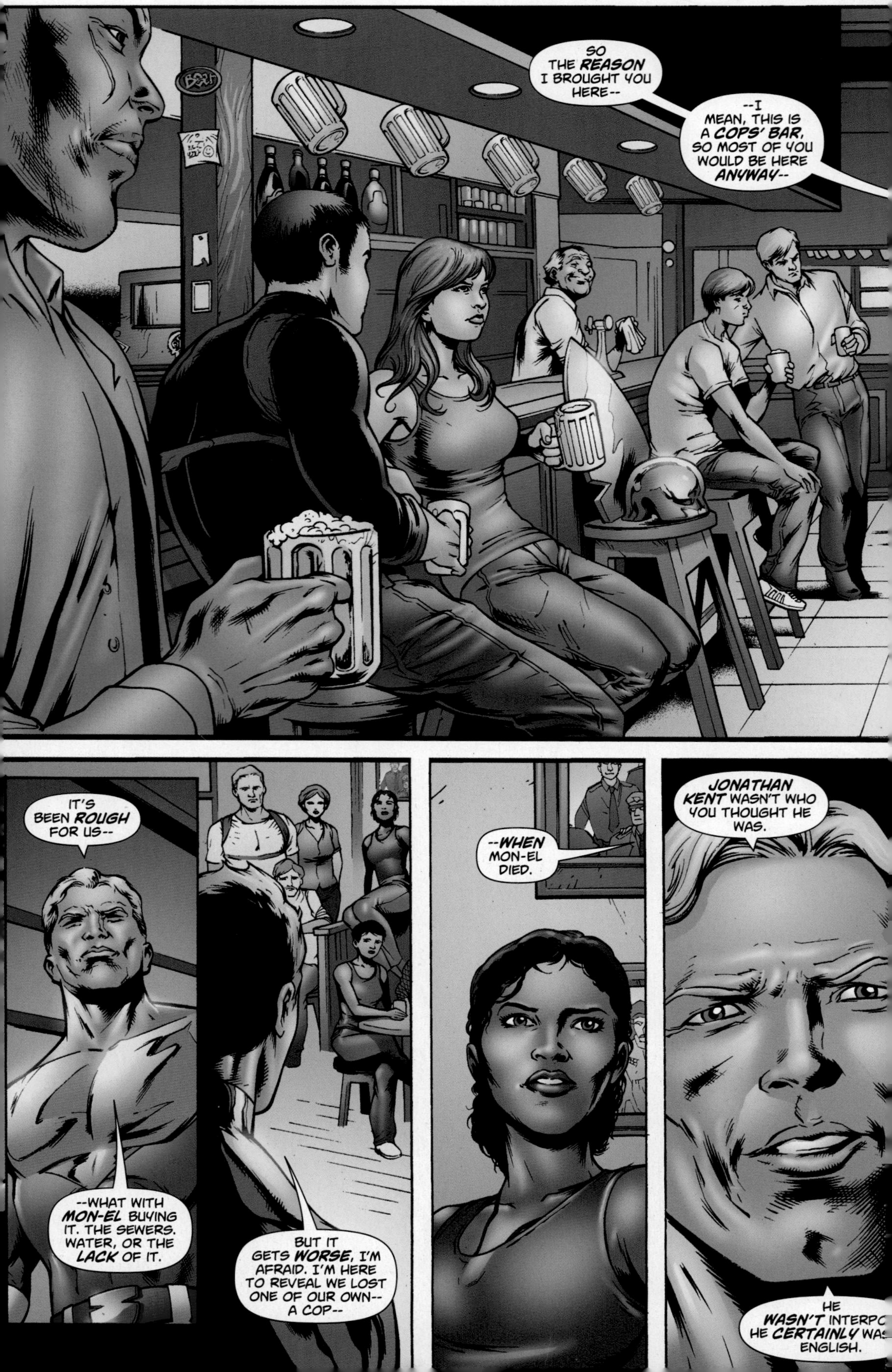
SO THE REASON I BROUGHT YOU HERE--
--I MEAN, THIS IS A COPS' BAR, SO MOST OF YOU WOULD BE HERE ANYWAY--
IT'S BEEN ROUGH FOR US--
--WHAT WITH MON-EL BUYING IT. THE SEWERS. WATER, OR THE LACK OF IT.
BUT IT GETS WORSE, I'M AFRAID. I'M HERE TO REVEAL WE LOST ONE OF OUR OWN--A COP--
--WHEN MON-EL DIED.
JONATHAN KENT WASN'T WHO YOU THOUGHT HE WAS.
HE WASN'T INTERPO
HE CERTAINLY WAS
ENGLISH.

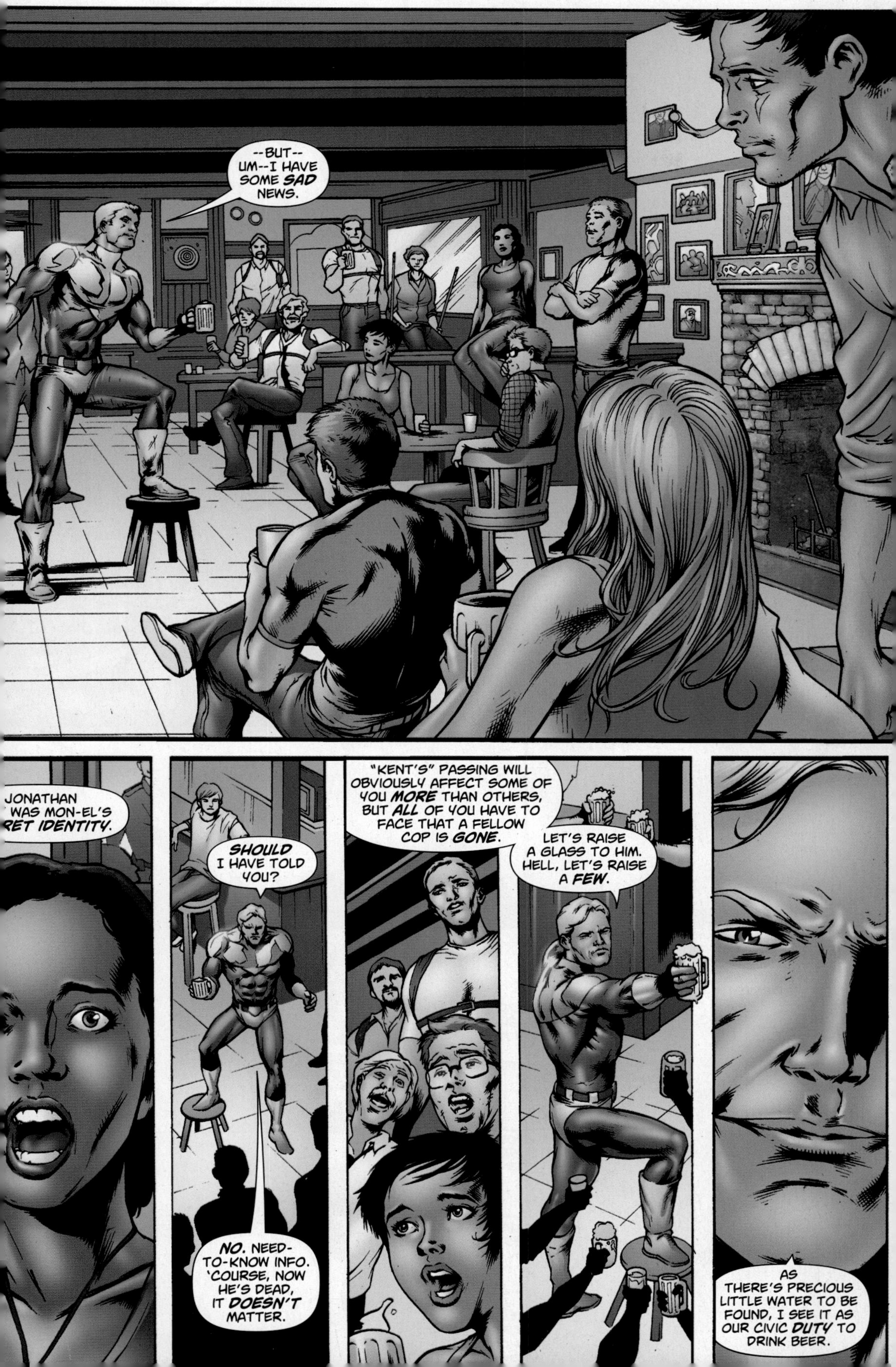

--BUT-- UM--I HAVE SOME SAD NEWS.
JONATHAN WAS MON-EL'S RET IDENTITY.
SHOULD I HAVE TOLD YOU?
NO. NEED-TO-KNOW INFO. 'COURSE, NOW HE'S DEAD, IT DOESN'T MATTER.
"KENT'S" PASSING WILL OBVIOUSLY AFFECT SOME OF YOU MORE THAN OTHERS, BUT ALL OF YOU HAVE TO FACE THAT A FELLOW COP IS GONE.
LET'S RAISE A GLASS TO HIM. HELL, LET'S RAISE A FEW.
AS THERE'S PRECIOUS LITTLE WATER TO BE FOUND, I SEE IT AS OUR CIVIC DUTY TO DRINK BEER.

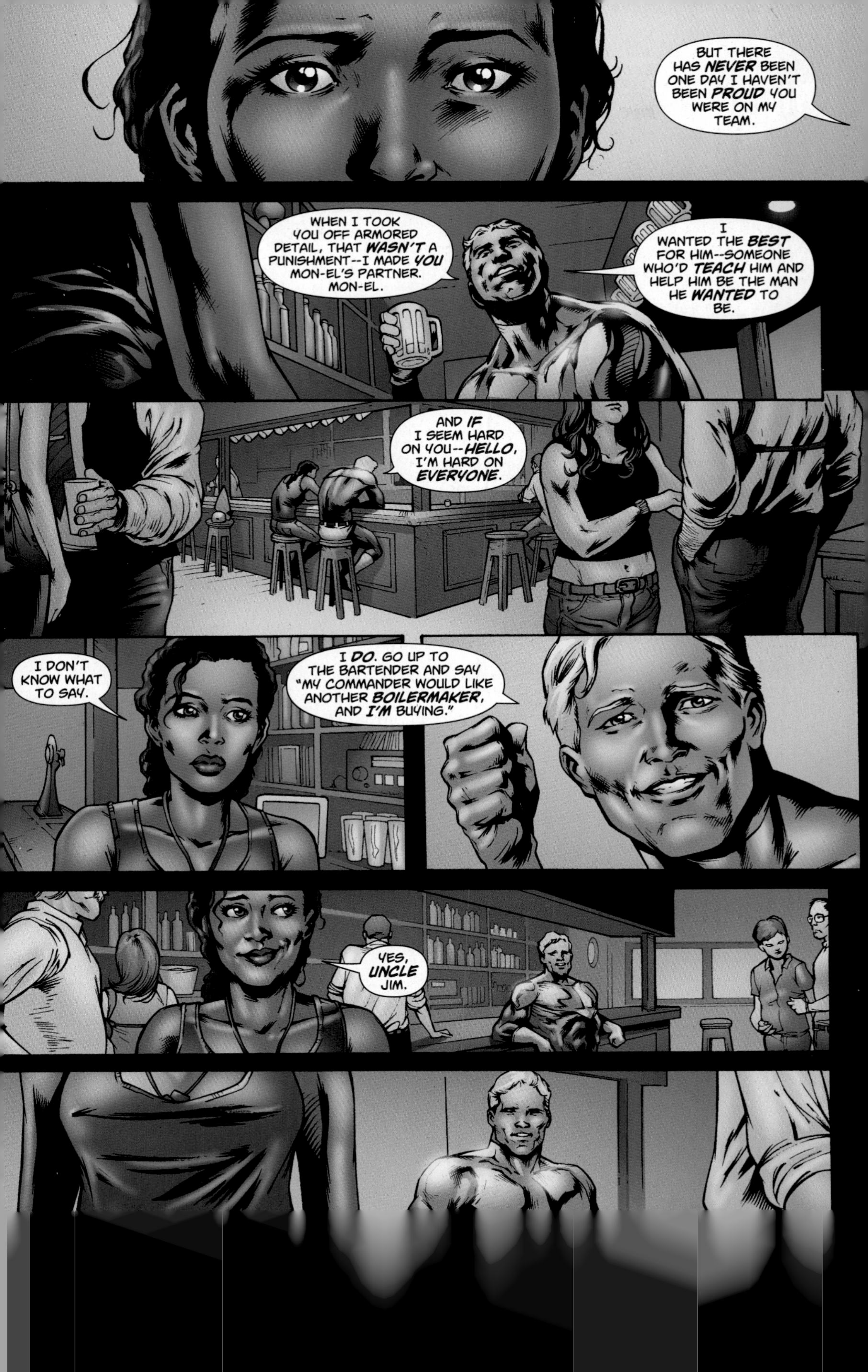
BUT THERE HAS NEVER BEEN ONE DAY I HAVEN'T BEEN PROUD YOU WERE ON MY TEAM.
WHEN I TOOK YOU OFF ARMORED DETAIL, THAT WASN'T A PUNISHMENT--I MADE YOU MON-EL'S PARTNER. MON-EL.
I WANTED THE BEST FOR HIM--SOMEONE WHO'D TEACH HIM AND HELP HIM BE THE MAN HE WANTED TO BE.
AND IF I SEEM HARD ON YOU--HELLO, I'M HARD ON EVERYONE.
I DON'T KNOW WHAT TO SAY.
I DO. GO UP TO THE BARTENDER AND SAY "MY COMMANDER WOULD LIKE ANOTHER BOILERMAKER, AND I'M BUYING."
YES, UNCLE JIM.

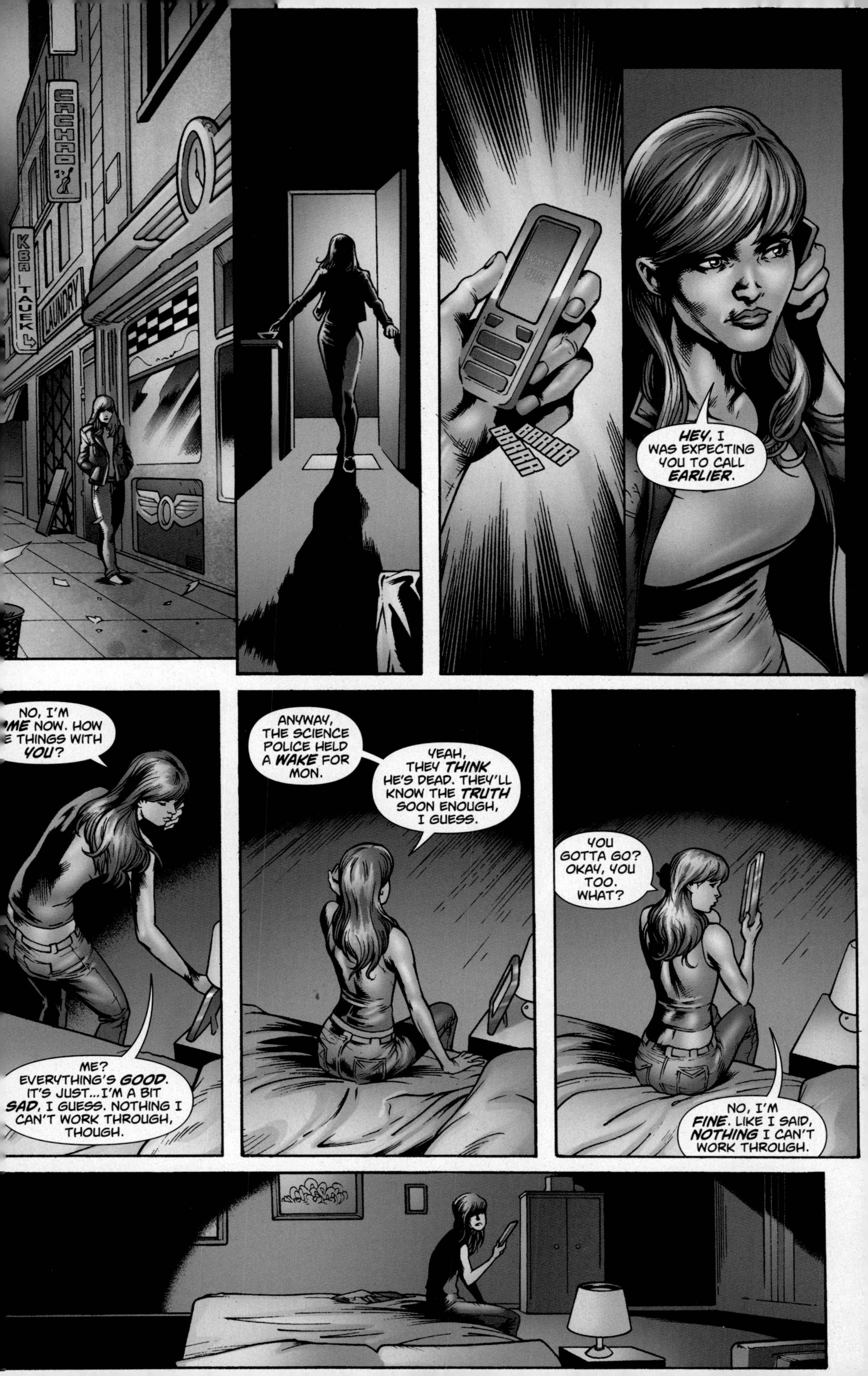
CACHRO
KBR TAUEK
LAUNDRY
BRRRR BRRRR
HEY, I WAS EXPECTING YOU TO CALL EARLIER.
NO, I'M ME NOW. HOW THINGS WITH YOU?
ME? EVERYTHING'S GOOD. IT'S JUST...I'M A BIT SAD, I GUESS. NOTHING I CAN'T WORK THROUGH, THOUGH.
ANYWAY, THE SCIENCE POLICE HELD A WAKE FOR MON.
YEAH, THEY THINK HE'S DEAD. THEY'LL KNOW THE TRUTH SOON ENOUGH, I GUESS.
YOU GOTTA GO? OKAY, YOU TOO. WHAT?
NO, I'M FINE. LIKE I SAID, NOTHING I CAN'T WORK THROUGH.

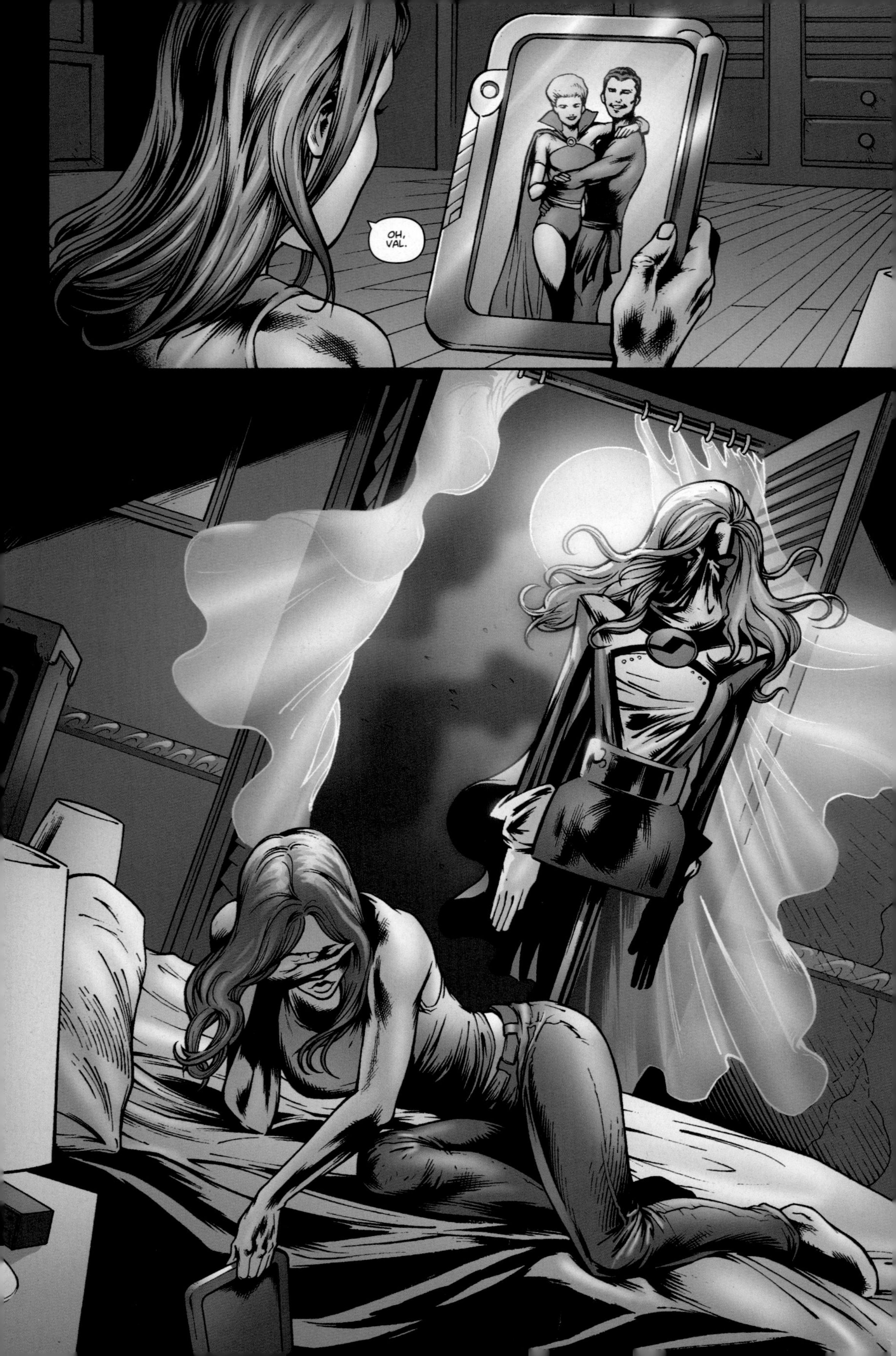
OH, VAL.

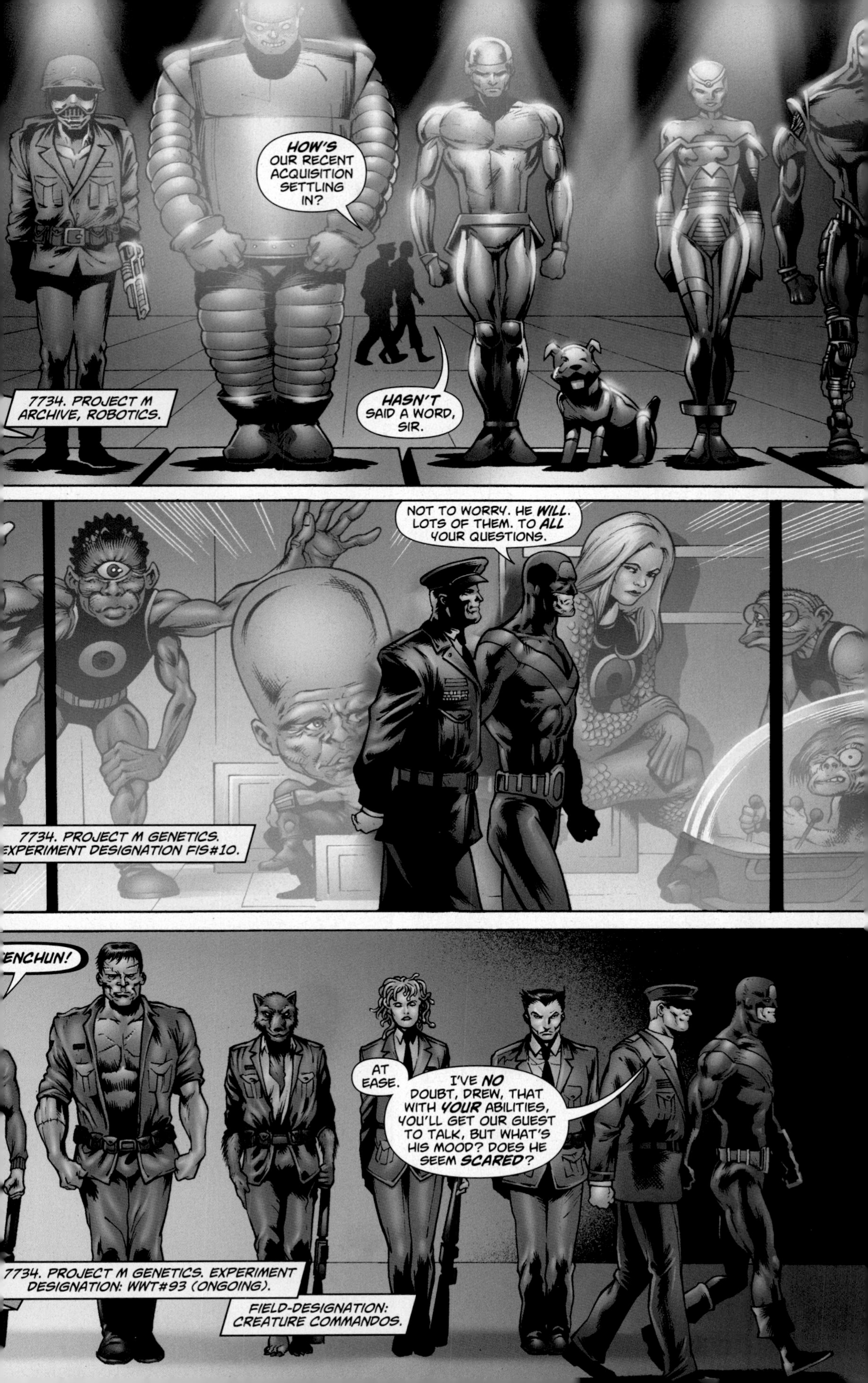

7734. PROJECT M ARCHIVE, ROBOTICS.
HOW'S OUR RECENT ACQUISITION SETTLING IN?
HASN'T SAID A WORD, SIR.
7734. PROJECT M GENETICS. EXPERIMENT DESIGNATION FIS#10.
NOT TO WORRY. HE WILL. LOTS OF THEM. TO ALL YOUR QUESTIONS.
ENCHUN!
7734. PROJECT M GENETICS. EXPERIMENT DESIGNATION: WWT#93 (ONGOING).
FIELD-DESIGNATION: CREATURE COMMANDOS.
AT EASE.
I'VE NO DOUBT, DREW, THAT WITH YOUR ABILITIES, YOU'LL GET OUR GUEST TO TALK, BUT WHAT'S HIS MOOD? DOES HE SEEM SCARED?

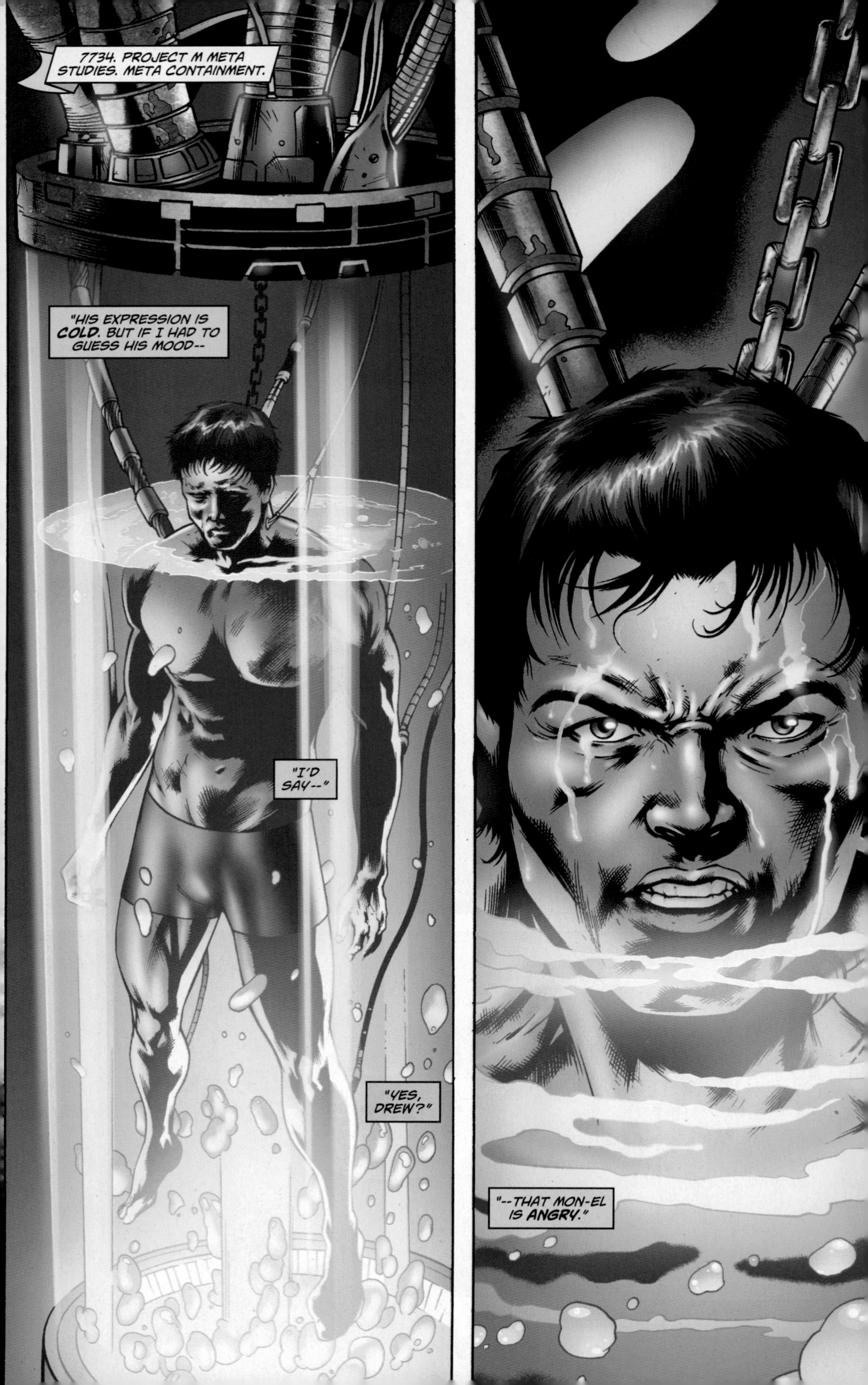
7734. PROJECT M META STUDIES. META CONTAINMENT.
"HIS EXPRESSION IS COLD. BUT IF I HAD TO GUESS HIS MOOD--
"I'D SAY--"
"YES, DREW?"
"--THAT MON-EL IS ANGRY."

COVER BY **CAFU** WITH **SANTIAGO ARCAS**

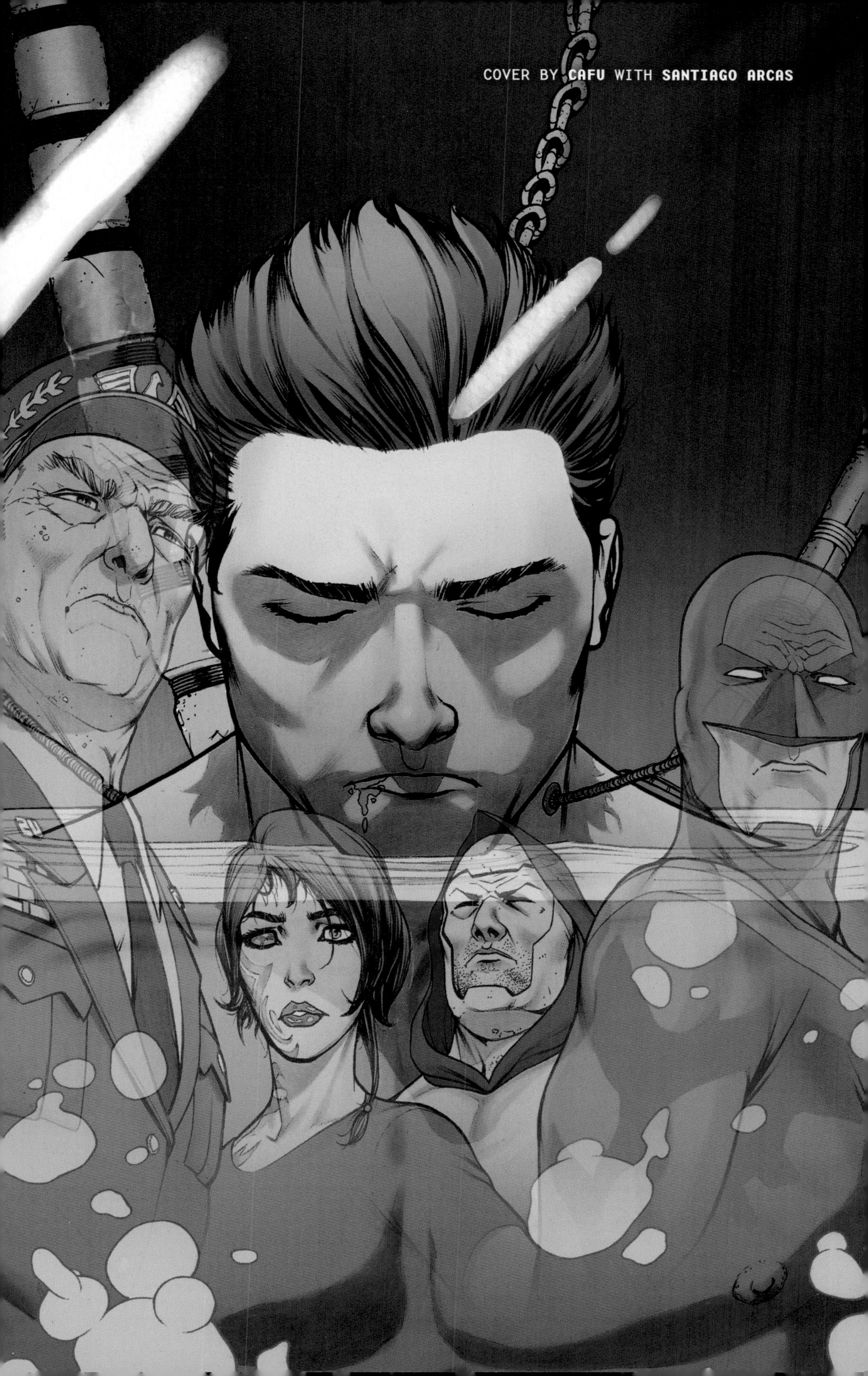

7734

FERNANDO DAGNINO <PENCILLER>
RAÚL FERNANDEZ <INKER>

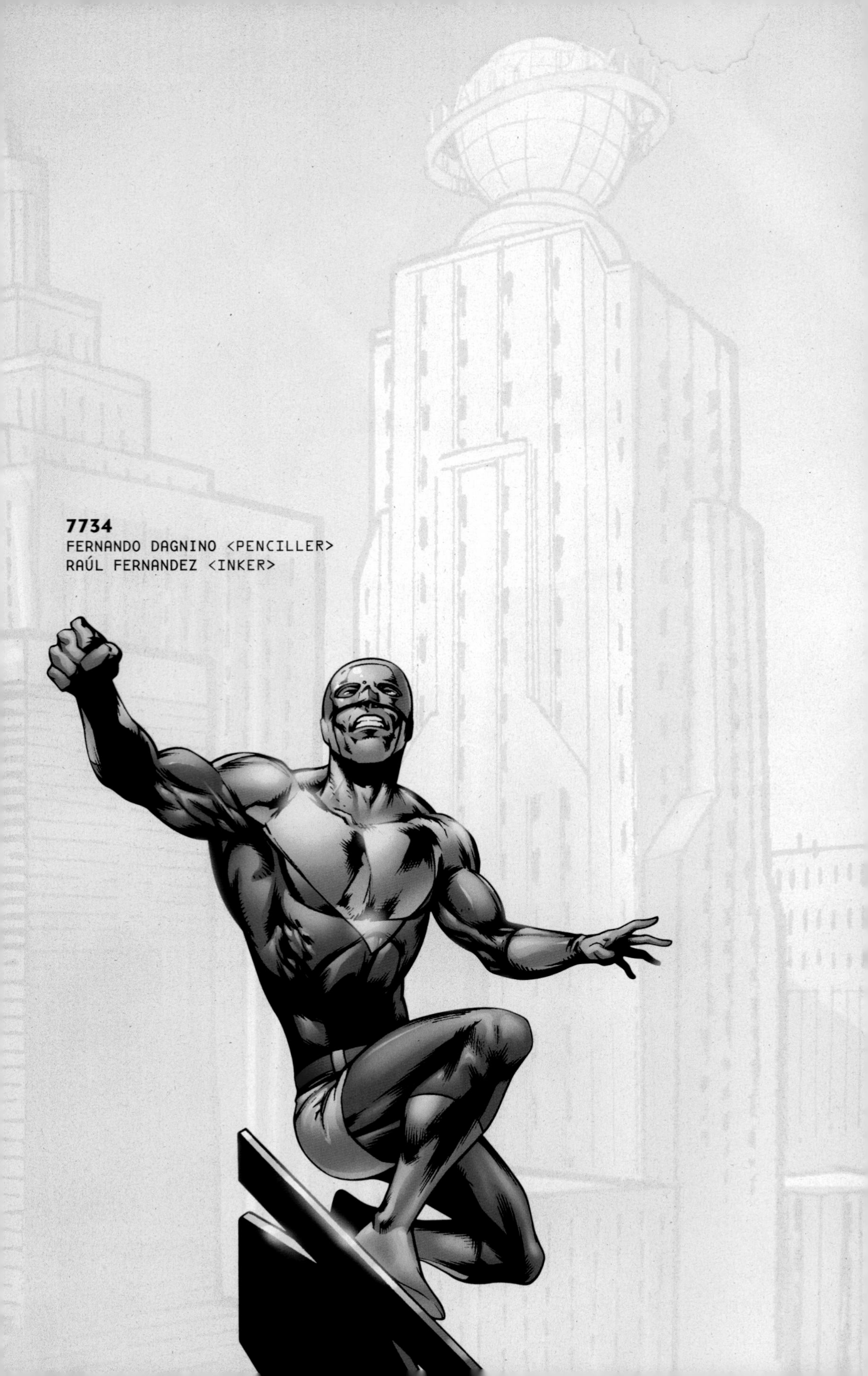

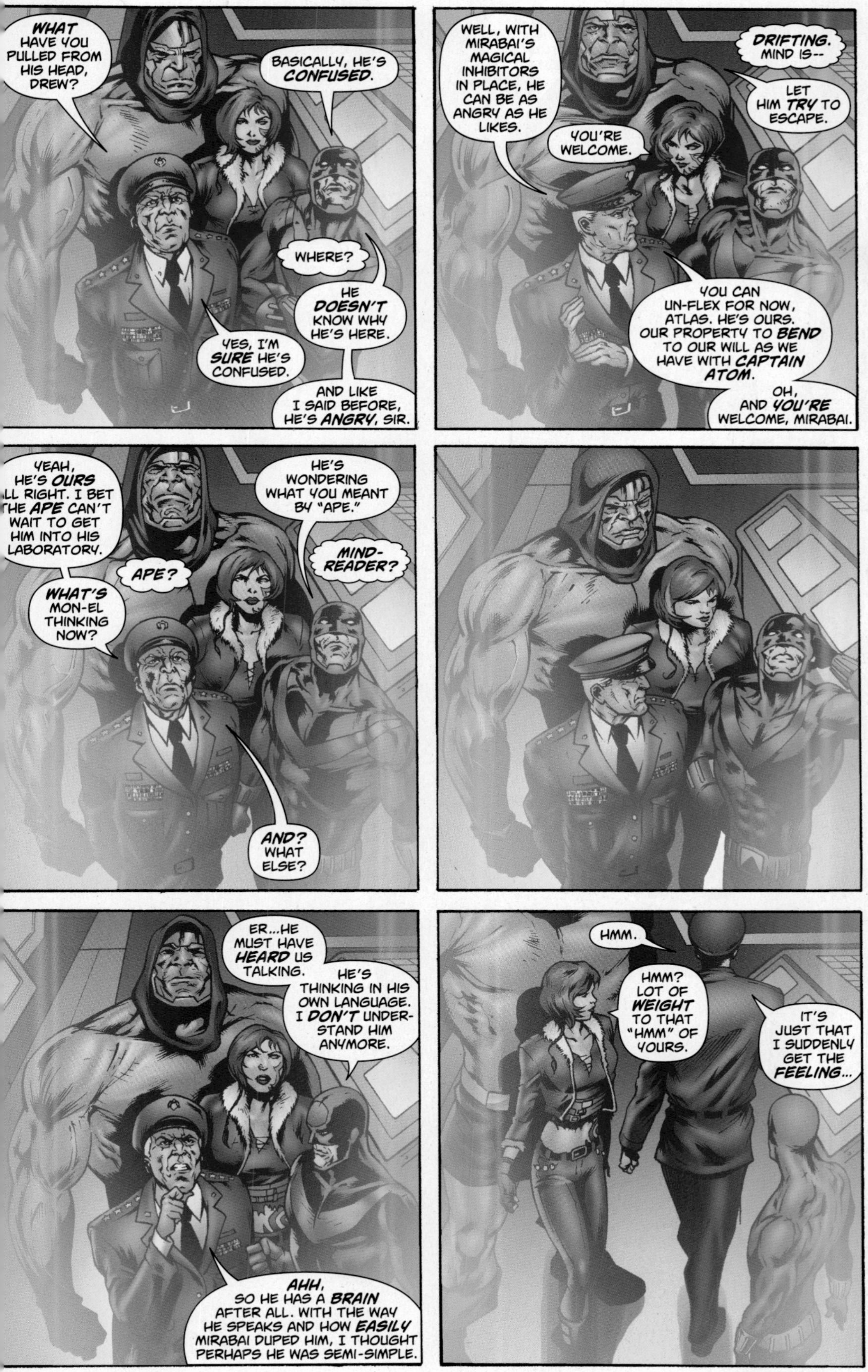
WHAT HAVE YOU PULLED FROM HIS HEAD, DREW?
BASICALLY, HE'S CONFUSED.
YES, I'M SURE HE'S CONFUSED.
WHERE?
HE DOESN'T KNOW WHY HE'S HERE.
AND LIKE I SAID BEFORE, HE'S ANGRY, SIR.
WELL, WITH MIRABAI'S MAGICAL INHIBITORS IN PLACE, HE CAN BE AS ANGRY AS HE LIKES.
YOU'RE WELCOME.
DRIFTING. MIND IS--
LET HIM TRY TO ESCAPE.
YOU CAN UN-FLEX FOR NOW, ATLAS. HE'S OURS. OUR PROPERTY TO BEND TO OUR WILL AS WE HAVE WITH CAPTAIN ATOM.
OH, AND YOU'RE WELCOME, MIRABAI.
YEAH, HE'S OURS ALL RIGHT. I BET THE APE CAN'T WAIT TO GET HIM INTO HIS LABORATORY.
APE?
HE'S WONDERING WHAT YOU MEANT BY "APE."
MIND-READER?
WHAT'S MON-EL THINKING NOW?
AND? WHAT ELSE?
ER...HE MUST HAVE HEARD US TALKING.
HE'S THINKING IN HIS OWN LANGUAGE. I DON'T UNDERSTAND HIM ANYMORE.
AHH, SO HE HAS A BRAIN AFTER ALL. WITH THE WAY HE SPEAKS AND HOW EASILY MIRABAI DUPED HIM, I THOUGHT PERHAPS HE WAS SEMI-SIMPLE.
HMM.
HMM? LOT OF WEIGHT TO THAT "HMM" OF YOURS.
IT'S JUST THAT I SUDDENLY GET THE FEELING...

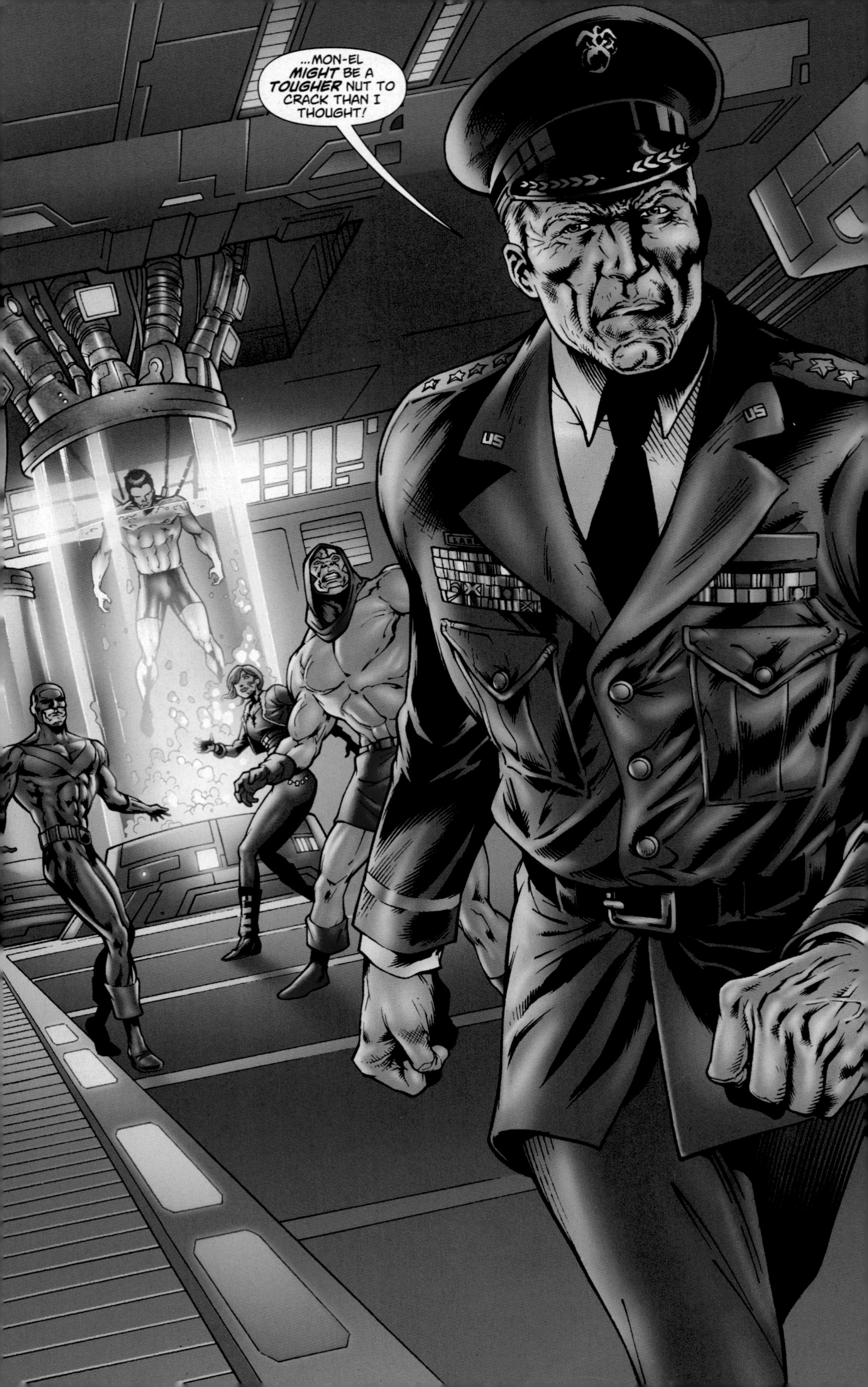
...MON-EL **MIGHT** BE A **TOUGHER** NUT TO CRACK THAN I THOUGHT!

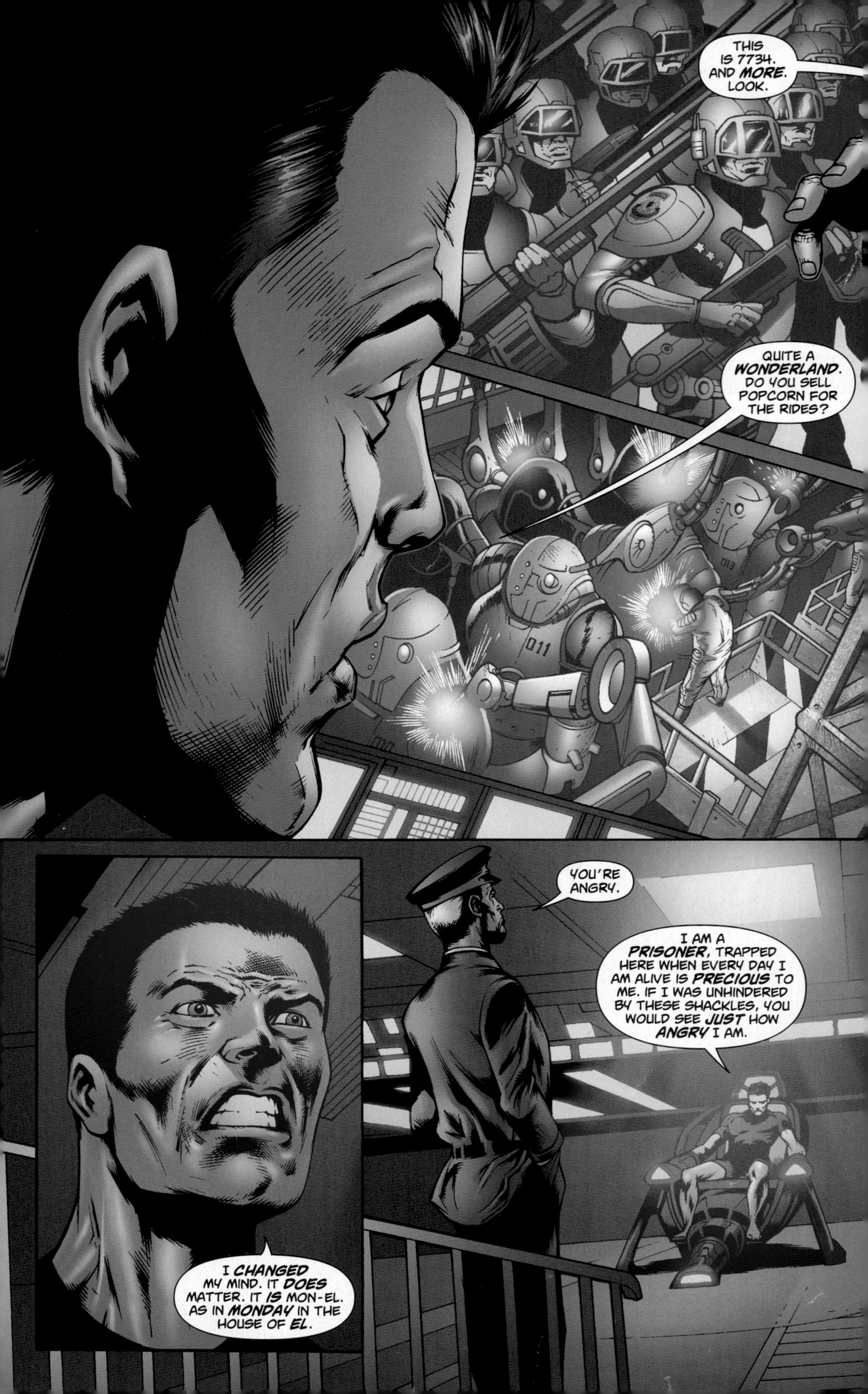
THIS IS 7734. AND MORE. LOOK.
QUITE A WONDERLAND. DO YOU SELL POPCORN FOR THE RIDES?
YOU'RE ANGRY.
I AM A PRISONER, TRAPPED HERE WHEN EVERY DAY I AM ALIVE IS PRECIOUS TO ME. IF I WAS UNHINDERED BY THESE SHACKLES, YOU WOULD SEE JUST HOW ANGRY I AM.
I CHANGED MY MIND. IT DOES MATTER. IT IS MON-EL. AS IN MONDAY IN THE HOUSE OF EL.

SUPERMAN **WAS** EARTH'S--

I **ALREADY** PROMISED SUPERMAN I WOULD BE THE PROTECTOR OF **METROPOLIS.**

WHY NOT "PROTECTOR OF THE **WORLD**"?

BEFORE HE DESERTED THE PLANET. NOW THAT'S **ME.** WHAT I AM GOING TO DO--

WITH THE HELP OF **AMAZING** BEINGS LIKE YOU--IS **PROTECT** THIS WORLD FROM THE **KRYPTONIAN THREAT.**

THREAT? THE KRYPTONIANS ARE **NOT** THE ONES WHO HAVE MADE ME A CAPTIVE.

YOU HAVE THE **POWER** OF SUPERMA— HELL, YOU'RE TECHNICA— **STRONGER** BY HAVIN— **INVULNERABILITY** BO— TO KRYPTONITE AS WEL— LEAD, UNLIKE **OTHER** DAXAMITES.

SIR! MAJOR **ZMECK** REPORTING, SIR. I'VE BEEN **ASSIGNED** TO YOU.

SPECIALIST **BLAKE.**

SIR.

PUT THE MAJOR ON— **PROJECT BREA**— WITH YOU. **AUXILI**— FOR NOW. LET'S S— HOW HE DOES—

SIR!

SO I'M **CAREFUL** WITH YOU, CAN YOU BLAME ME? BUT I'M **NOT** A BAD MAN.

YOU SAY THAT, BUT I CAN **FEEL** THE BLIND **HATRED** IN YOUR VOICE WHEN YOU SPEAK OF KRYPTON.

AH, **SGT. KELLY.** HOW'S YOUR UNIT'S SPELL-CASTING TRAINING PROGRESSING?

THE MEN ARE LEARNING **FAST,** SIR--THOSE WHO **AREN'T** BEING SENT TO THE MADHOUSE.

YES, **MAJOR FORCE.** YOU'VE A REPUTATION AS A **MAVERICK.** **NOT** HERE. NOT WITH **ME.** GOT IT, SON?

YES! SIR!

YOU REMIND ME OF THE **PRIESTS** OF MY OWN WORLD.

YES SIR.

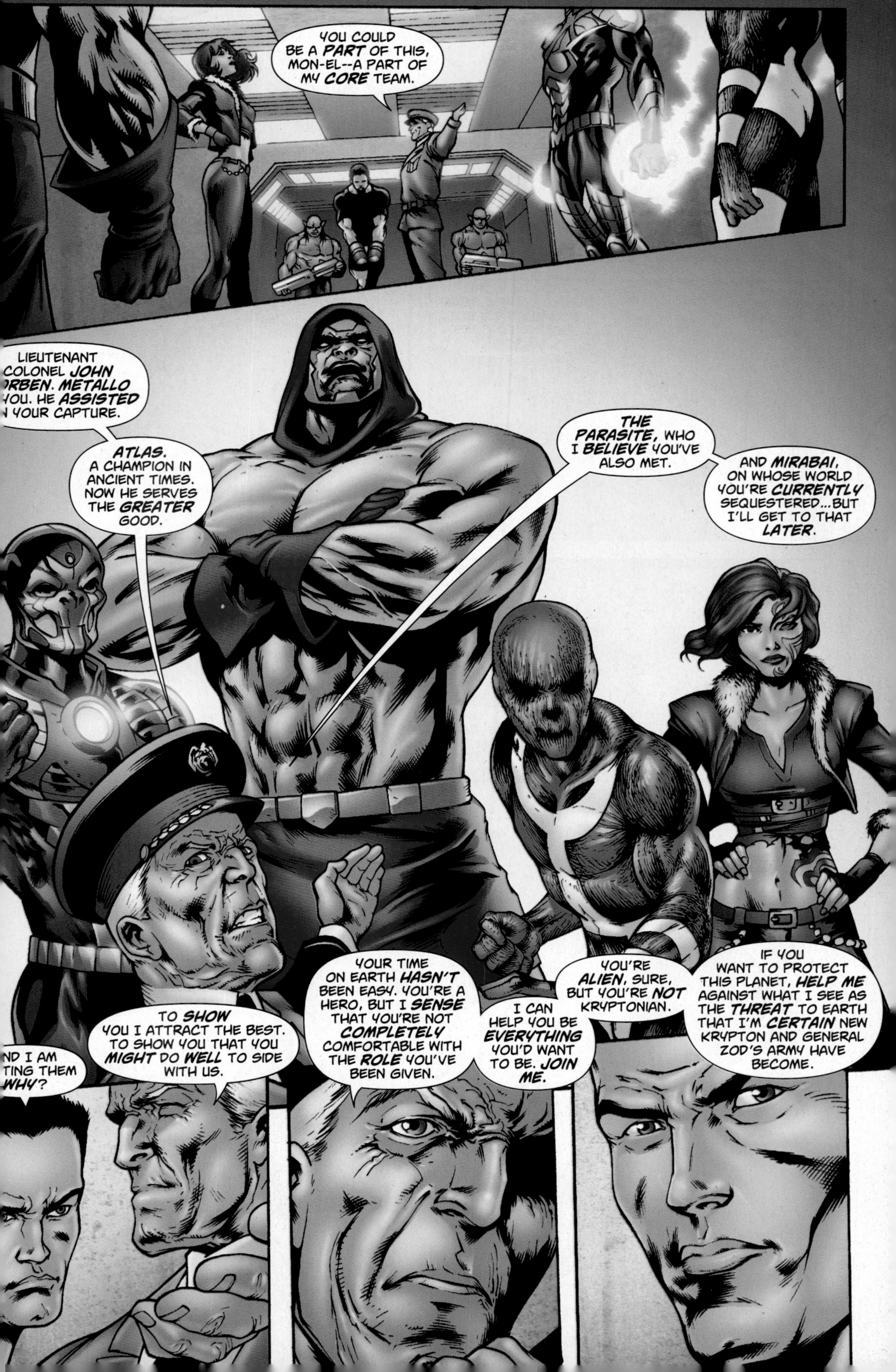

YOU COULD BE A PART OF THIS, MON-EL--A PART OF MY CORE TEAM.
LIEUTENANT COLONEL JOHN ...RBEN. METALLO ...YOU. HE ASSISTED ...N YOUR CAPTURE.
ATLAS. A CHAMPION IN ANCIENT TIMES. NOW HE SERVES THE GREATER GOOD.
THE PARASITE, WHO I BELIEVE YOU'VE ALSO MET.
AND MIRABAI, ON WHOSE WORLD YOU'RE CURRENTLY SEQUESTERED...BUT I'LL GET TO THAT LATER.
...ND I AM ...TING THEM ...WHY?
TO SHOW YOU I ATTRACT THE BEST. TO SHOW YOU THAT YOU MIGHT DO WELL TO SIDE WITH US.
YOUR TIME ON EARTH HASN'T BEEN EASY. YOU'RE A HERO, BUT I SENSE THAT YOU'RE NOT COMPLETELY COMFORTABLE WITH THE ROLE YOU'VE BEEN GIVEN.
I CAN HELP YOU BE EVERYTHING YOU'D WANT TO BE. JOIN ME.
YOU'RE ALIEN, SURE, BUT YOU'RE NOT KRYPTONIAN.
IF YOU WANT TO PROTECT THIS PLANET, HELP ME AGAINST WHAT I SEE AS THE THREAT TO EARTH THAT I'M CERTAIN NEW KRYPTON AND GENERAL ZOD'S ARMY HAVE BECOME.

THIS IS A **CHANCE** FOR YOU TO BE PART OF SOMETHING **GOOD**. NO, SOMETHING **GREAT!**

YOU PROMISED SUPERMAN YOU'D PROTECT EARTH, AND BELIEVE ME, YOU **WILL.**

OR IT'S THE LABORATORY OF DR. CALOMAR FOR YOU.

AND THE WORLD THINKS YOU'RE **DEAD,** SO **DON'T** EXPECT ANYONE TO COME LOOKING.

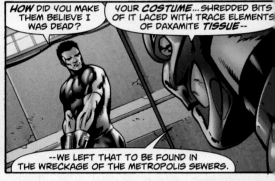

HOW DID YOU MAKE THEM BELIEVE I WAS DEAD?

YOUR **COSTUME**...SHREDDED BITS OF IT LACED WITH TRACE ELEMENTS OF DAXAMITE **TISSUE**--

--WE LEFT THAT TO BE FOUND IN THE WRECKAGE OF THE METROPOLIS SEWERS.

THEN **HOW** DID YOU GET DAXAMITE TISSUE? I AM **INVULNERABLE,** YOU COULD NOT SCRAPE IT OFF ME.

AND **HOW** DID YOU KNOW ABOUT MY RACE'S LEAD WEAKNESS, FOR THAT MATTER?

OH, WE KNOW **MORE** ABOUT DAXAM THAN YOU'D **THINK.**

NOW **ENOUGH** TALK, ALIEN. **CHOOSE.**

I MADE AN **OATH** TO SUPERMAN.

SUPERMAN IS KRYPTONIAN.

AND HE IS GOOD AND HE IS A **HERO,** WHICH IS MO... THAN I CAN SAY FOR ENTICING DISPLAY O... **GARBAGE** YOU HAV... COLLECTED.

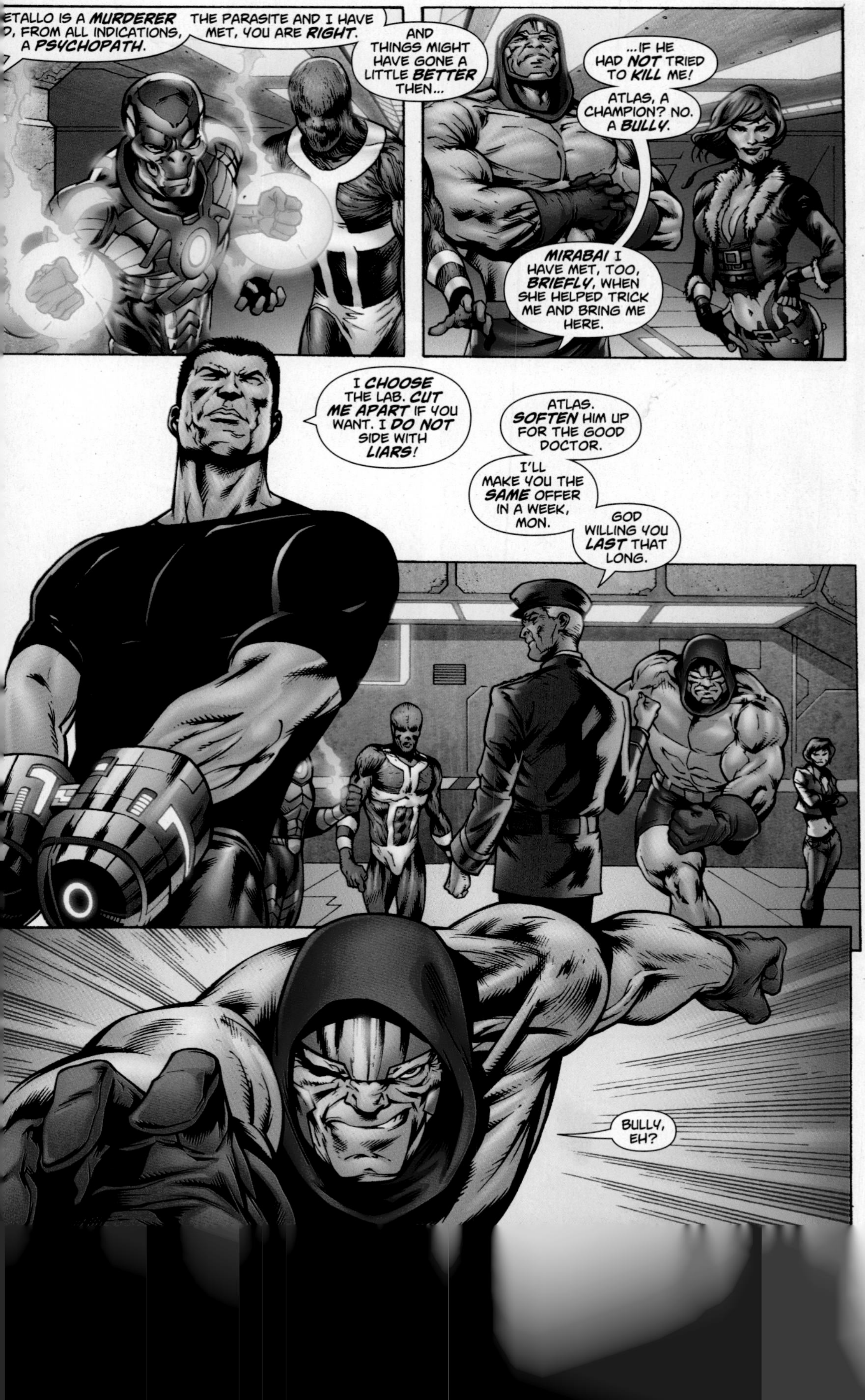
ETALLO IS A MURDERER
D, FROM ALL INDICATIONS, A PSYCHOPATH.
THE PARASITE AND I HAVE MET, YOU ARE RIGHT.
AND THINGS MIGHT HAVE GONE A LITTLE BETTER THEN...
...IF HE HAD NOT TRIED TO KILL ME!
ATLAS, A CHAMPION? NO. A BULLY.
MIRABAI I HAVE MET, TOO, BRIEFLY, WHEN SHE HELPED TRICK ME AND BRING ME HERE.
I CHOOSE THE LAB. CUT ME APART IF YOU WANT. I DO NOT SIDE WITH LIARS!
ATLAS. SOFTEN HIM UP FOR THE GOOD DOCTOR.
I'LL MAKE YOU THE SAME OFFER IN A WEEK, MON.
GOD WILLING YOU LAST THAT LONG.
BULLY, EH?

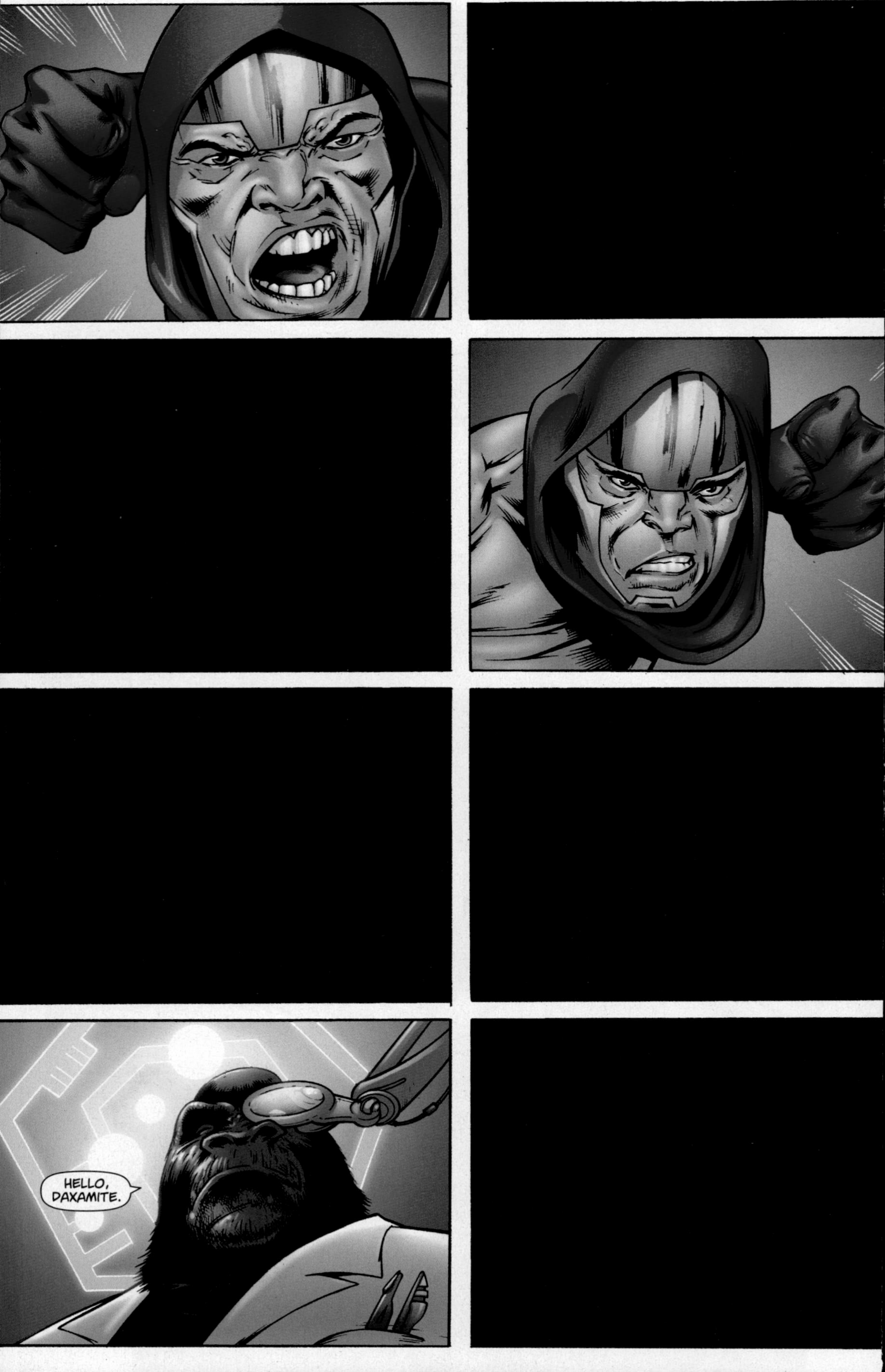
HELLO, DAXAMITE.

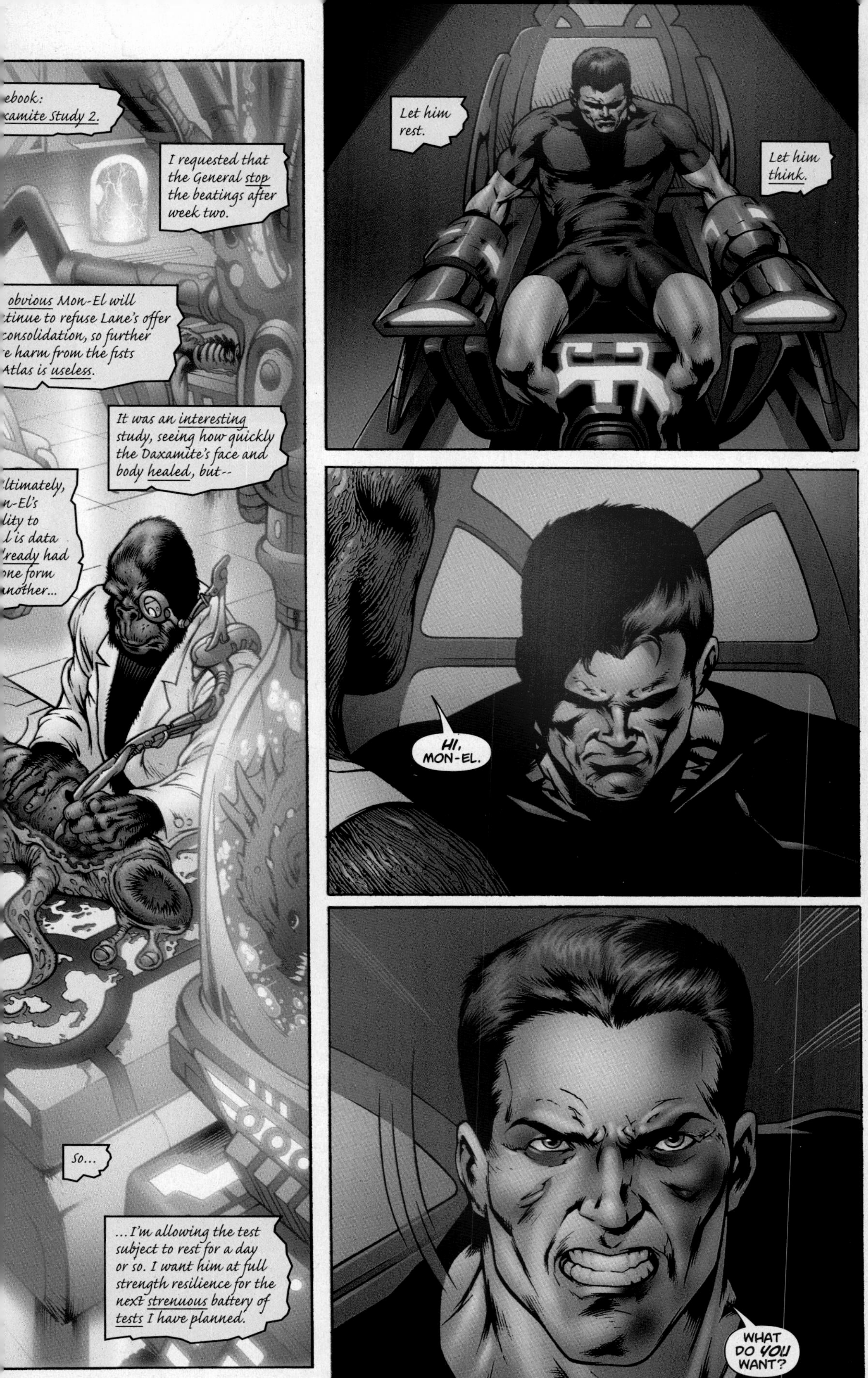

ebook:
xamite Study 2.
I requested that the General stop the beatings after week two.
obvious Mon-El will
ntinue to refuse Lane's offer
consolidation, so further
e harm from the fists
Atlas is useless.
It was an interesting study, seeing how quickly the Daxamite's face and body healed, but--
ltimately,
n-El's
lity to
l is data
lready had
one form
another...
So...
...I'm allowing the test subject to rest for a day or so. I want him at full strength resilience for the next strenuous battery of tests I have planned.
Let him rest.
Let him think.
HI, MON-EL.
WHAT DO YOU WANT?

THE PORTAL-CODE TO THE SISTER BASE ON *EARTH* CHANGES *EVERY* FIVE MINUTES.

I *STOLE* A SECURITY CHIEF'S MIND AND MEMORIES. I HAVE THE *DEACTIVATION INCANTATION* FOR YOUR POWER SUPPRESSORS AND, AND, *AND...*

HAVE THE PORTAL-ODE FOR *SEVEN MINUTES* FROM NOW.

BUT THERE'S A *GAUNTLET* OF TROUBLE AND WOE BETWEEN *HERE* AND THE *PORTAL* AND *THEN* GETTING FREE OF 7734 ON THE *OTHER* SIDE.

YOU *NEED* ME.

AND *I'LL* NEED YOUR POWER. AND YOU FIGHTING *ALONGSIDE* ME.

SEVEN MINUTES... NO, *SIX* MINUTES, MON-EL, AND *COUNTING.*

COME ON, THIS OFFER GOES STALE *QUICKLY,* SO--

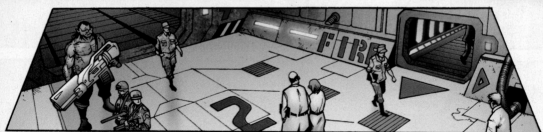

AAAEEEAAAEEEAAAEEEAAAEEEAAAEEEAAAEEE

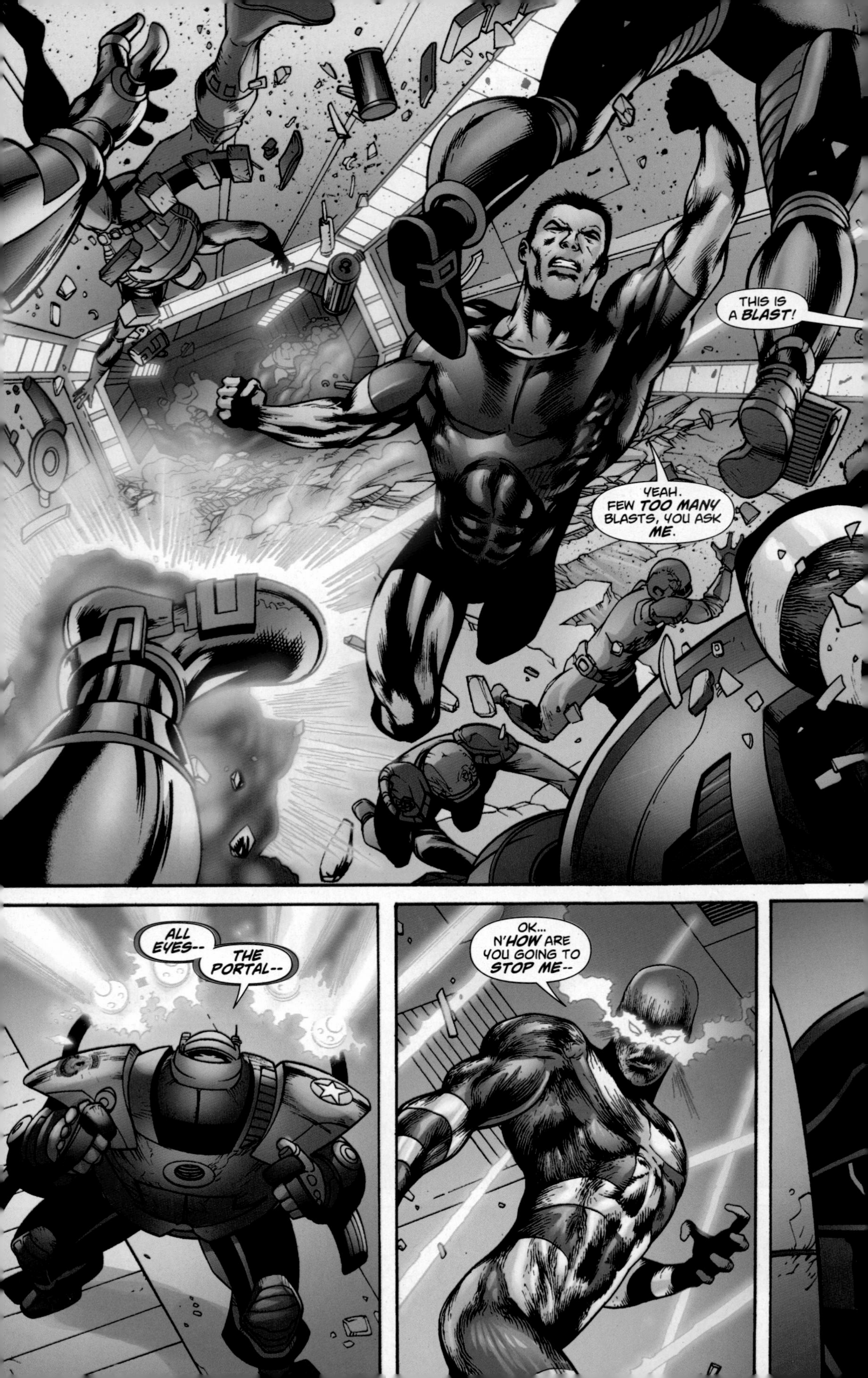
THIS IS A BLAST!
YEAH. FEW TOO MANY BLASTS, YOU ASK ME.
ALL EYES--
THE PORTAL--
OK... N'HOW ARE YOU GOING TO STOP ME--

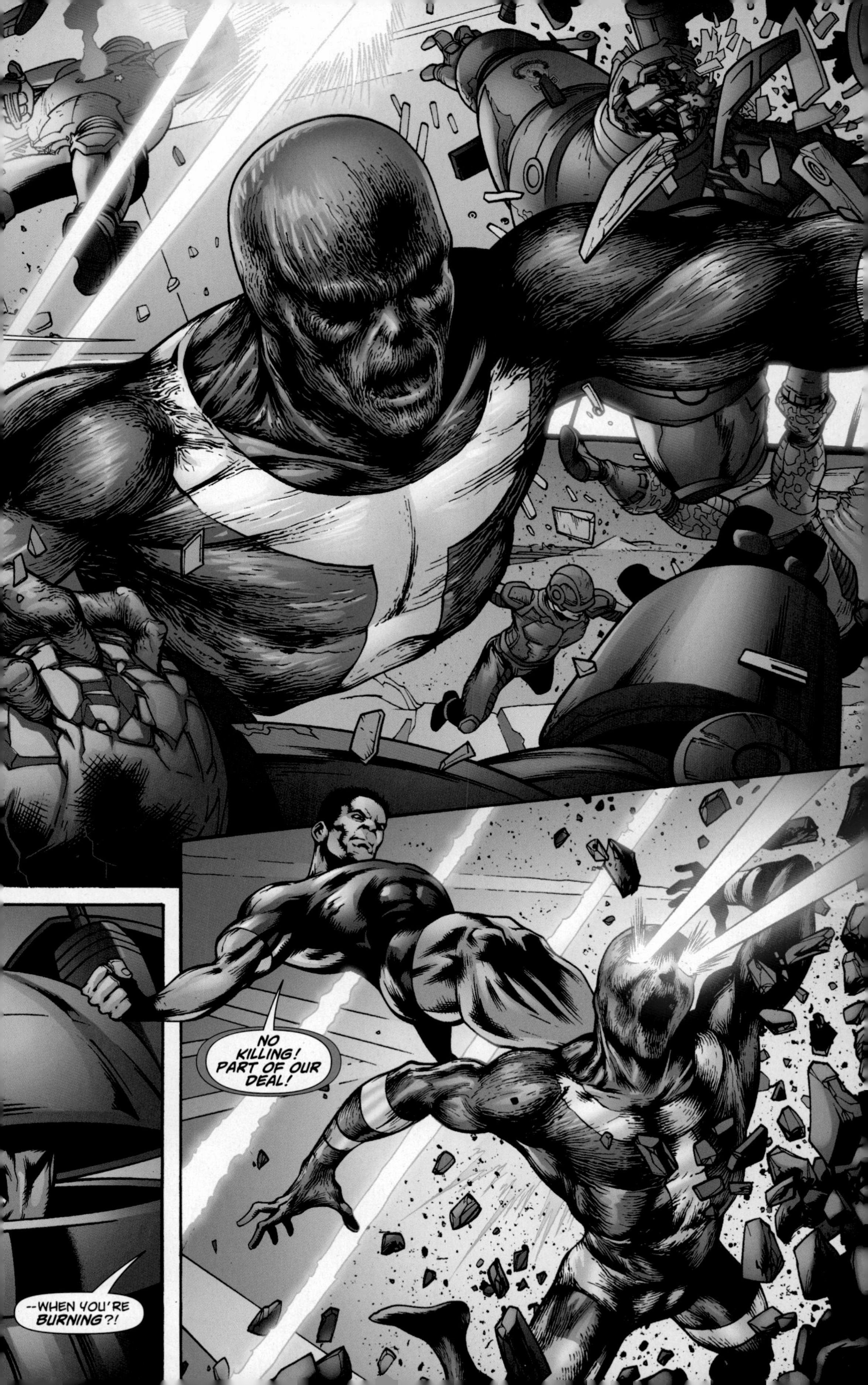
NO KILLING! PART OF OUR DEAL!
--WHEN YOU'RE BURNING?!

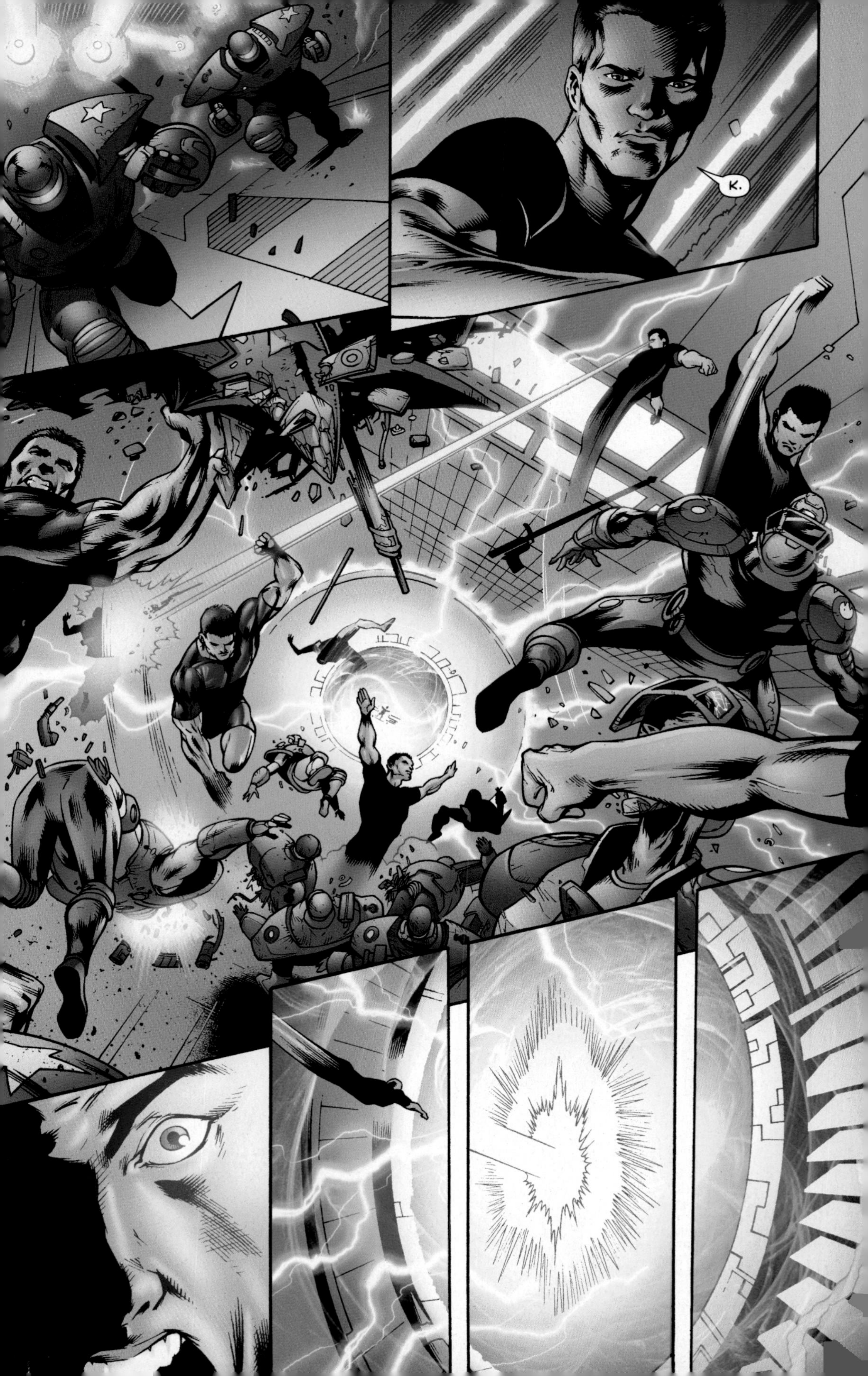
K.

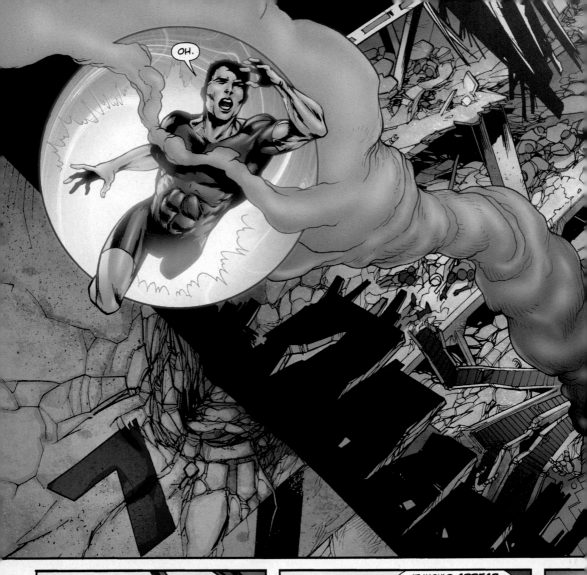

OH.

YOU *FLATTER* HIM. NO. THIS TOOK THE *COMBINED* SKILLS OF *BRAINIAC* AND *LUTHOR*. THEY'VE *ESCAPED*.

AND THEY TOOK THE *LIVES* OF MANY AMERICAN SOLDIERS WITH THEM.

SO IT IS JUST *YOU* AND *ME*.

IT WOULD *APPEAR* SO, WOULDN'T IT? DREW, ATLAS AND METALLO ARE ALL *OFF* LOOKING FOR BRAINIAC.

YOU'RE PRETTY MUCH *FREE* TO GO. *BESIDES*, THERE WILL BE A TIME WHEN YOU'LL *TAKE* MY ORDERS, LIKE IT OR NOT, COME THE *WAR*.

YOU, TOO?

THE PURPLE PEOPLE EATER *TOOK OFF* ALREADY.

YEAH, BUT PARASITE *COULD NOT* HAVE DONE ALL THIS. THERE *WAS NOT* TIME.

LOOKING AT THE *DEAD* AROUND ME, THERE'S *MORE* ON MY MIND THAN WHAT *BAD* THINGS YOU *MIGHT* HAVE TO SAY ABOUT ME TO THE DAILY PLANET.

...OU ...ED I WILL ...SE YOU ...OW?

YOU *CARE* ABOUT LIVES LOST? I AM *SURPRISED*.

I'M A *SOLDIER*. FOR ULTIMATE VICTORY, *SOMETIMES* LIVES MUST BE SACRIFICED. SOMETIMES THEY MUST BE *TAKEN*.

BUT I *HATE* TO SEE THEM *WASTED*.

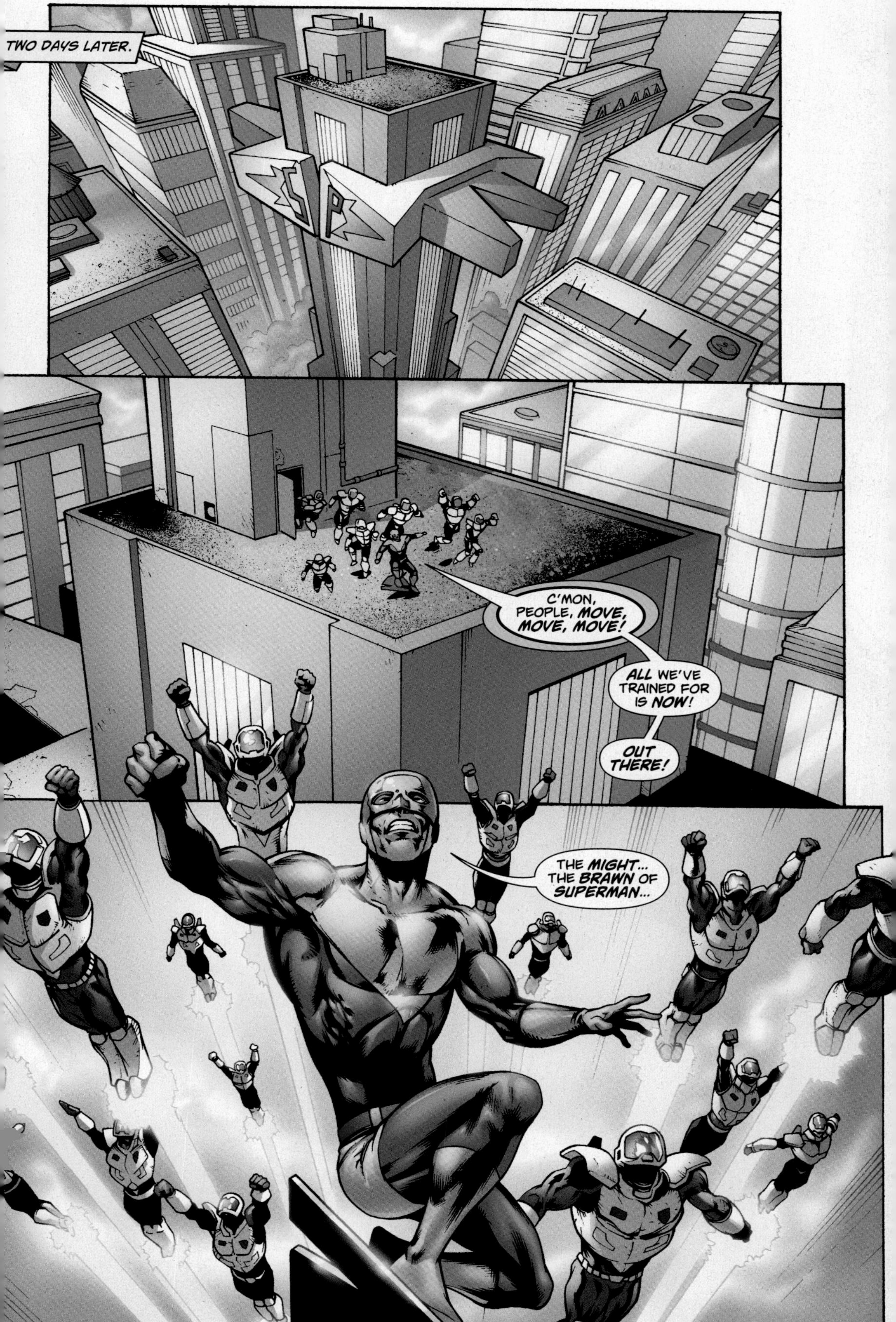
TWO DAYS LATER.
C'MON, PEOPLE, MOVE, MOVE, MOVE!
ALL WE'VE TRAINED FOR IS NOW!
OUT THERE!
THE MIGHT... THE BRAWN OF SUPERMAN...

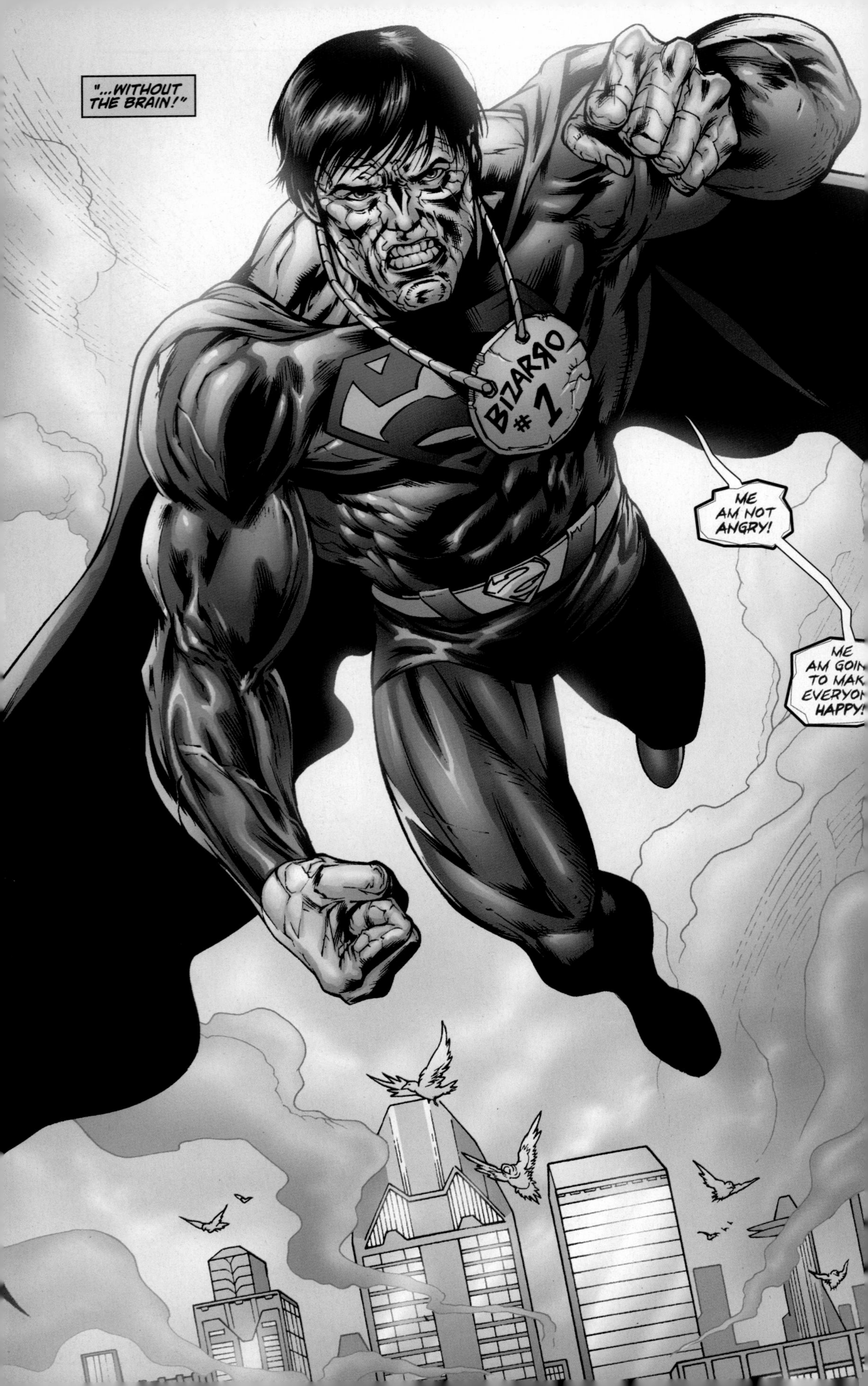
"...WITHOUT THE BRAIN!"
BIZARRO #1
ME AM NOT ANGRY!
ME AM GOIN TO MAK EVERYON HAPPY!

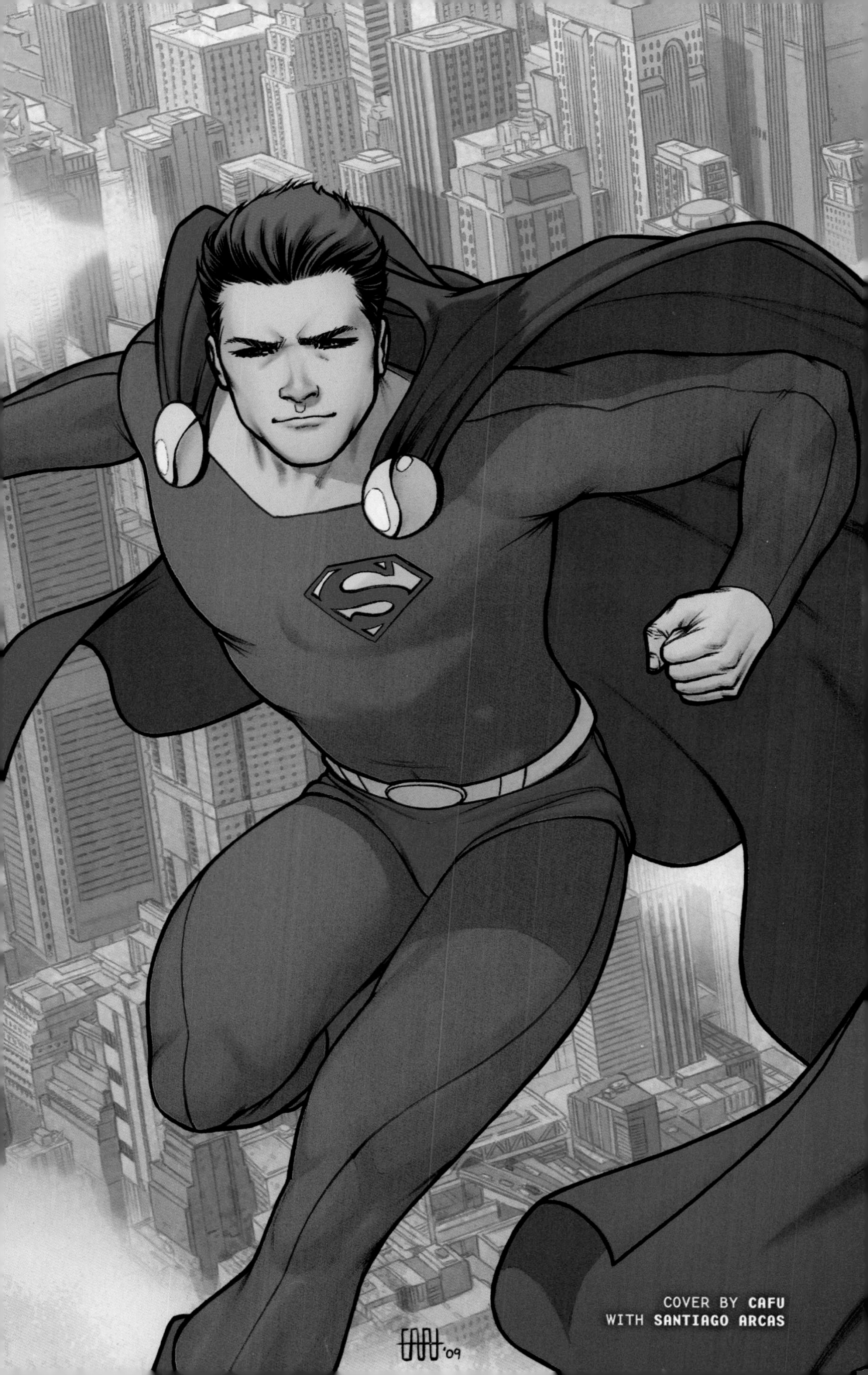

COVER BY **CAFU**
WITH **SANTIAGO ARCAS**

MAN OF VALOR PART ONE

JAVIER PINA <ARTIST>

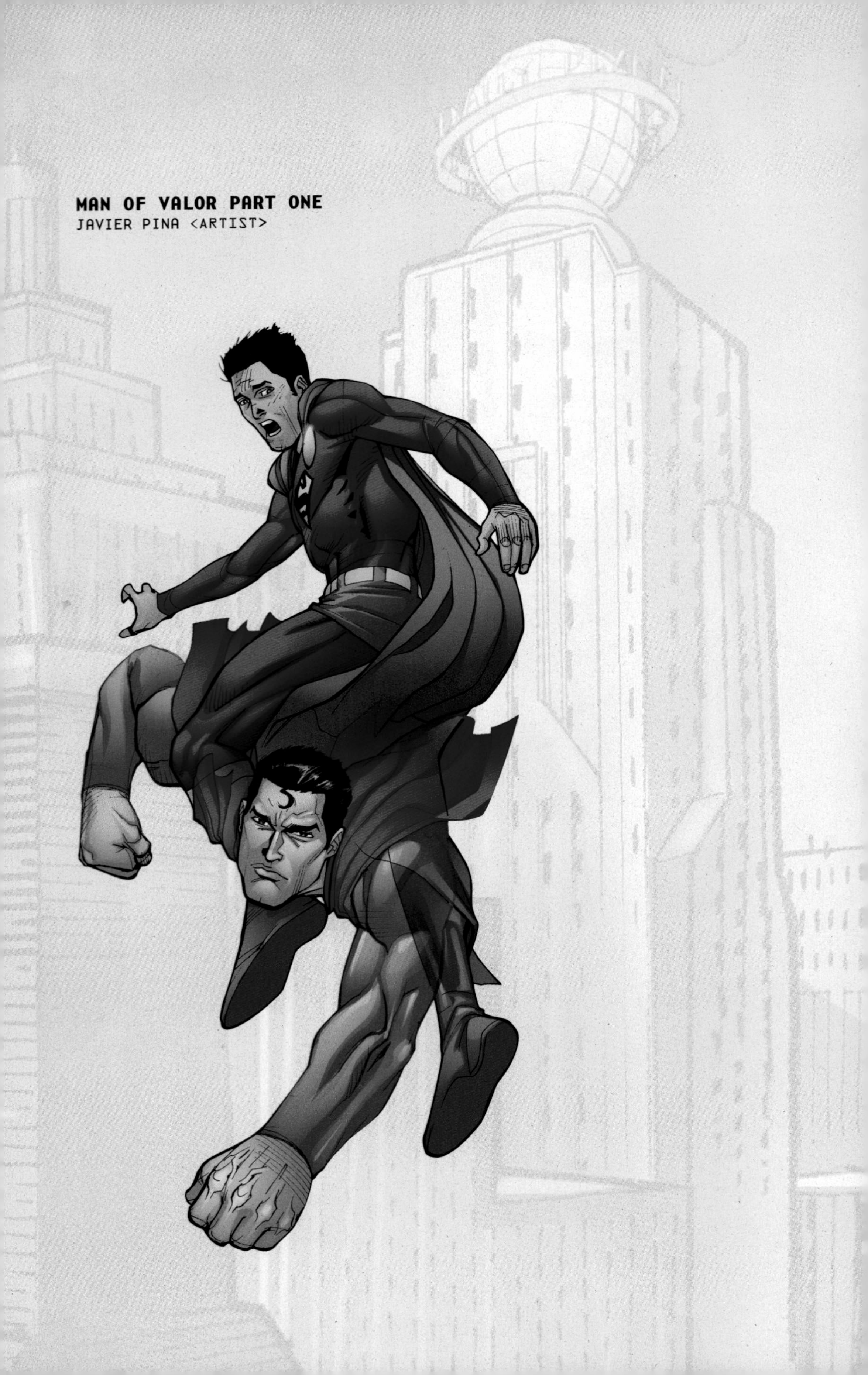

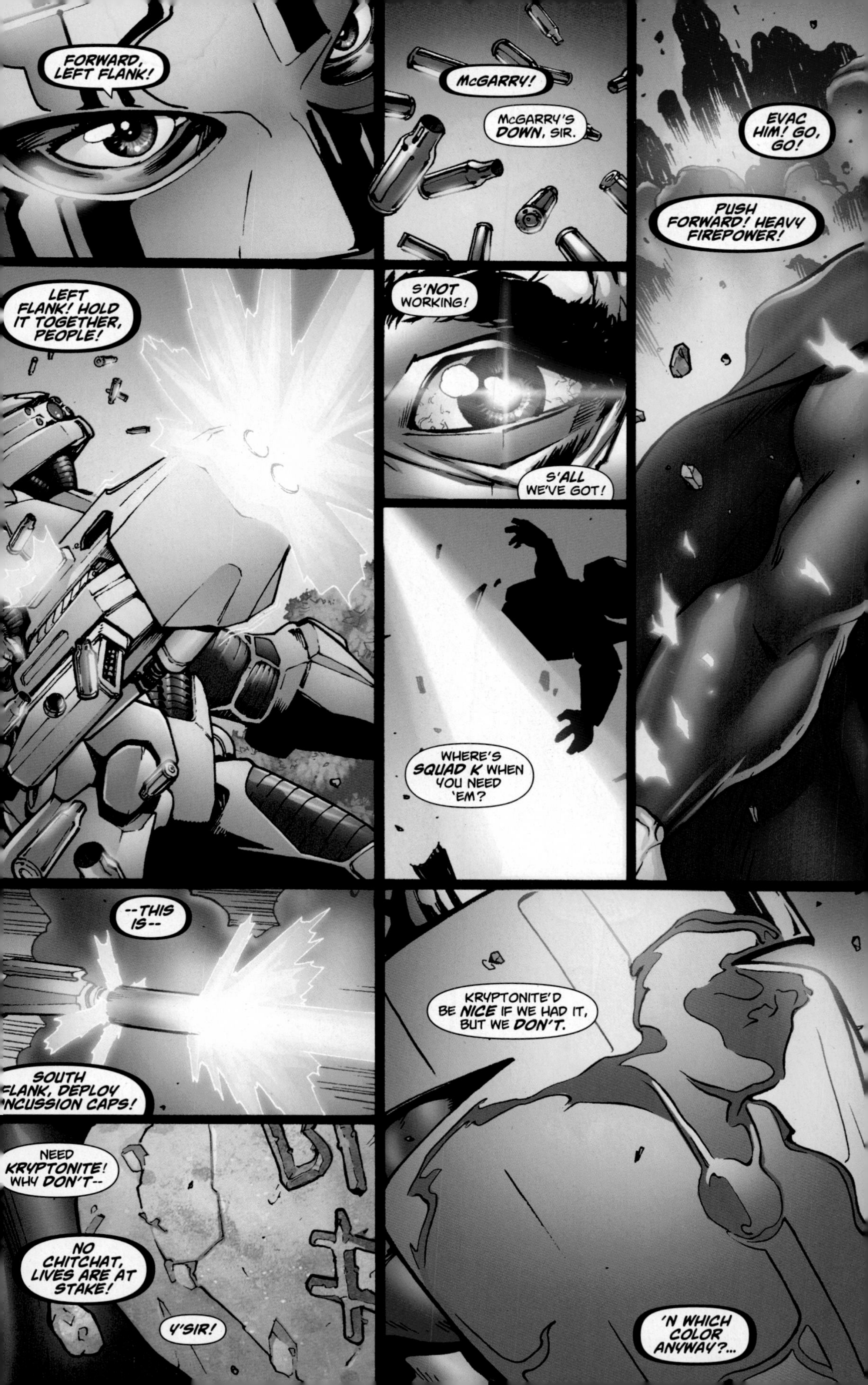
FORWARD, LEFT FLANK!
McGARRY!
McGARRY'S DOWN, SIR.
EVAC HIM! GO, GO!
PUSH FORWARD! HEAVY FIREPOWER!
LEFT FLANK! HOLD IT TOGETHER, PEOPLE!
S'NOT WORKING!
S'ALL WE'VE GOT!
WHERE'S SQUAD K WHEN YOU NEED 'EM?
--THIS IS--
SOUTH FLANK, DEPLOY NCUSSION CAPS!
NEED KRYPTONITE! WHY DON'T--
NO CHITCHAT, LIVES ARE AT STAKE!
Y'SIR!
KRYPTONITE'D BE NICE IF WE HAD IT, BUT WE DON'T.
'N WHICH COLOR ANYWAY?...

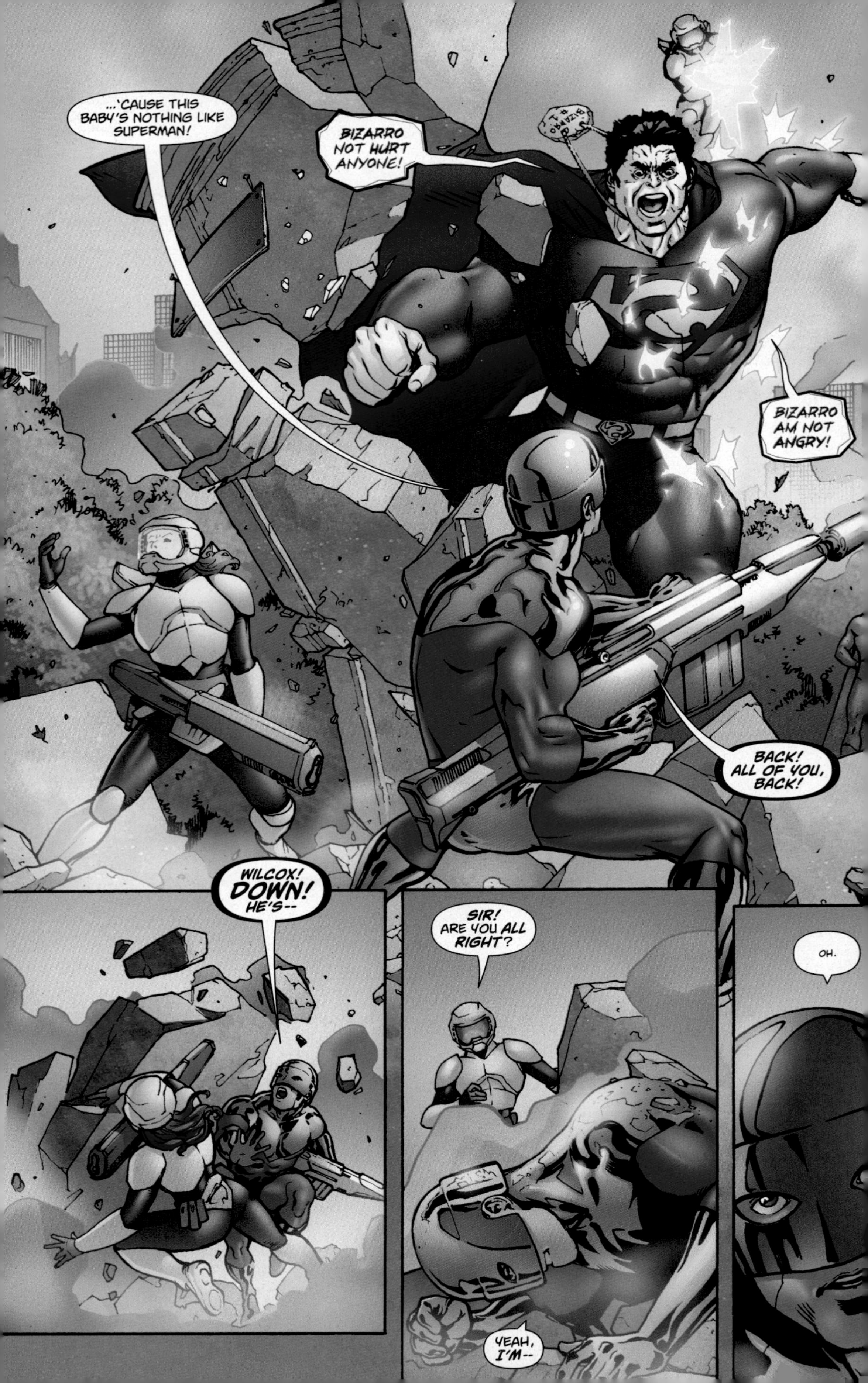
...'CAUSE THIS BABY'S NOTHING LIKE SUPERMAN!
BIZARRO NOT HURT ANYONE!
BIZARRO AM NOT ANGRY!
BACK! ALL OF YOU, BACK!
WILCOX! DOWN! HE'S--
SIR! ARE YOU ALL RIGHT?
YEAH, I'M--
OH.

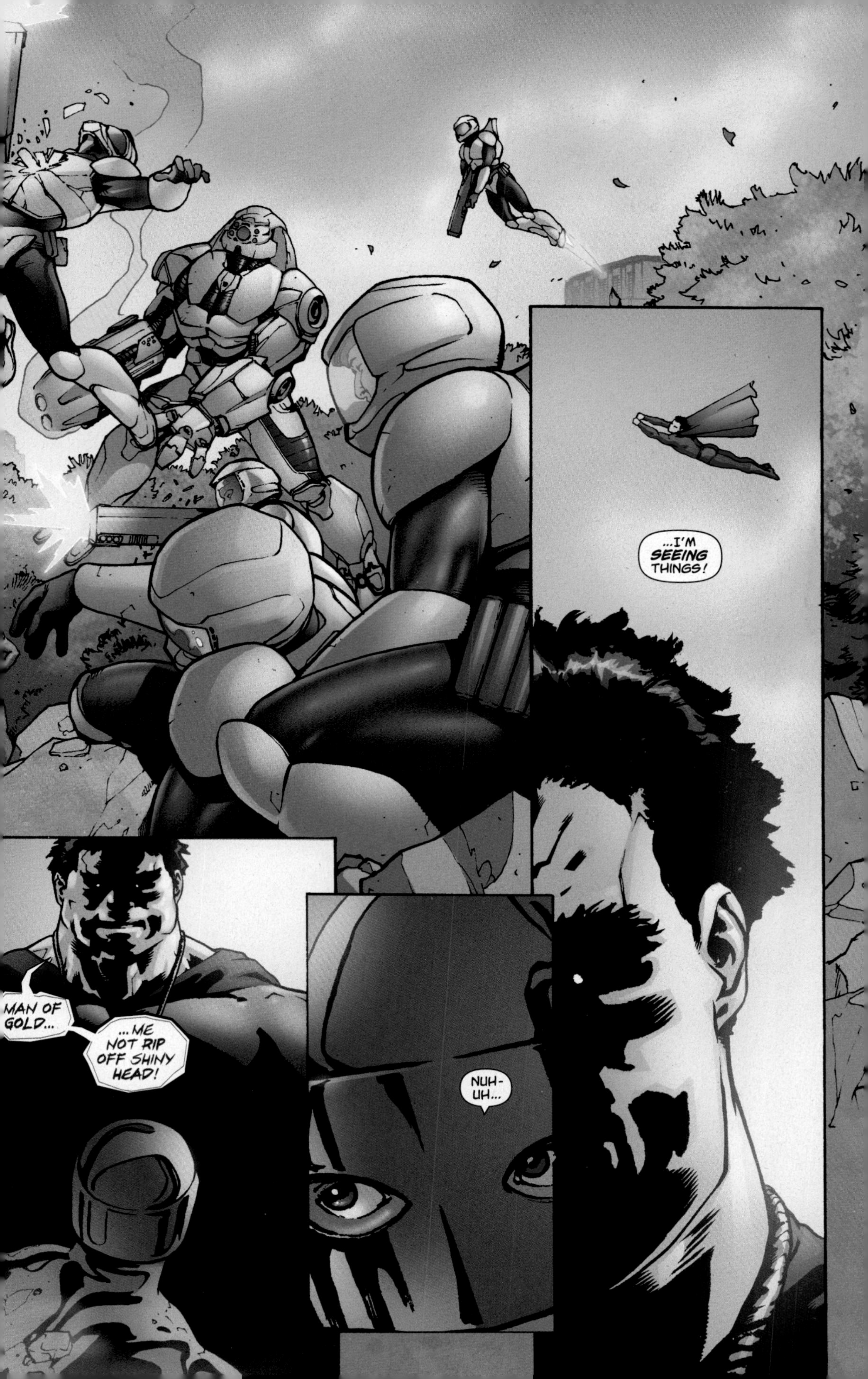
...I'M SEEING THINGS!
MAN OF GOLD...
...ME NOT RIP OFF SHINY HEAD!
NUH-UH...

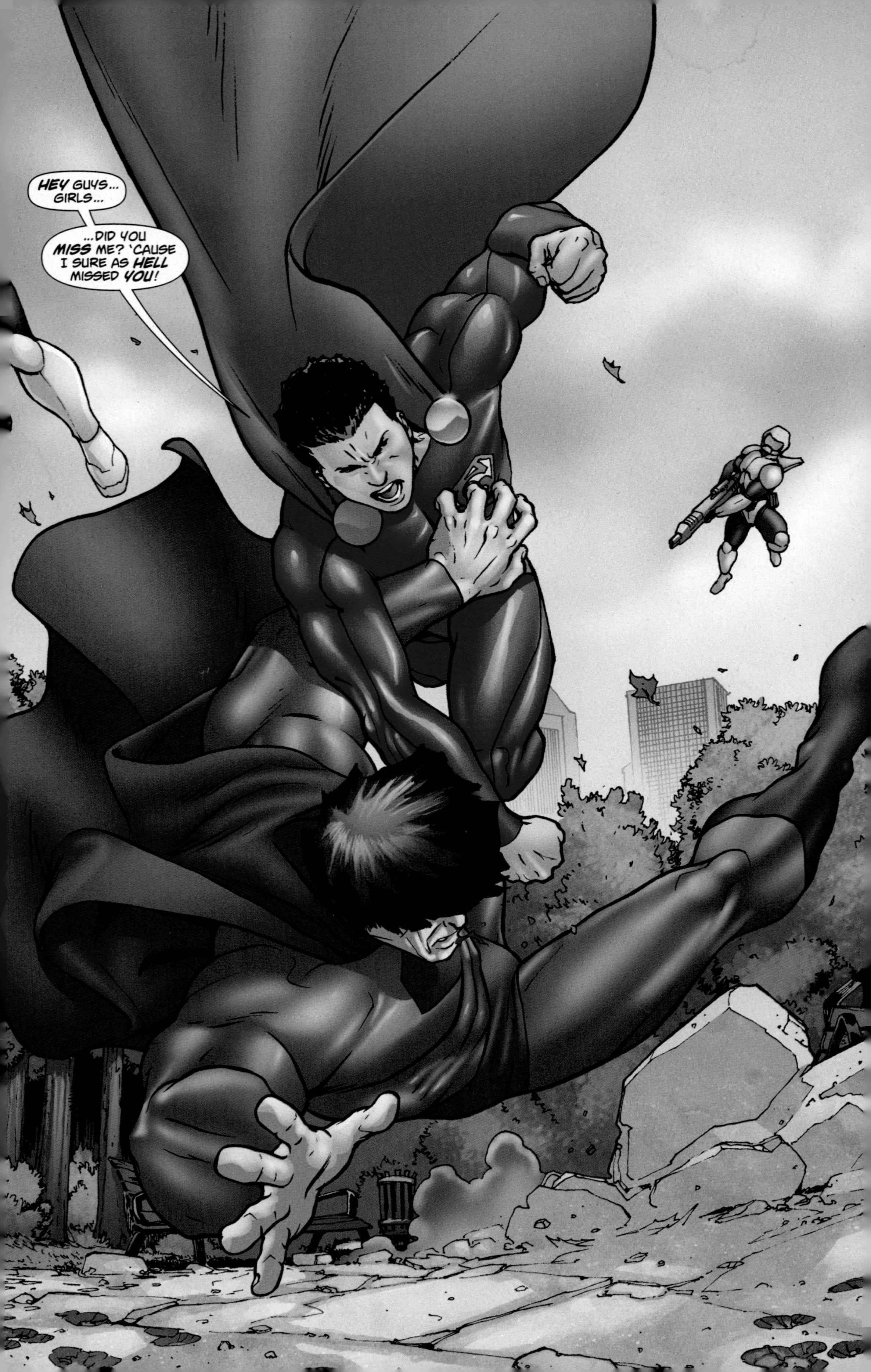
HEY GUYS... GIRLS...
...DID YOU MISS ME? 'CAUSE I SURE AS HELL MISSED YOU!

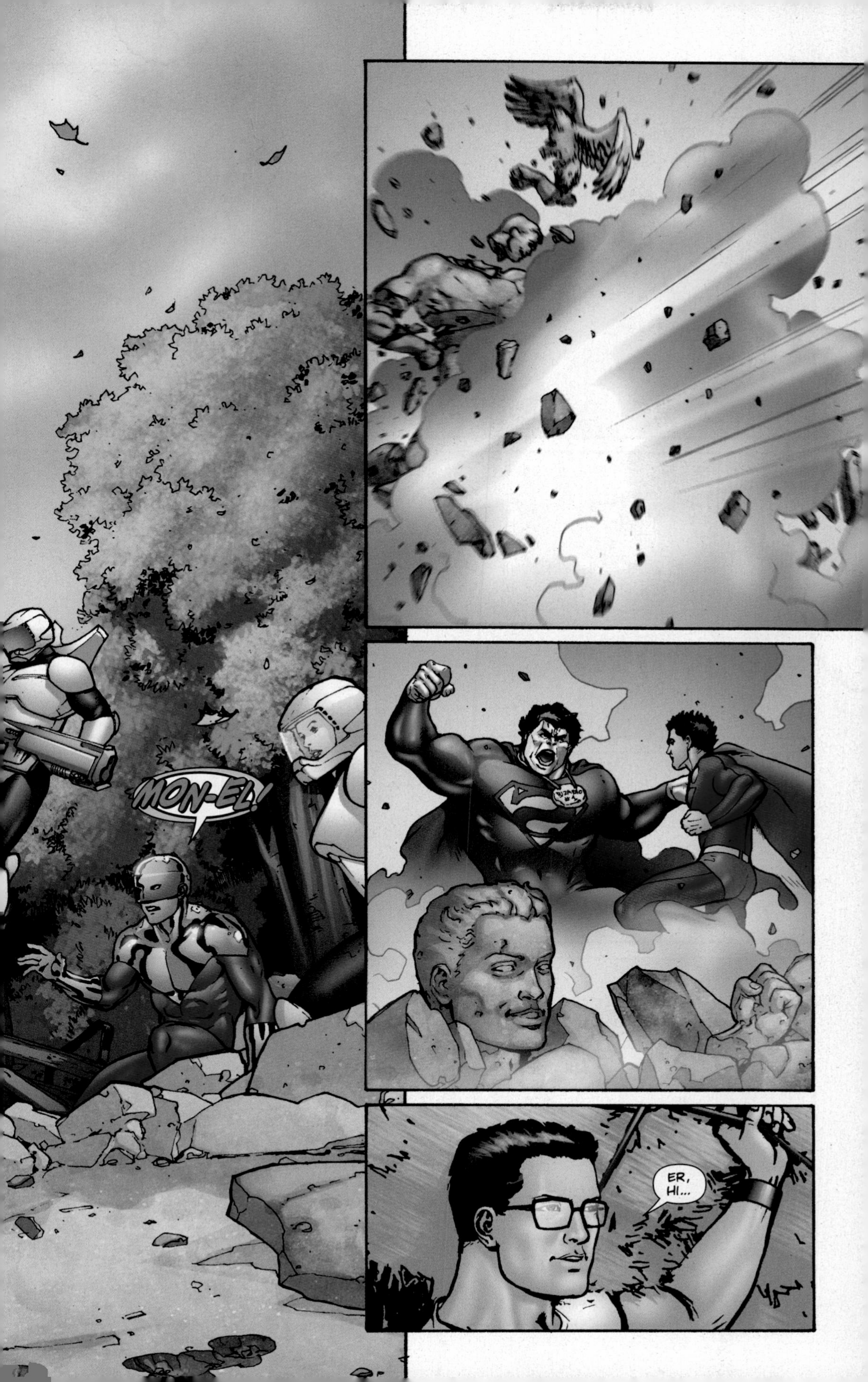
MON-EL!
ER, HI...

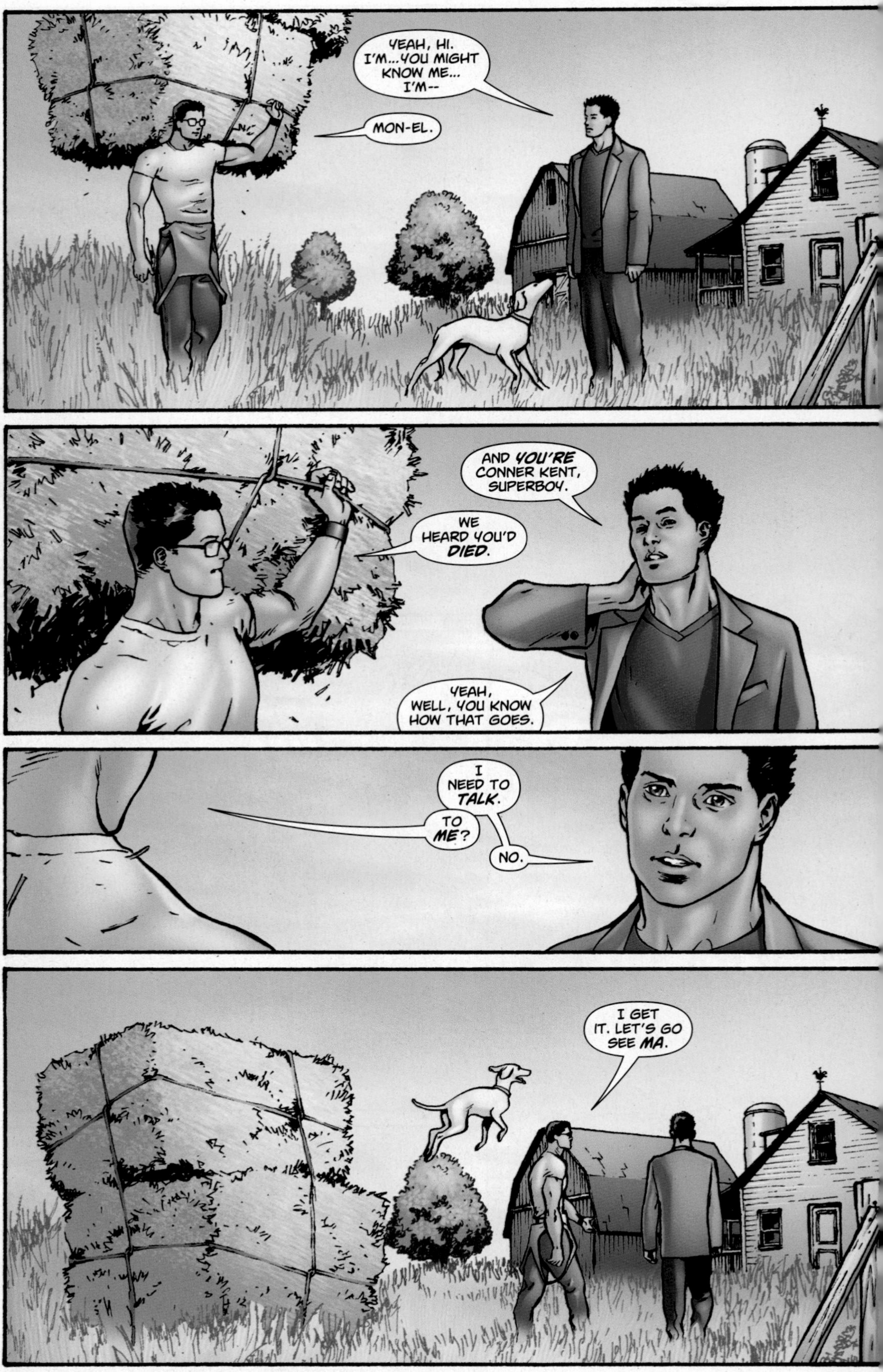
YEAH, HI. I'M...YOU MIGHT KNOW ME... I'M--
MON-EL.
AND YOU'RE CONNER KENT, SUPERBOY.
WE HEARD YOU'D DIED.
YEAH, WELL, YOU KNOW HOW THAT GOES.
I NEED TO TALK.
TO ME?
NO.
I GET IT. LET'S GO SEE MA.

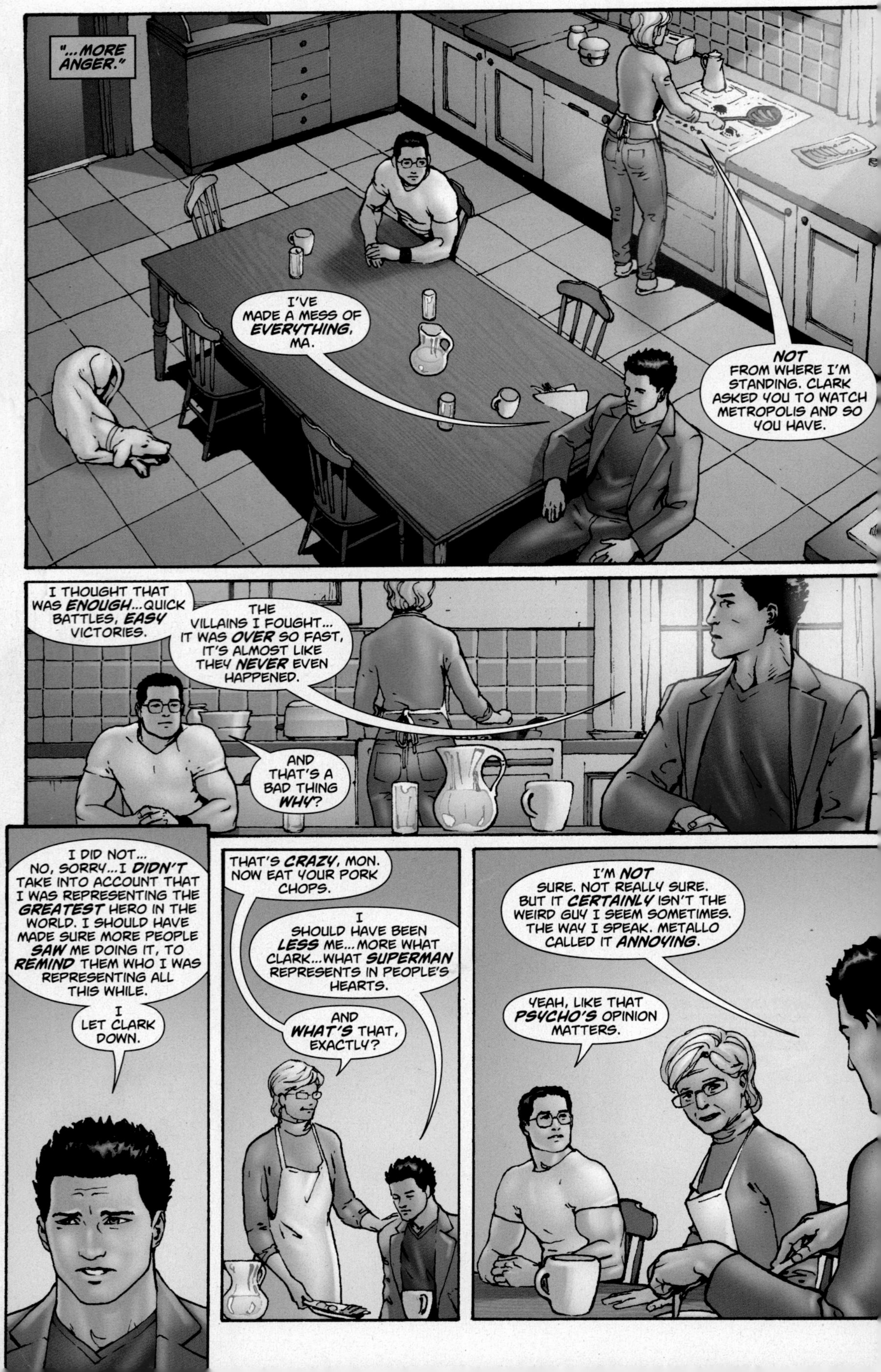
"...MORE ANGER."
I'VE MADE A MESS OF EVERYTHING, MA.
NOT FROM WHERE I'M STANDING. CLARK ASKED YOU TO WATCH METROPOLIS AND SO YOU HAVE.
I THOUGHT THAT WAS ENOUGH...QUICK BATTLES, EASY VICTORIES.
THE VILLAINS I FOUGHT... IT WAS OVER SO FAST, IT'S ALMOST LIKE THEY NEVER EVEN HAPPENED.
AND THAT'S A BAD THING WHY?
I DID NOT... NO, SORRY...I DIDN'T TAKE INTO ACCOUNT THAT I WAS REPRESENTING THE GREATEST HERO IN THE WORLD. I SHOULD HAVE MADE SURE MORE PEOPLE SAW ME DOING IT, TO REMIND THEM WHO I WAS REPRESENTING ALL THIS WHILE.
I LET CLARK DOWN.
THAT'S CRAZY, MON. NOW EAT YOUR PORK CHOPS.
I SHOULD HAVE BEEN LESS ME...MORE WHAT CLARK...WHAT SUPERMAN REPRESENTS IN PEOPLE'S HEARTS.
AND WHAT'S THAT, EXACTLY?
I'M NOT SURE. NOT REALLY SURE. BUT IT CERTAINLY ISN'T THE WEIRD GUY I SEEM SOMETIMES. THE WAY I SPEAK. METALLO CALLED IT ANNOYING.
YEAH, LIKE THAT PSYCHO'S OPINION MATTERS.

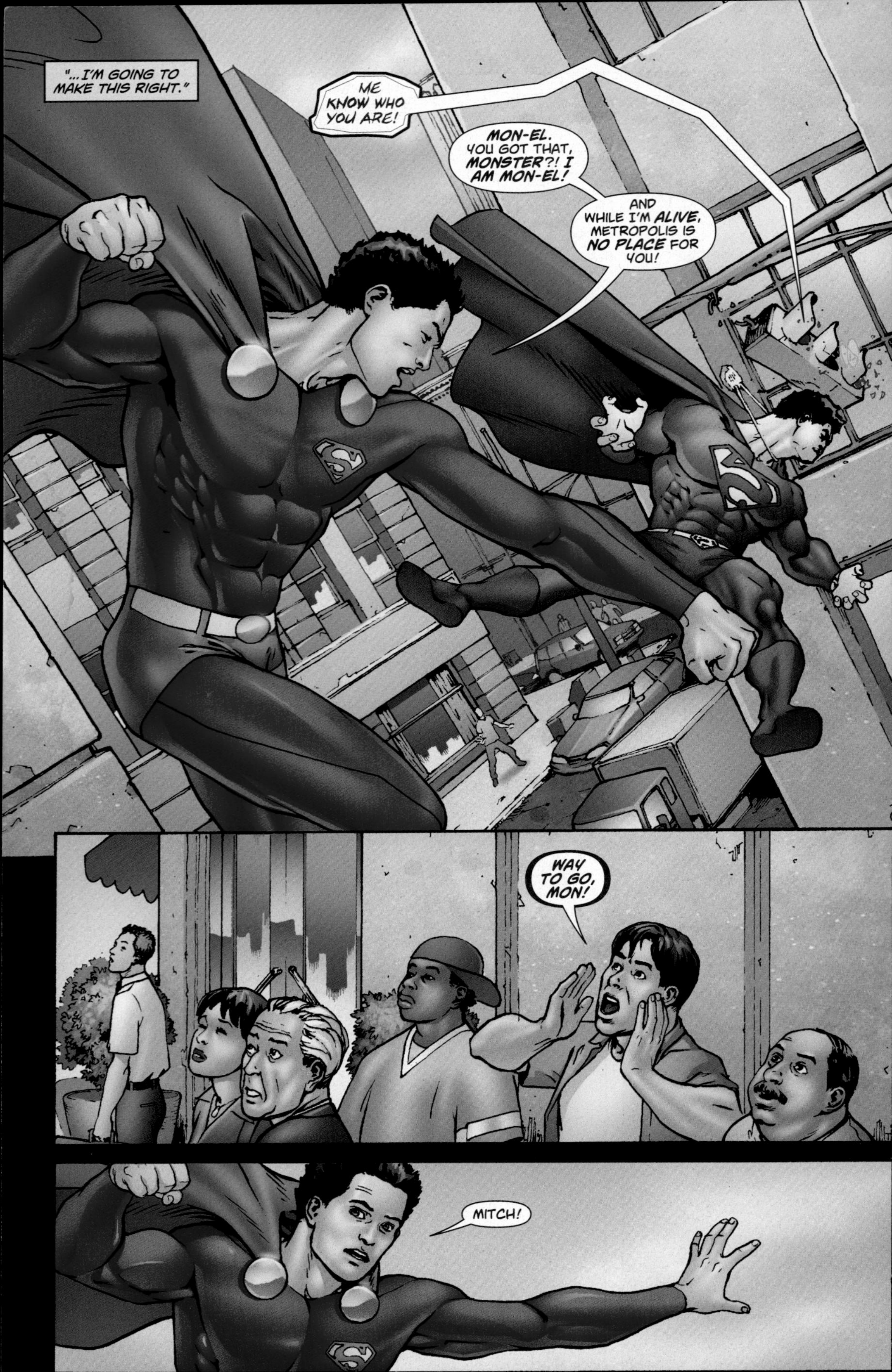
"...I'M GOING TO MAKE THIS RIGHT."
ME KNOW WHO YOU ARE!
MON-EL. YOU GOT THAT, MONSTER?! I AM MON-EL!
AND WHILE I'M ALIVE, METROPOLIS IS NO PLACE FOR YOU!
WAY TO GO, MON!
MITCH!

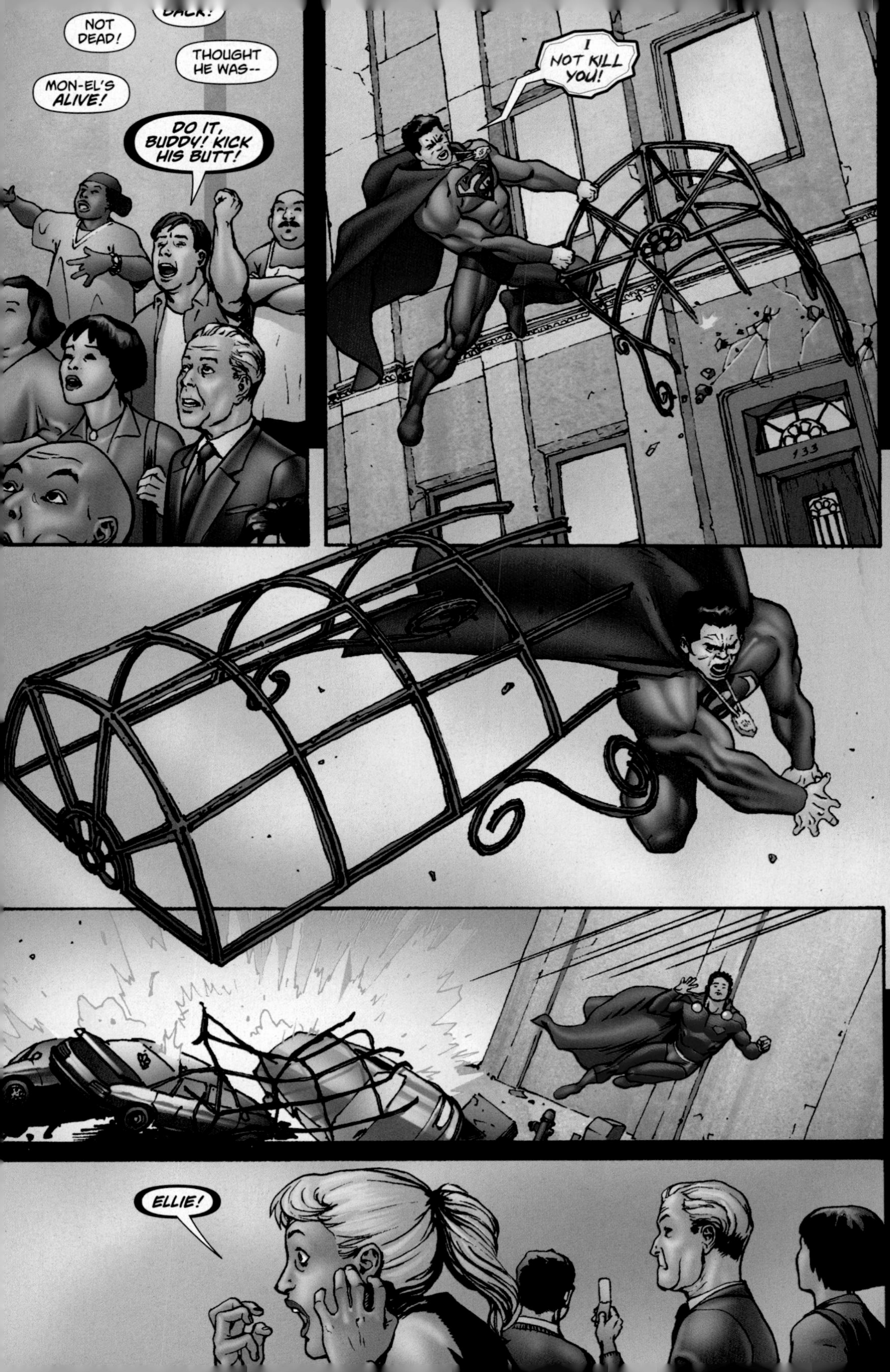
NOT DEAD!
THOUGHT HE WAS--
MON-EL'S ALIVE!
DO IT, BUDDY! KICK HIS BUTT!
I NOT KILL YOU!
133
ELLIE!

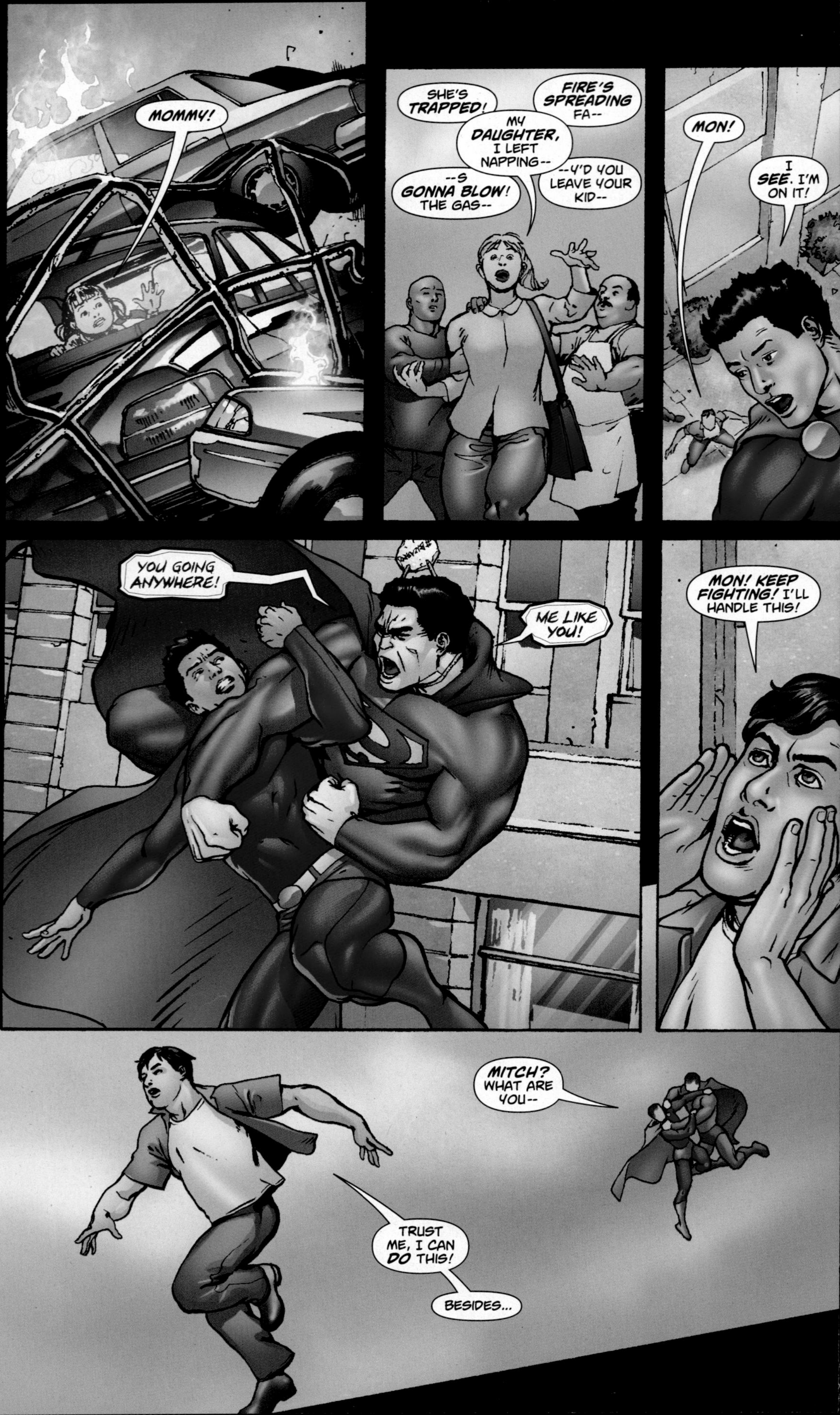
MOMMY!
SHE'S TRAPPED!
FIRE'S SPREADING FA--
MY DAUGHTER, I LEFT NAPPING--
--S GONNA BLOW! THE GAS--
--Y'D YOU LEAVE YOUR KID--
MON!
I SEE. I'M ON IT!
YOU GOING ANYWHERE!
ME LIKE YOU!
MON! KEEP FIGHTING! I'LL HANDLE THIS!
MITCH? WHAT ARE YOU--
TRUST ME, I CAN DO THIS!
BESIDES...

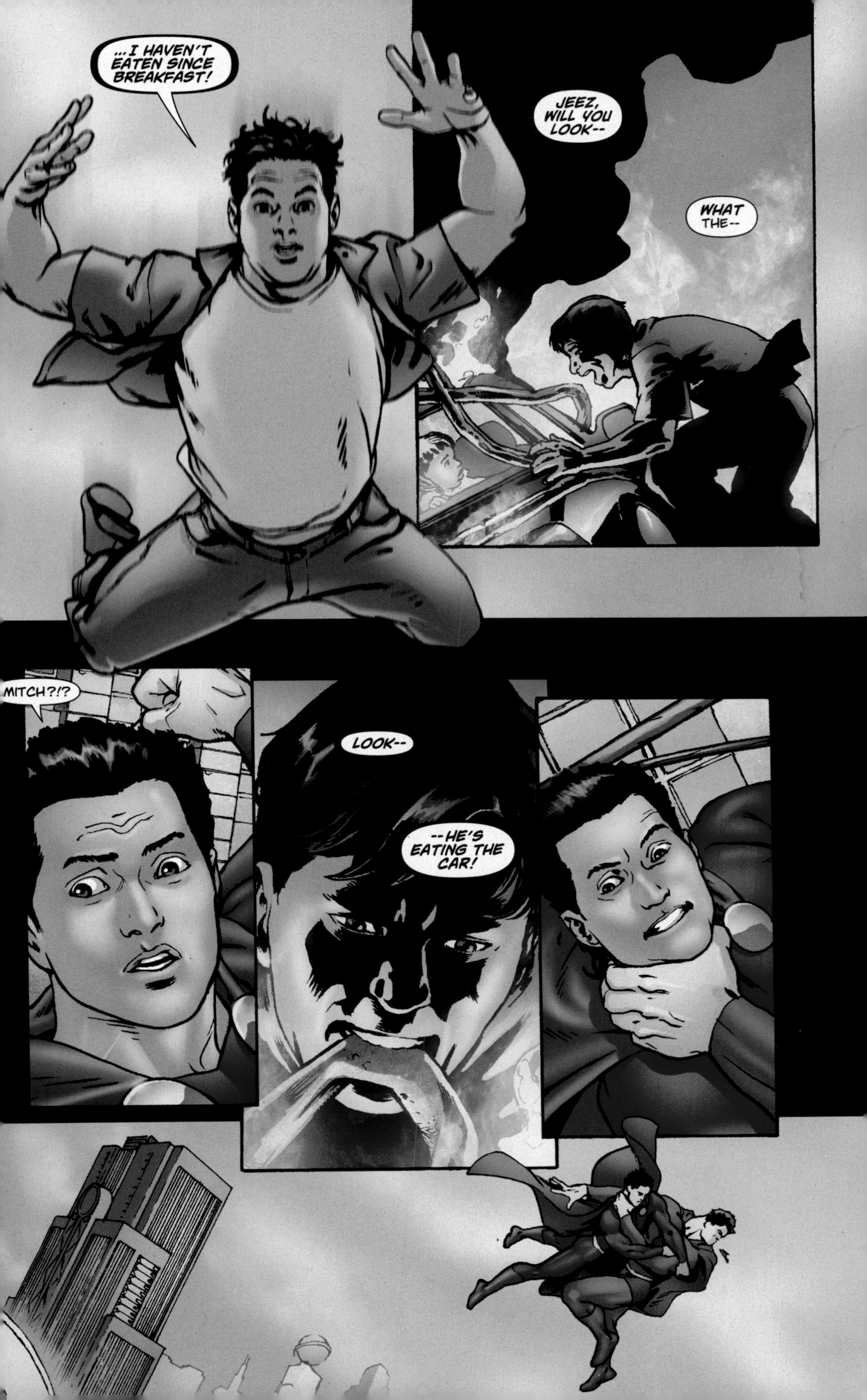
...I HAVEN'T EATEN SINCE BREAKFAST!
JEEZ, WILL YOU LOOK--
WHAT THE--
MITCH?!?
LOOK--
--HE'S EATING THE CAR!

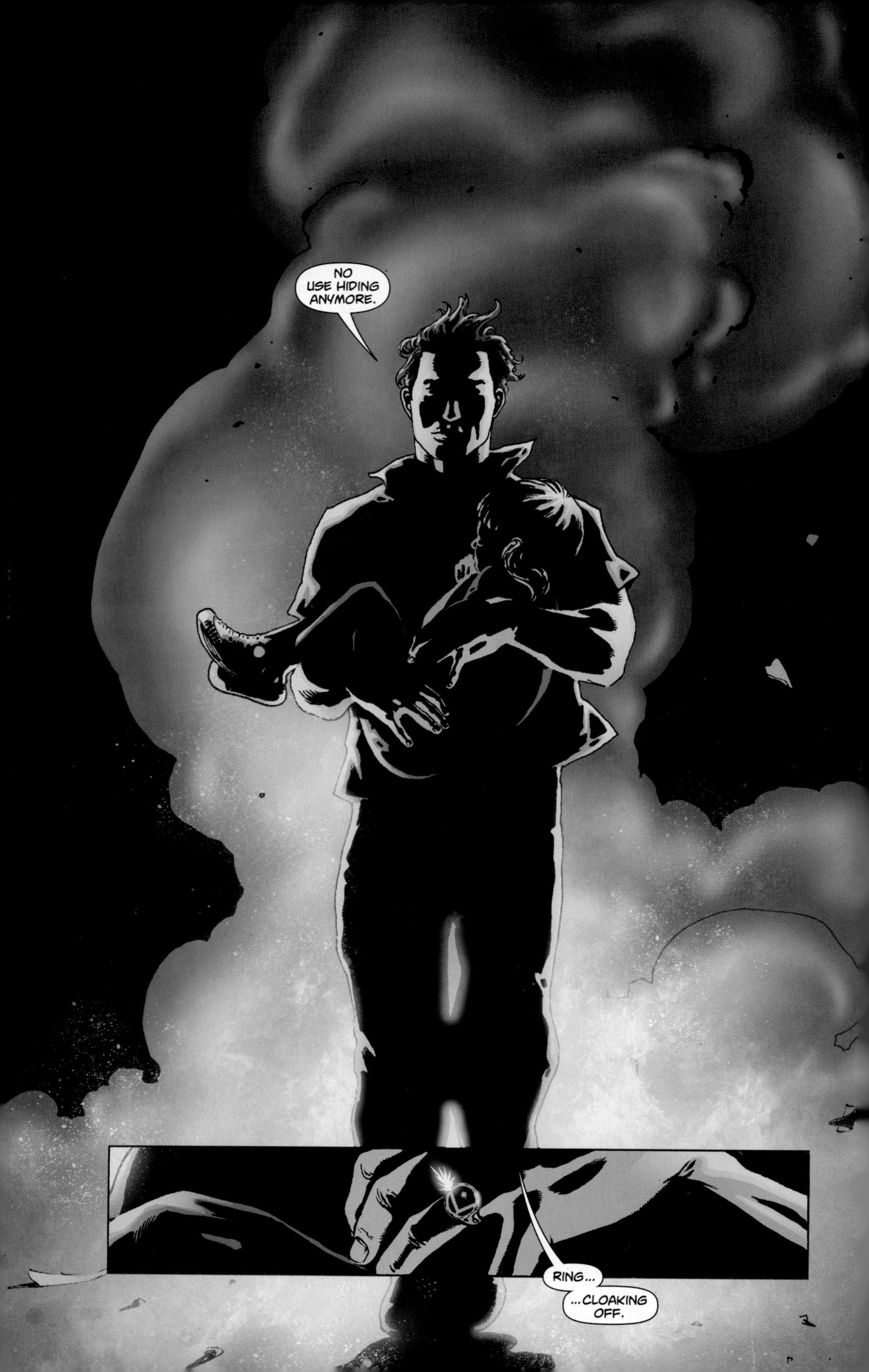
NO USE HIDING ANYMORE.
RING...
...CLOAKING OFF.

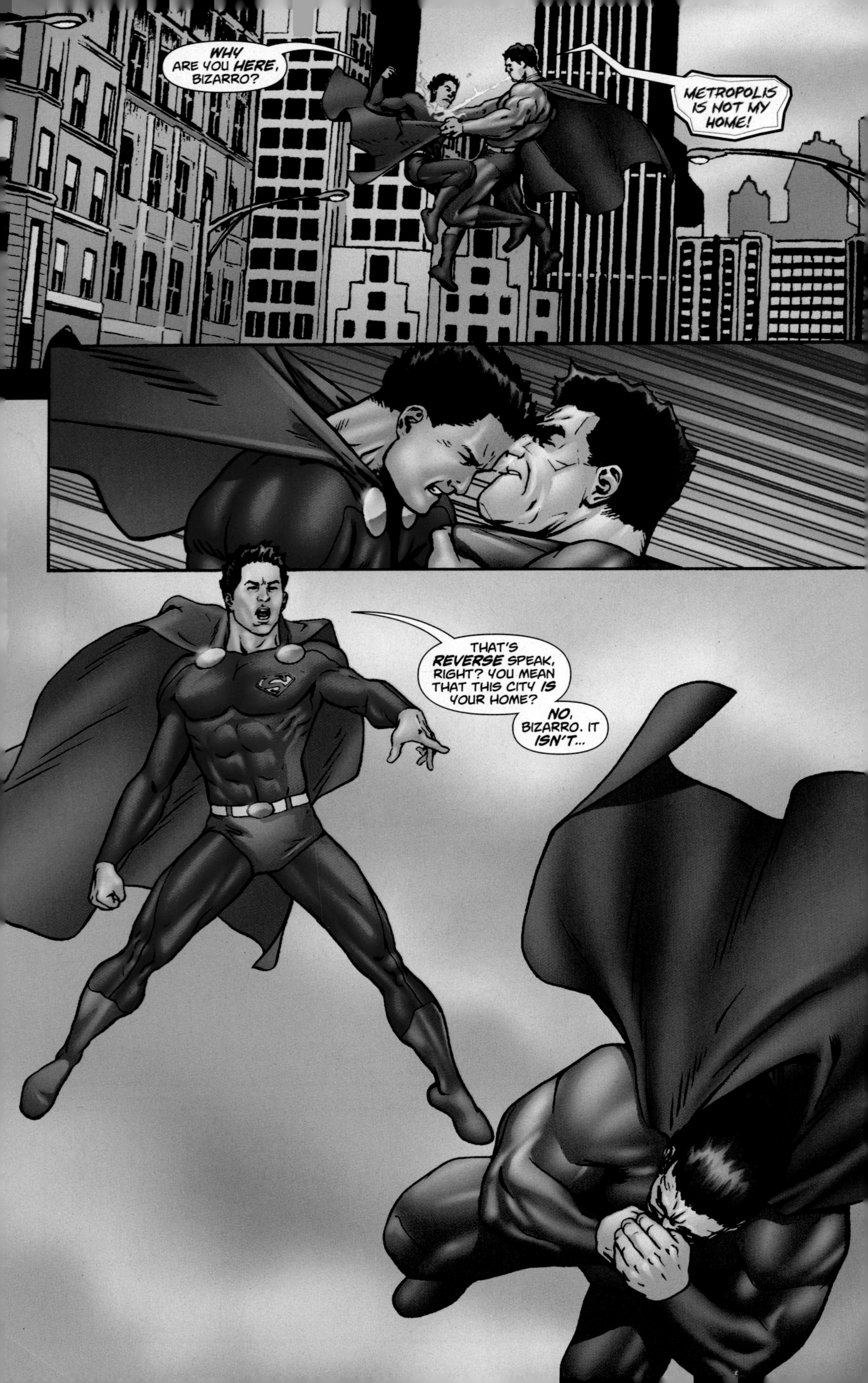
WHY ARE YOU HERE, BIZARRO?
METROPOLIS IS NOT MY HOME!
THAT'S REVERSE SPEAK, RIGHT? YOU MEAN THAT THIS CITY IS YOUR HOME?
NO, BIZARRO. IT ISN'T...

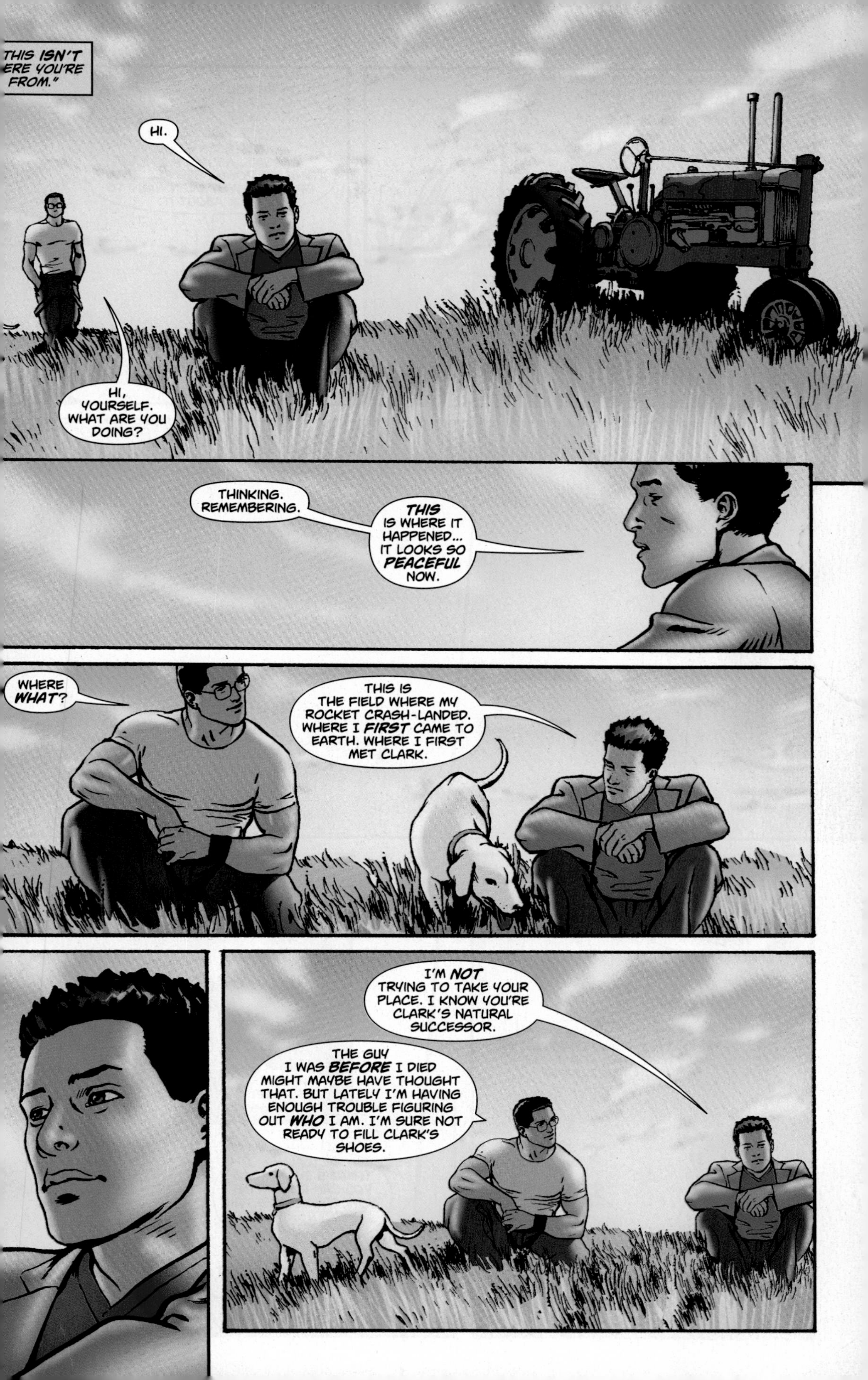

THIS ISN'T ERE YOU'RE FROM."
HI.
HI, YOURSELF. WHAT ARE YOU DOING?
THINKING. REMEMBERING.
THIS IS WHERE IT HAPPENED... IT LOOKS SO PEACEFUL NOW.
WHERE WHAT?
THIS IS THE FIELD WHERE MY ROCKET CRASH-LANDED. WHERE I FIRST CAME TO EARTH. WHERE I FIRST MET CLARK.
I'M NOT TRYING TO TAKE YOUR PLACE. I KNOW YOU'RE CLARK'S NATURAL SUCCESSOR.
THE GUY I WAS BEFORE I DIED MIGHT MAYBE HAVE THOUGHT THAT. BUT LATELY I'M HAVING ENOUGH TROUBLE FIGURING OUT WHO I AM. I'M SURE NOT READY TO FILL CLARK'S SHOES.

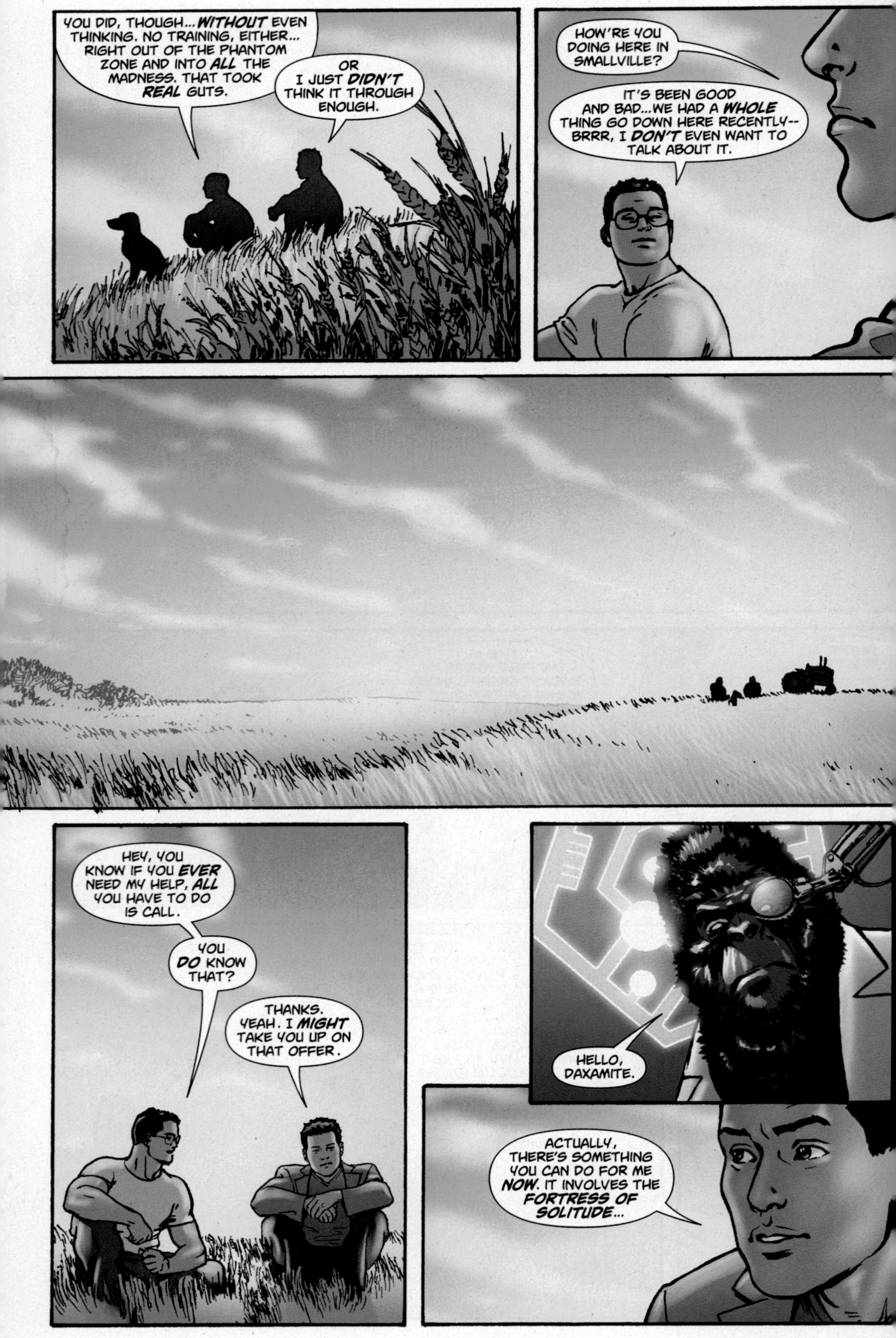
YOU DID, THOUGH... WITHOUT EVEN THINKING. NO TRAINING, EITHER... RIGHT OUT OF THE PHANTOM ZONE AND INTO ALL THE MADNESS. THAT TOOK REAL GUTS.
OR I JUST DIDN'T THINK IT THROUGH ENOUGH.
HOW'RE YOU DOING HERE IN SMALLVILLE?
IT'S BEEN GOOD AND BAD...WE HAD A WHOLE THING GO DOWN HERE RECENTLY-- BRRR, I DON'T EVEN WANT TO TALK ABOUT IT.
HEY, YOU KNOW IF YOU EVER NEED MY HELP, ALL YOU HAVE TO DO IS CALL.
YOU DO KNOW THAT?
THANKS. YEAH. I MIGHT TAKE YOU UP ON THAT OFFER.
HELLO, DAXAMITE.
ACTUALLY, THERE'S SOMETHING YOU CAN DO FOR ME NOW. IT INVOLVES THE FORTRESS OF SOLITUDE...

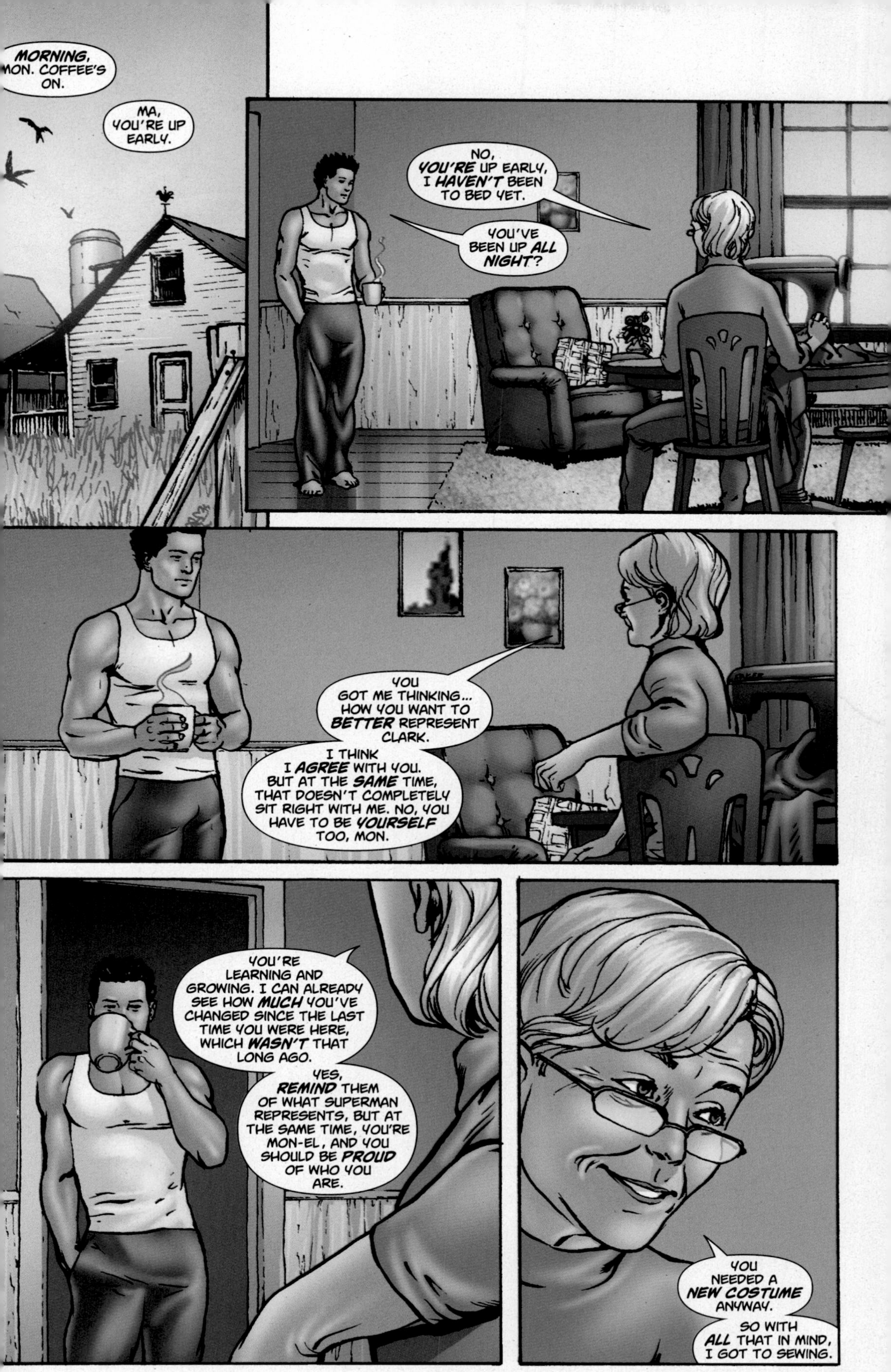
MORNING, MON. COFFEE'S ON.
MA, YOU'RE UP EARLY.
NO, YOU'RE UP EARLY, I HAVEN'T BEEN TO BED YET.
YOU'VE BEEN UP ALL NIGHT?
YOU GOT ME THINKING... HOW YOU WANT TO BETTER REPRESENT CLARK.
I THINK I AGREE WITH YOU. BUT AT THE SAME TIME, THAT DOESN'T COMPLETELY SIT RIGHT WITH ME. NO, YOU HAVE TO BE YOURSELF TOO, MON.
YOU'RE LEARNING AND GROWING. I CAN ALREADY SEE HOW MUCH YOU'VE CHANGED SINCE THE LAST TIME YOU WERE HERE, WHICH WASN'T THAT LONG AGO.
YES, REMIND THEM OF WHAT SUPERMAN REPRESENTS, BUT AT THE SAME TIME, YOU'RE MON-EL, AND YOU SHOULD BE PROUD OF WHO YOU ARE.
YOU NEEDED A NEW COSTUME ANYWAY.
SO WITH ALL THAT IN MIND, I GOT TO SEWING.

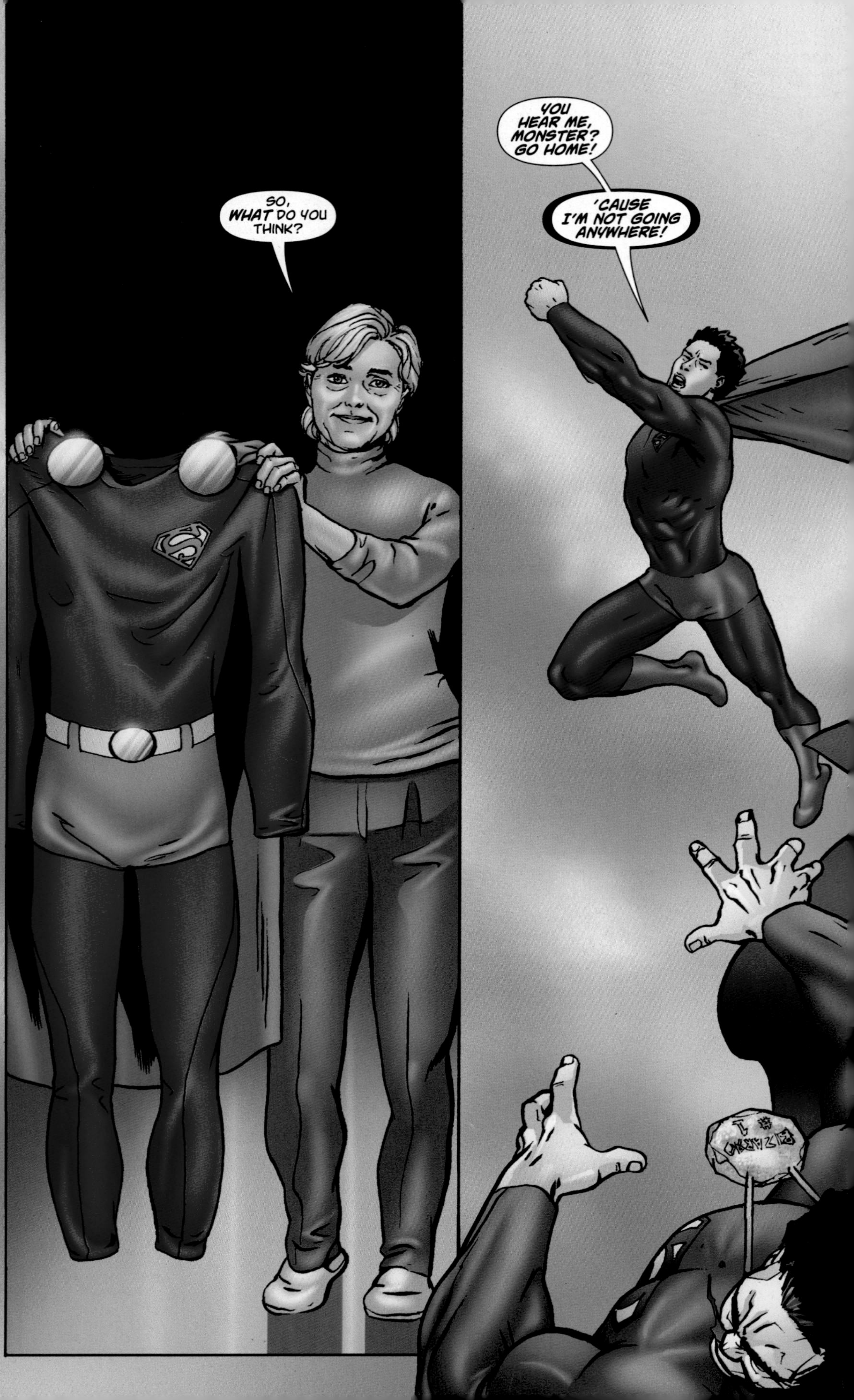
SO, WHAT DO YOU THINK?
YOU HEAR ME, MONSTER? GO HOME!
'CAUSE I'M NOT GOING ANYWHERE!

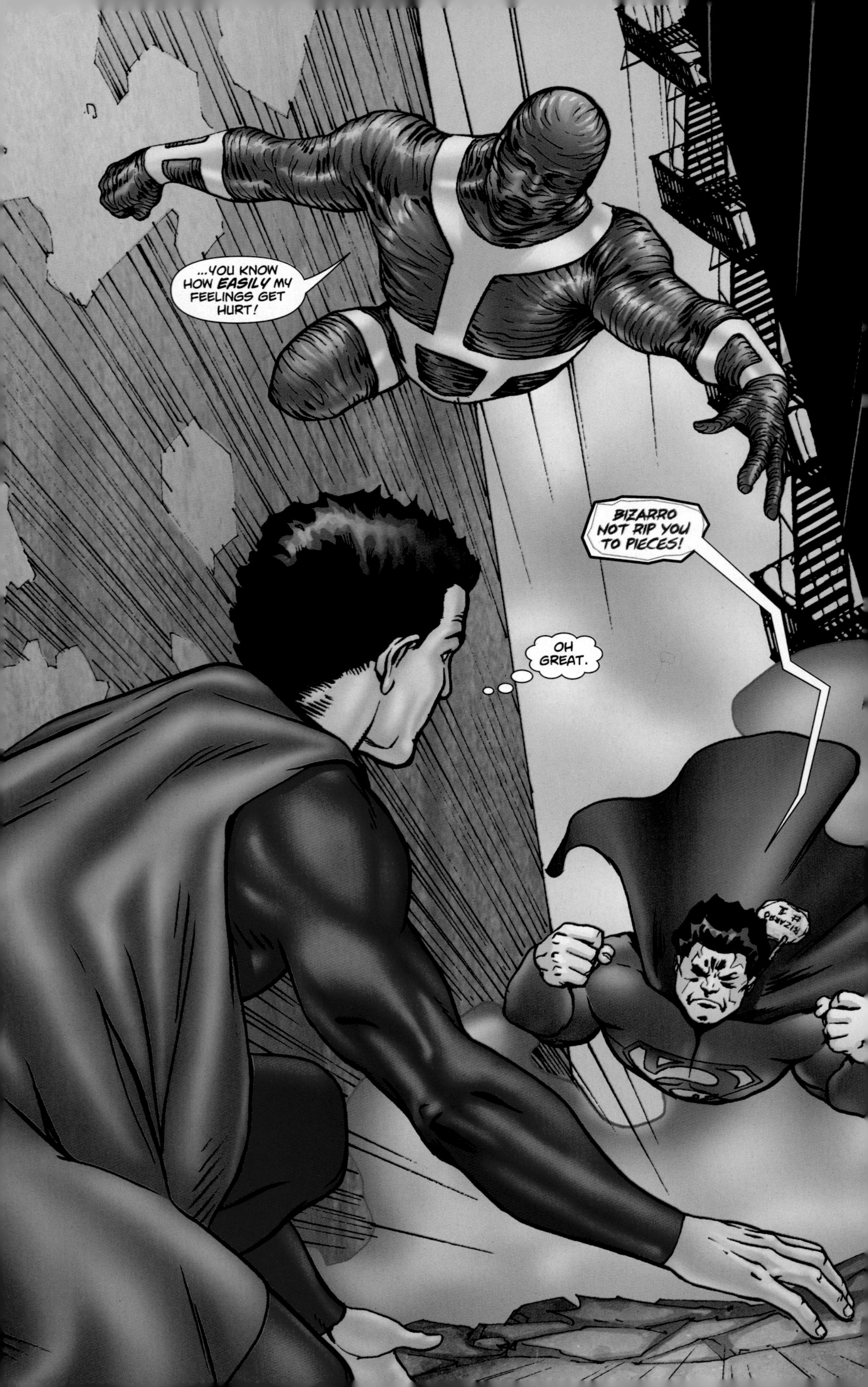
...YOU KNOW HOW EASILY MY FEELINGS GET HURT!
BIZARRO NOT RIP YOU TO PIECES!
OH GREAT.

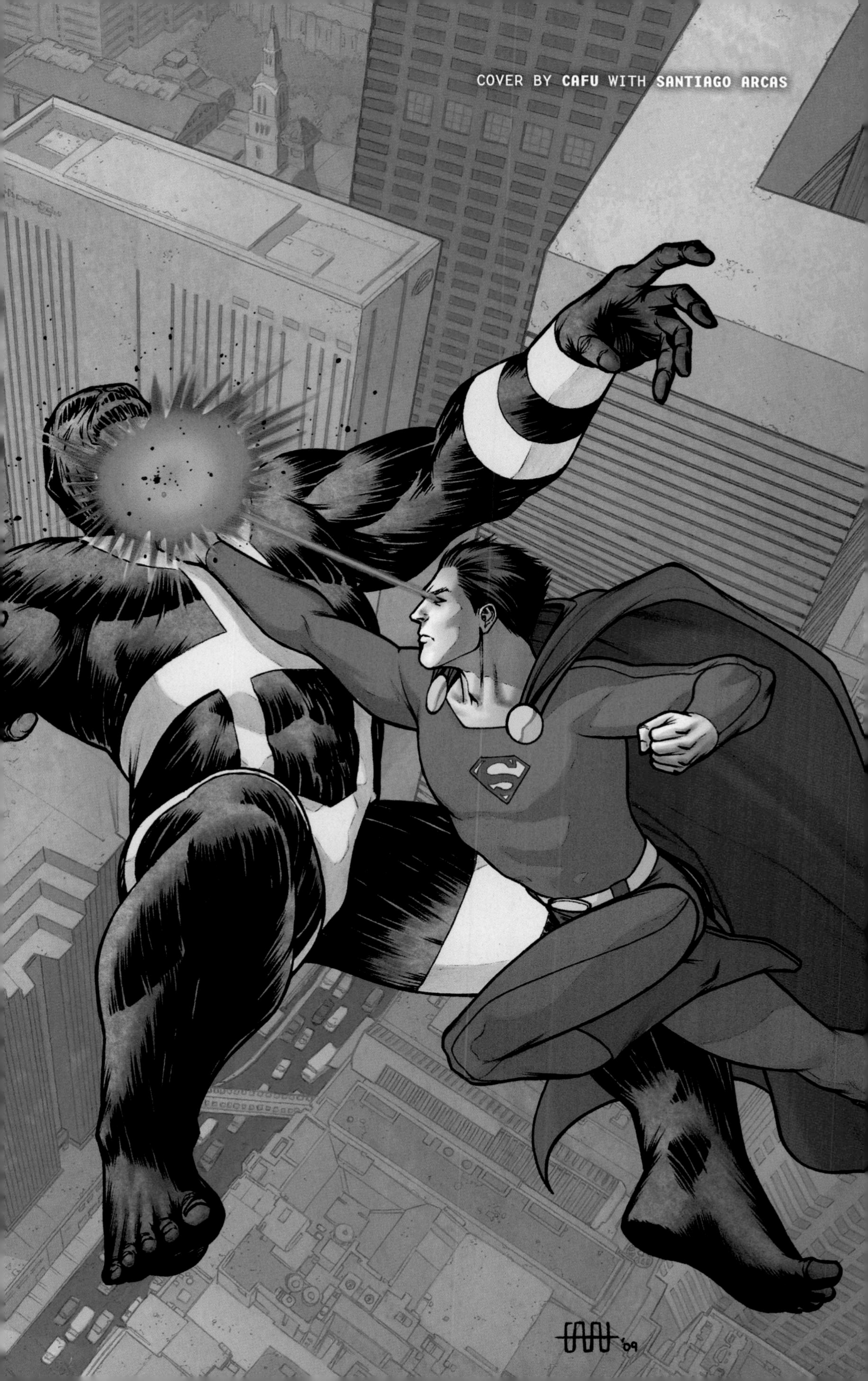
COVER BY CAFU WITH SANTIAGO ARCAS
CAFU '09

MAN OF VALOR PART TWO

BERNARD CHANG <ARTIST>

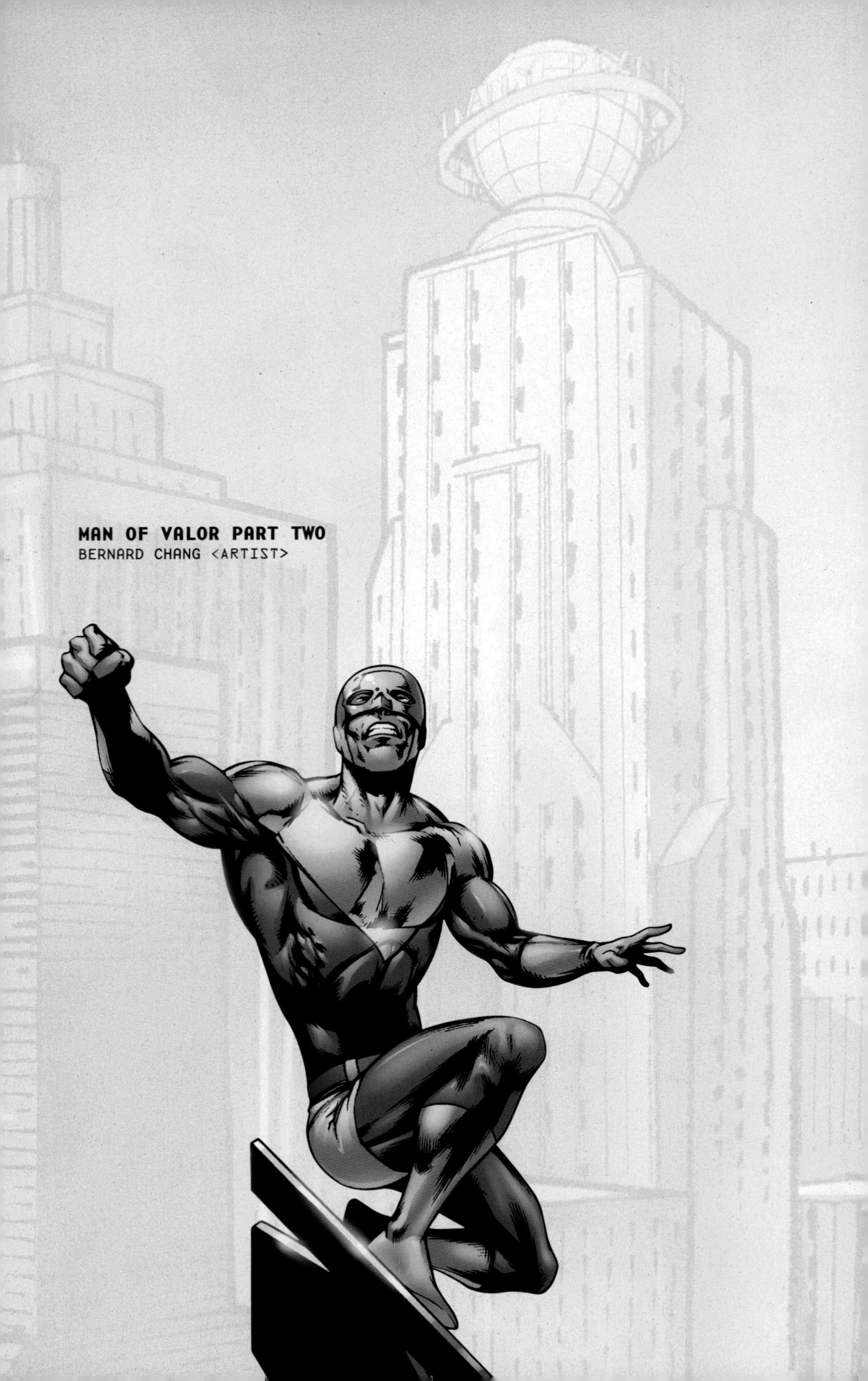

THE S.P.s,
THE GUARDIAN--
TOO FAR *AWAY*--
TOO *LATE* TO--

NO.

NOT TOO
LATE.

HE
TAUGHT
ME--

...TRAIN ME
TO FIGHT LIKE YOU--
FOR THE TIMES WHEN
I DO *NOT* HAVE MY
POWERS.

IF I AM
GOING TO KEEP
DOING THIS, I NEED
TO BE ON WHETHER I
AM SUPER-STRONG
OR NOT.

--IF
YOU GOT
A *BIGGER,*
STRONGER
ENEMY--

--USE YOUR
OPPONENT'S WEIGHT
AND STRENGTH. *LIKE*
THIS!

IT'S
NOTHING
FANCY--BASIC
JUDO--BUT IT
SAVED MY BUTT
MORE THAN
ONCE.

ANYWAY,
DON'T JUST L
THERE LIKE A
PANCAKE...

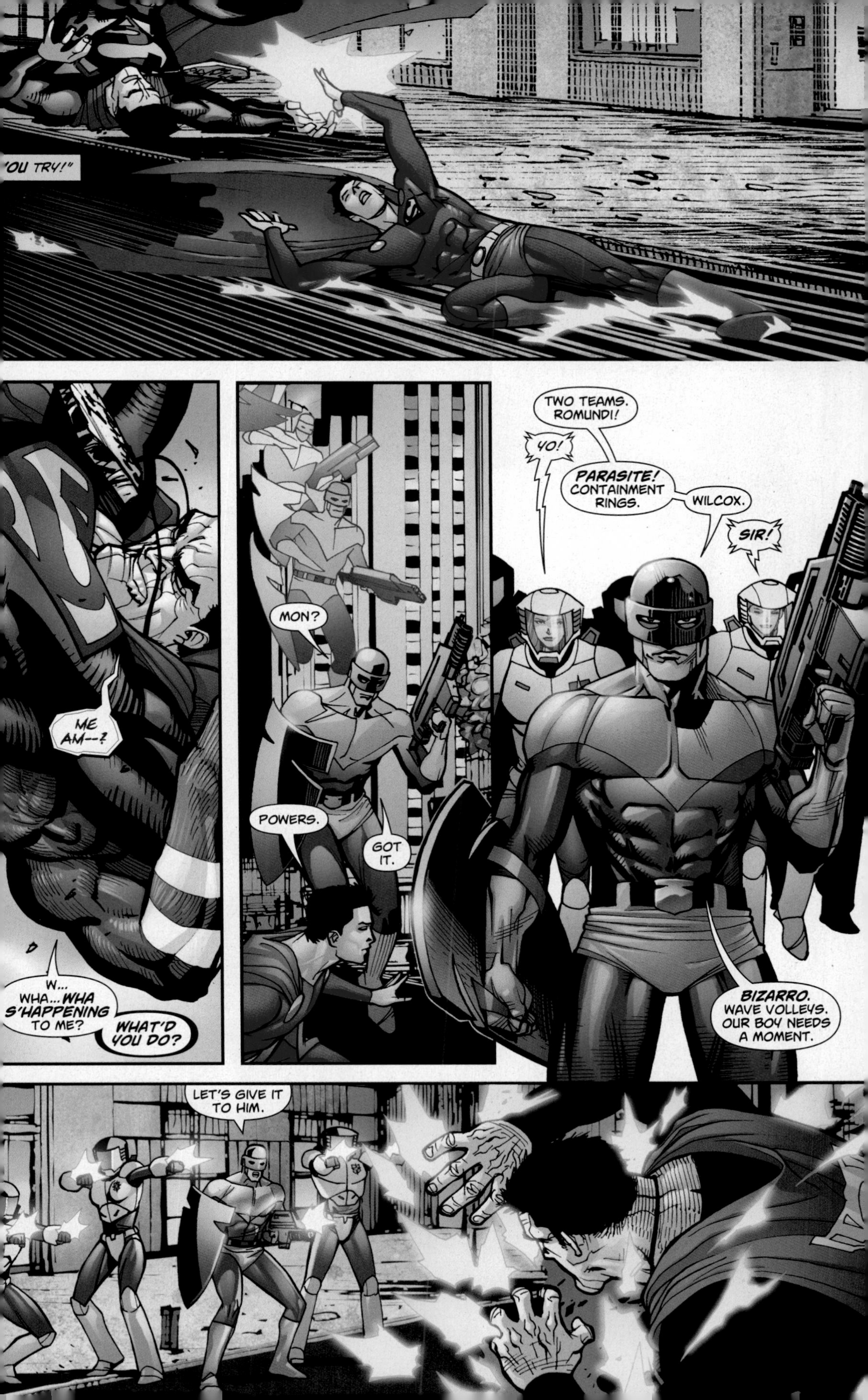

'OU TRY!"
ME AM--?
W... WHA... WHA S'HAPPENING TO ME?
WHAT'D YOU DO?
MON?
POWERS.
GOT IT.
TWO TEAMS. ROMUNDI!
YO!
PARASITE! CONTAINMENT RINGS.
WILCOX.
SIR!
BIZARRO. WAVE VOLLEYS. OUR BOY NEEDS A MOMENT.
LET'S GIVE IT TO HIM.

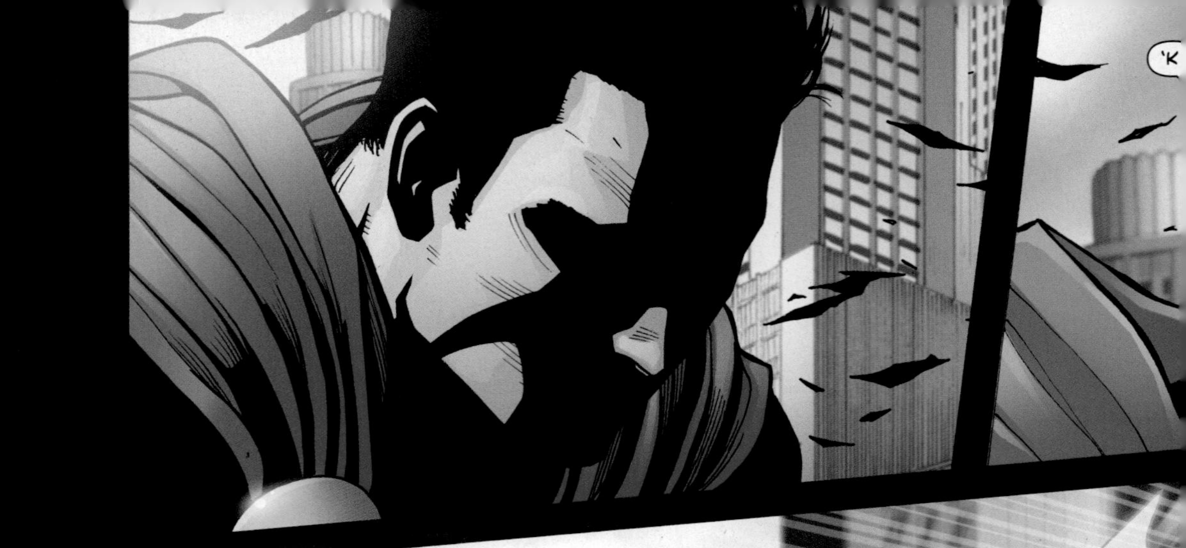
'K

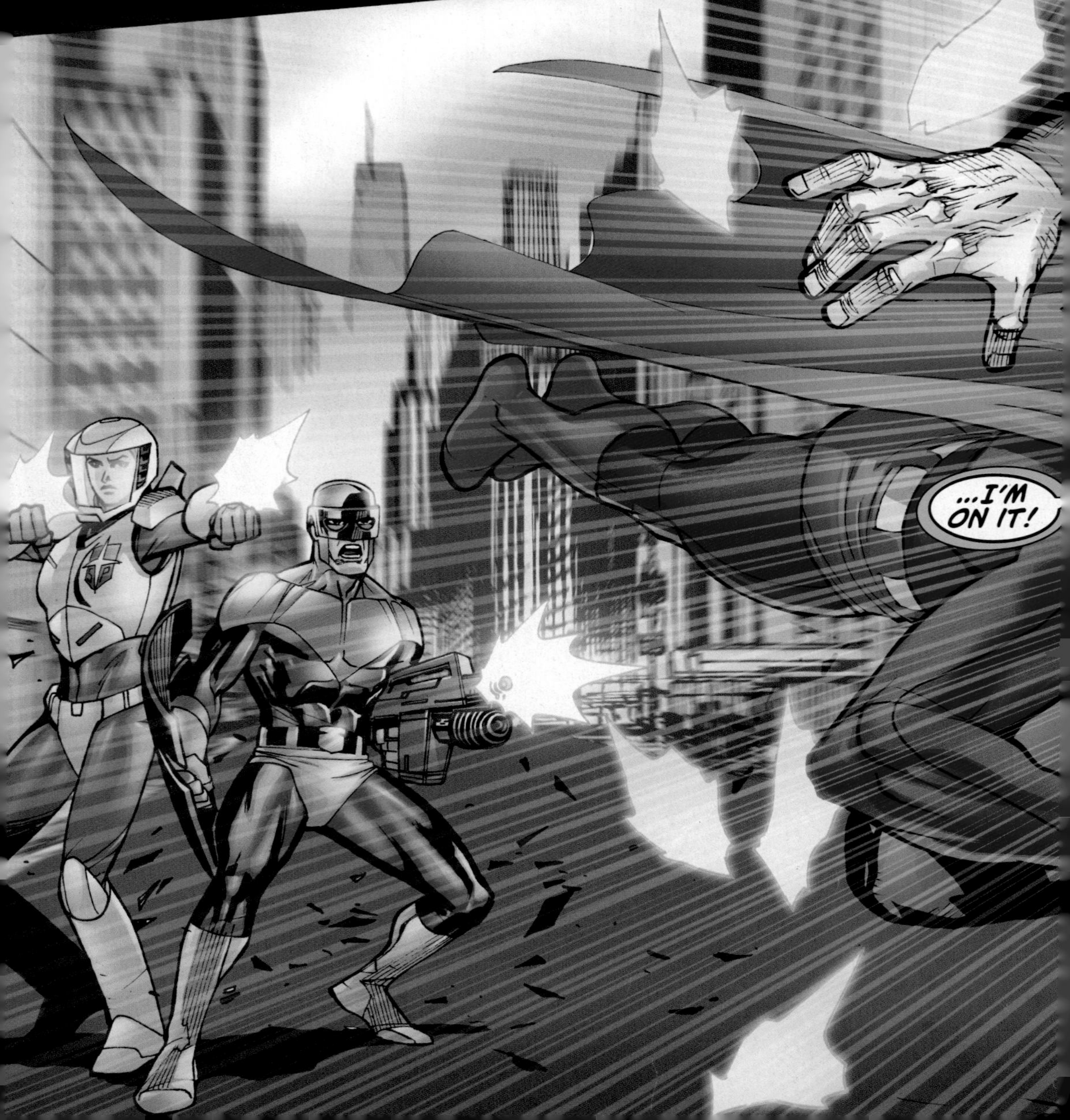
...I'M ON IT!

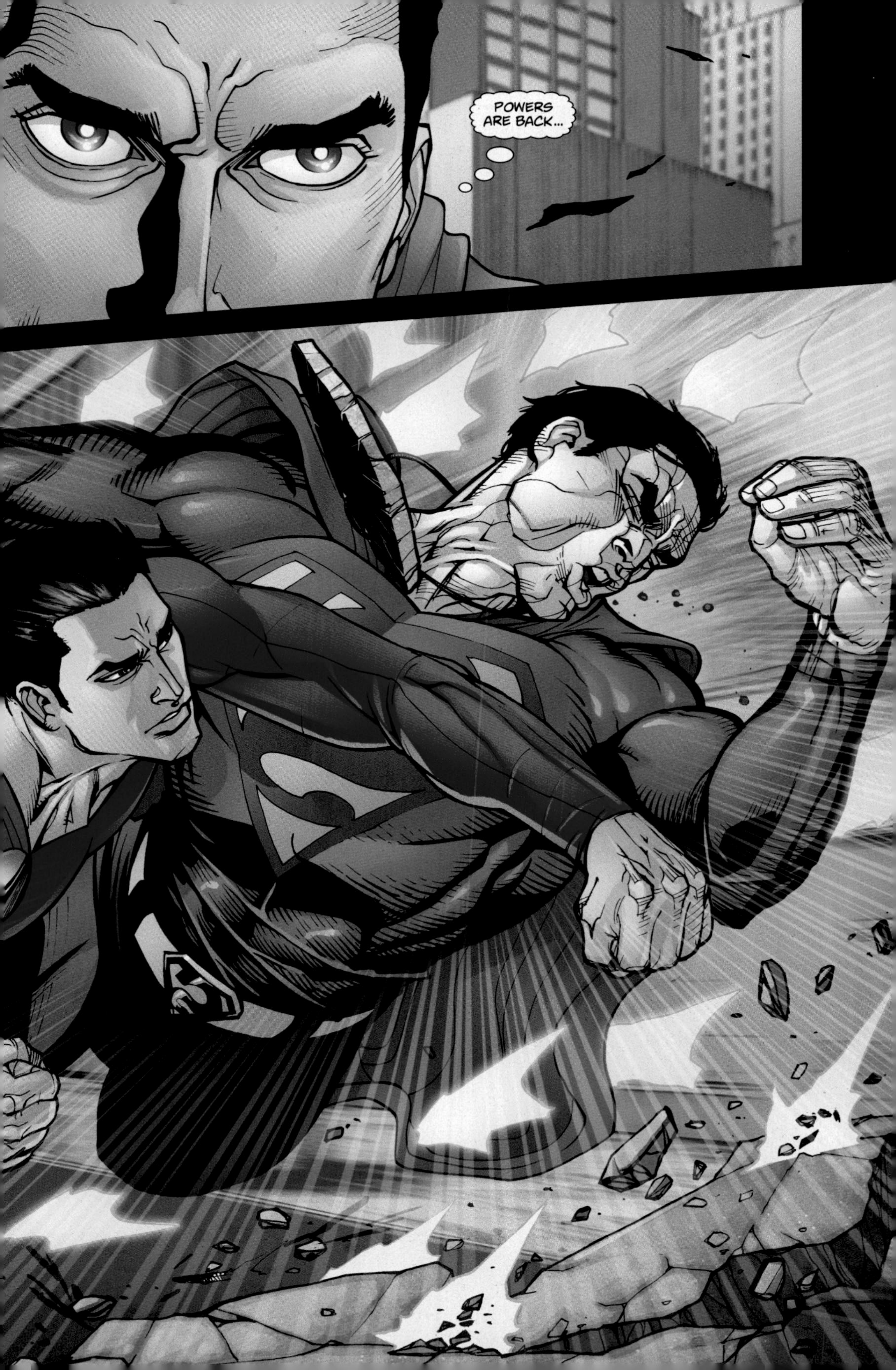
POWERS ARE BACK...

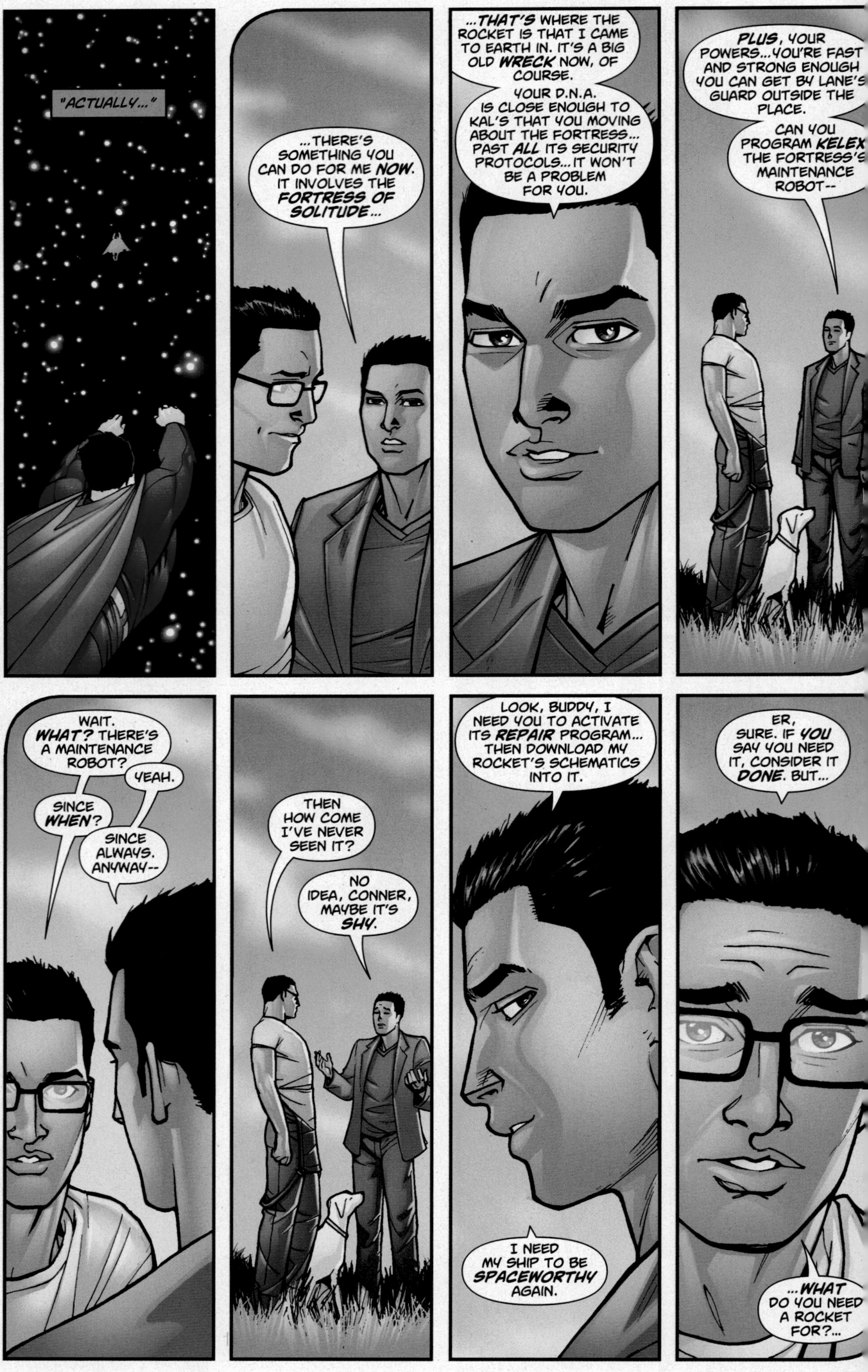
"ACTUALLY..."
...THERE'S SOMETHING YOU CAN DO FOR ME NOW. IT INVOLVES THE FORTRESS OF SOLITUDE...
...THAT'S WHERE THE ROCKET IS THAT I CAME TO EARTH IN. IT'S A BIG OLD WRECK NOW, OF COURSE.
YOUR D.N.A. IS CLOSE ENOUGH TO KAL'S THAT YOU MOVING ABOUT THE FORTRESS... PAST ALL ITS SECURITY PROTOCOLS...IT WON'T BE A PROBLEM FOR YOU.
PLUS, YOUR POWERS...YOU'RE FAST AND STRONG ENOUGH YOU CAN GET BY LANE'S GUARD OUTSIDE THE PLACE.
CAN YOU PROGRAM KELEX THE FORTRESS'S MAINTENANCE ROBOT--
WAIT. WHAT? THERE'S A MAINTENANCE ROBOT?
YEAH.
SINCE WHEN?
SINCE ALWAYS. ANYWAY--
THEN HOW COME I'VE NEVER SEEN IT?
NO IDEA, CONNER, MAYBE IT'S SHY.
LOOK, BUDDY, I NEED YOU TO ACTIVATE ITS REPAIR PROGRAM... THEN DOWNLOAD MY ROCKET'S SCHEMATICS INTO IT.
I NEED MY SHIP TO BE SPACEWORTHY AGAIN.
ER, SURE. IF YOU SAY YOU NEED IT, CONSIDER IT DONE. BUT...
...WHAT DO YOU NEED A ROCKET FOR?...

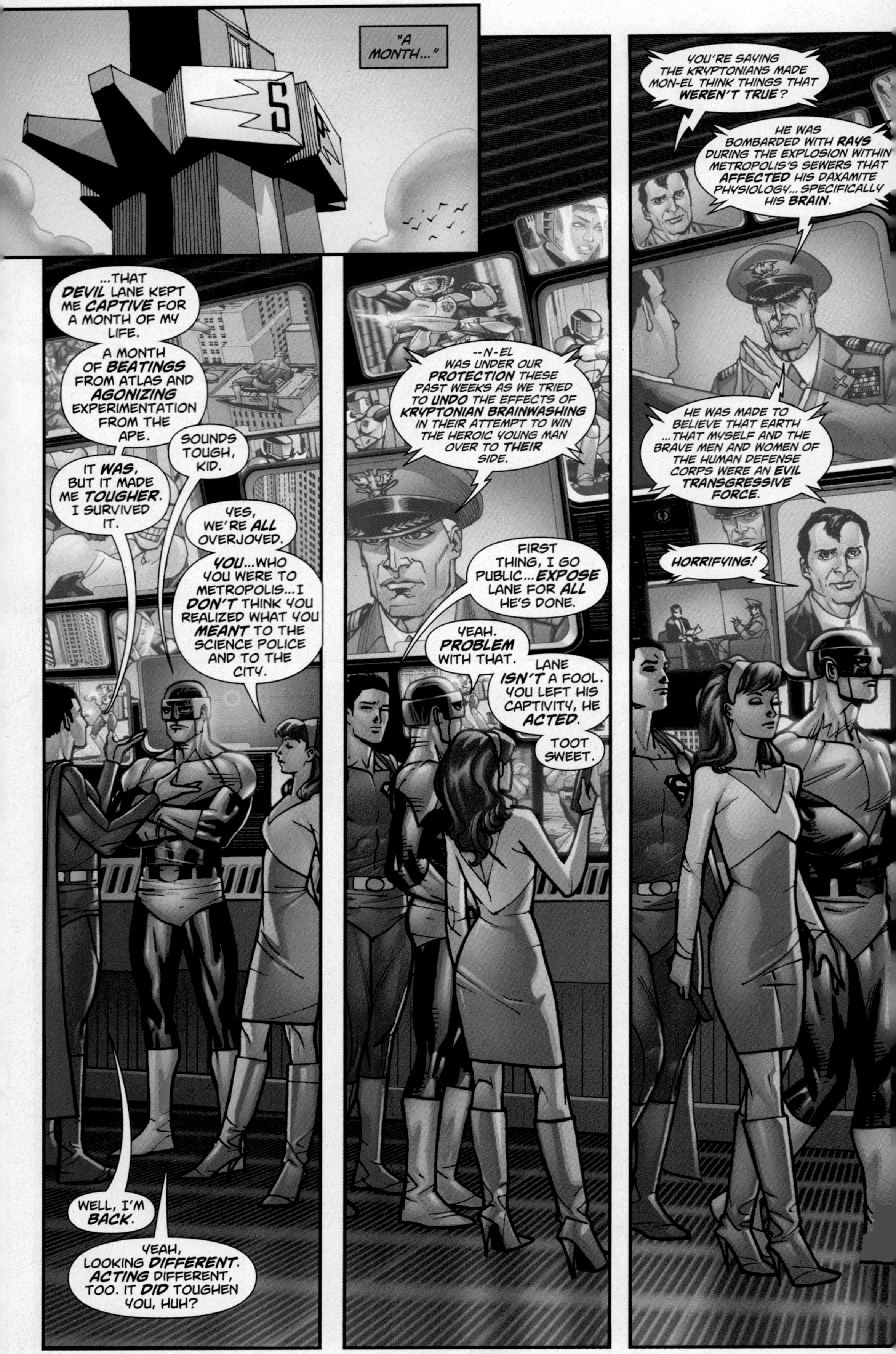
"A MONTH..."
YOU'RE SAYING THE KRYPTONIANS MADE MON-EL THINK THINGS THAT WEREN'T TRUE?
HE WAS BOMBARDED WITH RAYS DURING THE EXPLOSION WITHIN METROPOLIS'S SEWERS THAT AFFECTED HIS DAXAMITE PHYSIOLOGY... SPECIFICALLY HIS BRAIN.
...THAT DEVIL LANE KEPT ME CAPTIVE FOR A MONTH OF MY LIFE.
A MONTH OF BEATINGS FROM ATLAS AND AGONIZING EXPERIMENTATION FROM THE APE.
SOUNDS TOUGH, KID.
IT WAS, BUT IT MADE ME TOUGHER. I SURVIVED IT.
YES, WE'RE ALL OVERJOYED.
YOU... WHO YOU WERE TO METROPOLIS... I DON'T THINK YOU REALIZED WHAT YOU MEANT TO THE SCIENCE POLICE AND TO THE CITY.
WELL, I'M BACK.
YEAH, LOOKING DIFFERENT. ACTING DIFFERENT, TOO. IT DID TOUGHEN YOU, HUH?
--N-EL WAS UNDER OUR PROTECTION THESE PAST WEEKS AS WE TRIED TO UNDO THE EFFECTS OF KRYPTONIAN BRAINWASHING IN THEIR ATTEMPT TO WIN THE HEROIC YOUNG MAN OVER TO THEIR SIDE.
FIRST THING, I GO PUBLIC... EXPOSE LANE FOR ALL HE'S DONE.
YEAH. PROBLEM WITH THAT.
LANE ISN'T A FOOL. YOU LEFT HIS CAPTIVITY, HE ACTED.
TOOT SWEET.
HE WAS MADE TO BELIEVE THAT EARTH ...THAT MYSELF AND THE BRAVE MEN AND WOMEN OF THE HUMAN DEFENSE CORPS WERE AN EVIL TRANSGRESSIVE FORCE.
HORRIFYING!

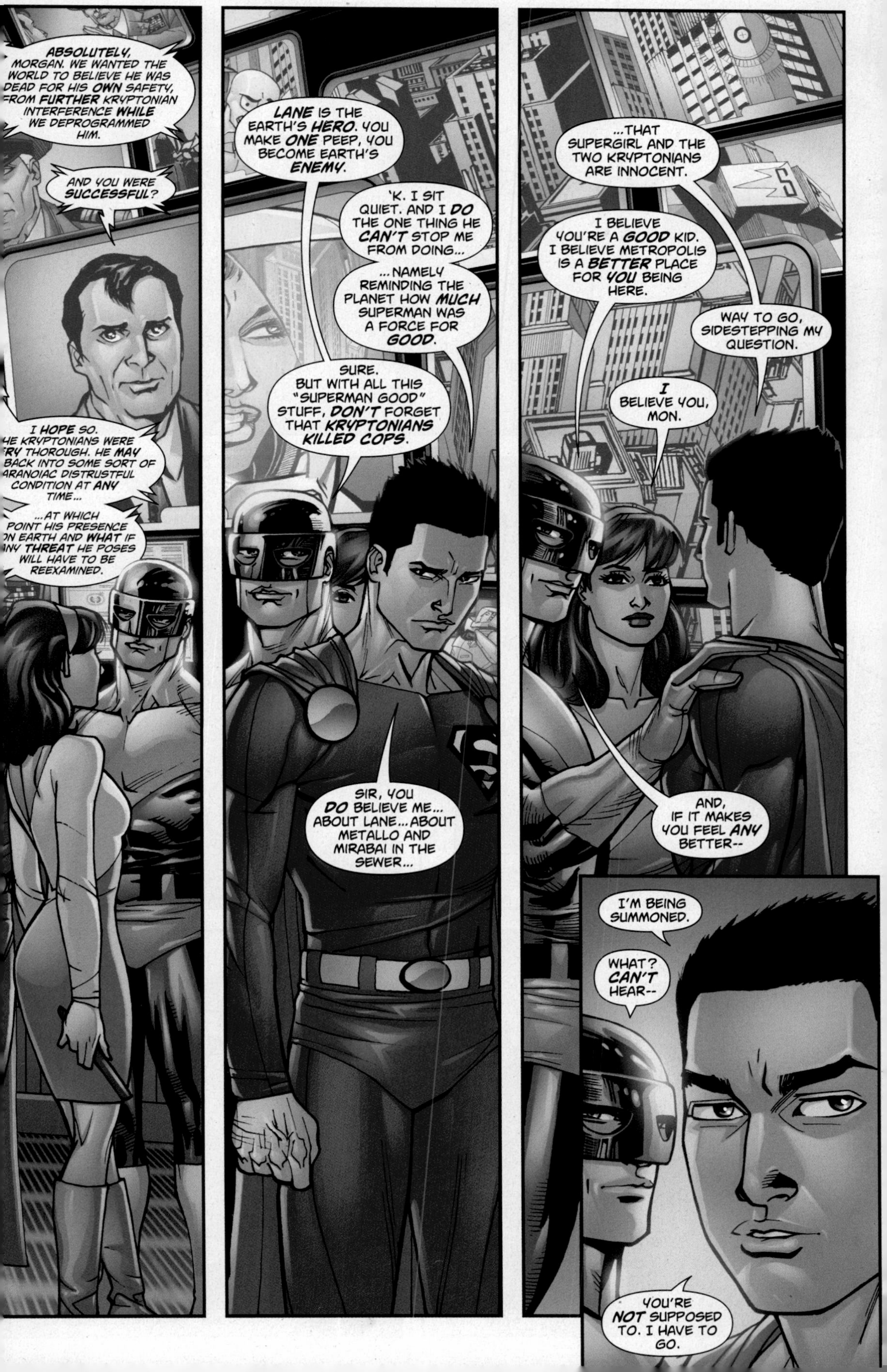
ABSOLUTELY, MORGAN. WE WANTED THE WORLD TO BELIEVE HE WAS DEAD FOR HIS OWN SAFETY, FROM FURTHER KRYPTONIAN INTERFERENCE WHILE WE DEPROGRAMMED HIM.
AND YOU WERE SUCCESSFUL?
I HOPE SO. HE KRYPTONIANS WERE FRY THOROUGH. HE MAY BACK INTO SOME SORT OF ARANOIAC DISTRUSTFUL CONDITION AT ANY TIME...
...AT WHICH POINT HIS PRESENCE ON EARTH AND WHAT IF ANY THREAT HE POSES WILL HAVE TO BE REEXAMINED.
LANE IS THE EARTH'S HERO. YOU MAKE ONE PEEP, YOU BECOME EARTH'S ENEMY.
'K. I SIT QUIET. AND I DO THE ONE THING HE CAN'T STOP ME FROM DOING...
...NAMELY REMINDING THE PLANET HOW MUCH SUPERMAN WAS A FORCE FOR GOOD.
SURE. BUT WITH ALL THIS "SUPERMAN GOOD" STUFF, DON'T FORGET THAT KRYPTONIANS KILLED COPS.
SIR, YOU DO BELIEVE ME... ABOUT LANE... ABOUT METALLO AND MIRABAI IN THE SEWER...
...THAT SUPERGIRL AND THE TWO KRYPTONIANS ARE INNOCENT.
I BELIEVE YOU'RE A GOOD KID. I BELIEVE METROPOLIS IS A BETTER PLACE FOR YOU BEING HERE.
WAY TO GO, SIDESTEPPING MY QUESTION.
I BELIEVE YOU, MON.
AND, IF IT MAKES YOU FEEL ANY BETTER--
I'M BEING SUMMONED.
WHAT? CAN'T HEAR--
YOU'RE NOT SUPPOSED TO. I HAVE TO GO.

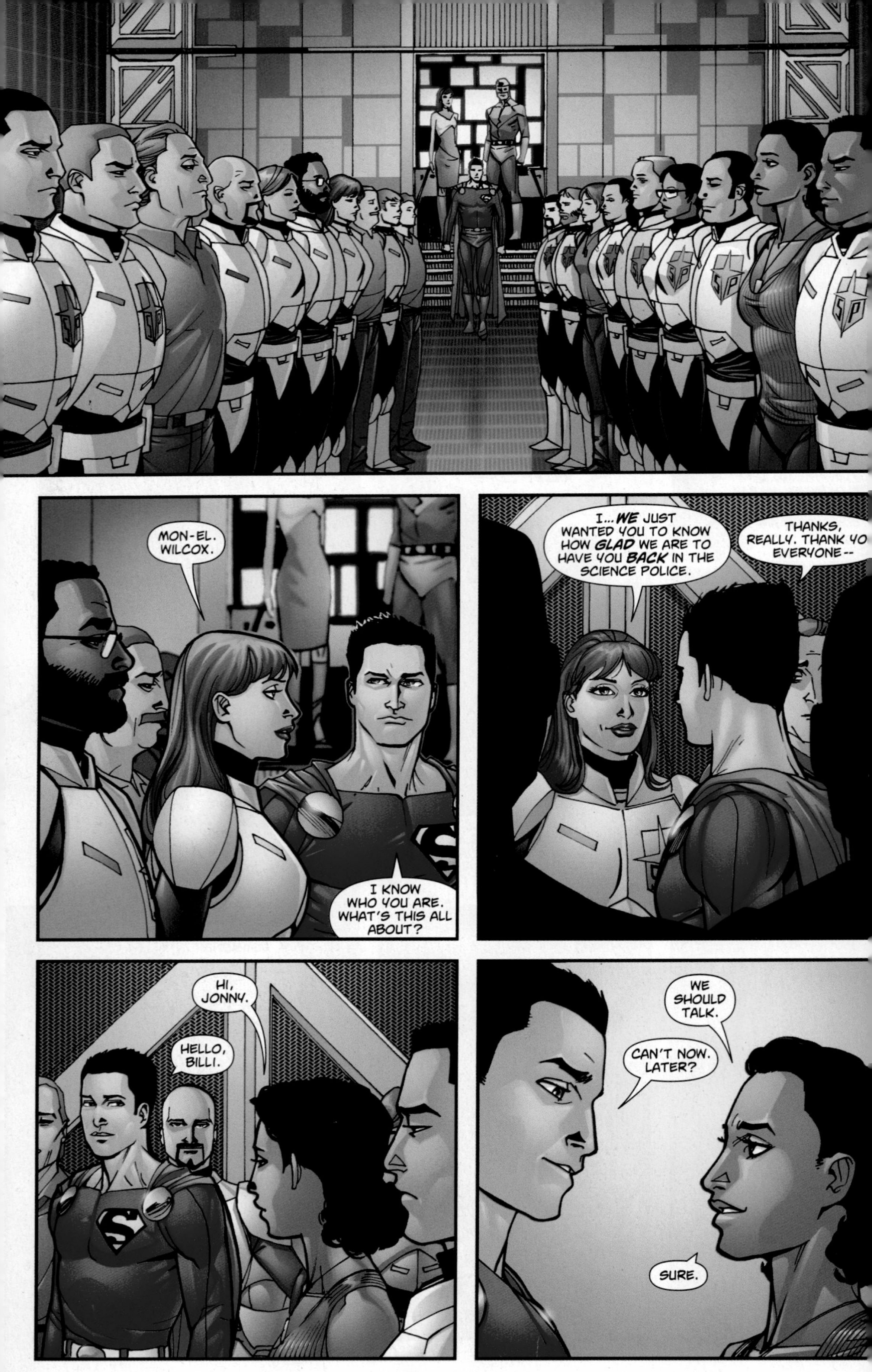
MON-EL. WILCOX.
I KNOW WHO YOU ARE. WHAT'S THIS ALL ABOUT?
I... WE JUST WANTED YOU TO KNOW HOW GLAD WE ARE TO HAVE YOU BACK IN THE SCIENCE POLICE.
THANKS, REALLY. THANK YO EVERYONE--
HI, JONNY.
HELLO, BILLI.
WE SHOULD TALK.
CAN'T NOW. LATER?
SURE.

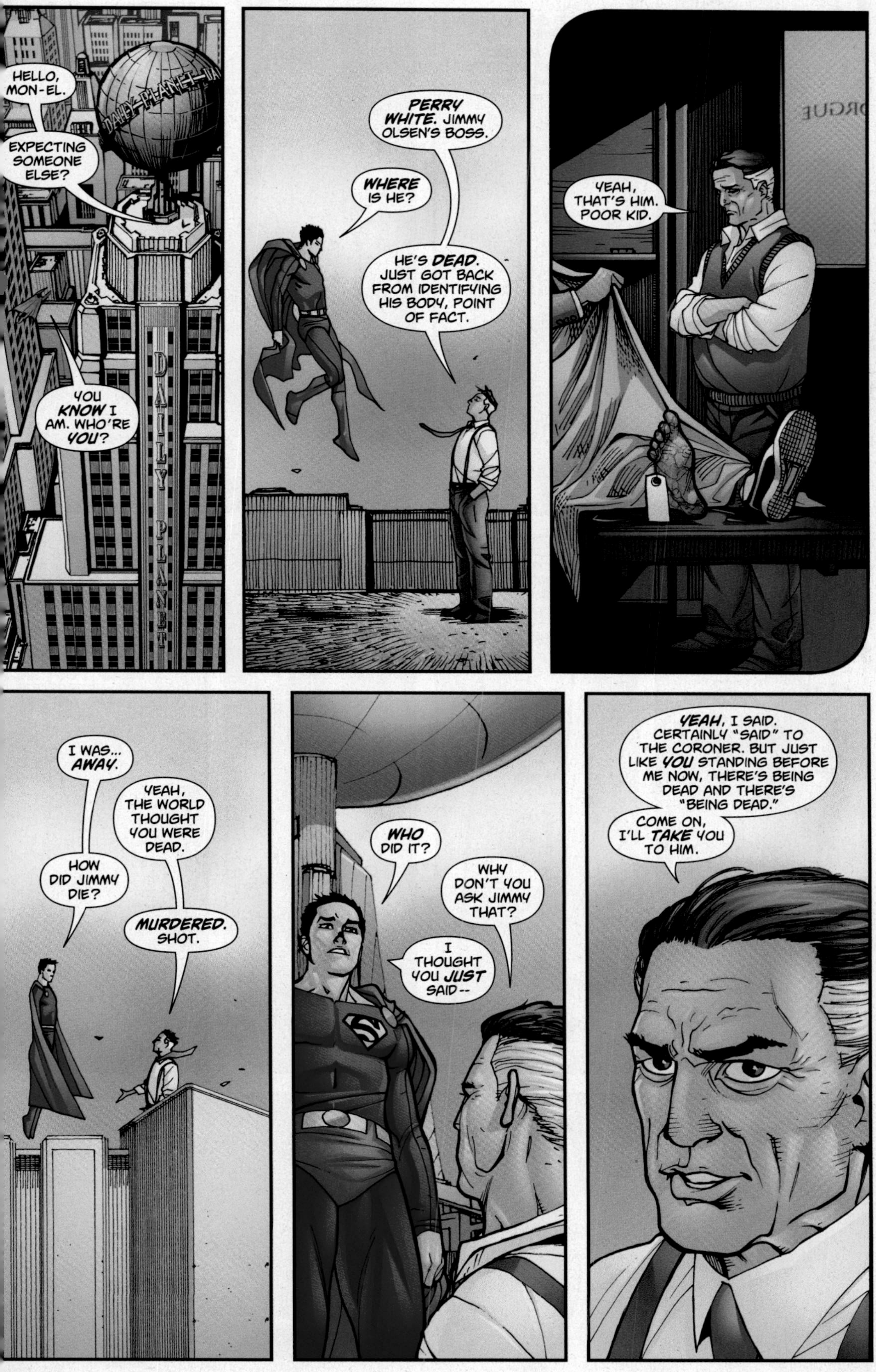
HELLO, MON-EL.
EXPECTING SOMEONE ELSE?
YOU KNOW I AM. WHO'RE YOU?
PERRY WHITE. JIMMY OLSEN'S BOSS.
WHERE IS HE?
HE'S DEAD. JUST GOT BACK FROM IDENTIFYING HIS BODY, POINT OF FACT.
YEAH, THAT'S HIM. POOR KID.
I WAS... AWAY.
YEAH, THE WORLD THOUGHT YOU WERE DEAD.
HOW DID JIMMY DIE?
MURDERED. SHOT.
WHO DID IT?
WHY DON'T YOU ASK JIMMY THAT?
I THOUGHT YOU JUST SAID--
YEAH, I SAID. CERTAINLY "SAID" TO THE CORONER. BUT JUST LIKE YOU STANDING BEFORE ME NOW, THERE'S BEING DEAD AND THERE'S "BEING DEAD."
COME ON, I'LL TAKE YOU TO HIM.

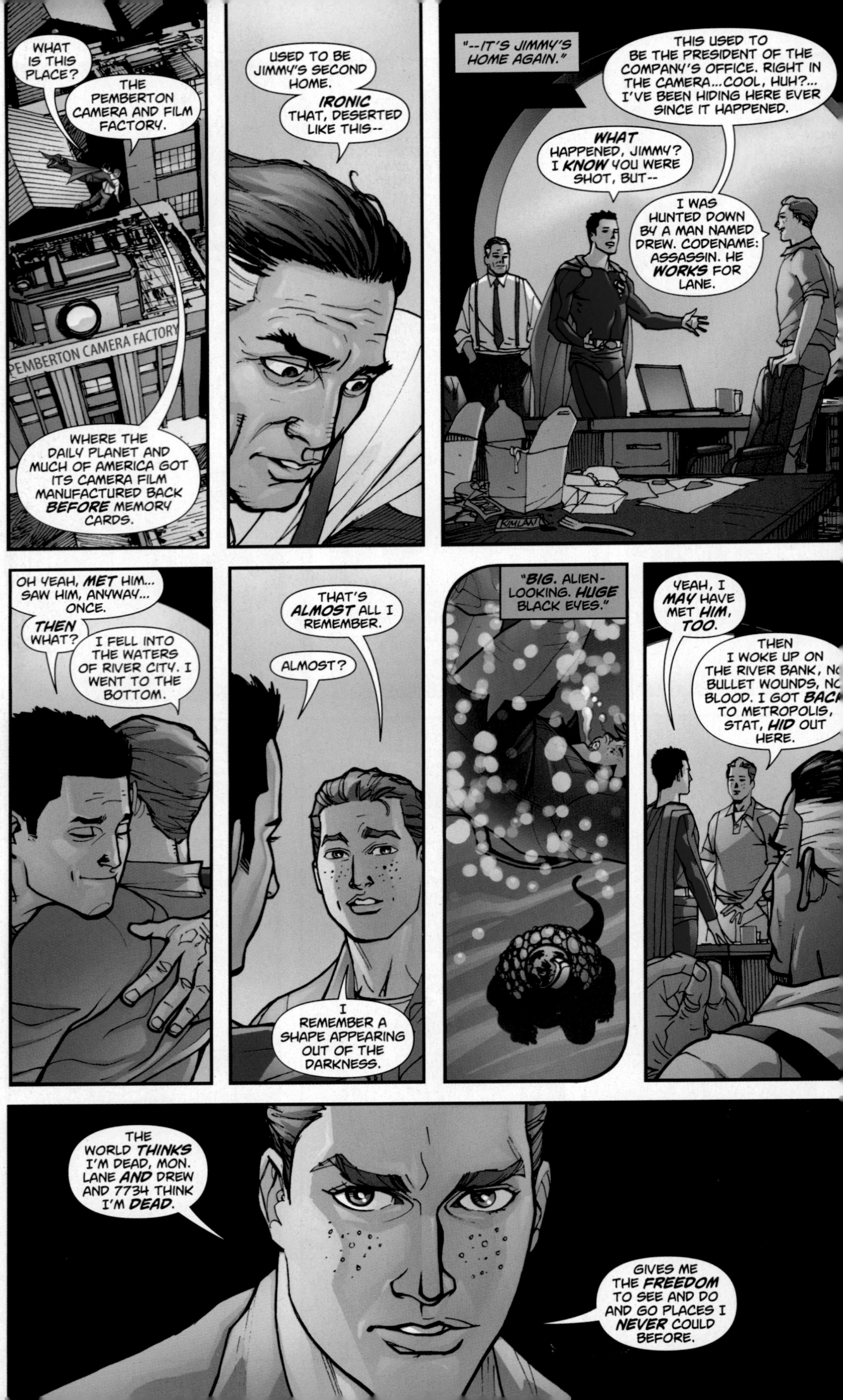
WHAT IS THIS PLACE?
THE PEMBERTON CAMERA AND FILM FACTORY.
PEMBERTON CAMERA FACTORY
WHERE THE DAILY PLANET AND MUCH OF AMERICA GOT ITS CAMERA FILM MANUFACTURED BACK BEFORE MEMORY CARDS.
USED TO BE JIMMY'S SECOND HOME.
IRONIC THAT, DESERTED LIKE THIS--
"--IT'S JIMMY'S HOME AGAIN."
THIS USED TO BE THE PRESIDENT OF THE COMPANY'S OFFICE. RIGHT IN THE CAMERA...COOL, HUH?... I'VE BEEN HIDING HERE EVER SINCE IT HAPPENED.
WHAT HAPPENED, JIMMY? I KNOW YOU WERE SHOT, BUT--
I WAS HUNTED DOWN BY A MAN NAMED DREW. CODENAME: ASSASSIN. HE WORKS FOR LANE.
OH YEAH, MET HIM... SAW HIM, ANYWAY... ONCE.
THEN WHAT?
I FELL INTO THE WATERS OF RIVER CITY. I WENT TO THE BOTTOM.
THAT'S ALMOST ALL I REMEMBER.
ALMOST?
I REMEMBER A SHAPE APPEARING OUT OF THE DARKNESS.
"BIG. ALIEN-LOOKING. HUGE BLACK EYES."
YEAH, I MAY HAVE MET HIM, TOO.
THEN I WOKE UP ON THE RIVER BANK, NO BULLET WOUNDS, NO BLOOD. I GOT BACK TO METROPOLIS, STAT, HID OUT HERE.
THE WORLD THINKS I'M DEAD, MON. LANE AND DREW AND 7734 THINK I'M DEAD.
GIVES ME THE FREEDOM TO SEE AND DO AND GO PLACES I NEVER COULD BEFORE.

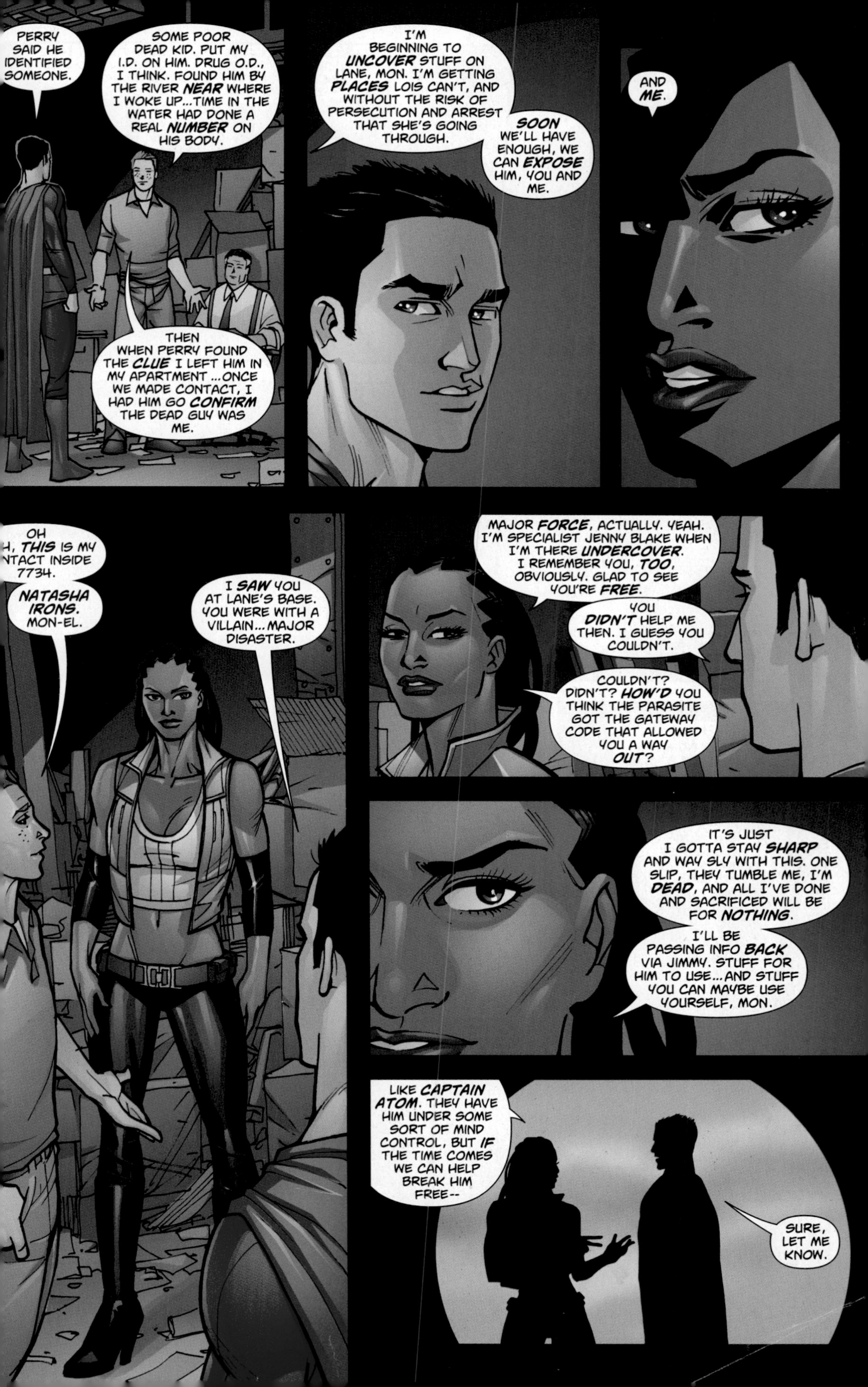
PERRY SAID HE IDENTIFIED SOMEONE.
SOME POOR DEAD KID. PUT MY I.D. ON HIM. DRUG O.D., I THINK. FOUND HIM BY THE RIVER NEAR WHERE I WOKE UP...TIME IN THE WATER HAD DONE A REAL NUMBER ON HIS BODY.
THEN WHEN PERRY FOUND THE CLUE I LEFT HIM IN MY APARTMENT ...ONCE WE MADE CONTACT, I HAD HIM GO CONFIRM THE DEAD GUY WAS ME.
I'M BEGINNING TO UNCOVER STUFF ON LANE, MON. I'M GETTING PLACES LOIS CAN'T, AND WITHOUT THE RISK OF PERSECUTION AND ARREST THAT SHE'S GOING THROUGH.
SOON WE'LL HAVE ENOUGH, WE CAN EXPOSE HIM, YOU AND ME.
AND ME.
NATASHA IRONS. MON-EL.
I SAW YOU AT LANE'S BASE. YOU WERE WITH A VILLAIN...MAJOR DISASTER.
MAJOR FORCE, ACTUALLY. YEAH. I'M SPECIALIST JENNY BLAKE WHEN I'M THERE UNDERCOVER. I REMEMBER YOU, TOO, OBVIOUSLY. GLAD TO SEE YOU'RE FREE.
YOU DIDN'T HELP ME THEN. I GUESS YOU COULDN'T.
COULDN'T? DIDN'T? HOW'D YOU THINK THE PARASITE GOT THE GATEWAY CODE THAT ALLOWED YOU A WAY OUT?
IT'S JUST I GOTTA STAY SHARP AND WAY SLY WITH THIS. ONE SLIP, THEY TUMBLE ME, I'M DEAD, AND ALL I'VE DONE AND SACRIFICED WILL BE FOR NOTHING.
I'LL BE PASSING INFO BACK VIA JIMMY. STUFF FOR HIM TO USE...AND STUFF YOU CAN MAYBE USE YOURSELF, MON.
LIKE CAPTAIN ATOM. THEY HAVE HIM UNDER SOME SORT OF MIND CONTROL, BUT IF THE TIME COMES WE CAN HELP BREAK HIM FREE--
SURE, LET ME KNOW.

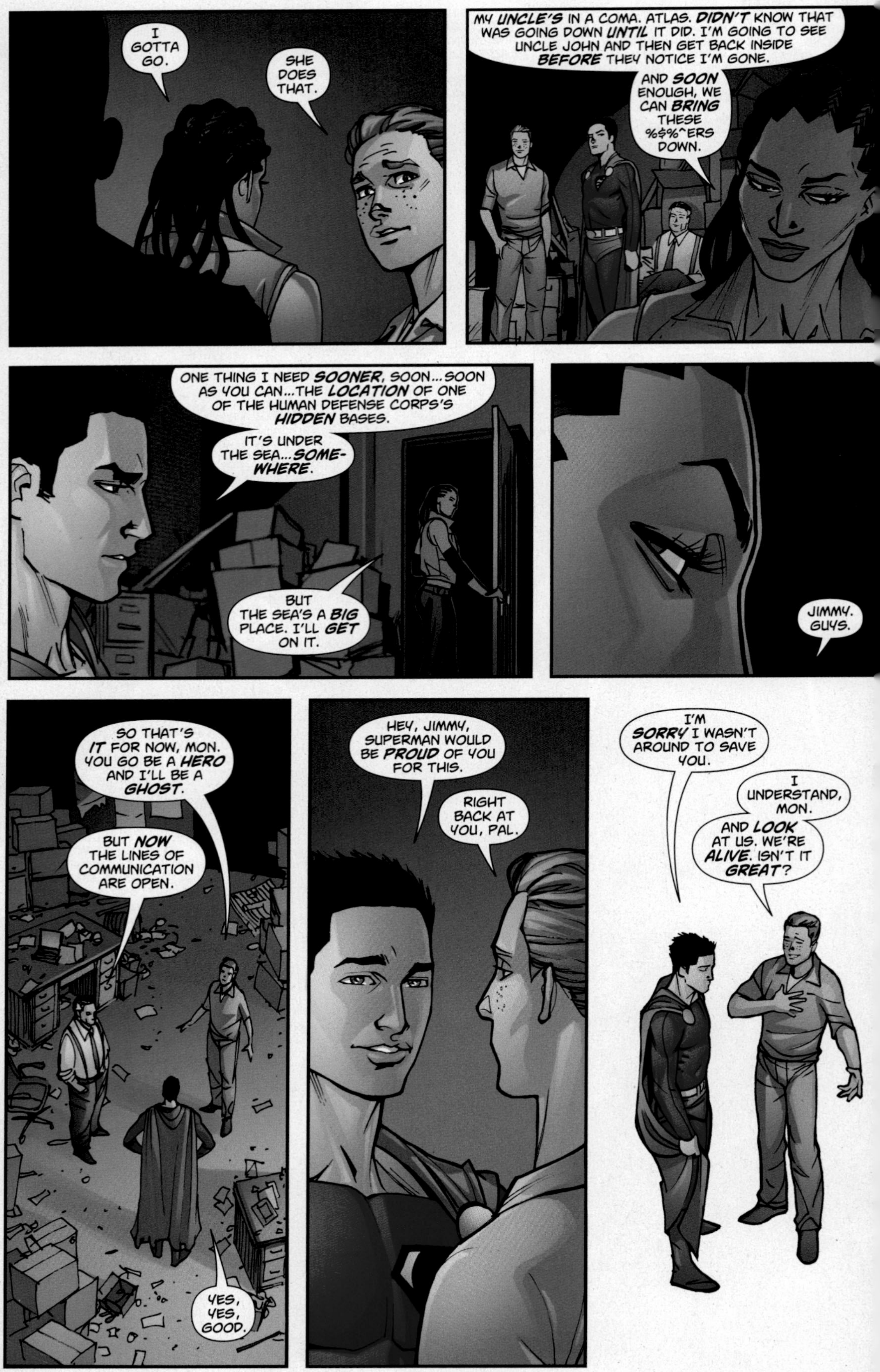
I GOTTA GO.
SHE DOES THAT.
MY UNCLE'S IN A COMA. ATLAS. DIDN'T KNOW THAT WAS GOING DOWN UNTIL IT DID. I'M GOING TO SEE UNCLE JOHN AND THEN GET BACK INSIDE BEFORE THEY NOTICE I'M GONE.
AND SOON ENOUGH, WE CAN BRING THESE %$%^ERS DOWN.
ONE THING I NEED SOONER, SOON... SOON AS YOU CAN... THE LOCATION OF ONE OF THE HUMAN DEFENSE CORPS'S HIDDEN BASES.
IT'S UNDER THE SEA... SOME-WHERE.
BUT THE SEA'S A BIG PLACE. I'LL GET ON IT.
JIMMY. GUYS.
SO THAT'S IT FOR NOW, MON. YOU GO BE A HERO AND I'LL BE A GHOST.
BUT NOW THE LINES OF COMMUNICATION ARE OPEN.
YES, YES, GOOD.
HEY, JIMMY, SUPERMAN WOULD BE PROUD OF YOU FOR THIS.
RIGHT BACK AT YOU, PAL.
I'M SORRY I WASN'T AROUND TO SAVE YOU.
I UNDERSTAND, MON.
AND LOOK AT US. WE'RE ALIVE. ISN'T IT GREAT?

UNCLE JOHN.

I **DON'T** HAVE LONG. I **BARELY** HAVE A MINUTE. LANE IS WATCHING YOU...WATCHING **WHO** VISITS YOU.

I CORRUPTED THEIR MONITOR PROGRAM, IT'LL TAKE THAT LONG TO REBOOT...**GIVES** ME THAT LONG, NO MORE.

YOU **HAVE** TO COME BACK, UNCLE JOHN.

THE CITY **NEEDS** YOU. AND I NEED YOU.

YOU'RE THE **STRONGEST**, BEST, MOST **WONDERFUL** PERSON I'VE EVER KNOWN.

TOO BUSY REBELLING AND BEING A **FOOL** BEFORE, DIDN'T SEE. I DIDN'T REALIZE.

TOO YOUNG THEN, MAYBE.

THE STEEL SUIT YOU MADE ME...NOT JUST BEAUTIFUL... **PERFECTION**.

I **SHOULD** HAVE TOLD YOU, SHOULD HAVE AND **DIDN'T**.

ALL YOU DID FOR ME. ALL THE **LOVE** YOU'VE GIVEN ME. **WHY** WAS I SO BLIND?

YOU'RE A GENIUS, SURE, BUT SO'S MAGNUS, HALEY, IRIGOYEN AND SO MANY OTHERS. GENIUS COMES CHEAP IN **OUR** WORLD.

YOU'RE NOT **JUST** THAT. YOU'RE **TRULY** GREAT. TRULY AMAZING.

PLEASE, **PLEASE**. COME **BACK** TO US.

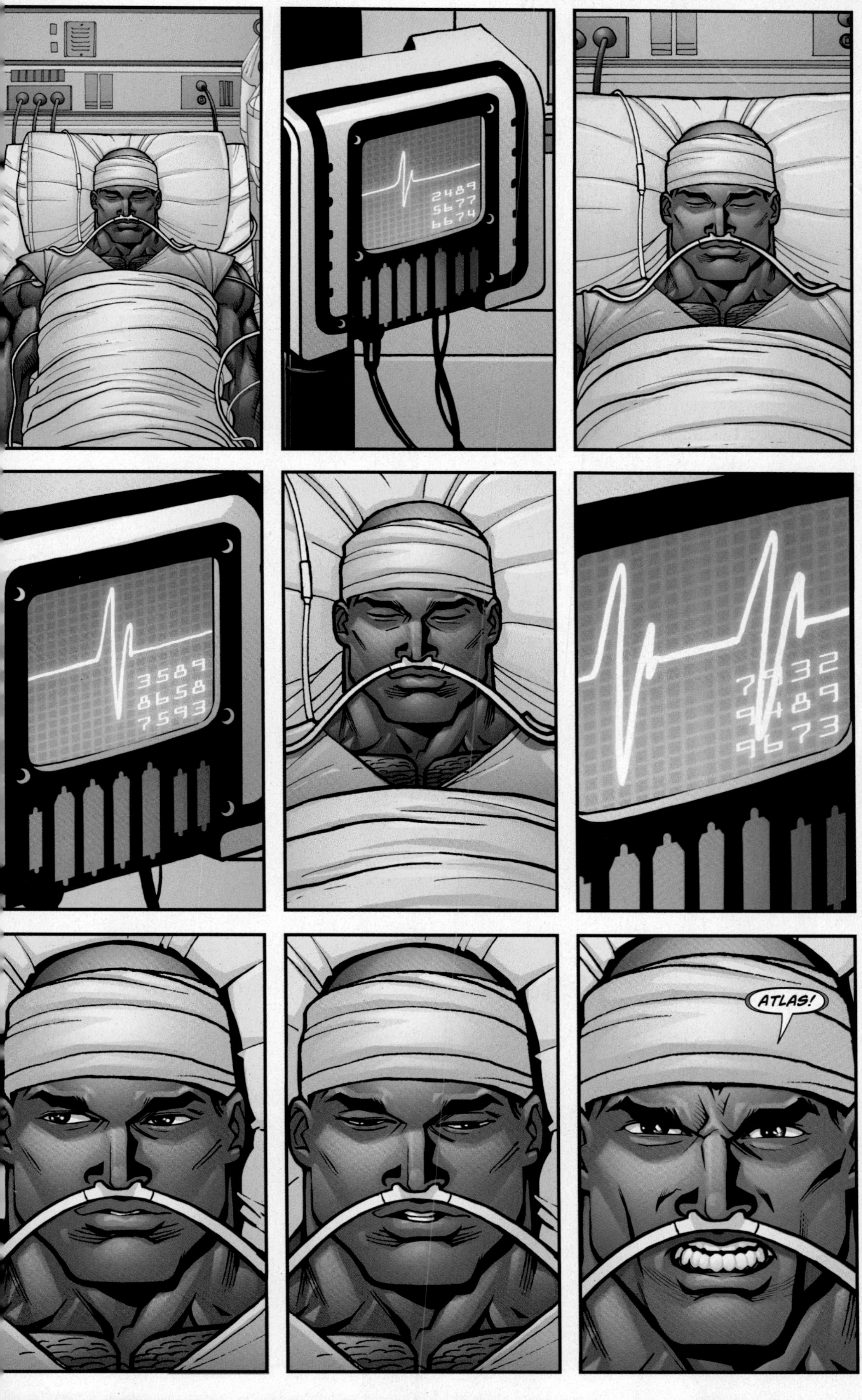
2489
5677
6674
3589
8658
7593
9673
ATLAS!

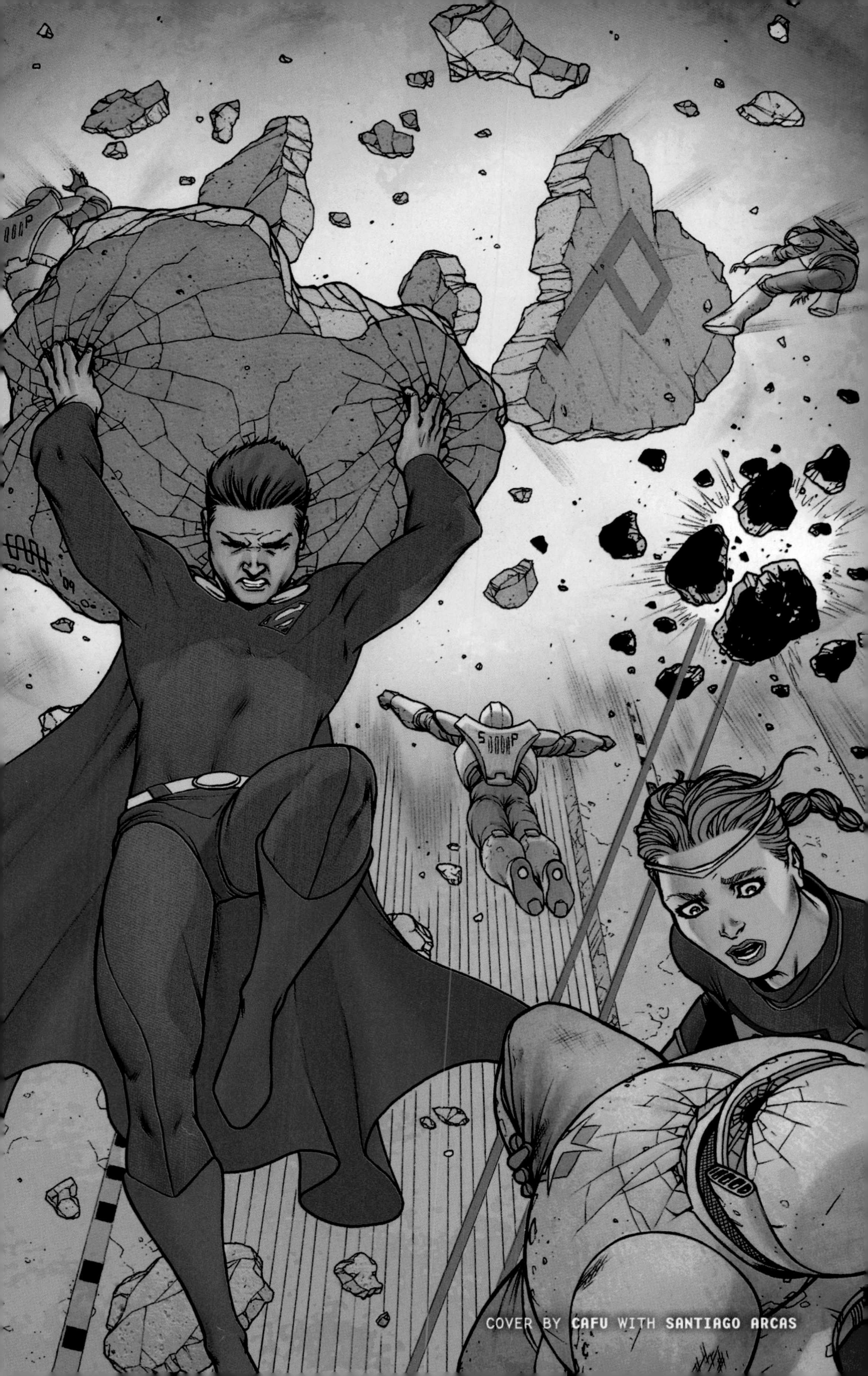

COVER BY **CAFU** WITH **SANTIAGO ARCAS**

MAN OF VALOR PART THREE

BERNARD CHANG <ARTIST>

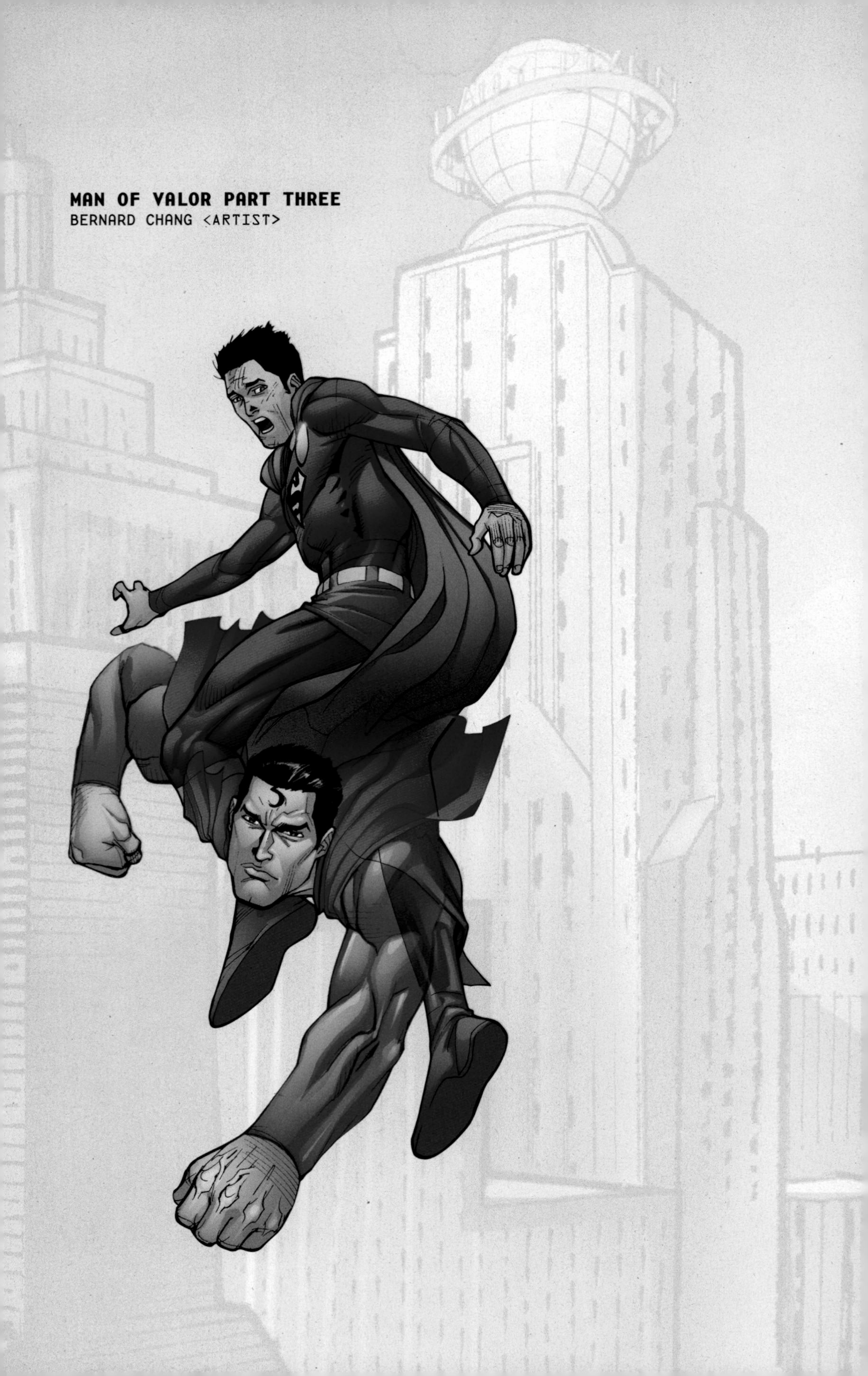

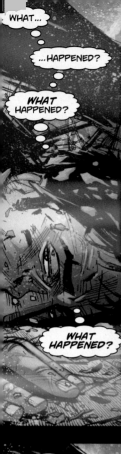

WHAT...

...HAPPENED?

WHAT HAPPENED?

WHAT HAPPENED?

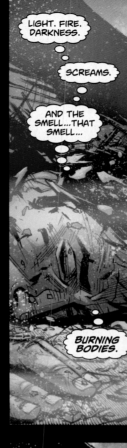

LIGHT. FIRE. DARKNESS.

SCREAMS.

AND THE SMELL...THAT SMELL...

BURNING BODIES.

BUT WHAT HAPPENED? HOW DID--

I'M IN SHOCK. I THINK...CAN'T THINK...

NO TIME FOR THAT.

COME ON, MON, GET IT TOGETHER.

RISE UP.

YEAH...

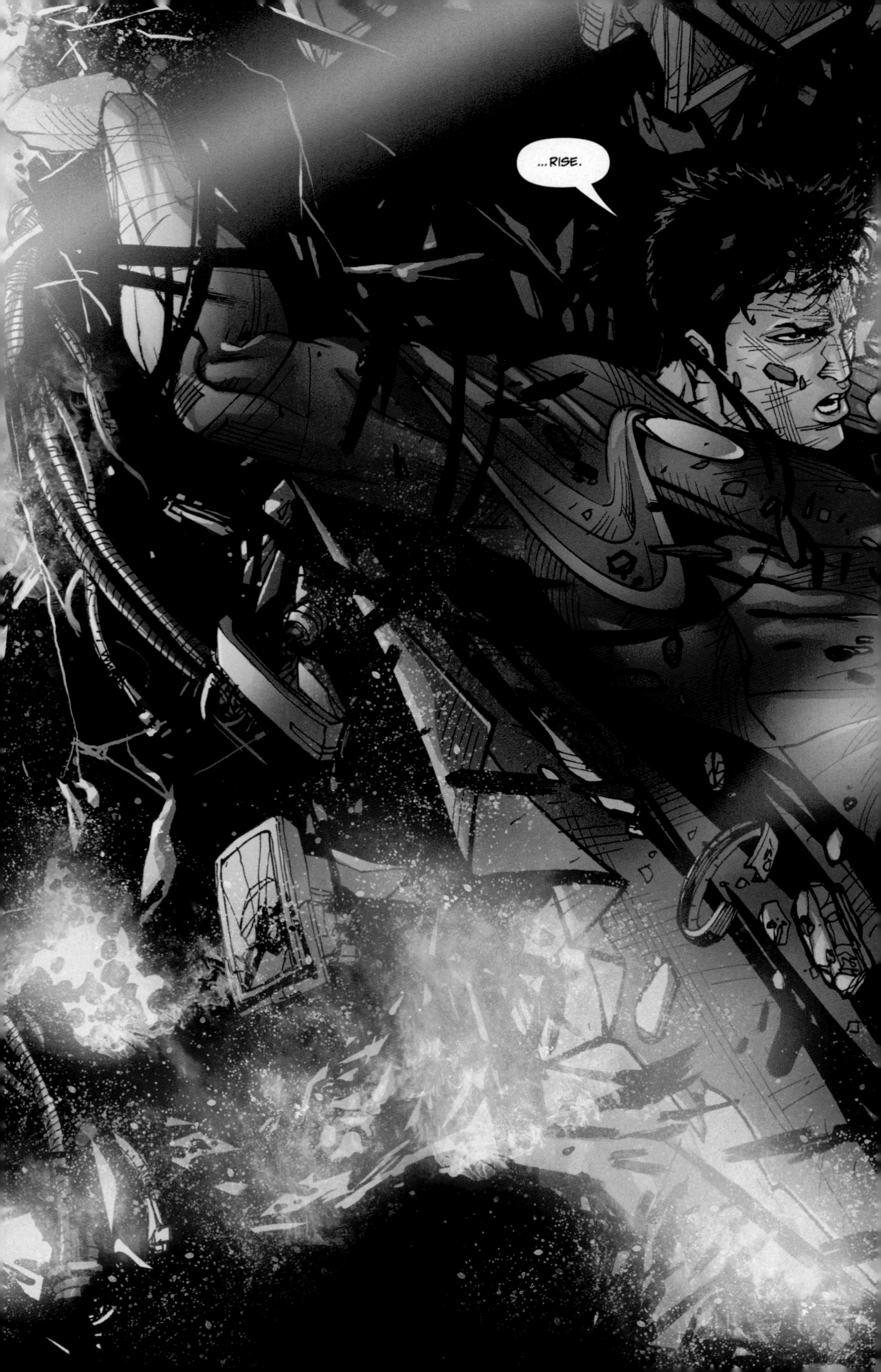
...RISE.

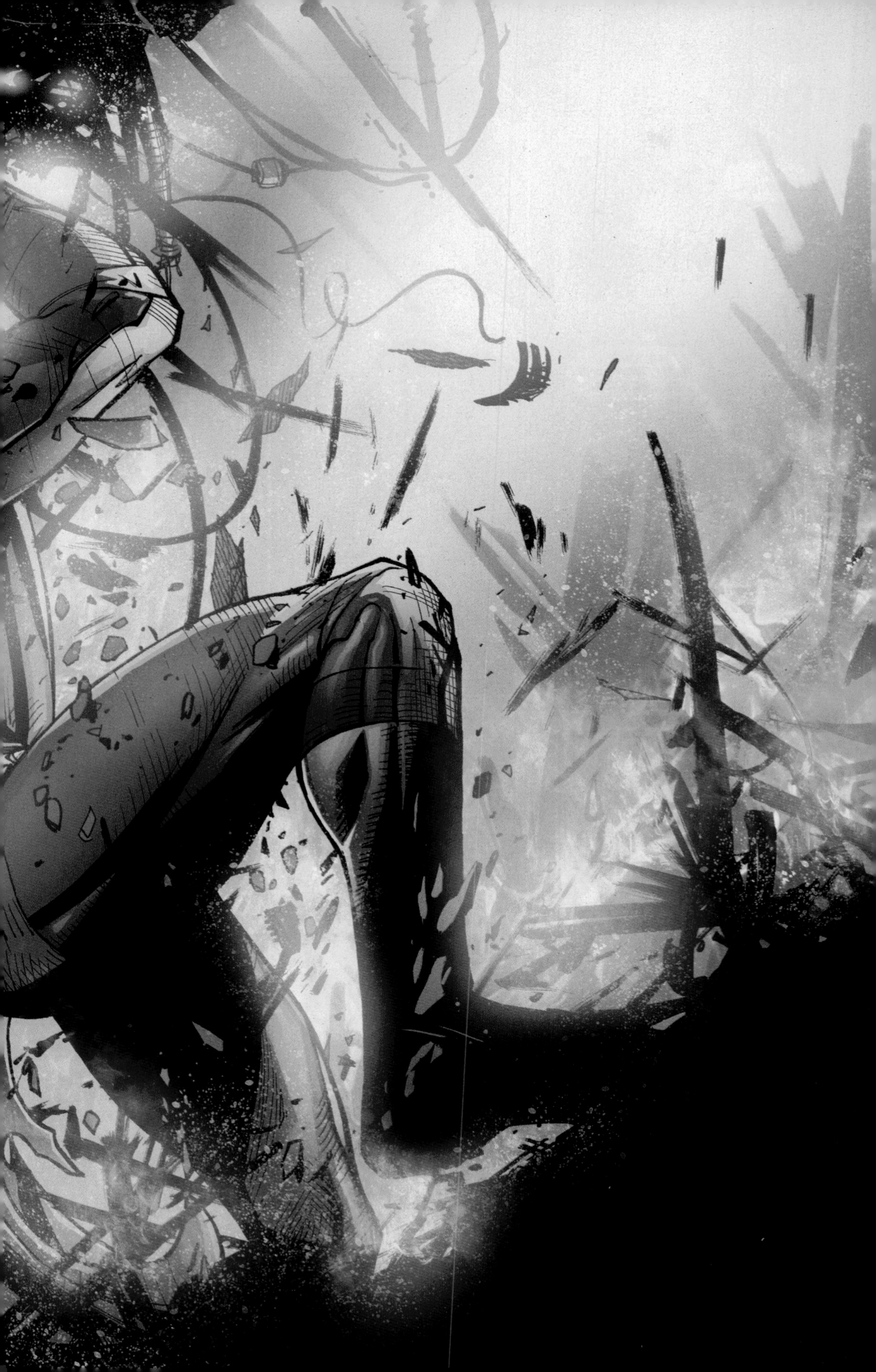

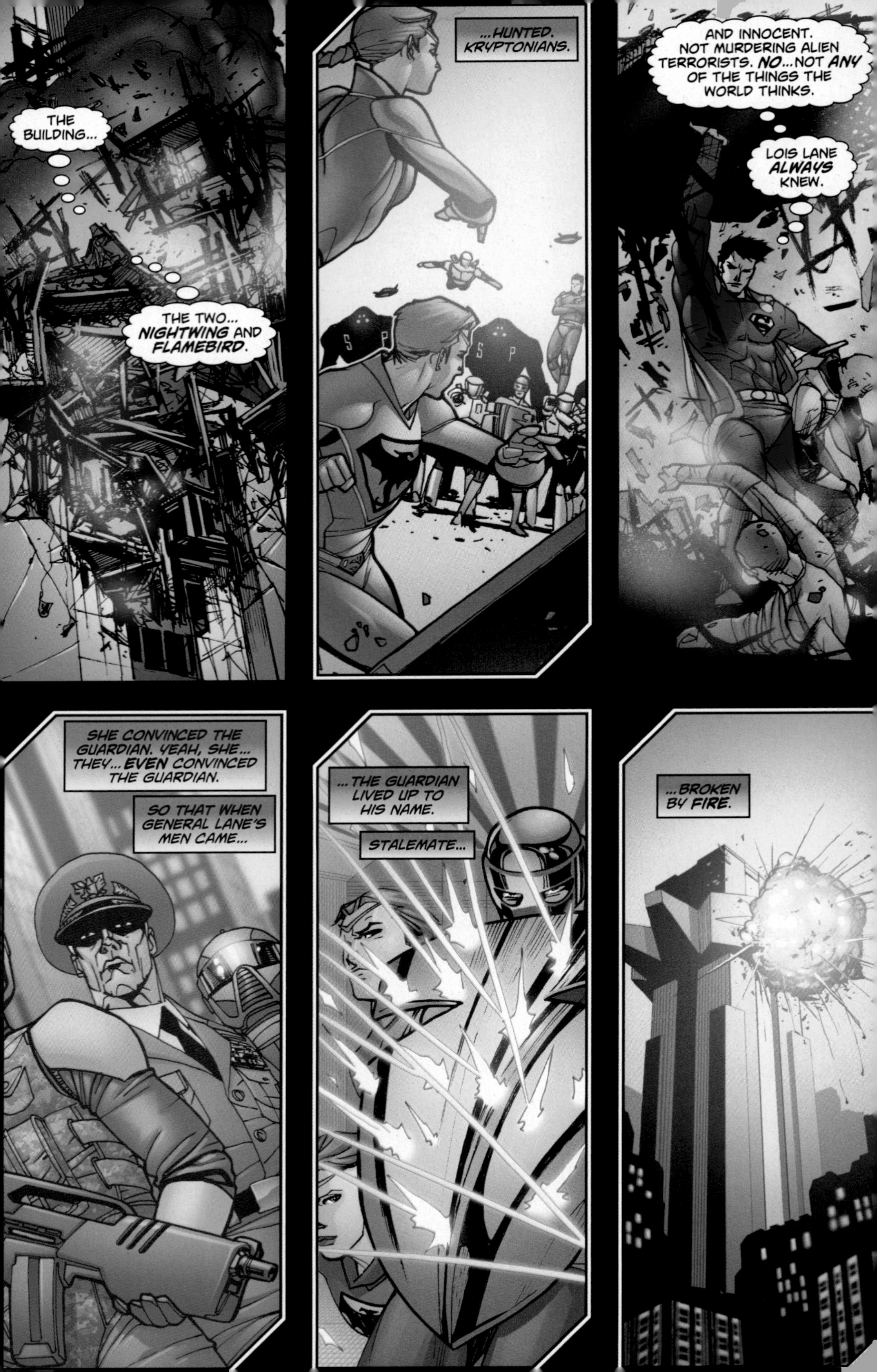
THE BUILDING...
THE TWO... NIGHTWING AND FLAMEBIRD.
...HUNTED. KRYPTONIANS.
AND INNOCENT. NOT MURDERING ALIEN TERRORISTS. NO...NOT ANY OF THE THINGS THE WORLD THINKS.
LOIS LANE ALWAYS KNEW.
SHE CONVINCED THE GUARDIAN. YEAH, SHE... THEY...EVEN CONVINCED THE GUARDIAN.
SO THAT WHEN GENERAL LANE'S MEN CAME...
...THE GUARDIAN LIVED UP TO HIS NAME.
STALEMATE...
...BROKEN BY FIRE.

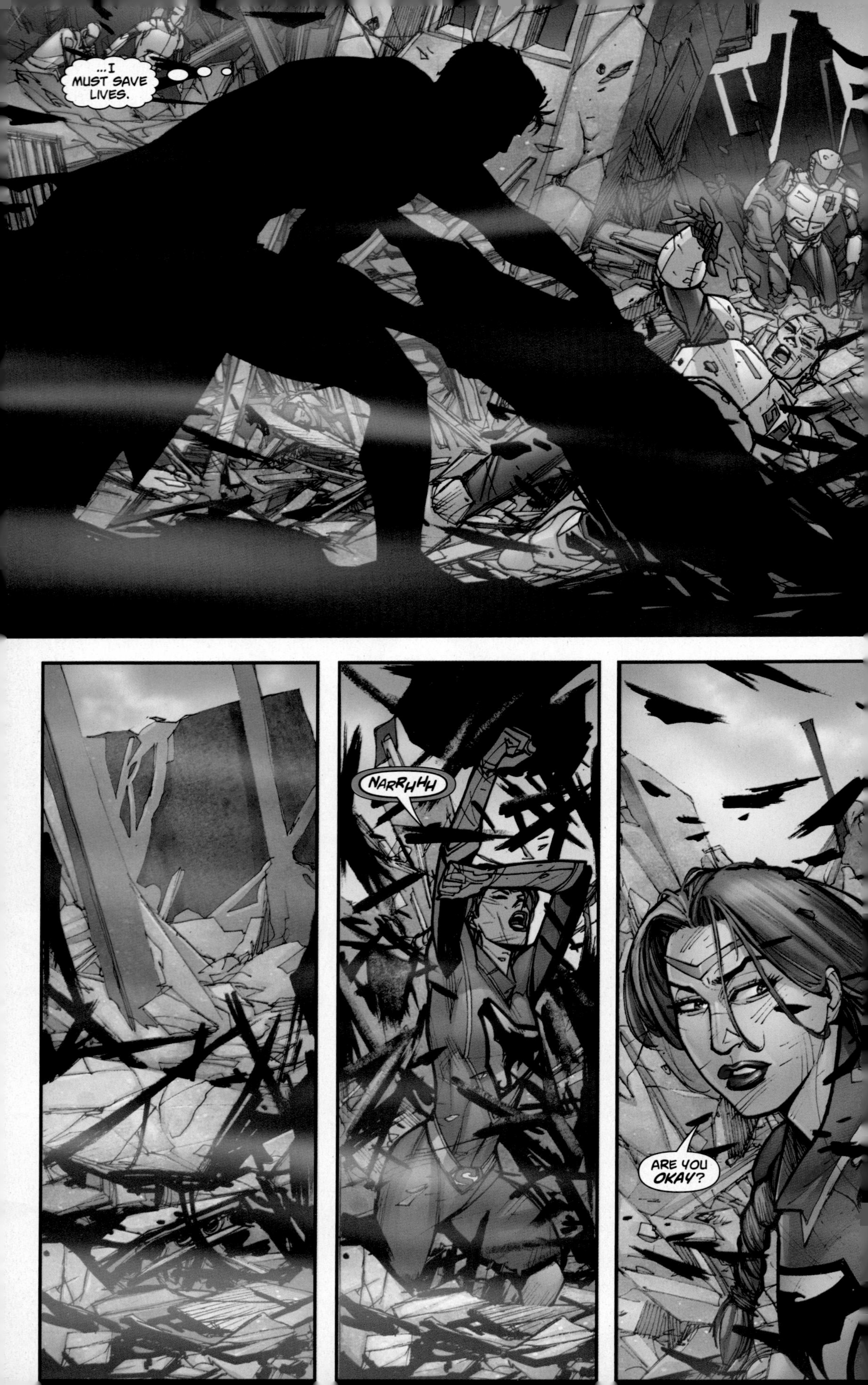
...I MUST SAVE LIVES.
NARRHHH
ARE YOU OKAY?

MOM?

I'M *FINE* CHRIS.

BUT YOU *HAVE* TO GO.

I *CAN'T* LEAVE THIS. AND...

...WE'RE *INNOCENT.* STAY AND MAY

THERE'S NO MAYBE, SON. NO CHANCE. *NOT* AFTER THIS.

I *KNOW* YOU'RE INNOCENT.

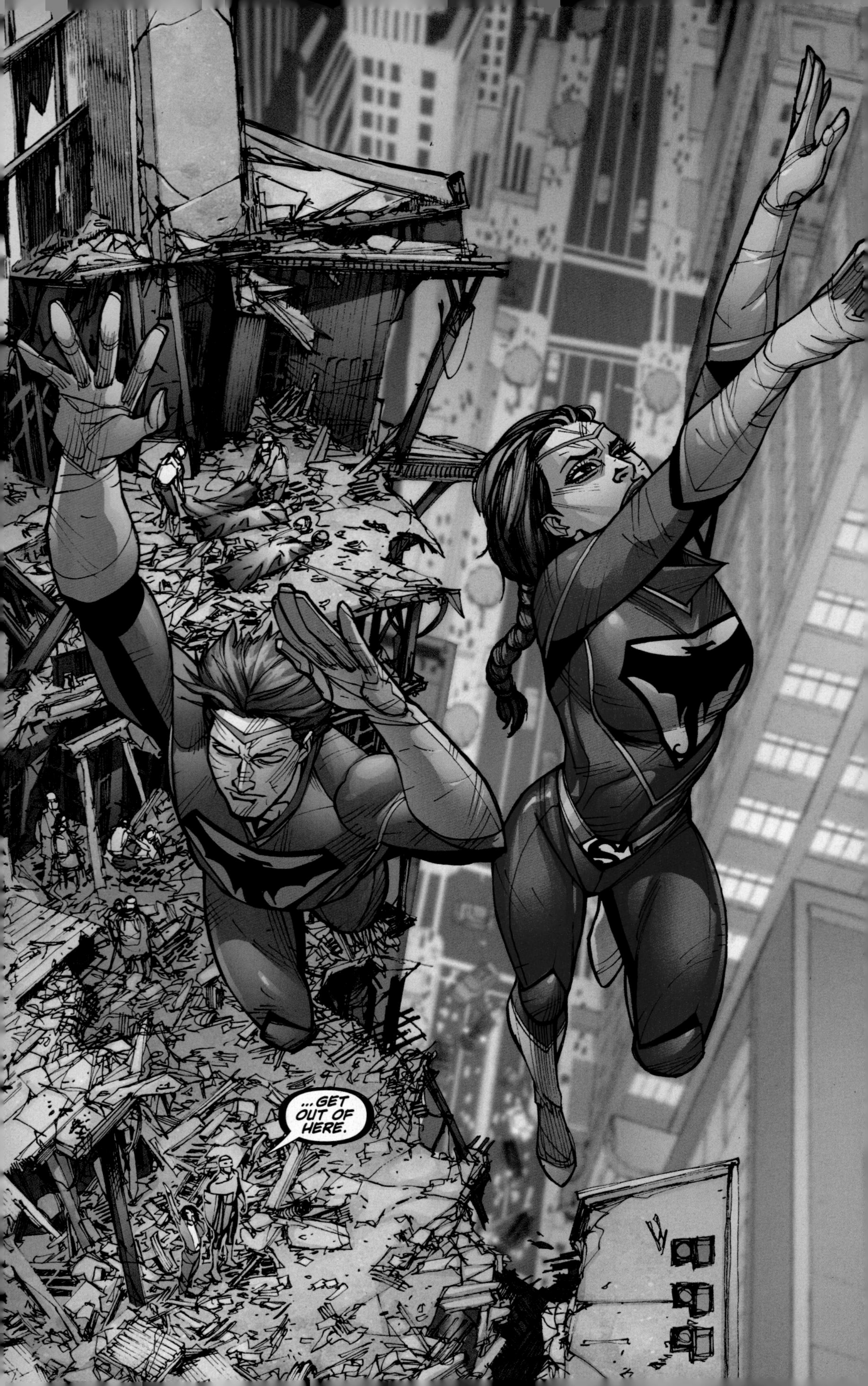
...GET OUT OF HERE.

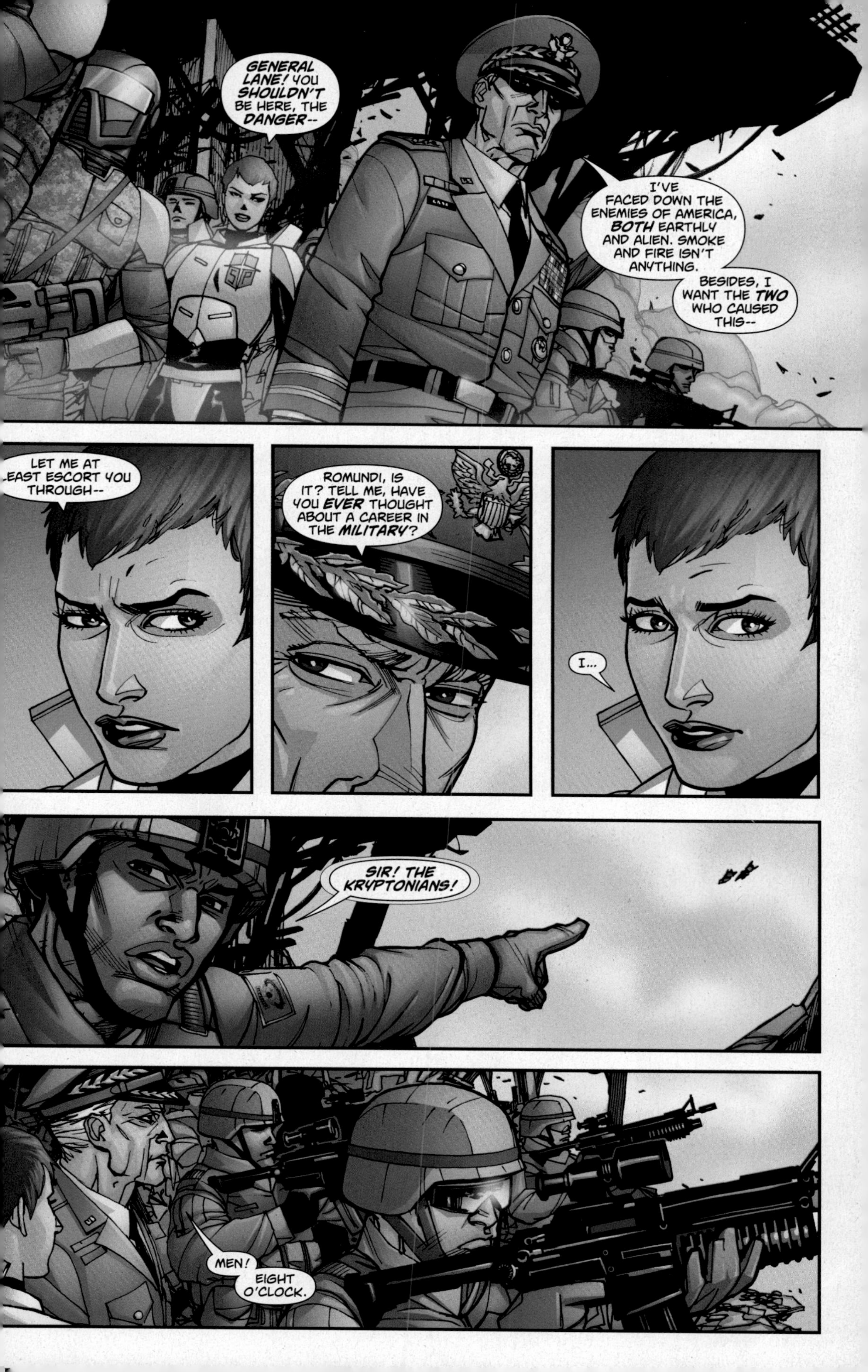
GENERAL LANE! YOU SHOULDN'T BE HERE, THE DANGER--
I'VE FACED DOWN THE ENEMIES OF AMERICA, BOTH EARTHLY AND ALIEN. SMOKE AND FIRE ISN'T ANYTHING.
BESIDES, I WANT THE TWO WHO CAUSED THIS--
LET ME AT LEAST ESCORT YOU THROUGH--
ROMUNDI, IS IT? TELL ME, HAVE YOU EVER THOUGHT ABOUT A CAREER IN THE MILITARY?
I...
SIR! THE KRYPTONIANS!
MEN! EIGHT O'CLOCK.

OHHH NO Y'DON'T!

◇‖‐◇–‡�‖‐
◇‡◇‖◇‐◇‖◇‐
⬡‐◇□◇▽◇‐
▽□‖‐□◇‡◇‐‐

MON-EL--HE'S IN SOME KIND OF TROUBLE--

THAT'S IT, MON. BE A GOOD LITTLE LURE.

TARGET LOCKED, SIR.

ARTILLERY!

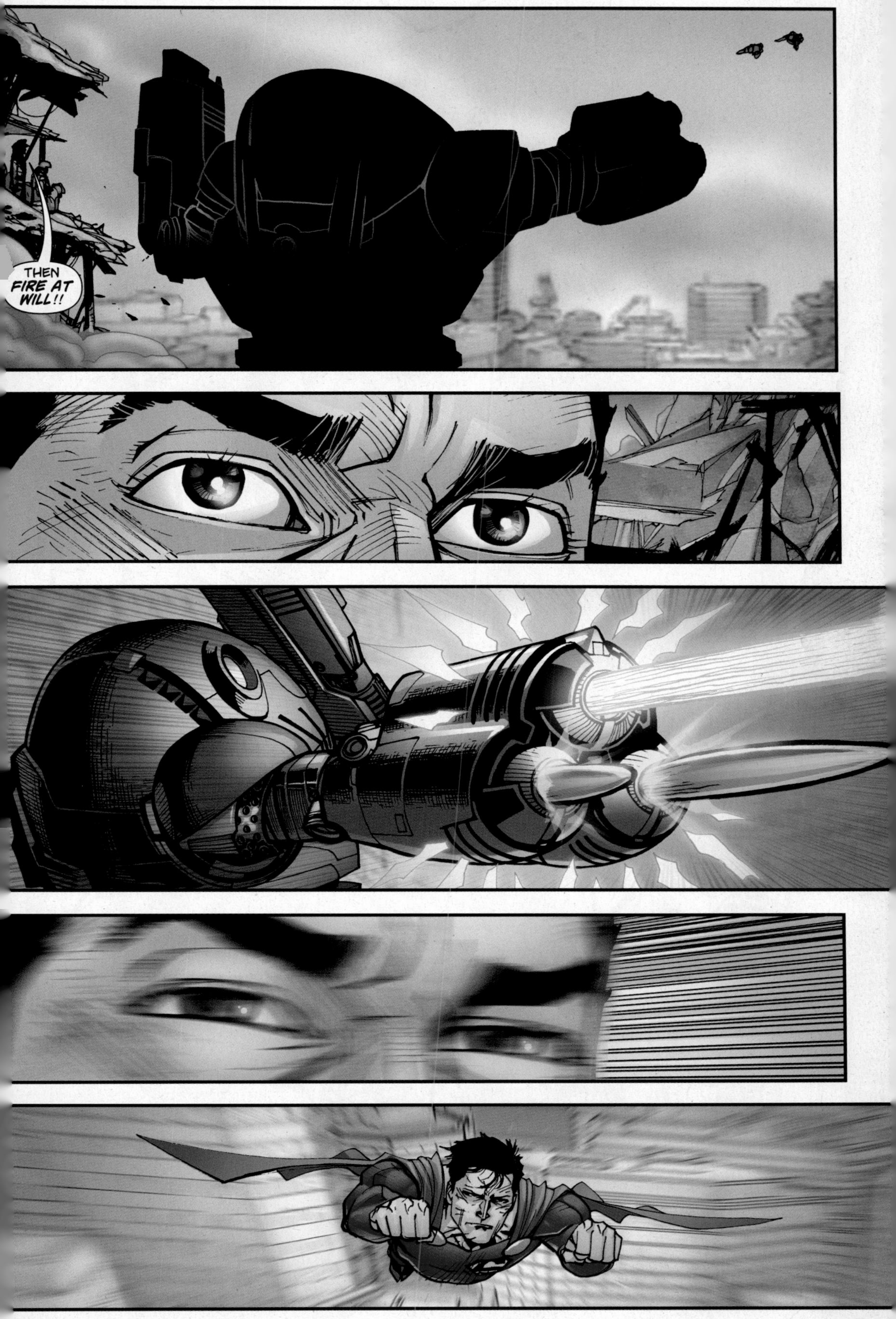
THEN FIRE AT WILL!!

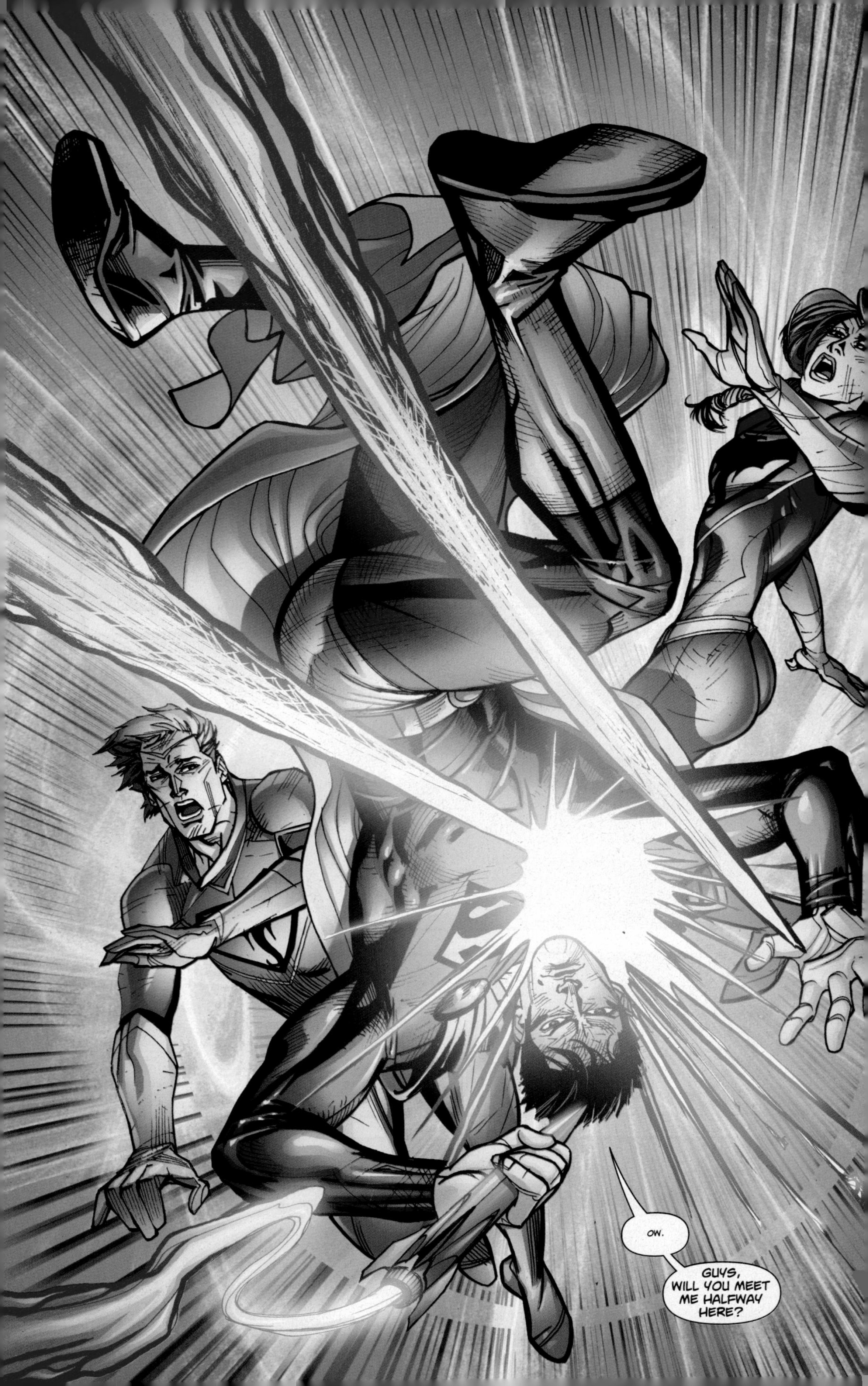
OW.
GUYS, WILL YOU MEET ME HALFWAY HERE?

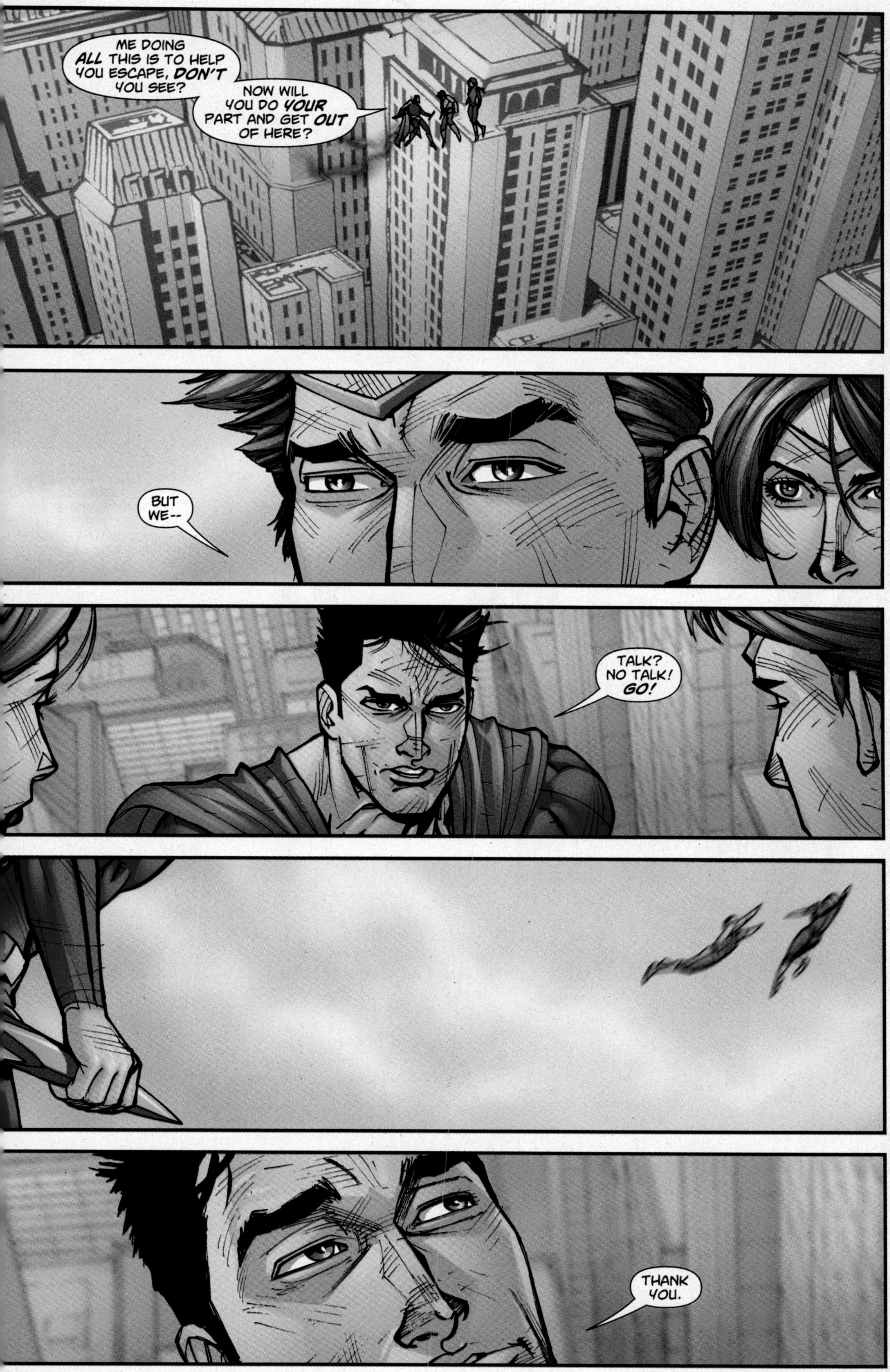
ME DOING ALL THIS IS TO HELP YOU ESCAPE, DON'T YOU SEE?
NOW WILL YOU DO YOUR PART AND GET OUT OF HERE?
BUT WE--
TALK? NO TALK! GO!
THANK YOU.

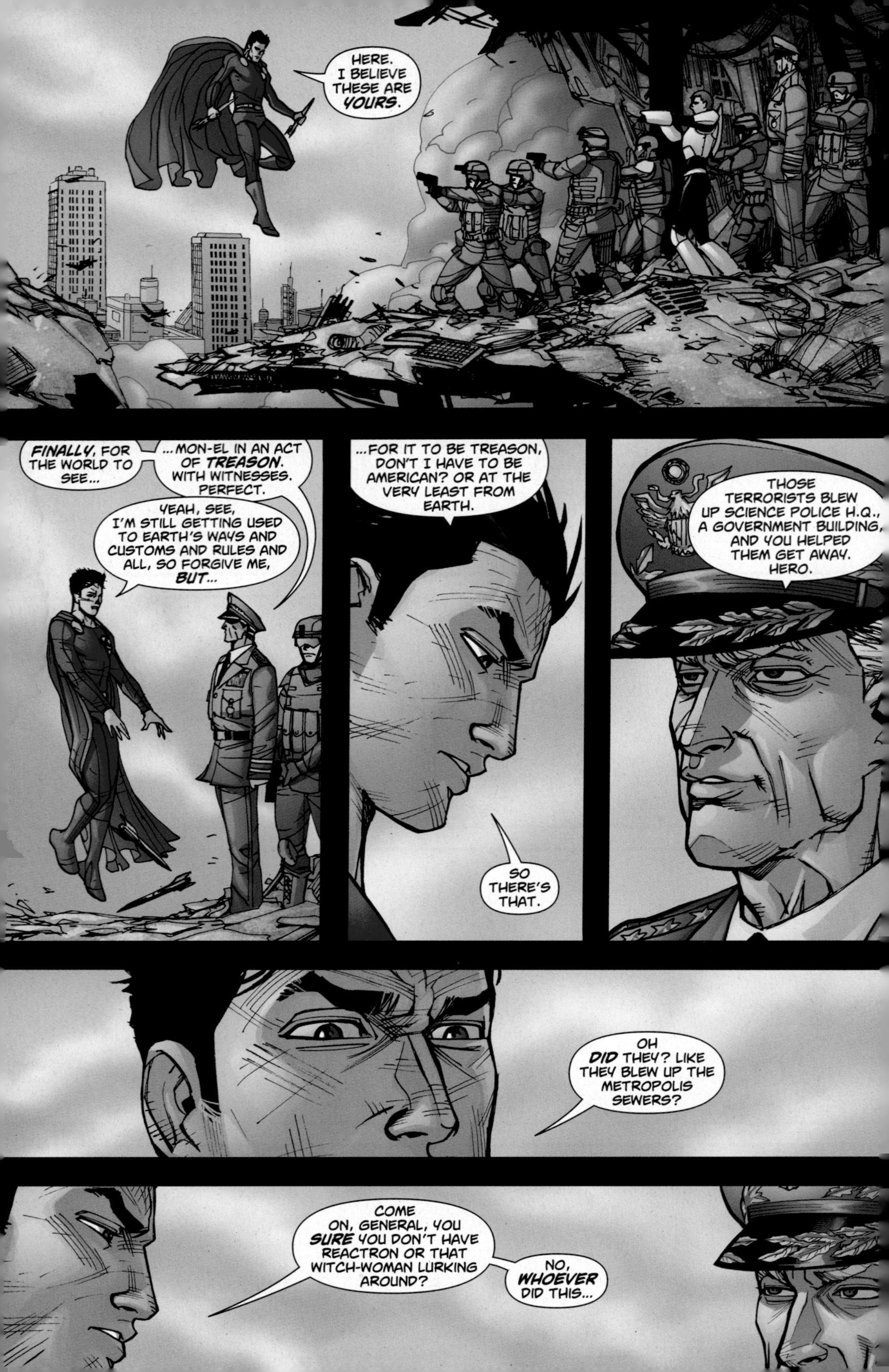
HERE. I BELIEVE THESE ARE YOURS.
FINALLY, FOR THE WORLD TO SEE...
...MON-EL IN AN ACT OF TREASON. WITH WITNESSES. PERFECT.
YEAH, SEE, I'M STILL GETTING USED TO EARTH'S WAYS AND CUSTOMS AND RULES AND ALL, SO FORGIVE ME, BUT...
...FOR IT TO BE TREASON, DON'T I HAVE TO BE AMERICAN? OR AT THE VERY LEAST FROM EARTH.
SO THERE'S THAT.
THOSE TERRORISTS BLEW UP SCIENCE POLICE H.Q., A GOVERNMENT BUILDING, AND YOU HELPED THEM GET AWAY. HERO.
OH DID THEY? LIKE THEY BLEW UP THE METROPOLIS SEWERS?
COME ON, GENERAL, YOU SURE YOU DON'T HAVE REACTRON OR THAT WITCH-WOMAN LURKING AROUND?
NO, WHOEVER DID THIS...

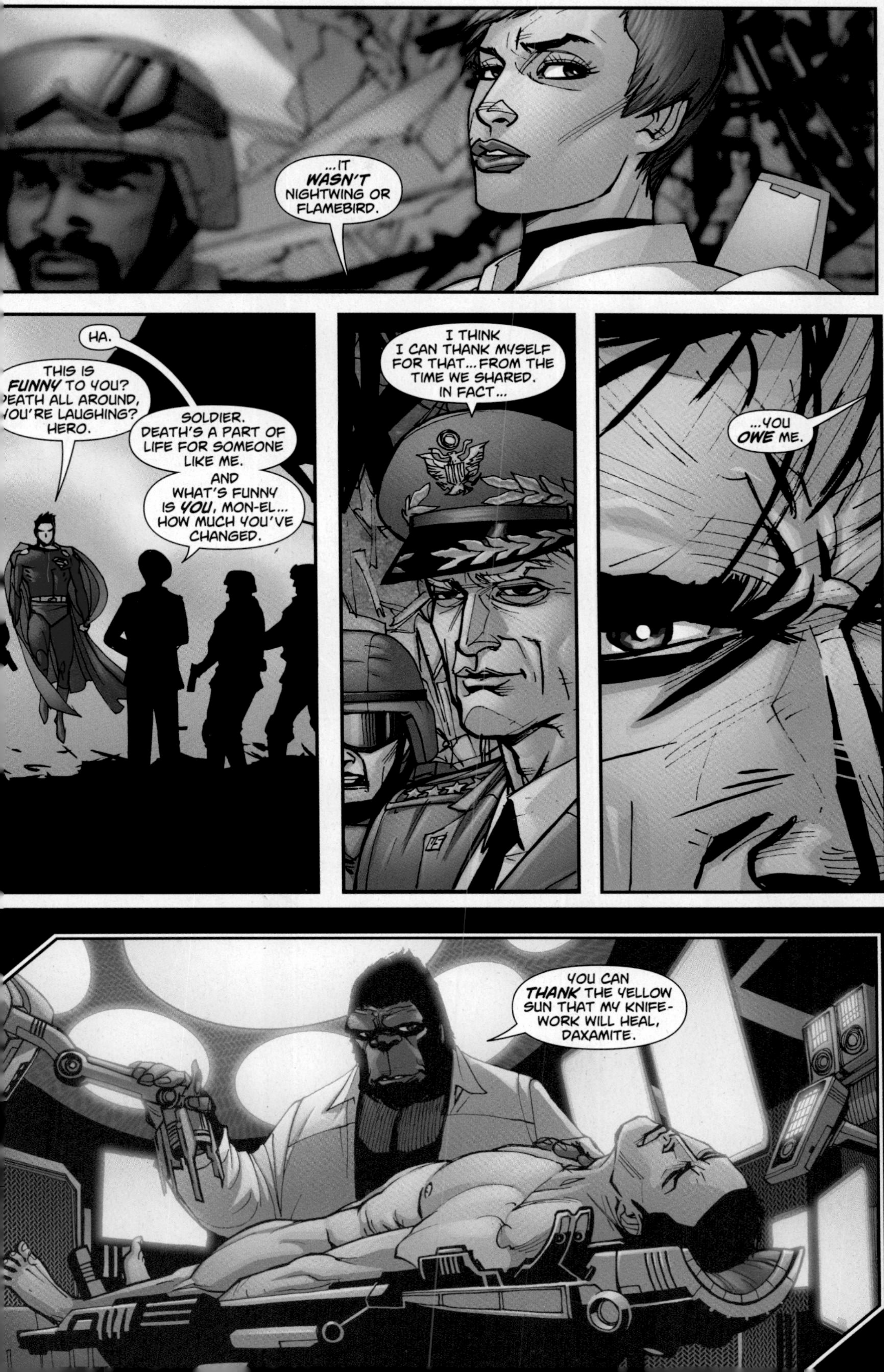
...IT WASN'T NIGHTWING OR FLAMEBIRD.
HA.
THIS IS FUNNY TO YOU? DEATH ALL AROUND, YOU'RE LAUGHING? HERO.
SOLDIER. DEATH'S A PART OF LIFE FOR SOMEONE LIKE ME.
AND WHAT'S FUNNY IS YOU, MON-EL... HOW MUCH YOU'VE CHANGED.
I THINK I CAN THANK MYSELF FOR THAT... FROM THE TIME WE SHARED. IN FACT...
...YOU OWE ME.
YOU CAN THANK THE YELLOW SUN THAT MY KNIFE-WORK WILL HEAL, DAXAMITE.

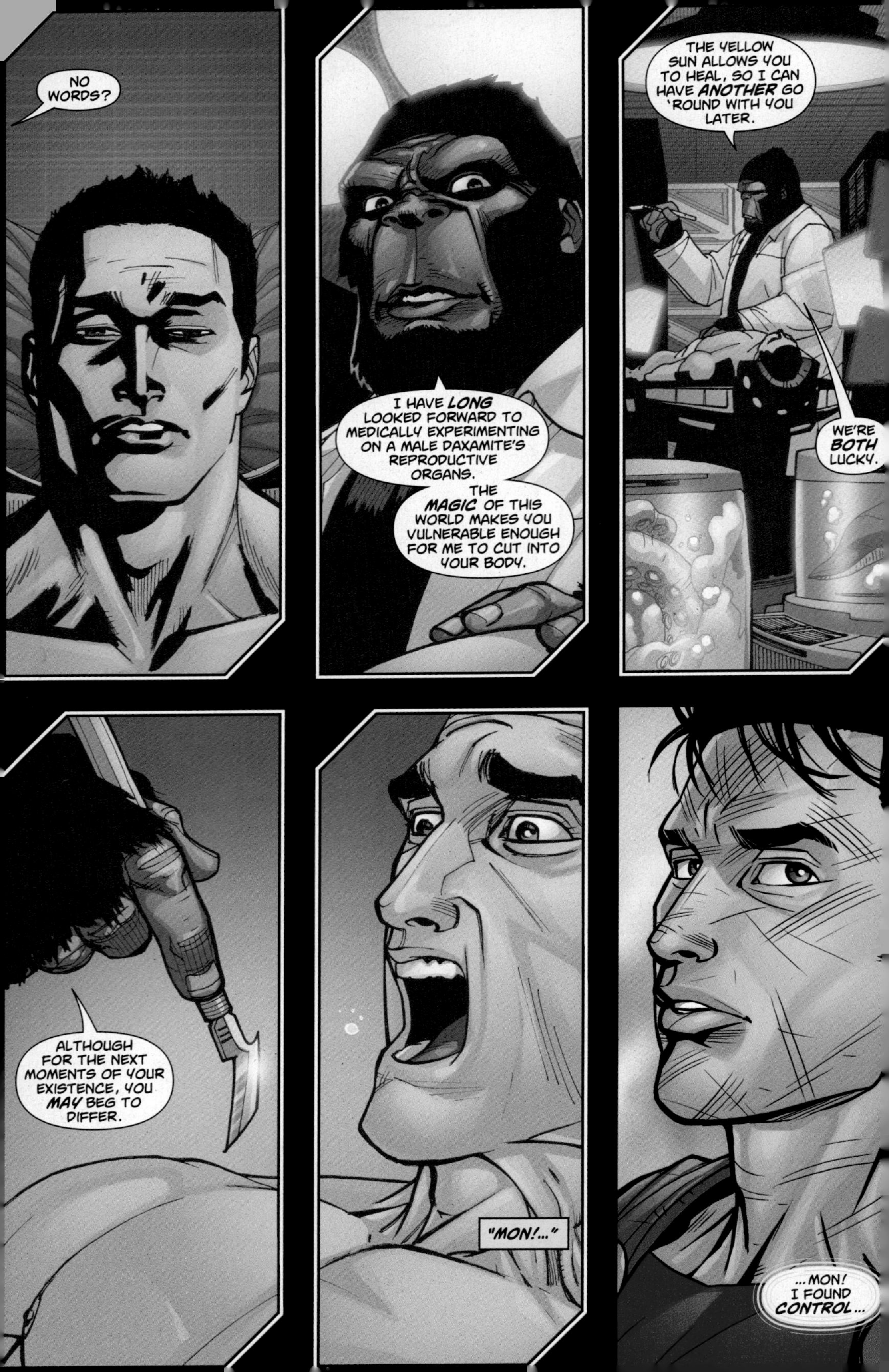
NO WORDS?
I HAVE LONG LOOKED FORWARD TO MEDICALLY EXPERIMENTING ON A MALE DAXAMITE'S REPRODUCTIVE ORGANS.
THE MAGIC OF THIS WORLD MAKES YOU VULNERABLE ENOUGH FOR ME TO CUT INTO YOUR BODY.
THE YELLOW SUN ALLOWS YOU TO HEAL, SO I CAN HAVE ANOTHER GO 'ROUND WITH YOU LATER.
WE'RE BOTH LUCKY.
ALTHOUGH FOR THE NEXT MOMENTS OF YOUR EXISTENCE, YOU MAY BEG TO DIFFER.
"MON!..."
...MON! I FOUND CONTROL...

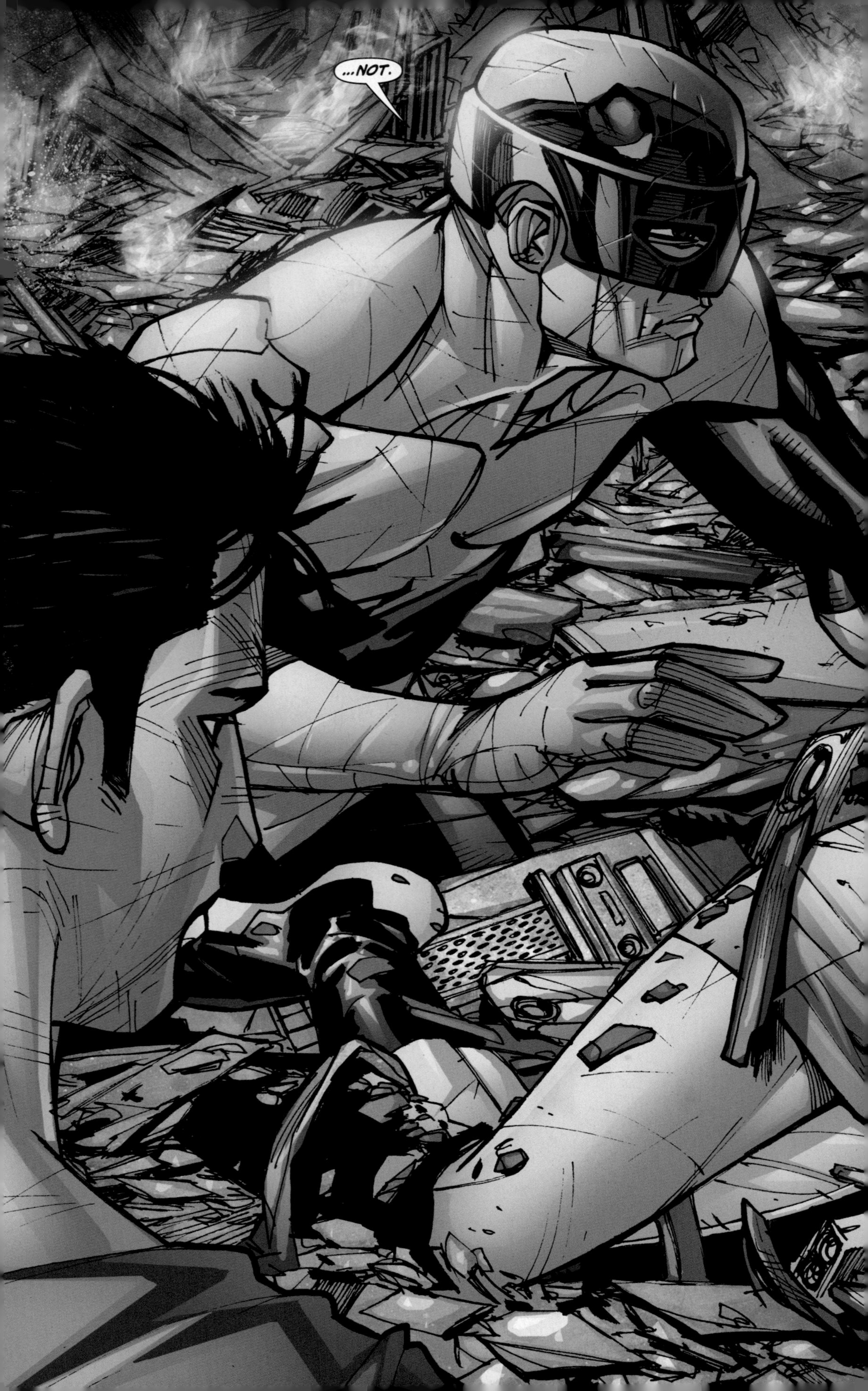
...NOT.

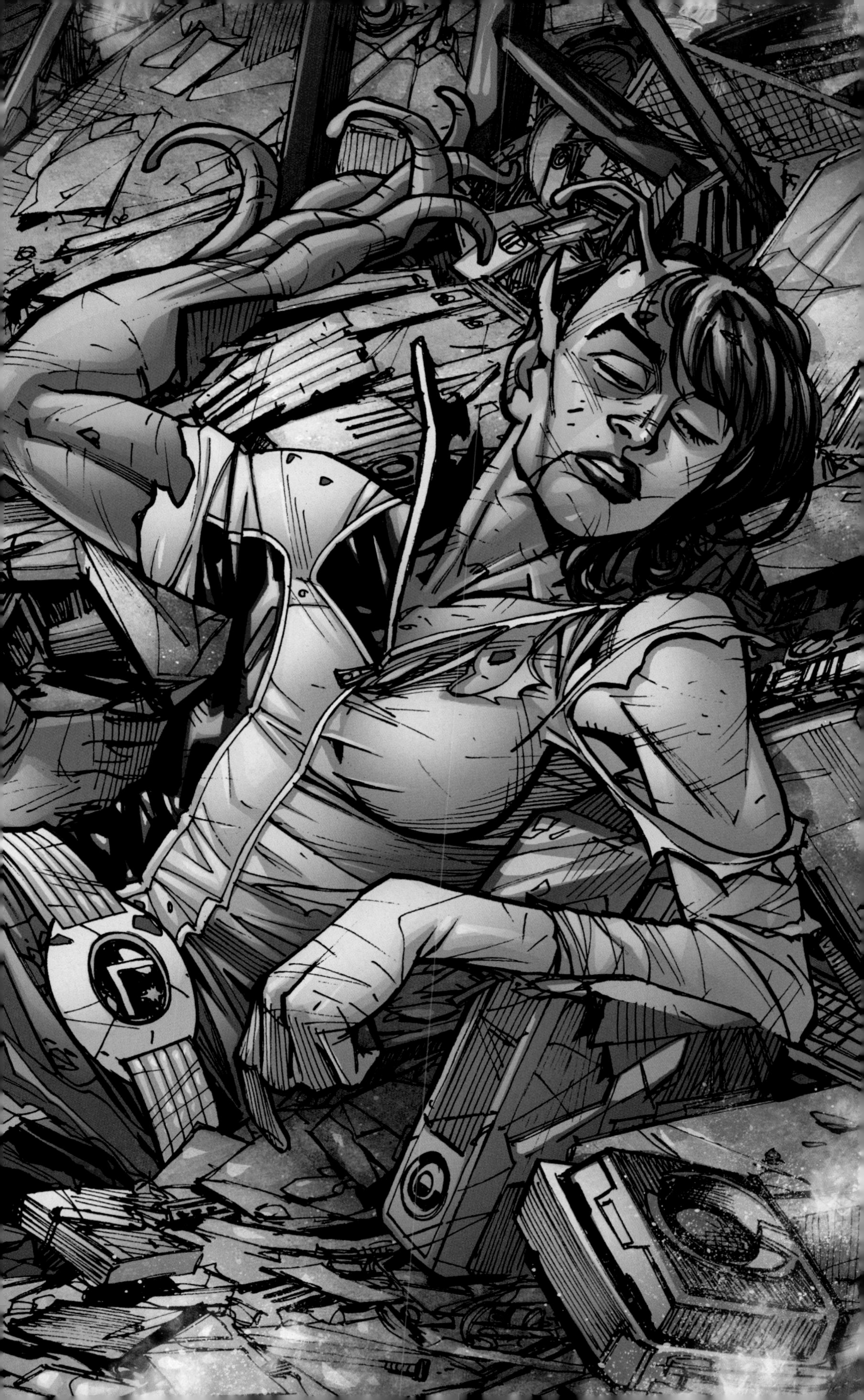

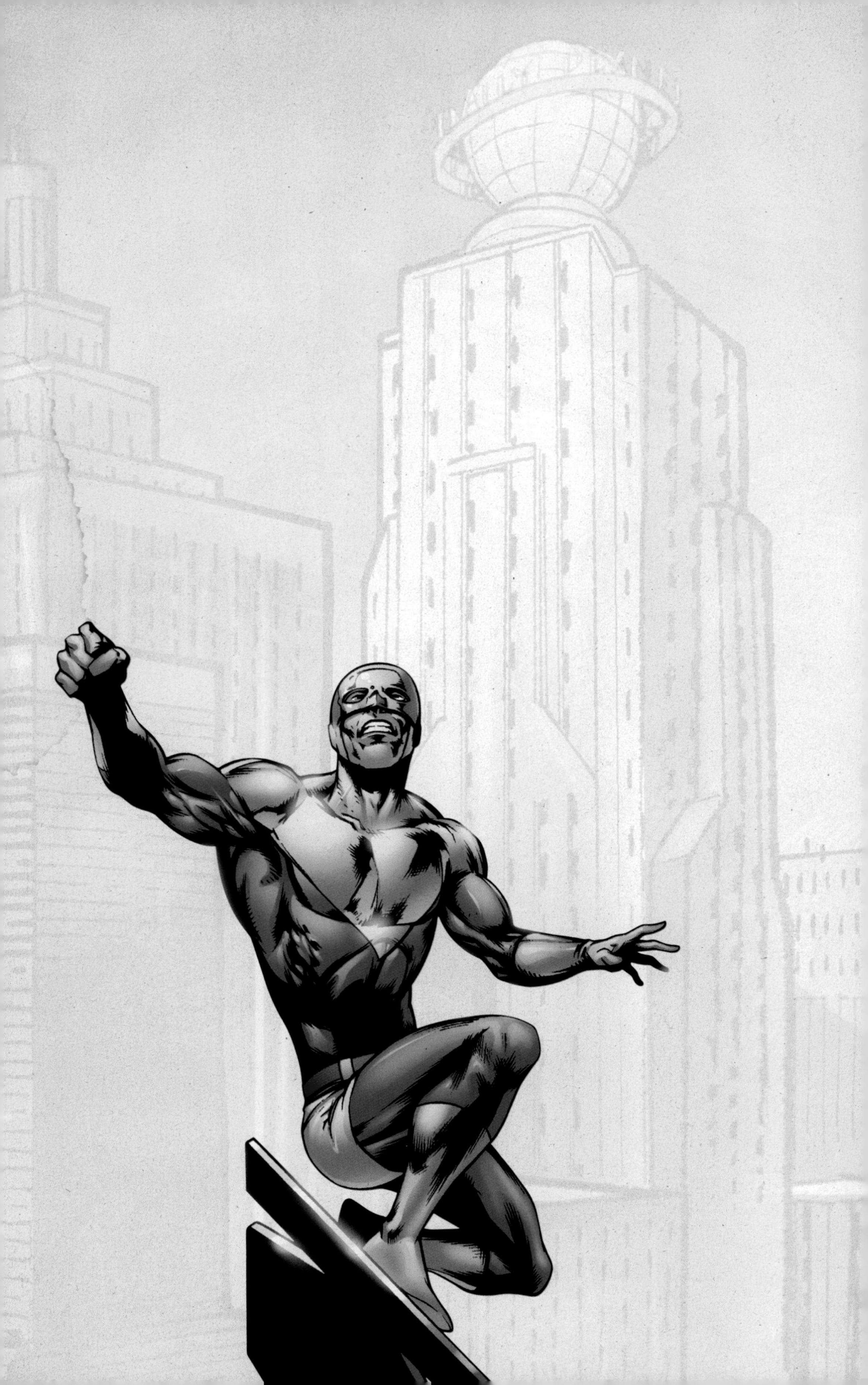

COVER BY **CAFU** WITH **SANTIAGO ARCAS**

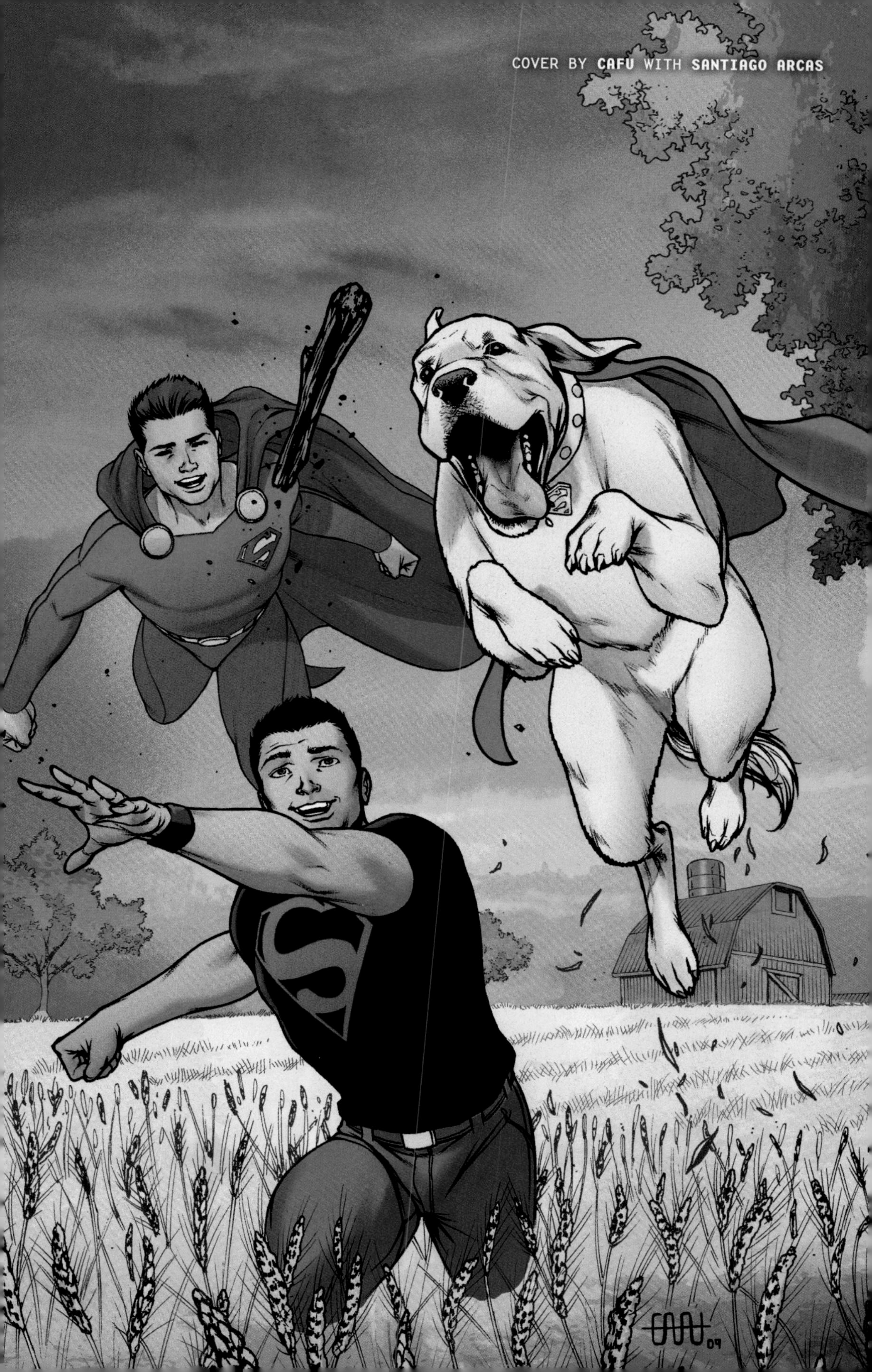

MAN OF VALOR PART FOUR

BERNARD CHANG <ARTIST - PAGES 175-185>
JAVIER PINA <ARTIST - PAGES 186-196>

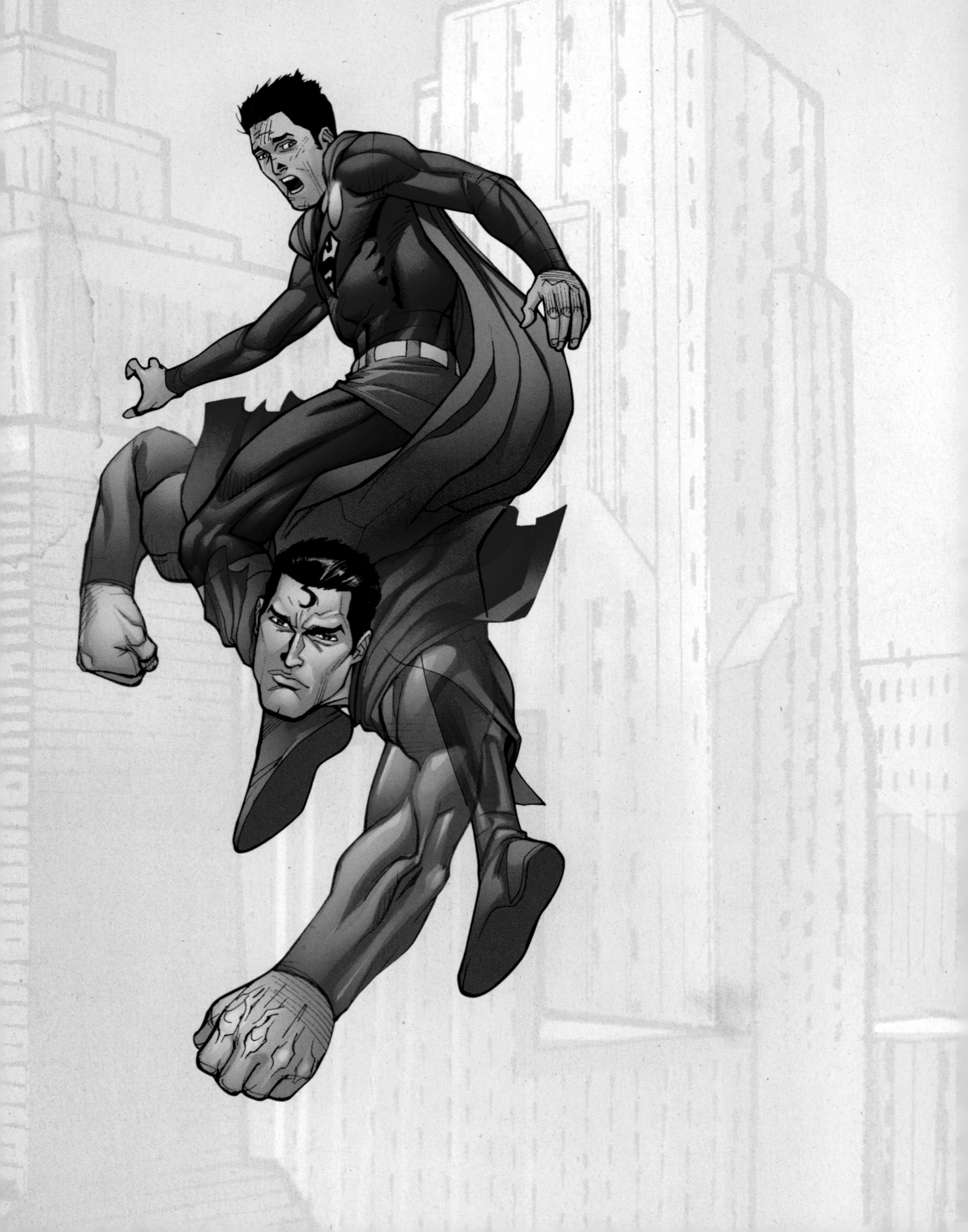

SORRY. I...REFLEX--

THE EXPLOSION-- WHAT--I...

...I GUESS MY LITTLE SECRET'S OUT, HUH?

"LITTLE"? CONTROL? WHO ARE YOU?

NO, SCRATCH THAT. WHAT ARE YOU?! COME ON, TALK! DID YOU KIDNAP THE REAL CONTROL AND--?

THERE NEVER WAS A REAL CONTROL, JIM. I'M A DURLAN...WE CAN SHAPE-SHIFT. I'VE BEEN CONTROL ALL ALONG...ME, LIVING AMONG YOU.

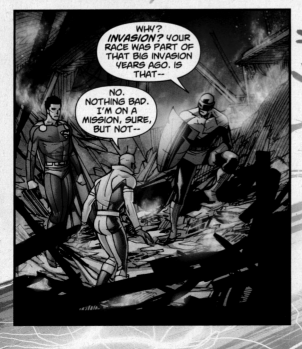

WHY? INVASION? YOUR RACE WAS PART OF THAT BIG INVASION YEARS AGO. IS THAT--

NO. NOTHING BAD. I'M ON A MISSION, SURE, BUT NOT--

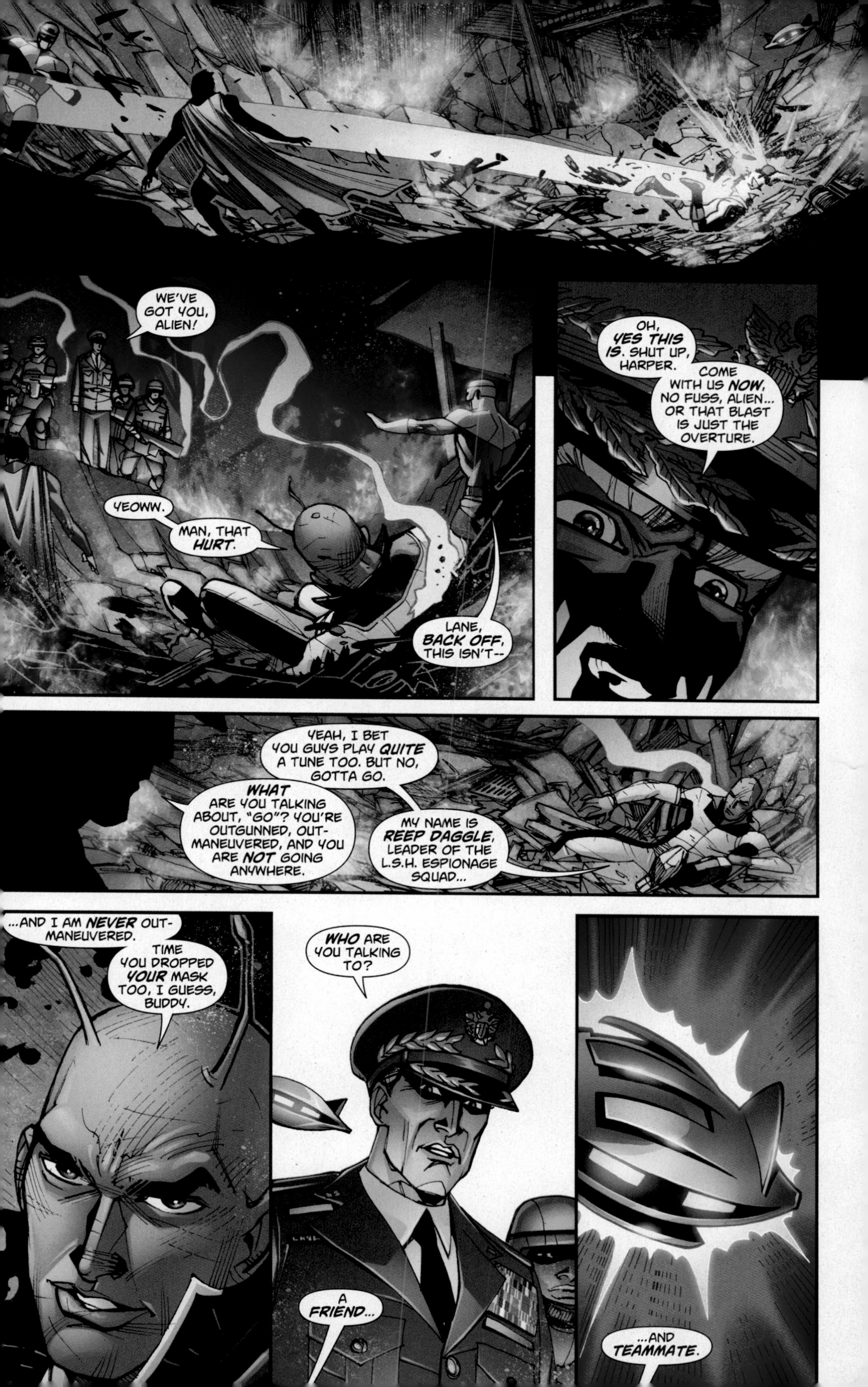
WE'VE GOT YOU, ALIEN!
YEOWW.
MAN, THAT HURT.
LANE, BACK OFF, THIS ISN'T--
OH, YES THIS IS. SHUT UP, HARPER.
COME WITH US NOW, NO FUSS, ALIEN... OR THAT BLAST IS JUST THE OVERTURE.
YEAH, I BET YOU GUYS PLAY QUITE A TUNE TOO. BUT NO, GOTTA GO.
WHAT ARE YOU TALKING ABOUT, "GO"? YOU'RE OUTGUNNED, OUT-MANEUVERED, AND YOU ARE NOT GOING ANYWHERE.
MY NAME IS REEP DAGGLE, LEADER OF THE L.S.H. ESPIONAGE SQUAD...
...AND I AM NEVER OUT-MANEUVERED.
TIME YOU DROPPED YOUR MASK TOO, I GUESS, BUDDY.
WHO ARE YOU TALKING TO?
A FRIEND...
...AND TEAMMATE.

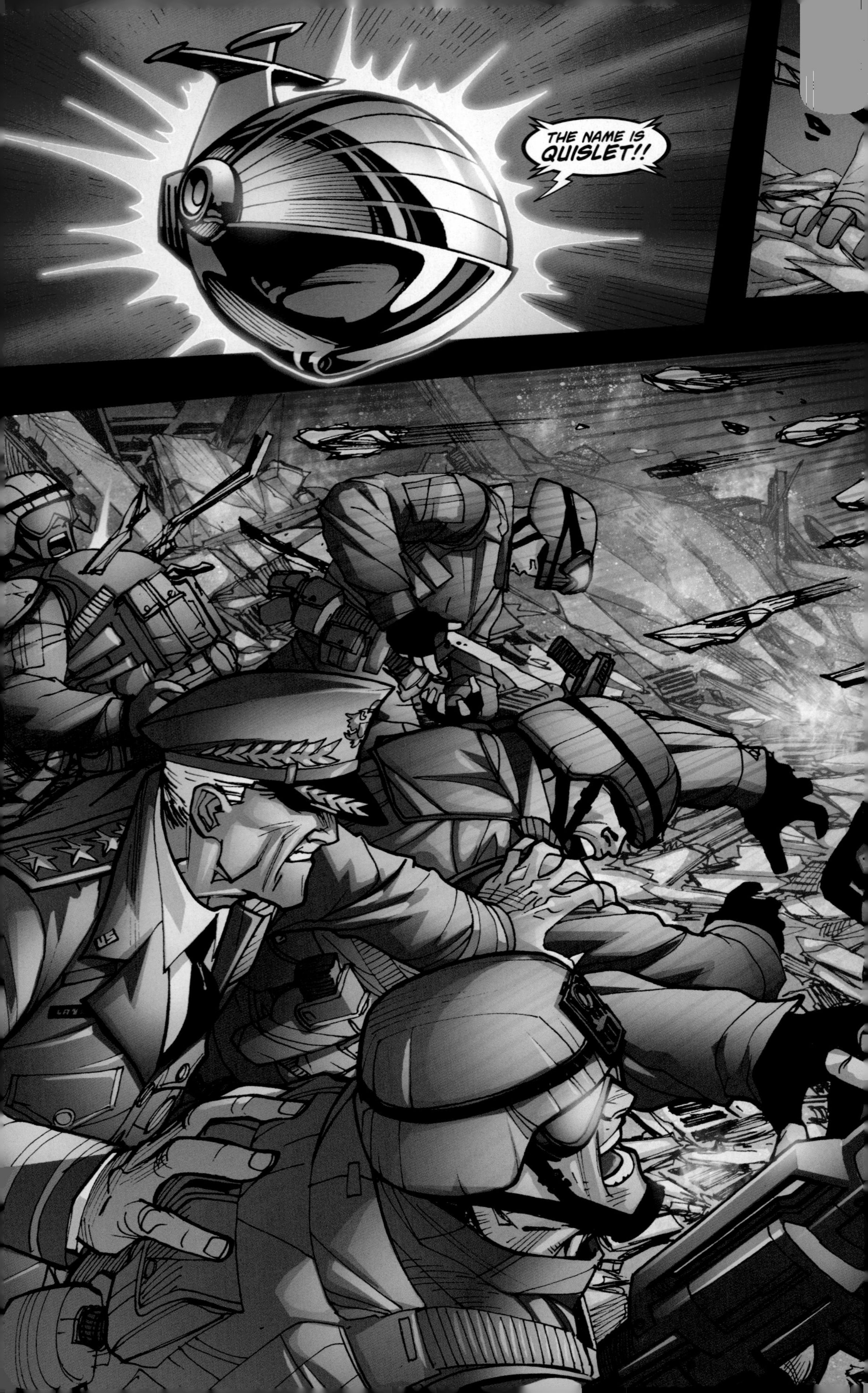
THE NAME IS QUISLET!!

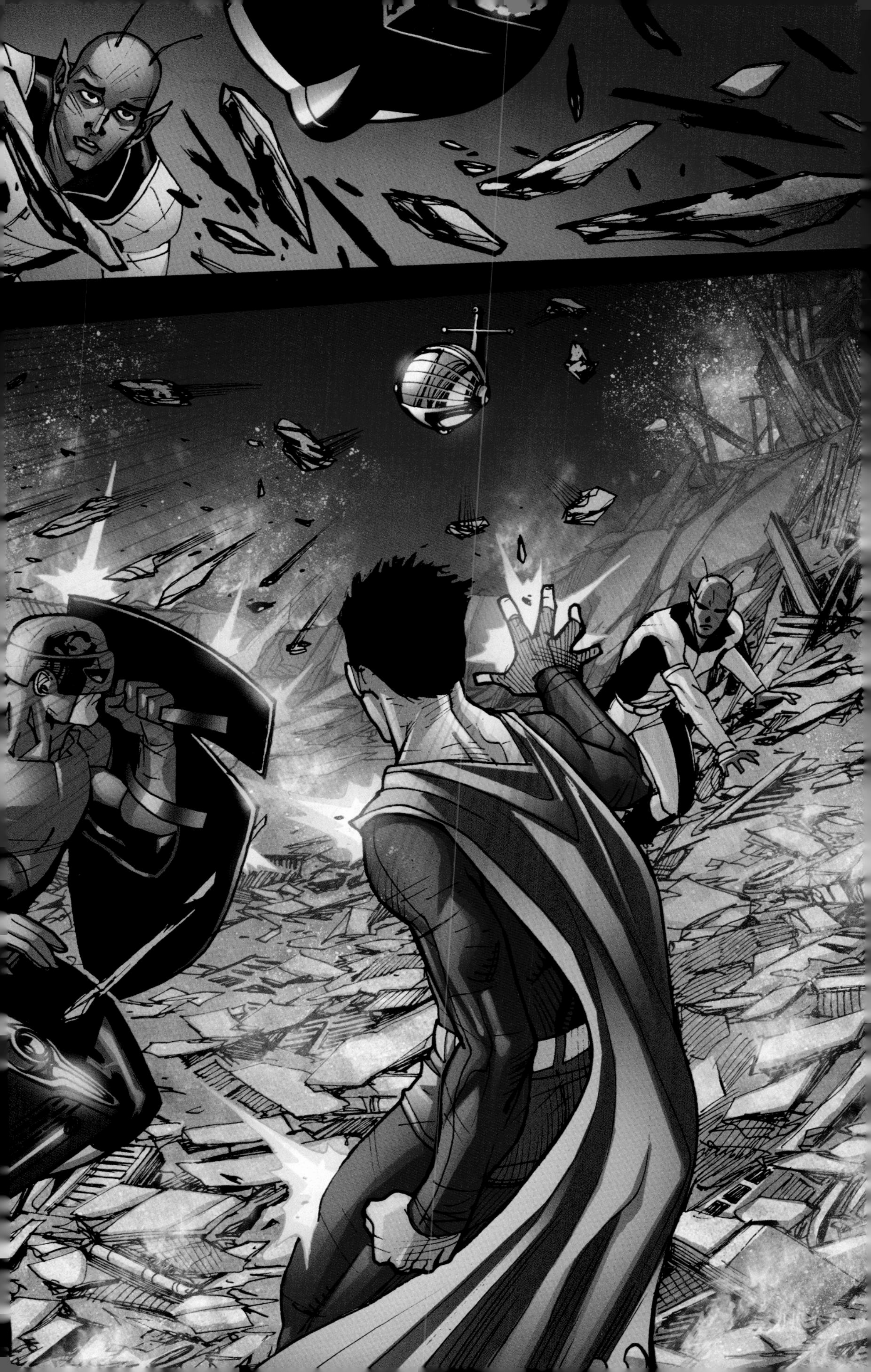

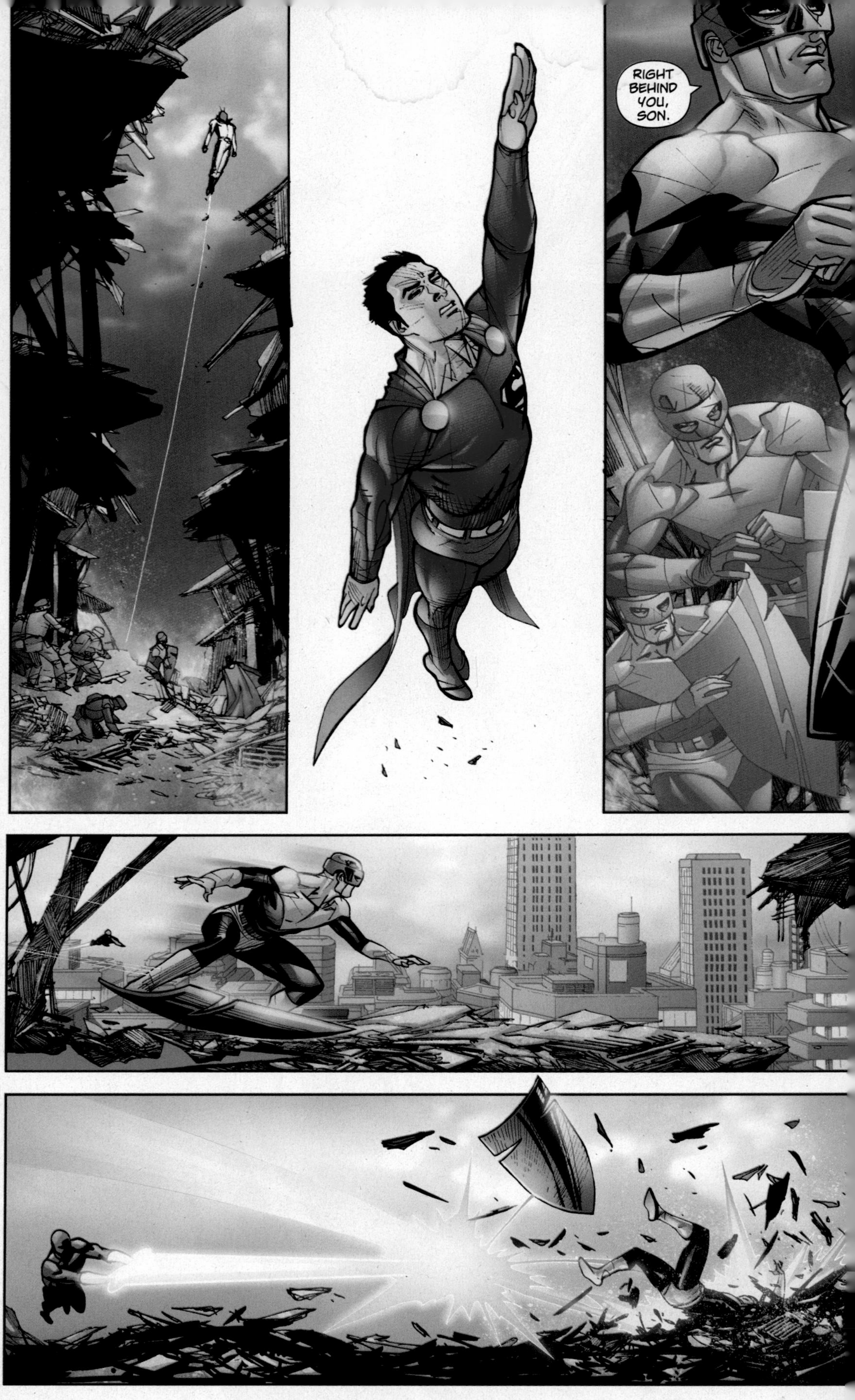
RIGHT BEHIND YOU, SON.

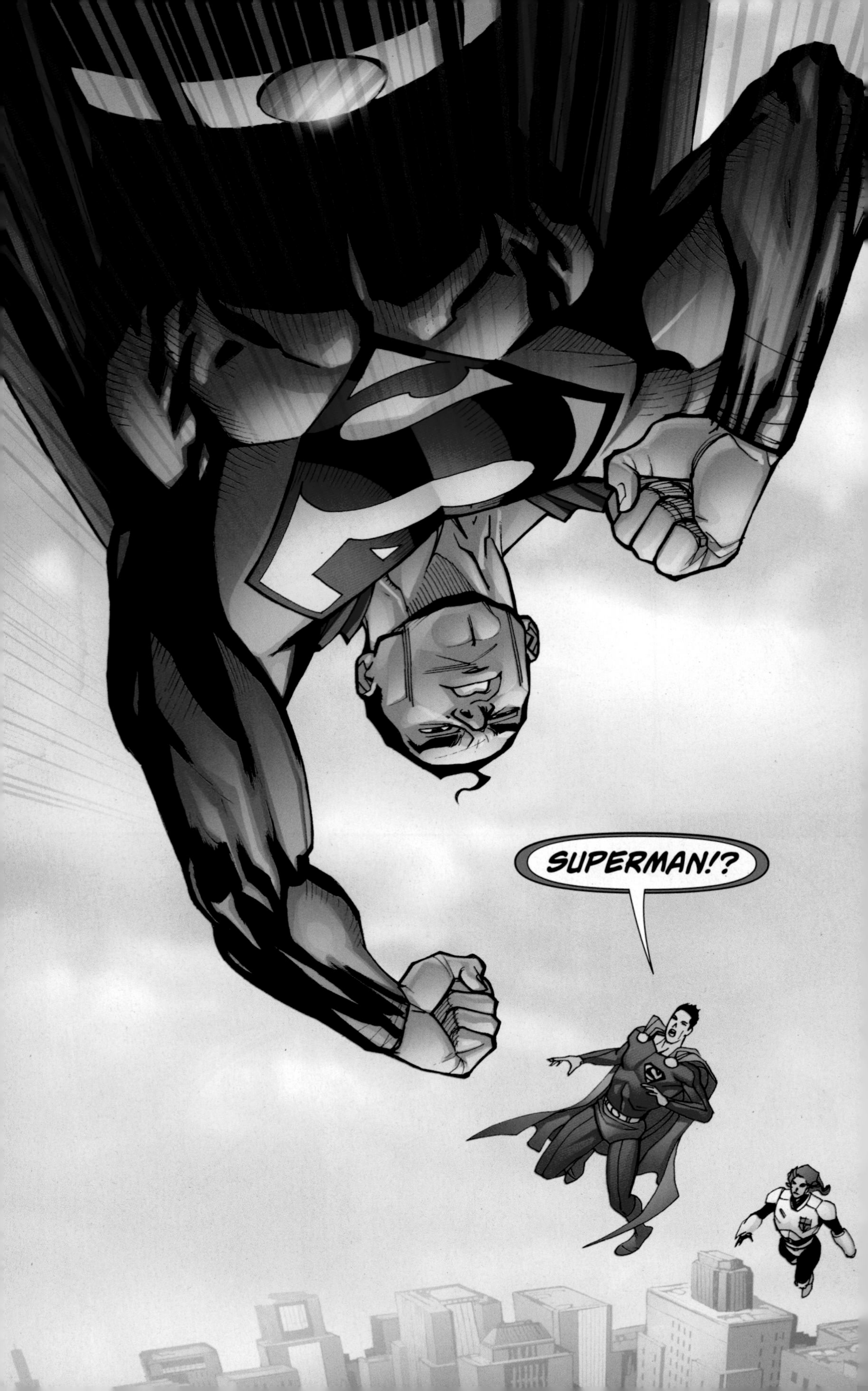
SUPERMAN!?

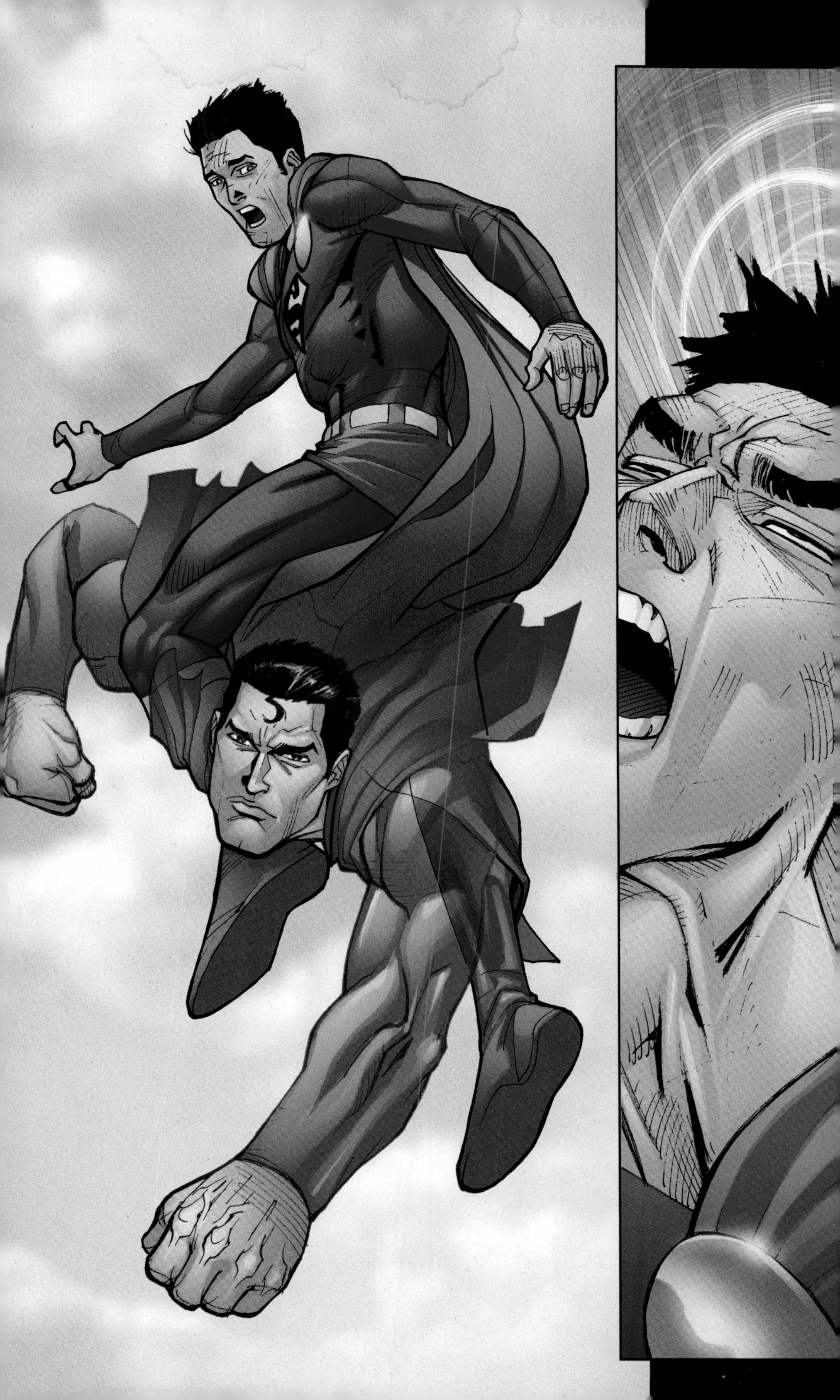

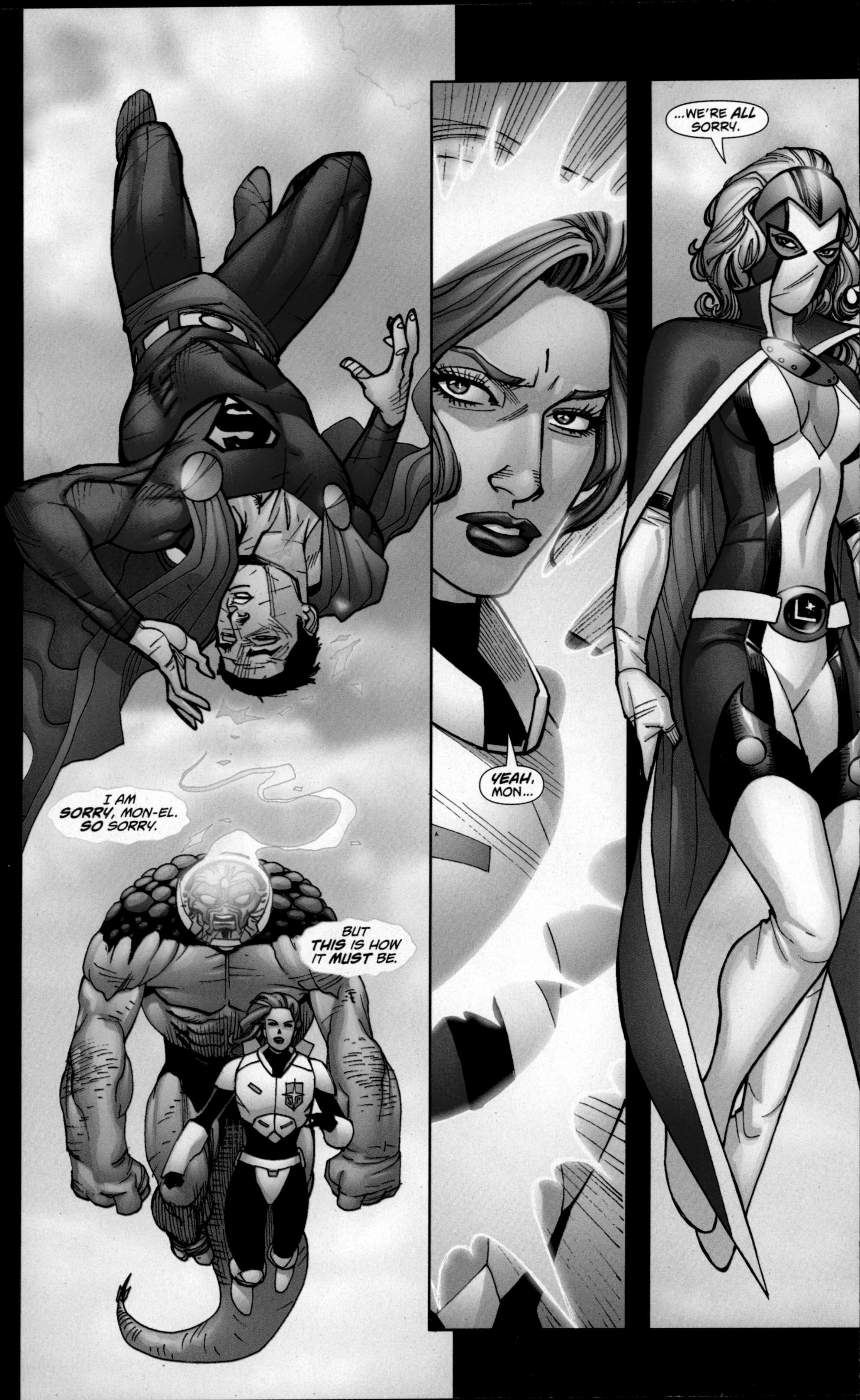
I AM SORRY, MON-EL. SO SORRY.
BUT THIS IS HOW IT MUST BE.
YEAH, MON...
...WE'RE ALL SORRY.

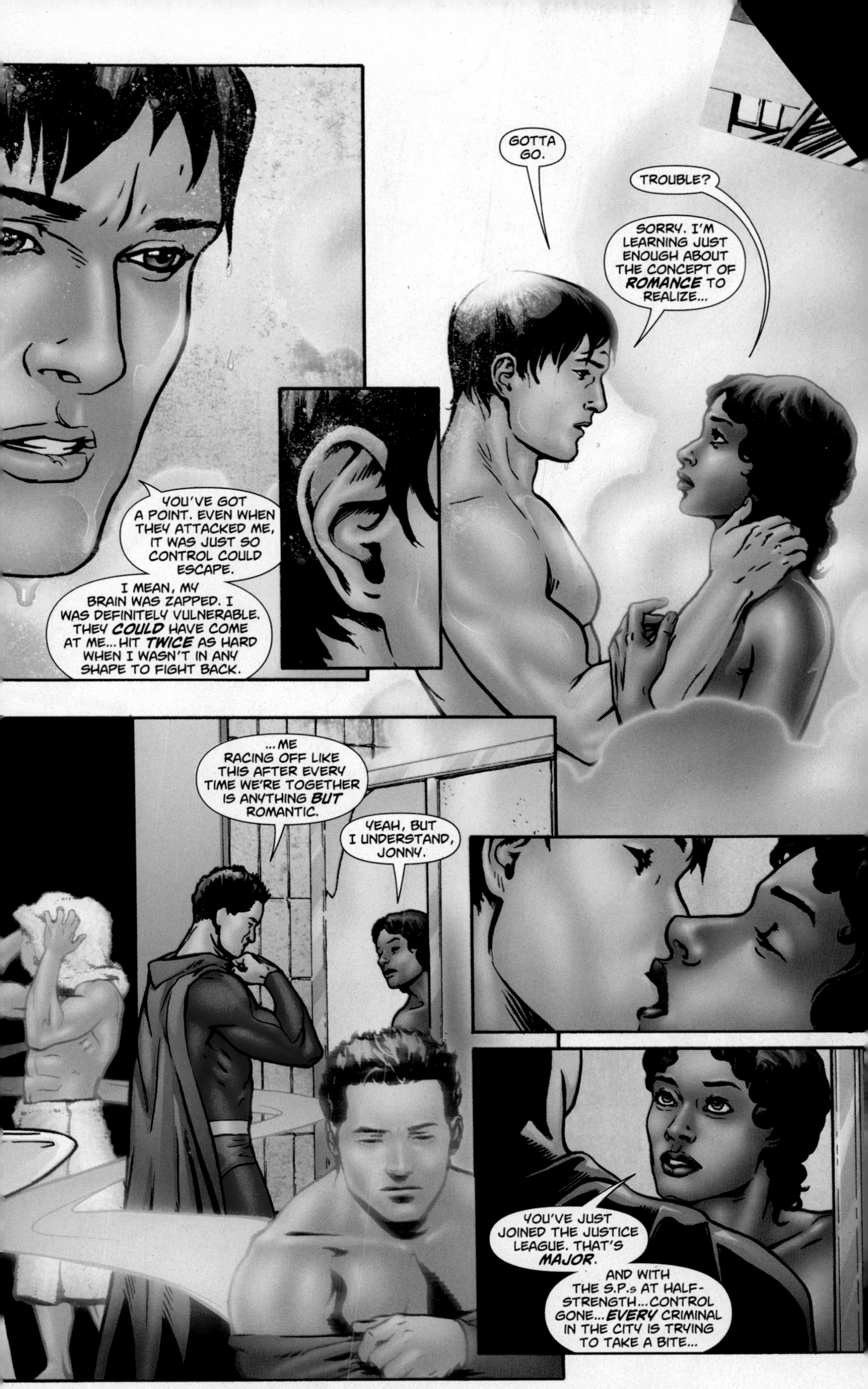
YOU'VE GOT A POINT. EVEN WHEN THEY ATTACKED ME, IT WAS JUST SO CONTROL COULD ESCAPE.
I MEAN, MY BRAIN WAS ZAPPED. I WAS DEFINITELY VULNERABLE. THEY COULD HAVE COME AT ME...HIT TWICE AS HARD WHEN I WASN'T IN ANY SHAPE TO FIGHT BACK.
GOTTA GO.
TROUBLE?
SORRY. I'M LEARNING JUST ENOUGH ABOUT THE CONCEPT OF ROMANCE TO REALIZE...
...ME RACING OFF LIKE THIS AFTER EVERY TIME WE'RE TOGETHER IS ANYTHING BUT ROMANTIC.
YEAH, BUT I UNDERSTAND, JONNY.
YOU'VE JUST JOINED THE JUSTICE LEAGUE. THAT'S MAJOR.
AND WITH THE S.P.s AT HALF-STRENGTH...CONTROL GONE...EVERY CRIMINAL IN THE CITY IS TRYING TO TAKE A BITE...

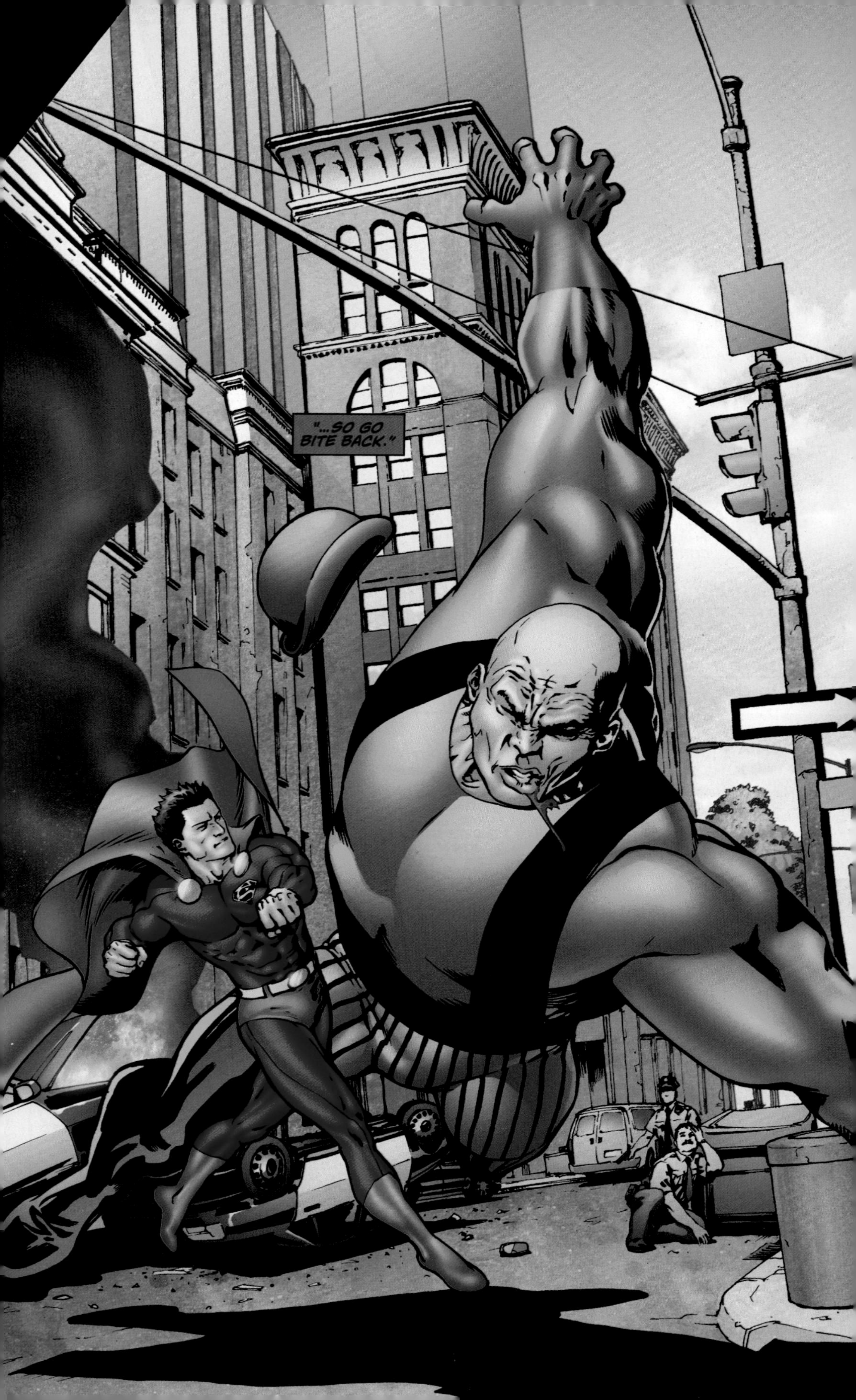
"...SO GO BITE BACK."

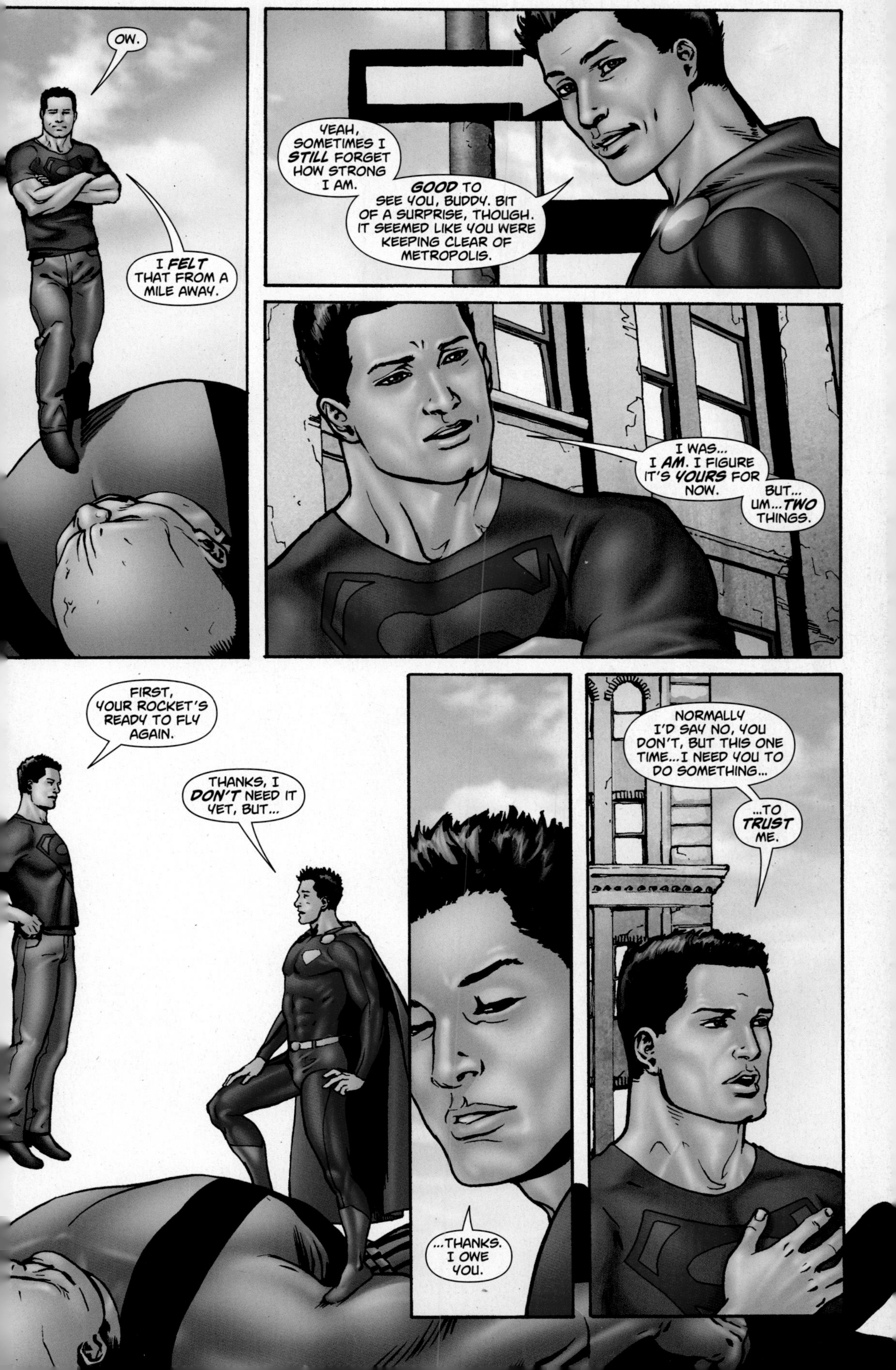
OW.
I FELT THAT FROM A MILE AWAY.
YEAH, SOMETIMES I STILL FORGET HOW STRONG I AM.
GOOD TO SEE YOU, BUDDY. BIT OF A SURPRISE, THOUGH. IT SEEMED LIKE YOU WERE KEEPING CLEAR OF METROPOLIS.
I WAS... I AM. I FIGURE IT'S YOURS FOR NOW.
BUT... UM...TWO THINGS.
FIRST, YOUR ROCKET'S READY TO FLY AGAIN.
THANKS, I DON'T NEED IT YET, BUT...
...THANKS. I OWE YOU.
NORMALLY I'D SAY NO, YOU DON'T, BUT THIS ONE TIME...I NEED YOU TO DO SOMETHING...
...TO TRUST ME.

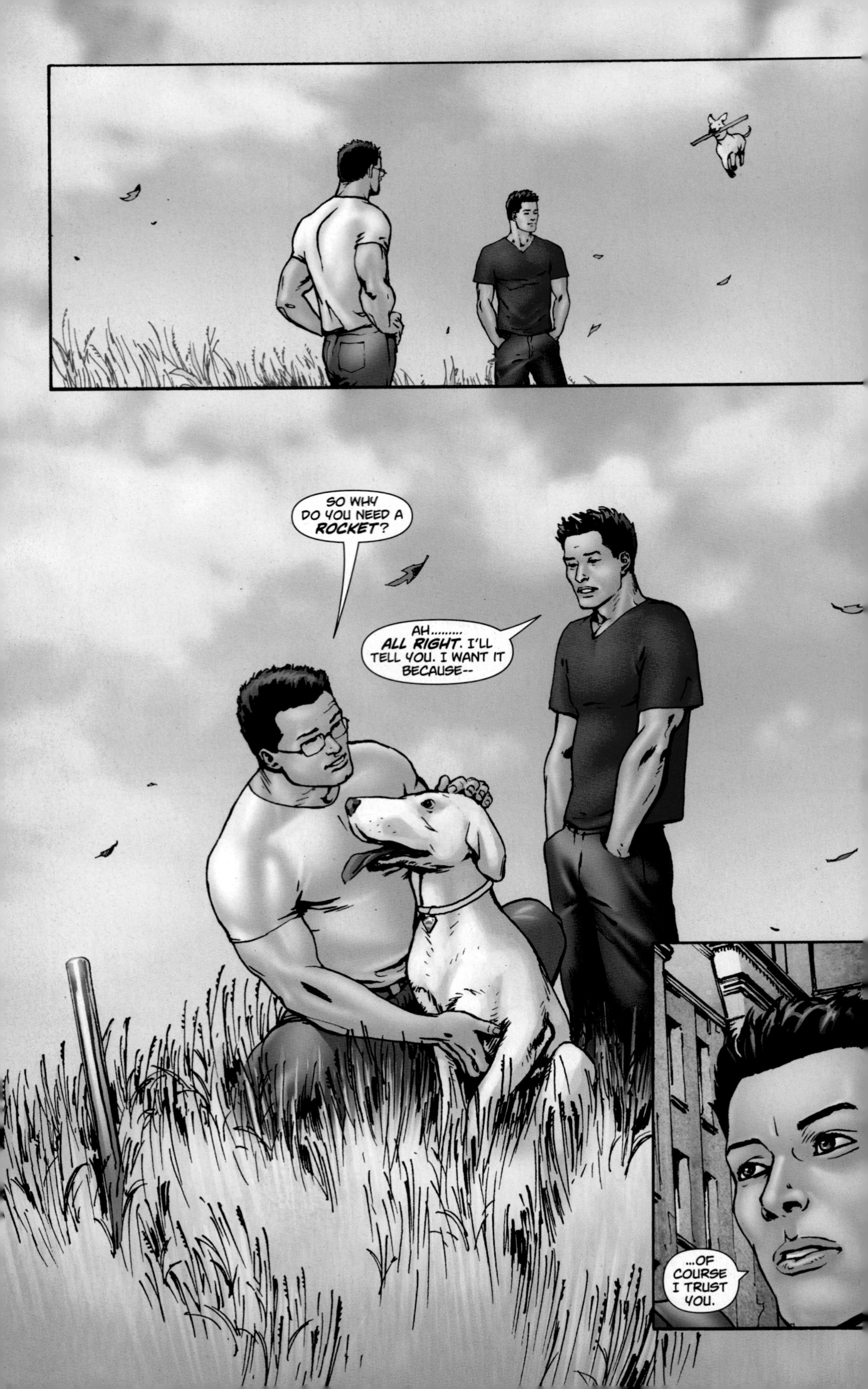
SO WHY DO YOU NEED A ROCKET?
AH......... ALL RIGHT. I'LL TELL YOU. I WANT IT BECAUSE--
...OF COURSE I TRUST YOU.

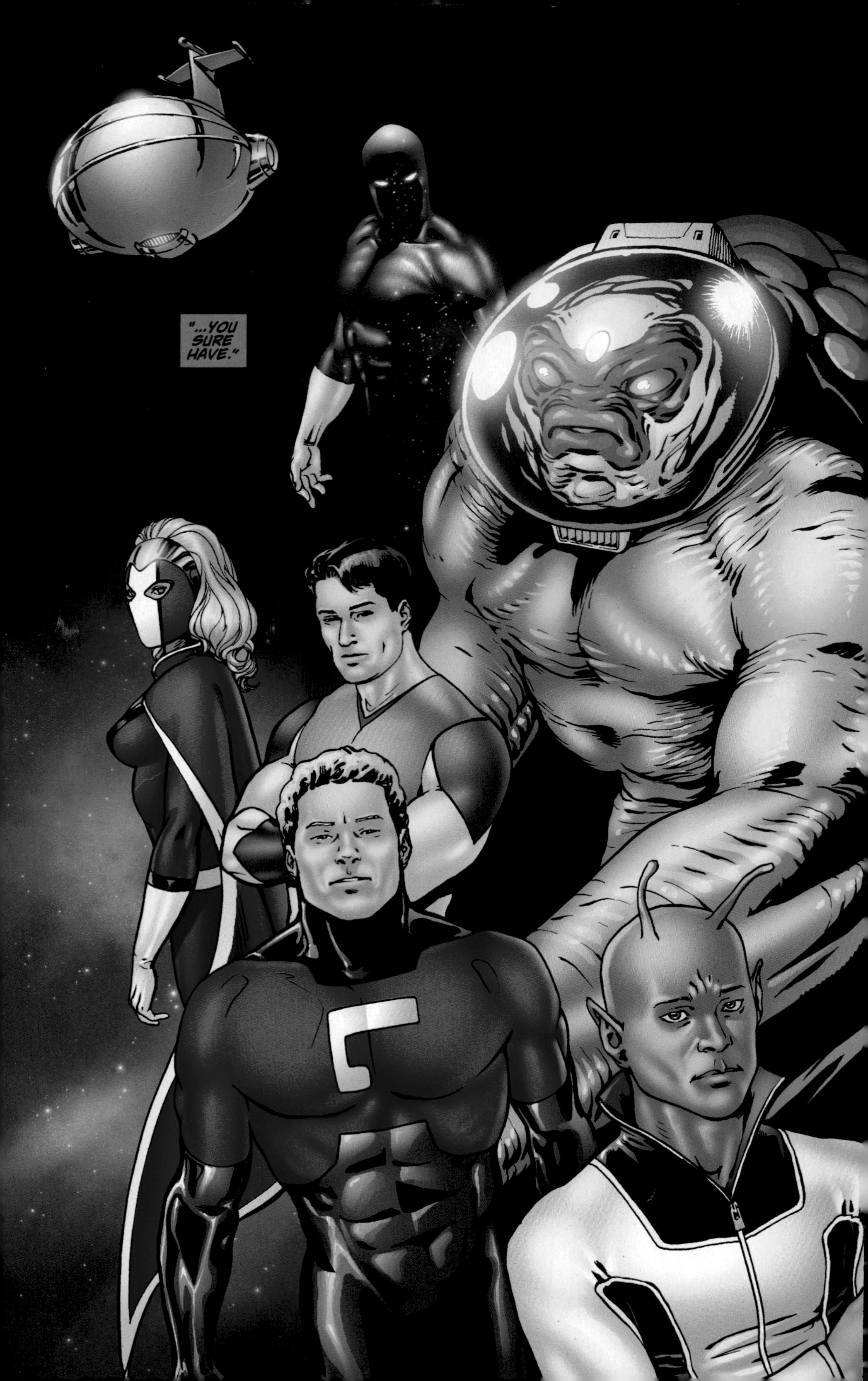
"...YOU SURE HAVE."

IN HONOR OF
MON-EL
FOR HIS NOBLE
SACRIFICE

‹PREVIOUSLY IN›
SUPERMAN:
LAST STAND OF
NEW KRYPTON

Mon-El and the Legion of Super-Heroes joined Superman in his battle to prevent Brainiac and Lex Luthor from destroying New Krypton. Their mission: save the bottle cities aboard Brainiac's ship to ensure that they will one day become the birthplaces of the Legionnaires.

At Superman's insistence, Mon-El and the Legion leave New Krypton with the bottle cities so that they can return them to their rightful places in the universe and save the future…

MAN OF VALOR FINALE

BERNARD CHANG ‹ARTIST›

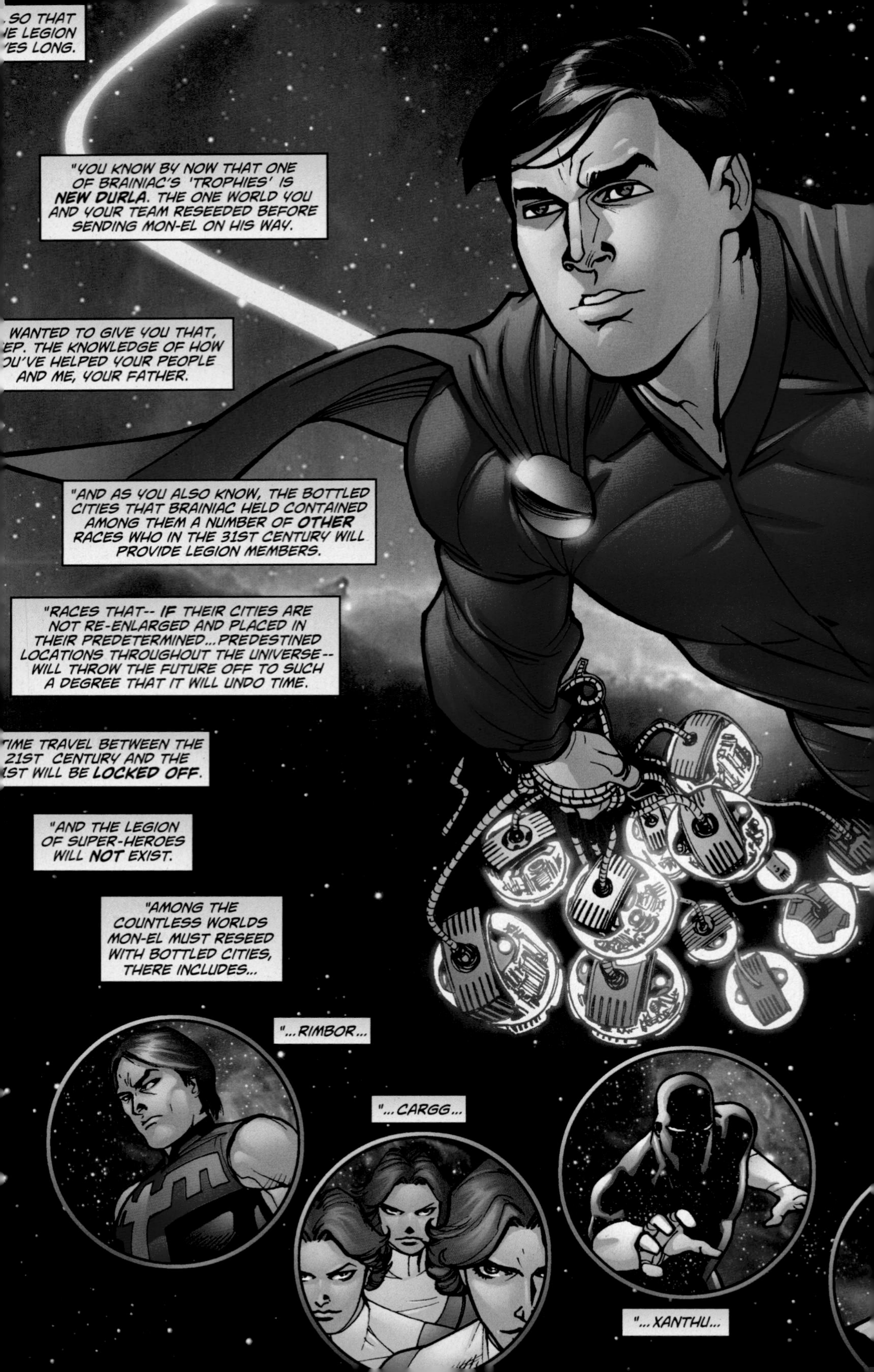
SO THAT
E LEGION
ES LONG.
"YOU KNOW BY NOW THAT ONE OF BRAINIAC'S 'TROPHIES' IS NEW DURLA. THE ONE WORLD YOU AND YOUR TEAM RESEEDED BEFORE SENDING MON-EL ON HIS WAY.
WANTED TO GIVE YOU THAT, EP. THE KNOWLEDGE OF HOW OU'VE HELPED YOUR PEOPLE AND ME, YOUR FATHER.
"AND AS YOU ALSO KNOW, THE BOTTLED CITIES THAT BRAINIAC HELD CONTAINED AMONG THEM A NUMBER OF OTHER RACES WHO IN THE 31ST CENTURY WILL PROVIDE LEGION MEMBERS.
"RACES THAT-- IF THEIR CITIES ARE NOT RE-ENLARGED AND PLACED IN THEIR PREDETERMINED...PREDESTINED LOCATIONS THROUGHOUT THE UNIVERSE-- WILL THROW THE FUTURE OFF TO SUCH A DEGREE THAT IT WILL UNDO TIME.
TIME TRAVEL BETWEEN THE 21ST CENTURY AND THE ST WILL BE LOCKED OFF.
"AND THE LEGION OF SUPER-HEROES WILL NOT EXIST.
"AMONG THE COUNTLESS WORLDS MON-EL MUST RESEED WITH BOTTLED CITIES, THERE INCLUDES...
"...RIMBOR...
"...CARGG...
"...XANTHU...

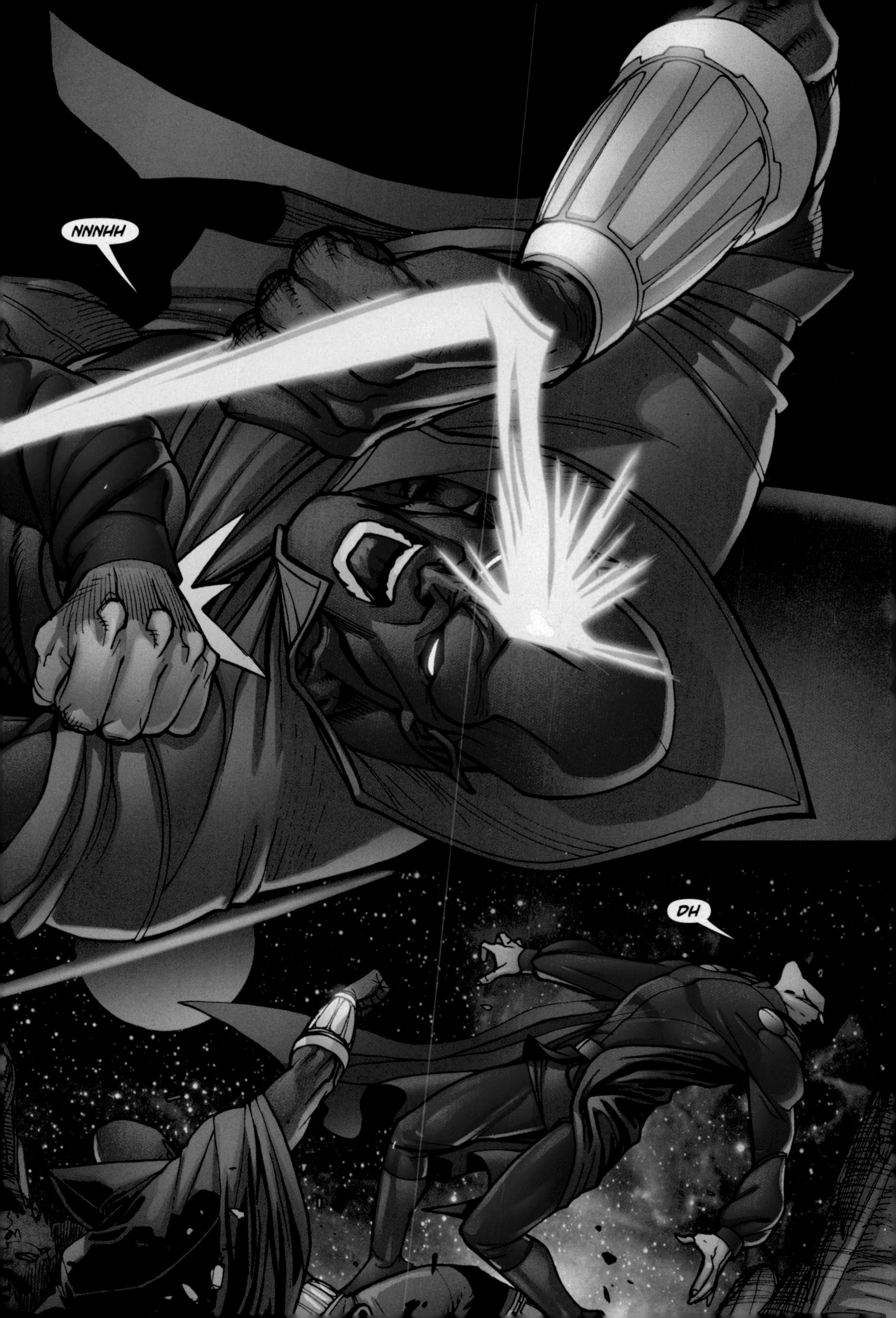
NNNHH
DH

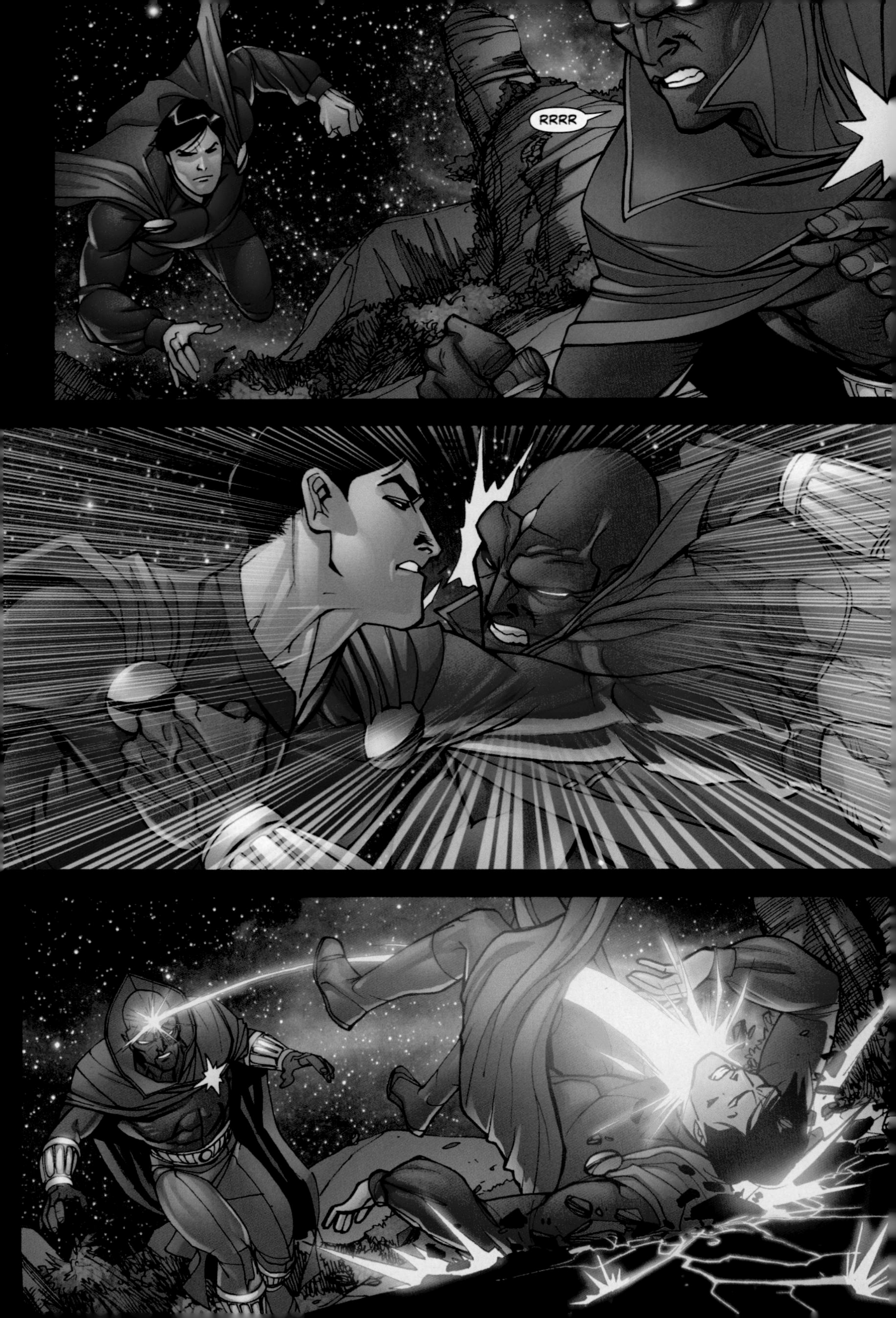
RRRR

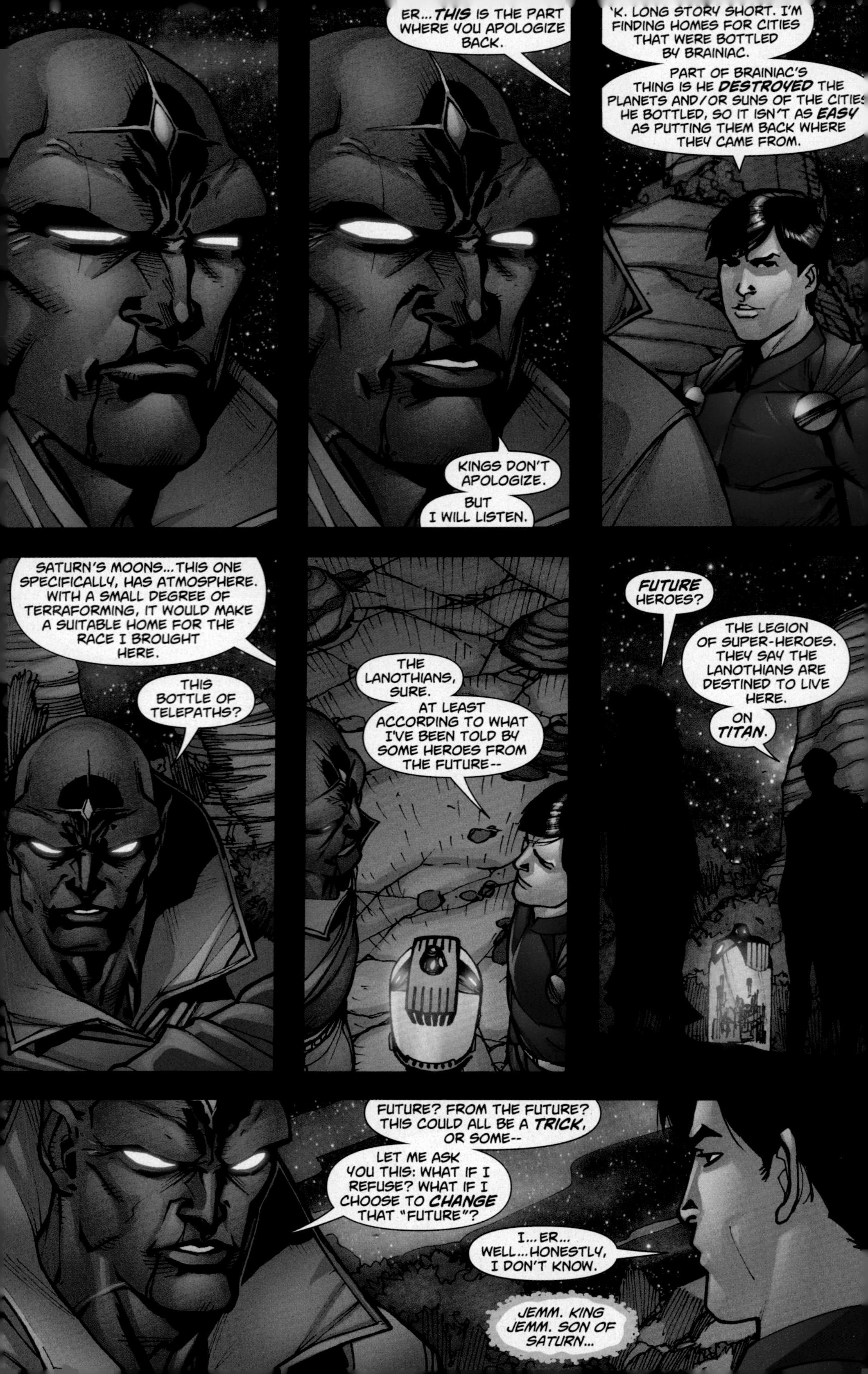
ER...THIS IS THE PART WHERE YOU APOLOGIZE BACK.
KINGS DON'T APOLOGIZE.
BUT I WILL LISTEN.
'K. LONG STORY SHORT. I'M FINDING HOMES FOR CITIES THAT WERE BOTTLED BY BRAINIAC.
PART OF BRAINIAC'S THING IS HE DESTROYED THE PLANETS AND/OR SUNS OF THE CITIES HE BOTTLED, SO IT ISN'T AS EASY AS PUTTING THEM BACK WHERE THEY CAME FROM.
SATURN'S MOONS...THIS ONE SPECIFICALLY, HAS ATMOSPHERE. WITH A SMALL DEGREE OF TERRAFORMING, IT WOULD MAKE A SUITABLE HOME FOR THE RACE I BROUGHT HERE.
THIS BOTTLE OF TELEPATHS?
THE LANOTHIANS, SURE.
AT LEAST ACCORDING TO WHAT I'VE BEEN TOLD BY SOME HEROES FROM THE FUTURE--
FUTURE HEROES?
THE LEGION OF SUPER-HEROES. THEY SAY THE LANOTHIANS ARE DESTINED TO LIVE HERE.
ON TITAN.
FUTURE? FROM THE FUTURE? THIS COULD ALL BE A TRICK, OR SOME--
LET ME ASK YOU THIS: WHAT IF I REFUSE? WHAT IF I CHOOSE TO CHANGE THAT "FUTURE"?
I...ER... WELL...HONESTLY, I DON'T KNOW.
JEMM. KING JEMM. SON OF SATURN...

...THAT MON-EL, THE MAN OF VALOR, DIDN'T HAVE MUCH TIME LEFT.

AND HE'D NEED THAT TIME, I WAS TO LEARN...EVERY SECOND. FOR HIS FINAL TASK...THE ONE HE BEGAN WHEN HE ASKED NATASHA IRONS (THEN UNDERCOVER IN LANE'S HUMAN DEFENSE CORPS) TO GET HIM SOME SPECIFIC INFORMATION.

ISN'T IT OBVIOUS...THE REASON LANE AND I KNOW SO MUCH ABOUT DAXAMITES ALREADY. WE...I...ALREADY HAVE ONE, CAPTURED YEARS AGO. A FEMALE. NO, NOT HERE, AT ANOTHER LOCATION.

SHE'S FUN. INTERESTING AND FUN TO TEST...TO PROBE.

THAT INFORMATION WAS UNCOVERED FINALLY BY NAT, WHO PASSED IT ON TO ME ON TO MON...

...THE LOCATION OF A HIDDEN HDC BASE (UNDER THE ATLANTIC, IT TURNED OUT) WHERE GORILLA SCIENTIST CALOMAR KEPT HIS COLLECTION OF "SCIENTIFIC ODDITIES."

AMONG THEM...

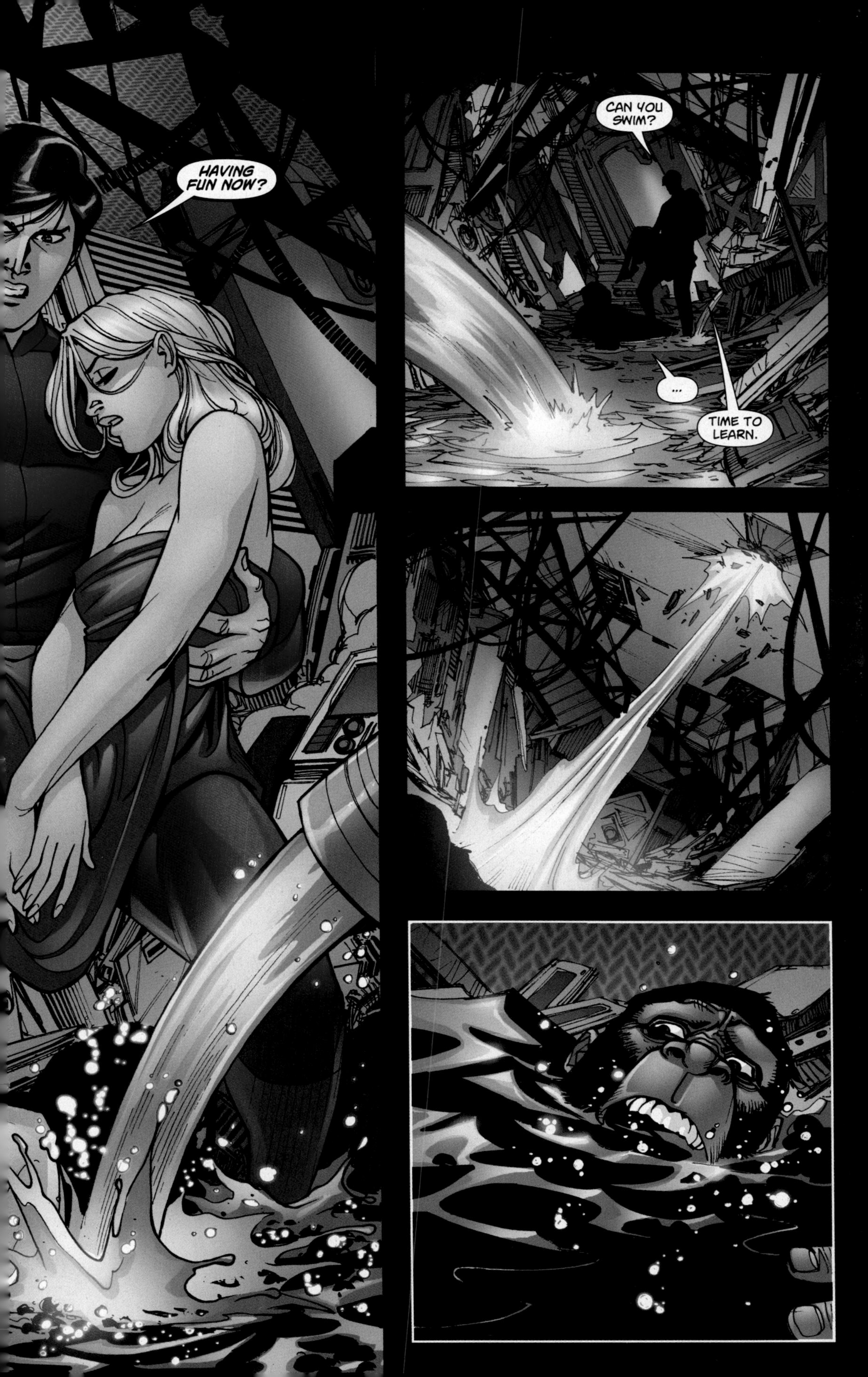
HAVING FUN NOW?
CAN YOU SWIM?
...
TIME TO LEARN.

BUT THERE IS SO *MUCH* I WANT TO ASK YOU...TO *SAY* TO YOU.

ALAS...

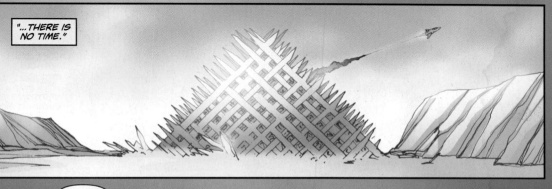

"...THERE IS NO TIME."

WE DONE NOW?

MON? DONE? WE *HAVE* TO GET YOU TO A DOCTOR, OR--

NO. IT'S TOO LATE. DONE? YEAH.

ME.

NO! NO, MON! WE CAN *SAVE* YOU. YOU CAN'T J--

IT'S ALL RIGHT, SUPERBOY...

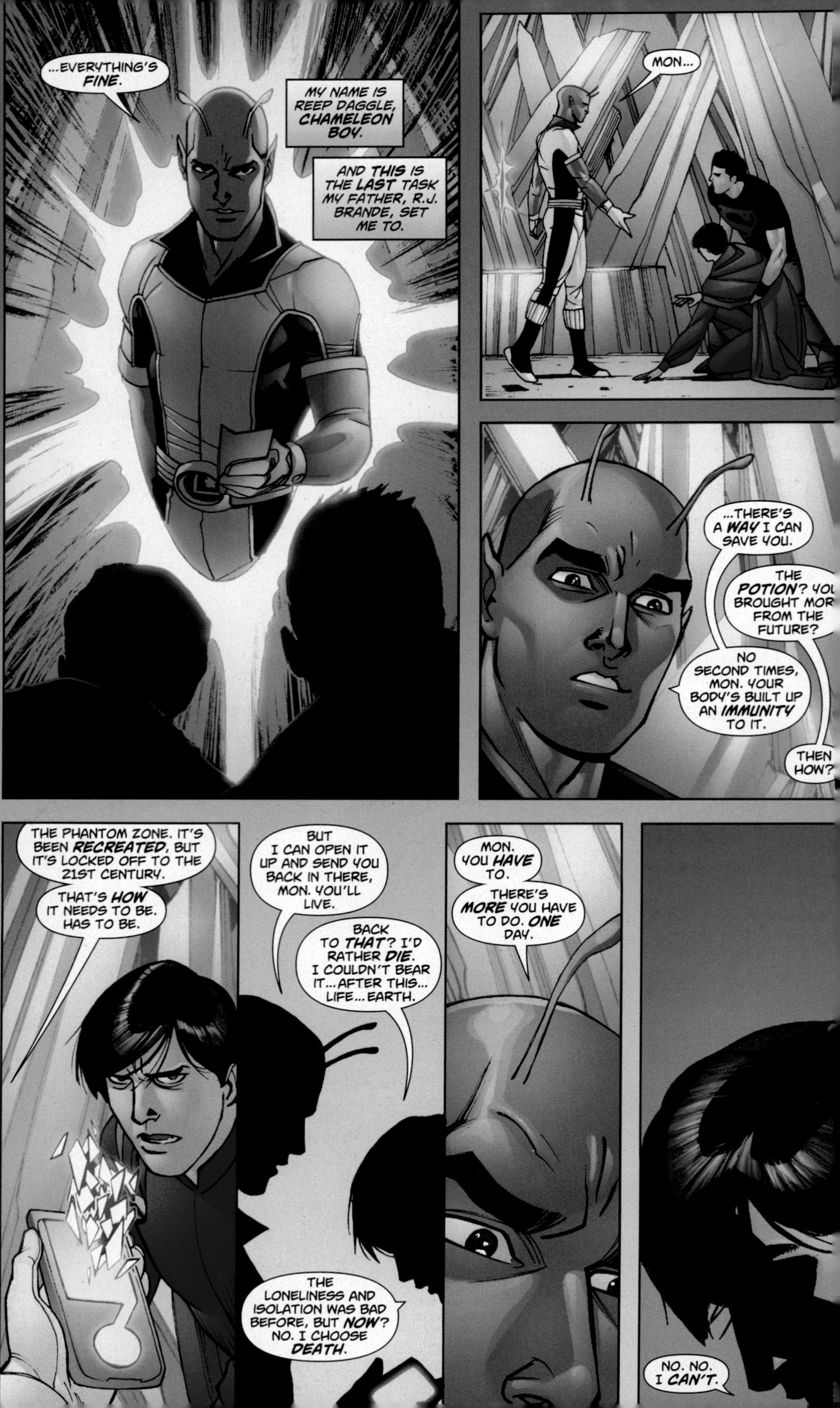
...EVERYTHING'S FINE.
MY NAME IS REEP DAGGLE, CHAMELEON BOY.
AND THIS IS THE LAST TASK MY FATHER, R.J. BRANDE, SET ME TO.
MON...
...THERE'S A WAY I CAN SAVE YOU.
THE POTION? YOU BROUGHT MORE FROM THE FUTURE?
NO SECOND TIMES, MON. YOUR BODY'S BUILT UP AN IMMUNITY TO IT.
THEN HOW?
THE PHANTOM ZONE. IT'S BEEN RECREATED, BUT IT'S LOCKED OFF TO THE 21ST CENTURY.
THAT'S HOW IT NEEDS TO BE. HAS TO BE.
BUT I CAN OPEN IT UP AND SEND YOU BACK IN THERE, MON. YOU'LL LIVE.
BACK TO THAT? I'D RATHER DIE. I COULDN'T BEAR IT... AFTER THIS... LIFE... EARTH.
THE LONELINESS AND ISOLATION WAS BAD BEFORE, BUT NOW? NO. I CHOOSE DEATH.
MON. YOU HAVE TO.
THERE'S MORE YOU HAVE TO DO. ONE DAY.
NO. NO. I CAN'T.

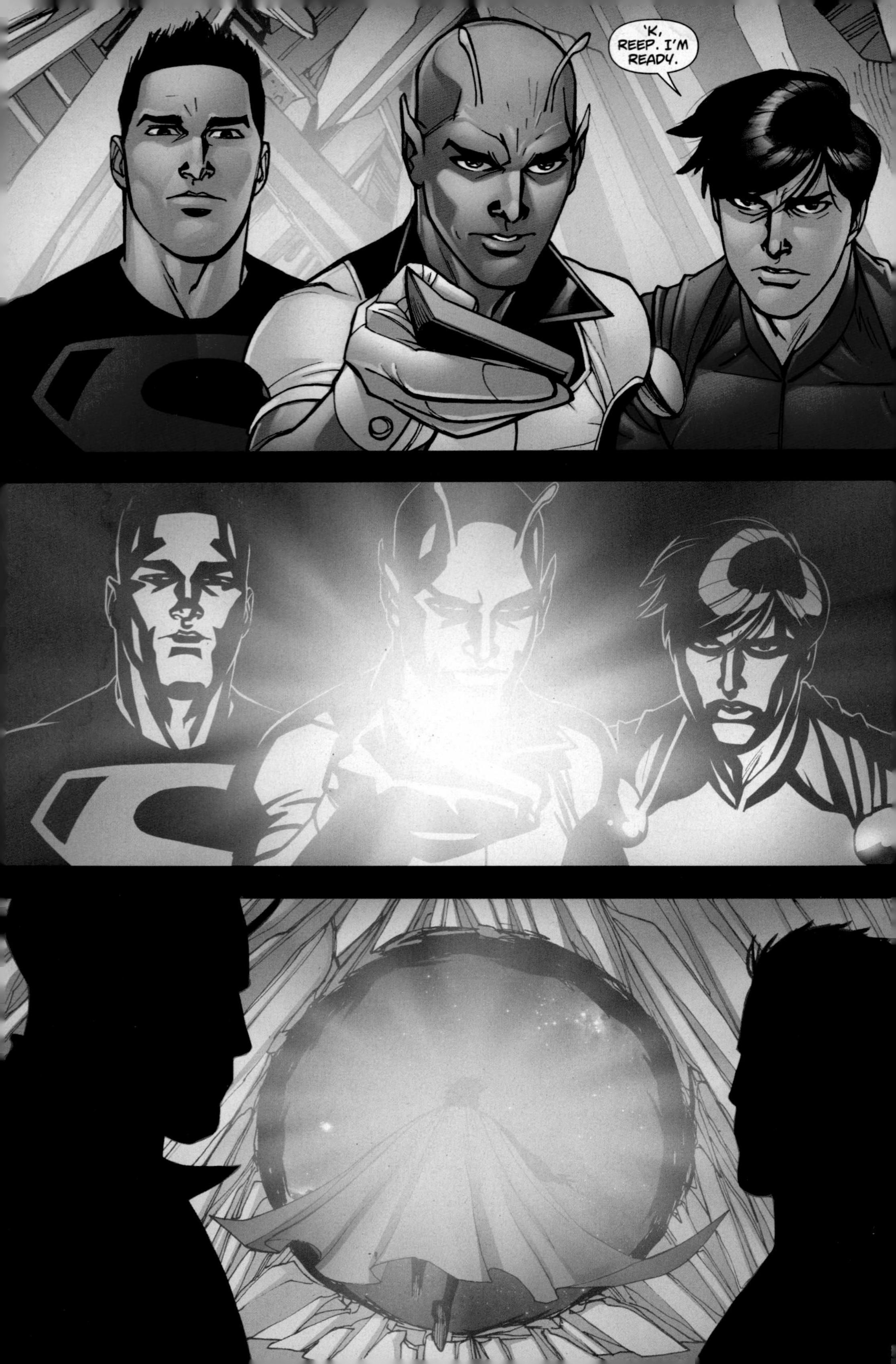
'K, REEP. I'M READY.

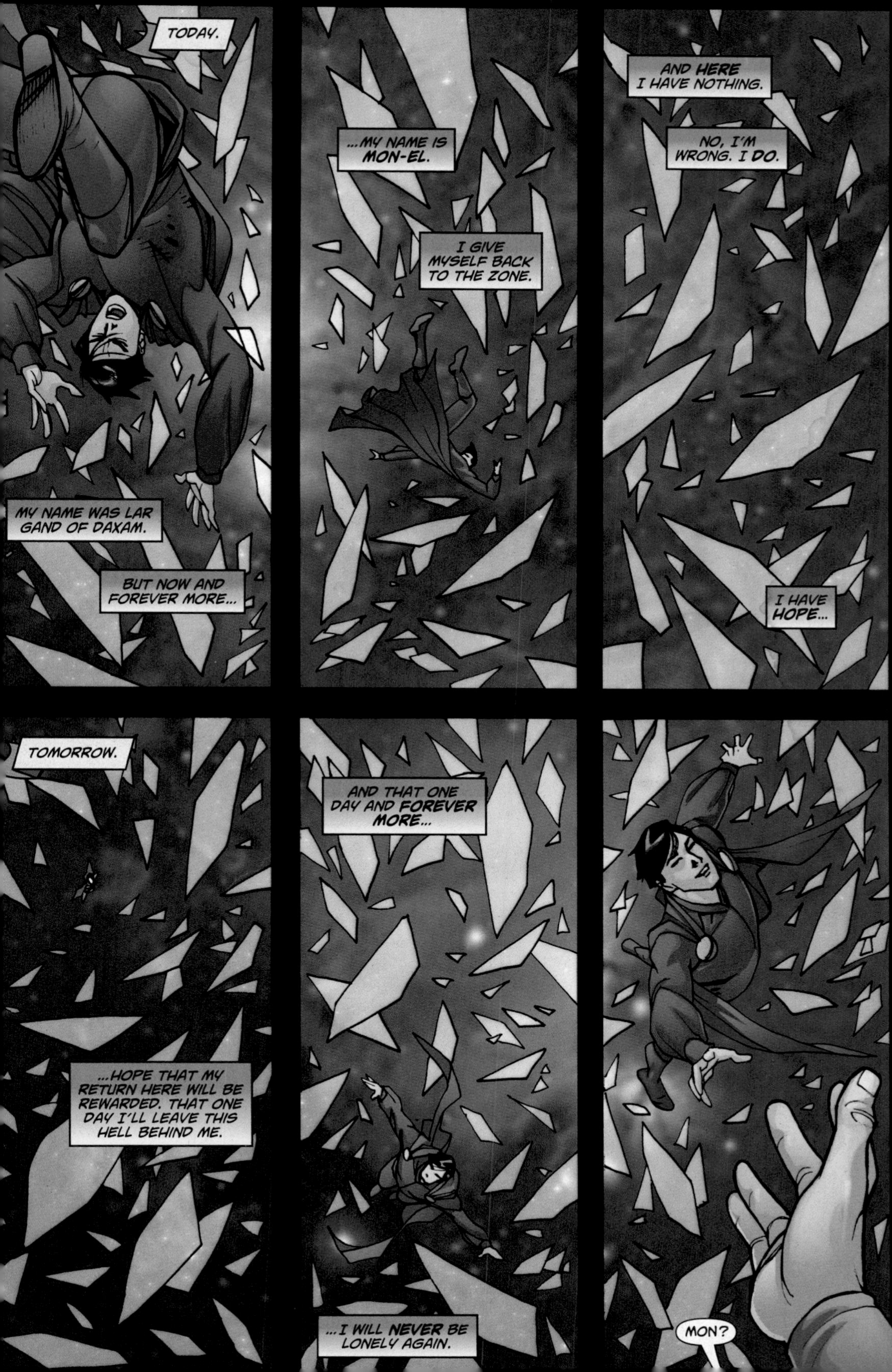
TODAY.
MY NAME WAS LAR GAND OF DAXAM.
BUT NOW AND FOREVER MORE...
...MY NAME IS MON-EL.
I GIVE MYSELF BACK TO THE ZONE.
AND HERE I HAVE NOTHING.
NO, I'M WRONG. I DO.
I HAVE HOPE...
TOMORROW.
...HOPE THAT MY RETURN HERE WILL BE REWARDED. THAT ONE DAY I'LL LEAVE THIS HELL BEHIND ME.
AND THAT ONE DAY AND FOREVER MORE...
...I WILL NEVER BE LONELY AGAIN.
MON?

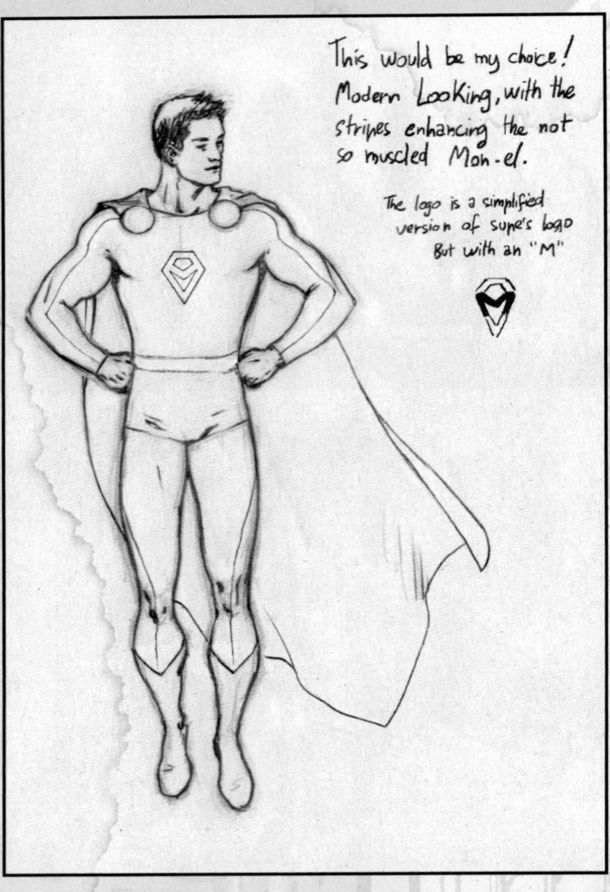
This would be my choice! Modern Looking, with the stripes enhancing the not so muscled Mon-el.
The logo is a simplified version of supe's logo But with an "M"

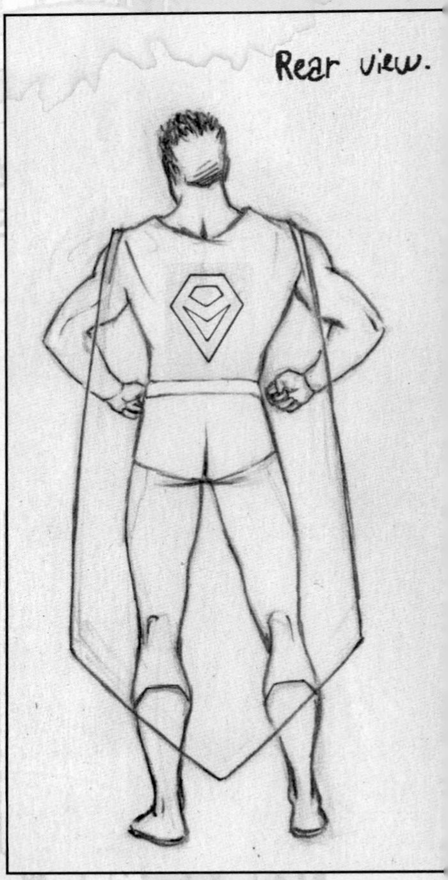
Rear view.

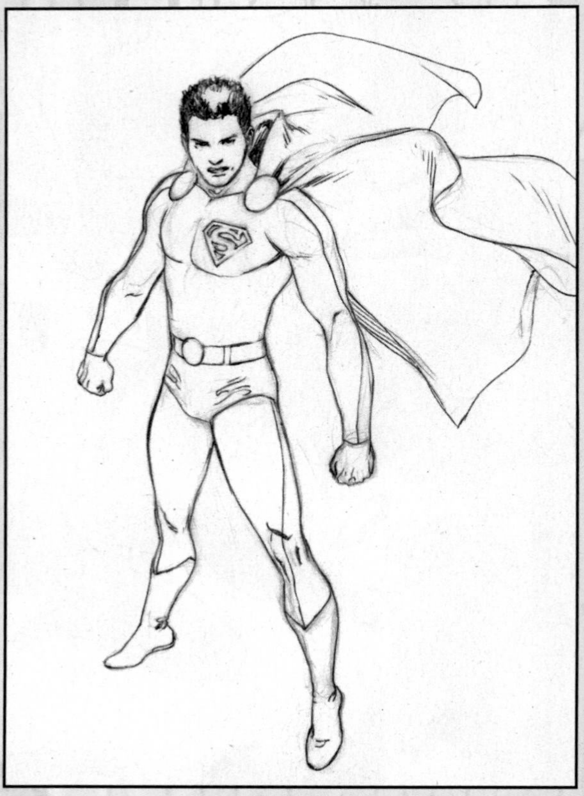

Mon-El sketches by **JAVIER PINA**

Mirabai

DIVINATION

EVOKATION

CONJURATION

NECROMANCY

TRANSMUTATION

Mirabai wears various fetishes and charms
she has collected from defeated rivals.
Not trophies— she only keeps what may
prove useful.

She is generally in her cloak or coat.
The runes on her gauntlets and cloak glow
a dull red.

The tattoo styles and colors vary based
on school. Illusion,curls like smoke. Dicination
is a stylized eye with lines radiating away
from it like roads or threads of fate.
Evokation can take the form of stylized
fire, water,or lightning (in Mirabai's case it
is fire). Conjuration can take the shape of
any variety of creature. Necromancy
is a stylized skull. Tramksmutation looks
something like a diagram of a molecule—
Circular "Atoms" with line arcing between
and conecting them representing a
shared electron.

Mirabai design by
PETE WOODS

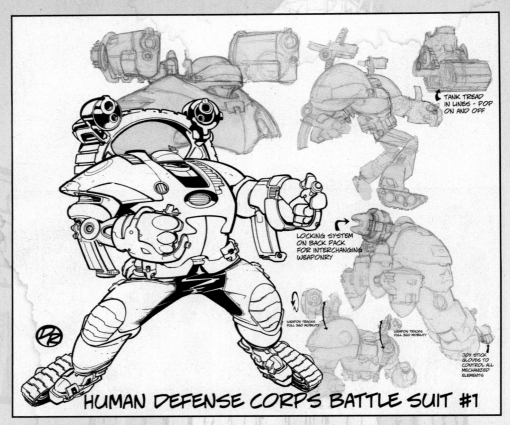

HUMAN DEFENSE CORPS BATTLE SUIT #1

TANK TREAD
IN LINES - POP
ON AND OFF

LOCKING SYSTEM
ON BACK PACK
FOR INTERCHANGING
WEAPONRY

WEAPON TRACKS
FULL 360 MOBILITY

WEAPON TRACKS
FULL 360 MOBILITY

JOY STICK
GLOVES TO
CONTROL ALL
MECHANIZED
ELEMENTS

EARTH DEFENSE CORP.
BATTLE SUIT 1

Human Defense Corps
designs by **DUNCAN ROULEAU**

BATTLE SUIT 2

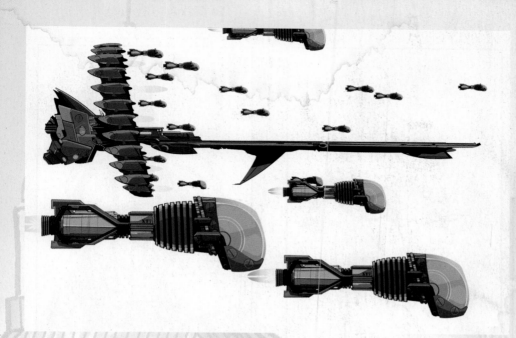

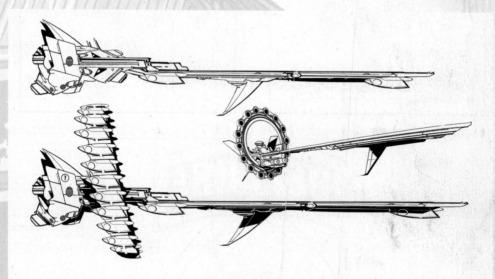

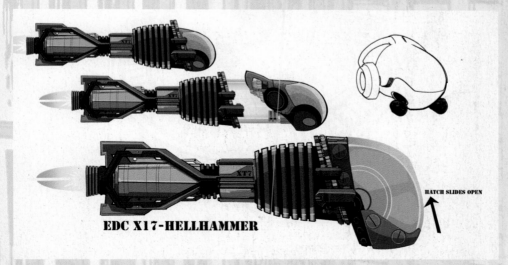

HATCH SLIDES OPEN

EDC X17-HELLHAMMER

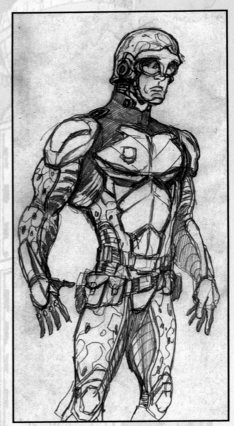

DEFENSE

AD INFEROS ET RETRORSUM

Human Defense Corps
design by **FERNANDO DAGNINO**